Chess Family Belavenets

Ludmila Belavenets, Sergey Yanovsky
and Vladimir Barsky

Chess Family Belavenets
Authors: Ludmila Belavenets, Sergey Yanovsky and Vladimir Barsky
Chess editor: Tibor Karolyi
Translated by Alexei Zakharov
Typesetting by Andrei Elkov
Photos in this book were provided by Boris Dolmatovsky, Eldar Mukhametov, Natalia Ushakova and Fabiano Ferreira, as well as taken from the authors' personal archives.
A previous edition of this book was published in Russian in 2012. Chess commentary in italics was added by the books' authors in the 2012 edition. The analysis was further revised by International Master Tibor Karolyi for the 2024 edition but we have not highlighted those changes in order not to disrupt the reading experience.
© LLC Elk and Ruby Publishing House, 2024
Follow us on Twitter/X: @ilan_ruby
www.elkandruby.com
ISBN 978-5-6045607-8-5 (black and white paperback); 978-5-6047848-6-0 (black and white hardback); 978-1-916839-38-0; (color hardback)

Contents

Index of Games 5
Foreword 7
    Yuri Averbakh
My Father Gifted Me Chess.. 9
    Ludmila Belavenets
Chess Lessons.. 50
    Sergei Belavenets
  GENERAL PRINCIPLES OF MIDDLEGAME PLAY 51
    THE CENTER.. 56
      Pawn centers... 57
      Piece centers... 64
  GENERAL PRINCIPLES OF ENDGAME PLAY............ 67
    PAWN ENDGAMES 75
      Material advantage... 75
      Outside passed pawns 77
      Protected passed pawns 78
      King activity 78
  SOME CONSIDERATIONS ON ENDGAMES WITH MULTIPLE MINOR PIECES 80
      Two bishops.. 80
      Bishop versus knight.. 82
      Bishop and rook versus knight and rook 90
      Same-colored bishops 93
      Knight endgames 96
      Multi-piece endgames.. 99
  MATERIAL ADVANTAGE IN A ROOK ENDGAME 111
      Pawn majority on the flank 111
      Rook positions: behind the passed pawn 113
      Rook positions: lateral to the passed pawn 115
      Rook positions: ahead of the passed pawn............... 117
      Maneuvering in rook endgames 119
Serezha Belavenets 124
    Mikhail Yudovich
The Triumph of Logic... 128
    Alexander Iglitsky
Two Chess Ajaxes.. 131
    Vasily Panov

The Training Camp at Koktebel 132
    Grigory Levenfish
Selection of Photos 133
Selected Games of Sergei Belavenets 165
    Ludmila Belavenets
Selected Games of Ludmila Belavenets 243
    Ludmila Belavenets
Afterword 290
    Sergei Belavenets's Final Resting Place 290
    The Sergei Belavenets Chess House in Brazil 291

Index of Games

No.	White	Black	Opening	Year
i	S. Belavenets	Lisitsin	Fragment	1937
ii	Euwe	Alekhine	Fragment	1937
iii	Flohr	Sultan Khan	Fragment	1932
iv	Budo	V. Makogonov	Fragment	1937
v	Bondarevsky	Botvinnik	Fragment	1941
vi	Pillsbury	Chigorin	Fragment	1895
vii	Ilyin-Zhenevsky	Botvinnik	Fragment	1931
viii	Botvinnik	Lilienthal	Fragment	1941
ix	Botvinnik	Kan	Fragment	1939
x	Capablanca	Ragozin	Fragment	1936
xi	Duz-Khotimirsky	Kotov	Fragment	1941
xii	Bogatyrchuk	Mazel	Fragment	1931
xiii	Alatortsev	Levenfish	Fragment	1940
xiv	Levenfish	Kotov	Fragment	1939
xv	E. Cohn	Rubinstein	Fragment	1909
xvi	Yudovich	Bondarevsky	Fragment	1937
xvii	Alekhine	Yates	Fragment	1925
xviii	Capablanca	Reshevsky	Fragment	1936
xix	Rubinstein	P. Johner	Fragment	1929
xx	S. Belavenets	Ilyin-Zhenevsky	Fragment	1937
xxi	Alekhine	Euwe	Fragment	1937
xxii	Botvinnik	Chekhover	Fragment	1934
xxiii	Kamyshev	Shamaev	Fragment	Corr.
xxiv	Eliskases	Capablanca	Fragment	1937
xxv	Duz-Khotimirsky	Kan	Fragment	1933
xxvi	Kamyshev	Zagoriansky	Fragment	1938
xxvii	Boleslavsky	Smyslov	Fragment	1940
xxviii	Flohr	Bondarevsky	Fragment	1939
xxix	Tarrasch	Teichmann	Fragment	1912
xxx	Factor	Rubinstein	Fragment	1916
xxxi	Stahlberg	Lasker	Fragment	1934
xxxii	Euwe	Alekhine	Fragment	1937
xxxiii	Alekhine	Capablanca	Fragment	1927
xxxiv	Lisitsin	Kan	Fragment	1935
xxxv	NN	NN	Fragment	Unknown
xxxvi	Flohr	Mikenas	Fragment	1939
1	S. Belavenets	Vygodchikov	Queen's Gambit D30	Unknown
2	S. Belavenets	L. Grigoriev	Queen's Gambit D63	Unknown
3	S. Belavenets	Yuriev	Queen's Gambit D52	1929
4	S. Belavenets	Veresov	Slav Defense D19	1934
5	S. Belavenets	Kotov	Nimzo-Indian Defense E23	1935
6	Zagoriansky	S. Belavenets	Grunfeld Defense D81	1936
7	S. Belavenets	Chistiakov	Queen's Gambit D61	1937
8	Rauzer	S. Belavenets	French Defense C12	1937

No.	White	Black	Opening	Year
9	S. Belavenets	Rauzer	Queen's Gambit D62	1937
10	Chekhover	S. Belavenets	Grunfeld Defense D95	1937
11	S. Belavenets	Lisitsin	Queen's Gambit D00	1937
12	Lilienthal	S. Belavenets	Grunfeld Defense D95	1937
13	S. Belavenets	Ilyin-Zhenevsky	Queen's Gambit D66	1937
14	S. Belavenets	Levenfish	Catalan Opening E00	1937
15	I. Rabinovich	S. Belavenets	French Defense C09	1937
16	S. Belavenets	Zagoriansky	Slav Defense D49	1937/38
17	Yudovich	S. Belavenets	Ruy Lopez C71	1937/38
18	Verlinsky	S. Belavenets	French Defense C19	1938
19	Freymann	S. Belavenets	Sicilian Defense B50	1938
20	S. Belavenets	M. Makogonov	Grunfeld Defense D96	1938
21	S. Belavenets	Duz-Khotimirsky	Dutch Defense A90	1938
22	S. Belavenets	Kaiev	Bogo-Indian Defense E11	1938
23	S. Belavenets	Panov	Queen's Gambit D31	1938
24	S. Belavenets	I. Rabinovich	Ruy Lopez C76	1939
25	Bondarevsky	S. Belavenets	Slav Defense D45	1939
26	S. Belavenets	Lisitsin	Sicilian Defense B75	1939
27	S. Belavenets	Ragozin	Queen's Gambit D44	1939
28	S. Belavenets	Tolush	Sicilian Defense B72	1939
29	Keres	S. Belavenets	Nimzo-Indian Defense E43	1939
30	S. Belavenets	Flohr	Caro-Kann Defense B15	1939
31	S. Belavenets	Panov	Old Indian Defense A54	1939
32	Van Elst	L. Belavenets	Sicilian Defense B80	1975–1980 *corr.*
33	L. Belavenets	Szalai-Horvath	Scandinavian Defense B01	1986–1991 *corr.*
34	L. Belavenets	Cunningham	Alekhine Defense B04	1984–1990 *corr.*
35	L. Belavenets	Manthey	Sicilian Defense B81	1984–1990 *corr.*
36	L. Belavenets	Praznik-Pezdirc	Pirc Defense B07	1984–1990 *corr.*
37	Orlova	L. Belavenets	Sicilian Defense B85	1984–1990 *corr.*
38	Vizdei	L. Belavenets	Sicilian Defense B81	1986–1991 *corr.*
39	L. Belavenets	Heigl	Sicilian Defense B99	1984–1990 *corr.*
40	Makai	L. Belavenets	Sicilian Defense B25	1975–1980 *corr.*
41	L. Belavenets	Skacelikova	Alekhine Defense B04	1975–1980 *corr.*
42	Hołuj-Radzikowska	L. Belavenets	King's Indian Defense E99	1986–1991 *corr.*
43	Staller-Reis	L. Belavenets	Sicilian Defense B40	1986–1991 *corr.*
44	L. Belavenets	Modrova	Ruy Lopez C78	1986–1991 *corr.*
45	Kattinger	L. Belavenets	Sicilian Defense B23	1980–1986 *corr.*
46	Berbecaru	L. Belavenets	Ruy Lopez C62	1980–1986 *corr.*
47	Vayrynen	L. Belavenets	Sicilian Defense B85	1980–1984 *corr.*
48	L. Belavenets	Bazaj-Bockaj	Sicilian Defense B81	1984–1990 *corr.*
49	Clarke	L. Belavenets	Reti Opening A11	1984–1990 *corr.*
50	L. Belavenets	Koroshinadze	French Defense C10	1978–1980 *corr.*
51	L. Belavenets	Voskresenskaya	Nimzo-Indian Defense E36	1978–1980 *corr.*
52	Gramignani	L. Belavenets	Sicilian Defense B85	1976
53	Popivoda	L. Belavenets	French Defense C02	1979

Foreword

Yuri Averbakh

In October 1941, the Moscow Sports Committee decided to hold an exhibition tournament to show the whole world that the capital of our Motherland, even though it was a frontline city back then, was still living a normal life. The atmosphere in the city was most anxious: "sausages" hanging over the streets (that's how we called airships), bombs falling; at night, I was sometimes on roof duty – catching the small firebombs and throwing them into boxes containing sand or water. During the blitzes, I would get up on the roof rather than running into a bomb shelter. Once, I went into the Sports Committee building on Markhlevsky Street *[now Milyutinsky Lane]*, and there I heard that they wanted to hold a tournament for masters and candidate masters.

The following masters took part: Yudovich, Belavenets, Blumenfeld, Zubarev, and Rabinovich. Abram Rabinovich worked at the Young Pioneers Stadium back then, and I studied there for a time. He was fascinated with openings, showed us some lines and then said, "White is better." And someone, for instance, Yura Gusev, would argue, "No, black is better!" Rabinovich would cry out angrily, "Then play, you peasants!" They would sit down and play blitz to decide whose position was better. Rabinovich was a most likeable man; he died during the war, in 1943.

They invited candidate masters as well: Khachaturov, Tarasov, Stanishnev, Aronin and me. Stanishnev, a textile institute student, was a very talented chess player; he achieved his master's norm after 9 rounds. Then he went to the front and never returned. Sergei Belavenets didn't return either. As it turned out, he played his last ever tournament game against me...

Sergei was a very good, pleasant man. There was never any friction between us, and I don't remember anyone saying a single bad word against him. Belavenets was friends with Mikhail Yudovich, whom I consider my teacher (he worked as a coach in the Pioneers House on Stopani Lane *[now Ogorodnaya Sloboda Lane]*). I still remember the old epigram, "I'm the master of the opening./ I'm the master of the ending./ Everyone knows Yudovich-Belavenets."

In a way, I projected my liking of Sergei onto Ludmila. I've always tried to help her. When the TV show *Shakhmatnaya Shkola (Chess School)* needed a female host, I decided to invite her. Ludmila was a natural fit. *Shakhmatnaya Shkola* was on air from 1969 to 1986. I gave endgame lessons for highly-qualified chess players, Alexander Kotov read lectures on middlegames, and Yudovich gave opening lessons. Later, Yudovich was replaced by Boris Voronkov, the father of the famous journalist Sergey Voronkov (Boris and I were childhood friends). Ludmila's lessons for beginners were very interesting.

The Belavenets family is a true chess family — the name of the book is just perfect. By the way, I knew not only Ludmila's father but also her father's father. He was also a chess fan and frequently visited tournaments. I knew her mother too, she worked in the Sports Committee. We're still friends with Ludmila, I gladly support her events, helping if needed. She serves an honorable cause — teaching young chess players, and I wish her every success with all of my heart.

Moscow, 2012

My Father Gifted Me Chess

Ludmila Belavenets

I consider my life to have worked out well. I have the most important thing for me: a job that I enjoy. I love chess and I love children, and my work combines both of them. What I earned from it (as we now like to say) is another matter... The first thing parents ask is whether their child will achieve anything. I answer to each of them: yes, as chess isn't an end in itself, but a means to an end. Because no matter whom your children become eventually, their fascination with chess will unite them when they grow up. It means that you belong to a special world.

Myachkovo – Koptelsky – Ordynka

I remember myself ever since the evacuation, when I was barely three years old. When the Nazi forces got close to Moscow, our family left for Gorkovskaya Oblast. My childhood memory still holds the name of the village we settled in – Myachkovo. To be honest, I'm not quite sure how this name is spelled – in my mind, it is just associated with football, which is why I remember it.

My first memories: we live in a small cottage, and it's very cold. So cold that snow has actually accumulated beside the bed I shared with my sister – in the corners between the floor and the walls. Mother was very anxious not to lose her children. Father wrote to her in one of his last letters, "Do whatever it takes, nothing else is particularly important, but you must save the children!" He said that he was not under any threat, he was young and healthy and about to be sent to some tank repair school (but this ultimately didn't happen). Anyway, what could really threaten him? Well, there's that small thing, war, but...

I still have this triangle-shaped letter from the front lines. The letter was sent to our home address, 1st Koptelsky Lane in Moscow. This building now hosts Dvorkovich's chess lounge, and before the revolution, it belonged to my grandfather, Fyodor Fyodorovich Malanyin. In 1942, we received a death notice from the front lines...

Since it was very cold in the cottage, I never left the bed for the entire winter. In the spring, I was put on the floor, and it turned out that I had forgotten how to walk. My sister, three years older than me, cried out, "Mom, Mom, look, Milka can't walk!" I was very upset: such a miserable situation for me, but everybody just laughed out loud!..

Father's letter from the front

When I grew a bit older, my sister taught me to say that my father died at the front lines. I gleefully and proudly announced that to everybody and was quite surprised that they didn't share my delight...

Later, we got back to Moscow, to 1st Koptelsky Lane. Mother's entire big family lived there; she was the youngest of eleven children. After 1917, our family was forced to "make room" for other tenants, but everyone still stayed in that building. After she married, my mother moved to my father's ground floor room on Bolshaya Ordynka Street, and we lived there until 1960. However, after evacuation ended we spent some time in the building on Koptelsky, I don't remember why. Perhaps we were waiting until a potbelly stove was installed in the Ordynka apartment; craftsmen would build them out of sheet iron and fit the pipe through the window. I remember the stove well: it didn't provide much heat, but at least you could make porridge on it. I spent most of my childhood and youth on Bolshaya Ordynka. When Khrushchev launched a building campaign in Moscow, we got relocated. Our old apartment block on Bolshaya Ordynka doesn't exist anymore, it was demolished.

There were four of us in our room in what had become a communal flat: my mother, sister, aunt and me. We had no gas, only kerosene heaters. Washing was a big hassle! We went to the bathhouse with our own tubs, because there were long queues for the sauna buckets. Standing in line was tiring and hot – no fun at all. But we had a great neighborhood with lots of friends. Now, the concept of neighborhood, the estate, is all but gone – nobody even knows their neighbors' names any more. But we knew everybody in the neighborhood.

With my big sister Nadezhda. 1943

Several two-story buildings, gates – all that was our territory. Our apartment block, #10, was very close to the center. I remember constant confrontations with the people from apartment block #14. We also played cops-and-robbers, and ran a lot...

An unforgettable childhood memory: preparations for the parade, tanks rumbling on Ordynka in the night. On the 1st May, the gates closed, the police cordoned off the street, not letting anybody through, and we stood at the gates, watching the vehicles from Red Square going down the Moskvoretsky Bridge

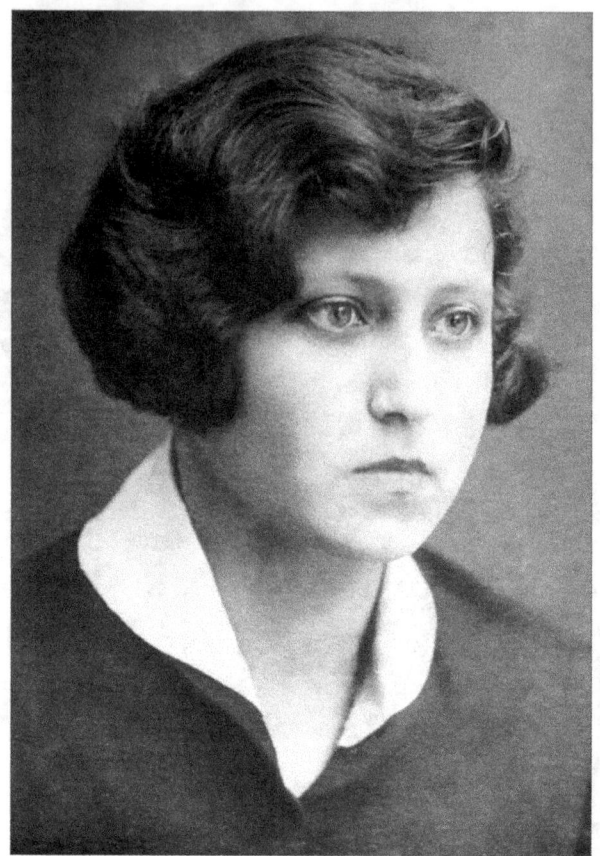
My mother Klavdia Fyodorovna. 1934

and Ordynka Street. Then the athletes and crowd followed. That day was great fun: we bought lollipops and yo-yos. A wonderful celebration!

Even later, when we grew up a bit, we were still excited on the bank holiday. My mother's boss at her job once allowed her to take me to the march. We walked through Red Square, and then everyone in the school was asking me, "Have you seen Stalin?" There was a girl in our class who actually saw Stalin: when their column walked through Red Square, he was watching from the stands. And everyone went to look at the girl who saw Stalin. But I wasn't as lucky as her.

In March 1953, I wanted to go and say farewell to Stalin, but the school teachers said that we shouldn't go. My older sister was much more active than me, she ran home and hurried me up, "Come on, get dressed, we're going to Stalin's funeral!" Our mother had already gone to the center that day, to a pharmacy on Trubnaya Street, and she saw what was happening there. She stood at the door and said, "No, you aren't going anywhere!" What could we do? We couldn't just push mother aside! So, my sister was running round in circles in the room while I watched... Finally, she grabbed a pillow and tore it apart, the feathers flew all around the room! But then she calmed down.

Such tragic pictures go hand in hand together with funny moments in life. Later, we learned that other girls from school who wanted to go to the funeral didn't go either. Our headmistress was a wise old woman, who judging by her manners had taught in a girls' grammar school even before the revolution. She invited the girls to her office, ostensibly to give them some instructions, and then locked the door! I think that she saved quite a few lives that day – now we know, if not precisely, how many people died in the crush during the funeral. Of course, nothing was said officially back then, but people passed the numbers between each other in hushed whispers, relating what was going on...

I was already 12 in March 1953, and I remember well that I felt deep grief. I didn't know how we would continue our lives! My child's consciousness must have been imbued with Soviet propaganda, even though my family didn't have too many reasons to like Stalin – quite a few of my family members were repressed. I remember that when I cried and asked, "How can that be?!" aunt Katya, mother's sister who lived with us and loved us with all her heart, said, "Well, honey, what can we do? He's an old man..." I was deeply offended by that: you could say that our neighbor was old, or granddad Petya, or uncle Vasya. But the aunt said, "People do die, your father also died..." But I couldn't comprehend how you could compare my dad and Stalin, just like that!.. Such a casual tone rubbed me the wrong way: well, some old man died, he was in his seventies already... Like it was nothing special. I was probably affected by the atmosphere in the kindergarten and school; radio anchors would often say, "Thanks to Comrade Stalin!" there were Stalin's five-year plans, Stalin's "ten victories"; everything was imbued with that.

"For Stalin!", the squad commander cried,
And through the lead, treading down the snow,
With his name on our lips
We would charge our foes like lions.

I read this poem by Surkov from the stage. We were all war children.

We defied death many times.
The way to Victory was hard and twisting.
Posterity will call us Stalinists
For this great feat.

I read it with great fervor, as expected. But, incredibly, even though it had been cultivated and accumulated for so long, all that disappeared very quickly! The next year, I was a bit surprised: his death anniversary came and went, but the previous grief had gone. And soon after that, they started to dismantle the cult of personality, and all that was quickly purged from our minds. If you ask school kids now what Stalin's real name was, or who Dzhugashvili was, I don't think that many would answer. And that's as it should be.

I went to School 556 on Pyatnitskaya Street, near Ordynka. Our Young Pioneer chapter was named after the writer and journalist Arkady Gaidar. His son Timur Gaidar, also a writer and journalist and father of the late politician Egor Gaidar, visited our school and made a speech, wearing military uniform. We staged a play based on *Timur and His Squad*. I played either Geika or some other boy. Our school was all-girls at first, co-education only started in the 8th grade [ages 14-15], so all the boys were played by girls – we wore trousers and hid our pigtails under caps. Were we good actors? Probably not, but we staged other plays as well – kids' plays, such as *The Snow Queen*. It was interesting for us, and Timur Gaidar liked our take on his father's book.

Experiments are constantly run in our schools: before the war, boys studied together with girls, then the classes got separated, then combined again, and now there is again talk about separation... When boys first came to our school, it was quite a shock for our poor headmistress, Nina Fyodorovna: she couldn't bear to watch boys sliding down the banisters in her school. Everything had been so nice and civil in our school: uniforms, pinafores, starched collars and cuffs, and then those "ruffians" came and ruined everything! I quickly saw, though, that the boys who joined our class viewed me with respect, because I played chess; other girls dismissed my interest as some kind of eccentricity. There weren't too many girls playing chess back then.

By the way, the famous explorer Dmitry Shparo went to our school. In 1998, he, together with his son Matvey, crossed the Bering Strait on skis for the first time in recorded history, making his way from Asia to the Americas on foot. Back then, he was just a boy from another class in my year; his sister Natasha was in my class.

The Portrait on the Wall

To be honest, I don't remember exactly how I learned to play chess. Boys played in the street, and I watched. We lived on the ground floor, so I could just climb out of the window to go outside, without having to go through the entrance hall. I had my father's chess set, a great rarity at the time, so I garnered much respect as "the equipment owner". The boys taught me as well. We didn't have a clear understanding of the actual chess rules. For instance, if the king reached the last rank, we put a pawn on the file the king was on. It's actually not that bad a rule; sometimes you really need something like that, when you're out of material and have nothing to win with!

My knowledge was corrected when I joined the Pioneers House. En passant was a nasty surprise for me: I was most irate when my pawn suddenly got captured. Castling in our street rules was also different. The boy who showed me how to castle did say that the king and the rook switched places, but he thought that you could also put the king on h1 and the rook on g1 if you wanted. And if you wanted to castle long, there were even more options. I played quite a lot of such games, we'd stay outside until dusk. My mother couldn't answer all my chess-related questions, so she once said, "Why don't you go to the Pioneers House? They have a chess circle there."

For the majority of my generation, war children, the father was above all a portrait on the wall. My father's framed photo hung over the sofa. I constantly felt like he was watching me, smiling a bit. When I was little, I thought that he was looking at me approvingly, but when you did something wrong (like stealing sweets intended for a party), his gaze became more stern. And he always saw everything! Sometimes it prevented me from doing something stupid. Yes, that's how I thought as a child.

I knew that my father was a chess player. We kept his prizes in our home, for instance, a really heavy inkstand. I don't know how he managed to haul it home: it was made of marble, with a paperweight, pencil stand and inkwell. The inkstand was engraved: "For a successful tournament performance." We also had his travel chess set with pieces on small pins inserted into the holes on the squares. My sister and I of course lost two of the pieces. Now this chess set is kept in a Smolensk museum. However, very few of father's chess books remained; my mother said that Kotov took some, and others were lost during the war. We also kept father's pocket watch. People don't wear them much anymore, but in the old days there were special pockets on suit jackets for the watches. This

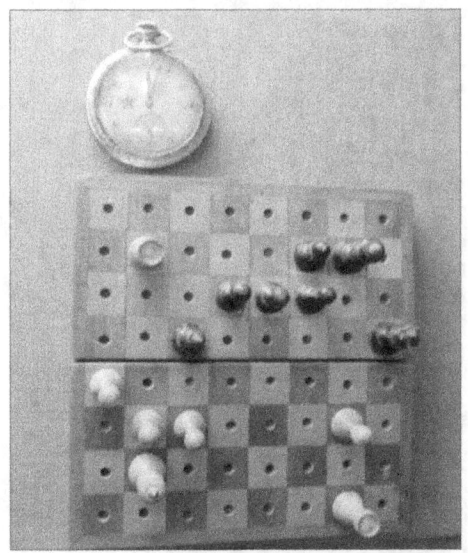

My father's travel chess set and pocket watch

watch was returned to us in 1944. An officer, I still remember his name, Leonid Shaida, came to our home and brought the watch for my mother. He said that he took it from the corpse of a Nazi. It was engraved: "For 4th place in the Belorussian championship." Shaida found my mother through the Sports Committee. I always think, what if items could talk? How many times has this watch changed hands? It's not valuable in itself, just a simple mechanical watch, but it's a memento nonetheless.

I learned of my father's chess career later, but not from my mother. She did accompany father to tournaments a couple of times, but she talked more about, for instance, Lasker's wife – how she looked, what she did. My mother never looked at the board but evaluated the position based on the way my father smoked cigarettes: if he did it calmly, without hurry, then all was well, but if he smoked quickly and nervously, then something was wrong.

Sergei Belavenets was a renowned master before the war. In 1939, he took 3rd place at the Soviet championship, behind only Mikhail Botvinnik and Alexander Kotov. My father was a highly talented and versatile man. After finishing school, he moved from Smolensk to Moscow to enroll in university. But he was, as they said back then, one of "the former", of noble lineage, and university education was severely restricted for students with such a background. After much effort, he was finally accepted by the Agricultural Mechanization and Electrification Research Institute, and his engineering talent really shone through. After his death, it turned out that my father had invented a lot of things that were applied in real life after the war. We learned about all that when his co-inventors came to our home and brought money. My mother tried to decline it at first, but they said, "We received that reward because we used Sergei's ideas. This is his fair share."

He only turned 31 years old in 1941. It seemed that his whole life was still ahead of him. But on 6 March 1942, he died in a battle near Staraya Russa. More detailed circumstances of his death are not known.

At the entrance to the Smolensk museum

Grigory Levenfish

When I was small, I thought that my father was just part of *our* family, *we* spoke about him at home, and all this was only of interest to *us*. But then I joined the chess circle of the Moskvoretsky Pioneers House on Polyanka Street. The coach was very happy to see a girl, because his other pupils were teenage boys, 16 or 17 years old. I knew that my surname was difficult, it was always mispronounced, with the accent on the wrong syllable; I had to repeat it several times, and I always felt very embarrassed. But the coach immediately wrote it down and said, "There was a master with that surname!" It turned out that he knew about Belavenets the chess player, and it was a true gift for him when I came along – he would say that many times. Our coach's name was Nikolai Kuptsov. I think he had gained first category. We usually just played chess, there were no lessons of the kind we're accustomed to today. Sometimes Nikolai showed us how to play a particular opening, so that you didn't end up losing immediately.

When I came home, I said, "Mom, our chess coach knows my dad!" She said, "Of course, chess players know him." Only then did I realize that my father was a really well-known chess player. I had heard that he took 3rd place in the Soviet Championship, but it didn't mean much to me at the time. Yes, he played chess, yes, there were some newspapers with photos. But it turned out that people actually knew and remembered him!

I joined the chess circle at the age of 12 and was considered very young. In the modern age, it sounds almost ludicrous – kids are usually about to give up chess at the age of 12 because they spend too much time on studying, going to a prestigious school on the other side of Moscow, private English lessons or whatever. Today's children are overloaded, but back then, there was nothing of the sort, we would just run about on the streets. Still, everyone went to school and even acquired some knowledge. Perhaps because the distances weren't too great: we lived on Bolshaya Ordynka, the school was on Pyatnitskaya, and the chess circle was on Polyanka – all within walking distance. I went everywhere by myself, nobody held my hand. My mom actually never saw me at a chess board. For many years, even when I started working as a chess coach myself, the majority of new pupils were older kids who wanted to learn chess. But now, parents come with children in tow, holding them in their arms – they'll probably start bringing babies in prams soon!

I think that back then, the process of initial learning was much quicker. The coach explained the concept of opposition to me once, and it was enough. But now, even first-category players often lack precision. Sometimes I randomly toss two kings and a pawn on the board and ask, "So, White to move, Black to move – how does this game end?" And I get different answers. Then I tell my pupils,

"You should stand up and quickly answer all at once, 'White to move – White wins, Black to move – draw!'" There are a lot of things in chess that require a certain degree of maturity, the ability to see the big picture. Earlier, it was thought that abstract thinking is formed when the child is about 11 years old, so we started to study algebra in fifth grade [ages 11-12]. Then, all these thoughts were turned on their heads, and now, first-grade kids are already learning that A is greater than B... I don't know how clearly they understand what they're told. Children's thinking is very concrete. When they are told that there were 5 flowers, and 3 were picked, they realize that they have to subtract 3 from 5. It's the same in chess. If you simply say that White is better, they immediately start asking, "But what if I make this move? Or that move?" You have to reckon with that.

I was very lucky: on Nikolskaya Street (which was called 25th October Street back then), in building #10/2, there was a chess club for the Krasnaya Shveya factory. One day, the club put up an ad – they invited girls for lessons with Grandmaster Levenfish. I think about 20 girls from various pioneers houses showed up, from all corners of Moscow. I first met Alla Kushnir from the Leninsky Pioneers House there. She was a year younger than me. Most of the girls were 15 or 16 years old, but Alla and I were smaller – she was 12, and I was 13. It's hard to say why such an illustrious grandmaster had decided to coach girls, and rather weak girls at that. He actually thought that there was no place for women in chess and didn't exactly hide it. He would often say, "This is awful, simply awful!" Grigory Yakovlevich was an acerbic and witty man and was quite harsh to us. Because of that, or maybe for some other reason, almost all the girls soon quit, and only three of us remained: Marina Shumilina (the daughter of Vera Chudova, another woman player), Alla Kushnir, and me. And later, only Alla and I remained.

Levenfish was constantly kvetching, "Why are you thinking like female elephants?" or, "Any boy would have figured that out ten times faster!" Maybe it was his coaching method – gaslighting us, so that we would work harder and prove him wrong. But could these silly girls really appreciate that?.. Levenfish was actually treating us like grown-ups. He didn't drop to our level – he tried to lift us to his level. And we were awfully embarrassed that we didn't live up to his hopes. I was sure that he considered us utterly stupid; perhaps he really did think so. But once I accidentally overheard Levenfish telling someone, "Belavenets and Kushnir – those two are talented." It was so unexpected that it really shocked me!

Much of my chess knowledge was imparted by him. I had no chess textbooks, but Levenfish explained concepts such as weak squares, backward pawns, and isolated pawns to us... Alla also said that she'd learned a lot in the year she trained with Grigory. Perhaps because we really craved the knowledge, and

With Grigory Levenfish and Alla Kushnir

wanted to study. Levenfish spoke to us on almost equal terms. Of course he berated us a lot, but he never tried to simplify his explanations. When I work as a coach now, I occasionally have to resort to kiddie's language: "Where's our pawnie, who's attacking it now, how do we save our pawnie now?" Of course, Levenfish never used that language with us. He just conversed with us, occasionally using unfamiliar terms. For instance, if you play this and that, you might get counterplay. We didn't quite understand what counterplay was, but Levenfish never condescended to such explanations. Still, two years later, aged 15, I played in the Moscow championship and defeated the reigning women's world champion, Olga Rubtsova. Although I can't say I played particularly well – she just missed a one-move tactic, a knight on d7 that forked a rook on f8 and a queen on b6, and then I barely managed to convert the extra exchange. Olga was not a young woman, and she probably underestimated the schoolgirl who came to the games wearing a white-collared uniform. And Kushnir won the Moscow women's chess championship at the age of 16. So, we did achieve a certain level, and, of course, Grigory should take much of the credit for this.

My First Travels

There weren't many tournaments back then, so I played anywhere I could. At home with my grandfather, in the Moscow girls championship, then in the Moscow women's semi-final and final.

After chess came into my life, my world significantly expanded, in the most literal sense of the word. I boarded a train for the first time that I could recall when I was 14. For the first time!.. I first saw a train carriage with couchettes from the inside. It was really something! What can you compare it to now? Even a sea cruise probably wouldn't do! I was going to Leningrad to take part in the first USSR under 18 girls championship. By the way, women's ex-world champion Ludmila Rudenko served as the arbiter.

At the age of 15, I was selected for the Moscow team, and we traveled to Riga for the USSR youth championship. Each team featured 8 boys and 4 girls. The pressure was enormous – Moscow was considered the main contender for first place. I slowly accumulated chess knowledge, bit by bit. One coach showed something, then another would analyze games, and I kept all that in my memory very well. I remember putting a rook on the seventh rank. I could have put my second rook there as well, but instead, I took the rook back to the fifth rank to attack a couple of stupid pawns. Viktor Khenkin said then, "How could you, it's the Gluttonous Row!" I usually remember such vivid images very well.

When we got to Riga, it felt like being abroad. The year was 1955. I remember going out on the street one day and seeing a man in SS uniform!.. We stood there, shocked – everyone still remembered the war very well. It turned out that a movie was being filmed there...

Several years after becoming acquainted with Ludmila Rudenko at the USSR girls championship I encountered her at the board

In Riga, we stayed at the Metropol Hotel. The name was famous, of course, but we four lodged in one room. Well, it wasn't too bad.

Vladimir Liberzon played first board in our team. At the opening ceremony, it was proudly announced that two candidate masters were playing in the championship: Liberzon and Aivars Gipslis from Latvia – I still remember him as a young, blond boy. Two candidate masters in 17 teams! It was a great chess festival! Sadly, many of the participants have since died.

I also first met Nona Gaprindashvili in Riga. She was a shy girl and didn't speak Russian well. But everyone thought she was very talented, and soon she proved that she indeed was.

Team tournaments were highly beneficial for me because I couldn't study chess alone – perhaps I wasn't assiduous enough. But every game was analyzed

With Boris Persits, Moscow, 1955

at team tournaments, so I watched and learned. Still, I didn't think of chess as my future profession, I treated it as a fun pastime. I never thought about quitting chess, regardless of my performance.

In general, team tournaments are great – everyone gathers in the evening and looks through the adjourned positions. I was lucky: I got to see Botvinnik and Korchnoi analyze. Viktor looked through the games of young boys from his team and even through my own, and, like Levenfish, made some acerbic remarks in the process. We played for the Trud society, and Grigory Goldberg was our captain. He would go to the youth tournaments with us and berate everyone. A huge man, he would sit on a chair cross-legged and say sternly, "Well now, show me what you were doing here!" All this was highly beneficial.

Our coach in the Trud society was Boris Persits. I was still a schoolgirl at that point. We studied at the same club, the unforgettable Krasnaya Shveya. Boris was a sweet man, fully devoted to chess; it's hard for me to judge his level as a player. Every coach definitely helped with my development, and they didn't solely expand my opening repertoire. Persits thought that, both in chess and life, a bird in the hand is worth two in the bush. You should grip the bird with all your strength and then pluck and pluck it. But then it might turn out that nothing was left of the bird... I followed such an approach for quite a while, and Alla complained that she did, too. Later, when Vladimir Yurkov became her coach, he would often chide her, "Away with these 'Persits' moves! I won't tolerate pawns on c3 and e3!" Vladimir did manage to retrain her, but Alla confessed that, in time trouble, when there was no time left to think, she would still occasionally make a "Persits" move – something solid and unambitious.

I owe much to Boris Persits. But in every life, there comes a moment when excessive care, even the most benevolent, becomes burdensome. So, I switched to another coach. Now, you understand a lot of things, but back then... Perhaps I wasn't tactful and gentle enough. But still, I'm thankful to Boris and everyone else who helped me in my chess career.

From Power Engineering to Young Pioneers

I didn't have a single role model I looked up to. I revered all famous chess players, especially the world champions – Botvinnik, Smyslov, Tal, Petrosian, Spassky, and the old-time greats too. I studied their games extensively and learned from them, but still, I can't say that any one of them was a role model. In general, I was most impressed by Mikhail Tal – he was incredibly charismatic! Always funny, friendly and witty, he had a truly magnetic personality, and you couldn't help but admire his colossal chess talent. Tal's career seemed unbelievable, fantastic to me. When I met him, he'd only just become a master.

And then – the sensational victory in the 1957 Soviet Championship, and three years later, Mikhail Tal – the same Misha Tal whose chess career was seemingly just beginning – climbed to the very top and became the world champion. I must admit that I was shocked by such a meteoric rise.

My father's chess motto was "Do not hurry!" I earned first category in 1955, in the Moscow women's championship semi-final, but became a master only in 1964, at the Sukhumi international tournament. I played at Sukhumi almost by accident: they needed a replacement literally one day before the tournament started, and I was in the right place at the right time. I played in ten Soviet women's championships. Now, it doesn't sound as much of a big deal as it was then. Back then, it meant that you were among the 18 strongest woman players: the championships were played in a round-robin system, not Swiss.

To be honest, I don't think that I had much chess talent. My father was talented, but chess talent is not hereditary – I'm sure of that, there are no cases in the entire history of chess. I didn't harbor great ambitions, either. But in women's chess, a bit of attitude and a certain playing ability could get you quite far.

Kushnir was both more talented and ambitious than me. I needed strong motivation to chase any ambitious goal. For instance, after Alla emigrated to Israel, I wanted to meet her at least one more time. There was only one way to do that – qualify for the Interzonal. And I won the Soviet zonal championship! But, let me reiterate, I was never greatly ambitious, in the vein of "either I get to the very top or I quit chess altogether". I liked playing chess, and I wanted it always to be a part of my life. And then Vladimir Yurkov invited me to the Young Pioneers Stadium. He said, "Why suffer in the institute? You get up so early each day. Go back to chess! You'll be a good coach, it's also interesting!"

After school, I graduated from a teacher's training college: physics and math department. I got a school teacher's degree, but actually working as a teacher meant quitting chess. Then, Botvinnik invited me to the mathematical department of VNIIE – the All-Union Research and Development Institute of Electrical Engineering. Chess was highly respected there. I met my future husband at the institute – he played last board for the VNIIE chess team, with Botvinnik himself taking first board. They worked in adjacent labs and knew each other well. But I had to cross the entire city each morning to get to the institute by 7:30 a.m. And we had only just obtained an apartment in the Khimki-Khovrino district, so I had to chase buses at 6:30 a.m. to get to work on time... Yurkov didn't mince words, he'd say, "You'll just drop dead!" He didn't have a particularly elegant way with words, but he made his thoughts clear – he saw that I was exhausted. So, he convinced me to get a job at the Young Pioneers Stadium. This probably helped me win the Soviet championship, too.

Above all, I finally started to sleep well. In 1974, I became a chess coach, and in 1975, I became Soviet champion.

Roughly at the same time, I also started playing correspondence chess, to entrench my presence in the game. It was a good way to enjoy myself, too. But, of course, it's very different from over-the-board play. When you play in over-the-board tournaments, you sit on the stage, you're a star! If you win, they print tables in magazines and congratulate you. You get public acclaim. On the other hand, correspondence chess is pure creativity. You can't exactly boast of your successes, but correspondence chess gave me inspiration, the pure, true joy I never felt at the board. Every correspondence player is convinced that their games are the most interesting thing in life! You say the sweet words, "Here, let me show you!..", then you put a position on the board and show it to your colleagues, fellow crazy correspondence players. They look and say, "Wonderful!"

It's a special class of people: always sitting with a pocket chess set, searching for something... At training camps, I saw the following situation many times: a player receives a postcard and says thoughtfully: "Mmm, I didn't consider this." And then they go in a trance until they find the best reply in the new position. I remember people telling Vladimir Zagorovsky, "Let's go to lunch, and then come and look at the position." He would answer, "Yes, let's look at it later." But I would see him already deep in thought, and he couldn't think of anything but the position. And then he emerges from his room and says joyfully, "All right, let's go, we found the move!" These people love chess with all their heart, and correspondence chess didn't even bring you any income. On the contrary, you only spent money on it constantly – on the postcards and stamps. The games took away a big chunk of your time: it's like having 20 or 25 adjourned positions at once, at various stages of the game. Older chess players will understand me.

The Test Abroad

I played in my first Soviet women's championship final when I was 19. I was proud to qualify. I didn't play too badly, sharing seventh place with Gaprindashvili; I defeated Nona and even got a prize for the best endgame (though I can't remember exactly why I won that prize). Nona wasn't the world champion back then, but she became it the following year. I actually defeated all women's world champions up to Chiburdanidze, except for Vera Menchik.

My first international tournament was in Romania in 1967. For some reason, they wanted a player from Moscow, and I had shared 1st–2nd place in the Moscow championship that year. Medyanikova was the champion, but she was unable to take part. I had to go alone, and I was incredibly anxious. Another big problem was what to wear. When Alla Kushnir went abroad, everyone also helped her with clothes. I wore someone else's coat, because everybody decided that my own coat looked too shabby; I still had to rearrange the buttons. They brought me gloves, and Alla gave me a headscarf and said, "If you tie it this way, it'll look wonderful!" Now it's funny to remember all that, but back then, it was quite an important issue.

I remember that I couldn't go to banquets because I didn't have a formal dress. For instance, I worked as a demonstrator at the Bykova – Rubtsova match. I'd already finished school by that point, but still wore my school uniform dress because it was the most presentable one I had. After the closing ceremony, everyone involved in the match was invited to dinner in a restaurant, but I simply went home – you can't go to a restaurant in school uniform... Any modern girl would have probably laughed at that – everyone has a lot of clothes now.

Also, modern children usually know foreign languages. I learned German in school, but didn't have any practice. At the tournament, I lived in a room with Porubszky, a Hungarian player. She also spoke a bit of German, but her vocabulary barely intersected with mine. Still, we managed to understand each other.

I arrived at the tournament on the opening day, so I had to hit the ground running (there weren't flights from Moscow the day before, and they didn't want to send me two days earlier). I didn't even know the time control. I thought I had to make 40 moves, but it turned out that I had to make 45. I learned that when I was already in time trouble, played some random moves and undeservedly lost. After that, the entire tournament went badly.

There was another incident as well. I played against Jurczynska from Poland (she was quite an unpleasant person), and I promoted my pawn. I put it on the 8th rank and said, "It's a queen," then I looked around quickly, but there was no goddamned queen in sight! I repeated, "It's a queen!" The clock was ticking, I had no other pieces, so I pressed the clock. She jumped up and cried, "That's no queen! That's a pawn!" I was incredibly afraid – I didn't know how the international rules treated such a situation. Popescu, the chief arbiter, came to our board, talked to Jurczynska for a while, and then asked me why I hadn't put the correct piece onto the board. I answered, "Because I didn't have it." Then he explained that in that case, I had to stop my clock and call the arbiter, and since I didn't do any of that, this was all my fault. They brought the tournament regulations in Romanian and read from it for a long time. Then they formally reprimanded me and brought a full set of pieces for me to choose from – queen, rook, everything. I put the queen on the board, and Jurczynska resigned immediately – her position was hopeless. And I learned that you couldn't expect any sporting behavior away from home. I shared 3rd-4th at that tournament in Romania.

My second international tournament was in Halle, East Germany. The players lived in the Rotes Ross hotel – "Red Horse". I won the tournament and thought of myself as a great player. I was really happy. Going to East Germany was interesting, it was basically a different world. But still, the contrast with our country wasn't too great. I only felt a bit embarrassed because everyone spoke a different language, and I constantly had to concentrate to understand what was being discussed. I only felt a stark contrast with our life when I traveled to the Netherlands in 1976 to play in the Roosendaal Interzonal. As I said before, I wanted to meet Alla Kushnir, who'd already emigrated to Israel at that point.

Before the trip, I had to endure an unpleasant briefing at our "competent organs". That year, Korchnoi had defected to the West. I was ordered to convey to him if we met, "Why did you run away? You could have just asked, and we would have let you go!" Yes, that's exactly what they wanted to tell him – even though Korchnoi and I weren't close friends. The Staraya Square official who told me that looked like a decent man, but I think he just didn't understand what he was saying. I listened quietly and nodded. I can imagine the scene that would have happened had I actually told Viktor that... After his defection, Korchnoi lived in the Netherlands for a while and visited our tournament. We looked at each other from a distance, then I passed him some things from his wife through Alla, but asked Alla to tell him not to come close to me.

Alla Kushnir

Alla and I were friends for two decades – very close friends, our lives were tightly intertwined. I remember going to the Sukhumi Interzonal with her in 1964. A month earlier, Alla had given birth to her son, Pavel, and our duties were quite complicated: Alla played, and I babysat Pavlik; then she would return and nurse him. That's how we took care of him, and her husband helped as well. Once, Kira Zvorykina came to our room, looked at us taking care of the baby, and exclaimed, "What a circus!" It's really unbelievable: taking a month-old son on a plane, just to play in some tournament! But Alla won the Interzonal – she shared 1st–3rd place with Lazarevic and Zatulovskaya and then won the play-off.

Both Alla and I represented the Trud sports society, and we helped each other at tournaments. As a chess player, she was stronger: she played three world championship matches against Nona Gaprindashvili – in 1965, 1969 and 1972. I was involved in all three matches as Alla's second. She was first coached

A luxury feast – lemonade and cakes

by Boris Persits, and then Vladimir Yurkov (he was also my coach at many tournaments, and we all worked together; this partnership was what made me a chess player). Now, Kushnir is almost forgotten; when I wrote an article for the *64* magazine in honor of her 60th birthday, I looked in the *Chess Encyclopedia* and saw that they even got her birth date wrong.

I was in Riga at the 1972 world championship when Alla blundered a mate on g2: she protected the h2 square, but forgot about g2. There's a photo of her sitting on the stage, head in her hands... Yurkov jumped up and ran out of the hall, muttering some choice words under his breath. But when Alla came to us, he was already composed. He said, "Never mind, bad things happen. After winning two games in a row, Nona may play something stupid." And indeed, Alla won the third game. She fought valiantly, but Gaprindashvili was truly the strongest woman player in the world back then.

The world championship match is a grueling test, both for the players and the spectators. Nona would always arrive with a big entourage: she was supported by the whole of Georgia. Compared with her, we had only a handful of fans. Nona was probably much more determined – it's no accident that she's still an active and relatively successful player.

Alla left the Soviet Union on 27th August 1974, and, sadly, we parted ways. In the next Candidates cycle, she had to play a match against Marta Shul (Litinskaya). Alla wanted to play the match as an Israeli representative, but nobody in the USSR would agree to that. Viktor Baturinsky had a long conversation with Kushnir; he was very delicate, pouring her coffee. Alexander Konstantinopolsky, the women's national team coach, tried to persuade her as well. As a result, Alla just forfeited the match and left.

It was a blow for me: I was accustomed to us always being together. Back then, leaving the country was similar to jumping into a black hole... Now, you can just go abroad, then return and go abroad again. But then, you had to gather an impressive amount of documents even to arrange a short trip to another socialist country: questionnaires, character references, all that. And you had to jump through many more hoops to emigrate...

At Roosendaal, Alla told me that no matter how she performed in the cycle, even if she became world champion, she would quit chess. I've never understood how one can just quit chess. But Alla changed her life drastically: she enrolled in university there, her personal life changed as well, and so on. Kushnir really did quit chess for good and pursued a new passion — archeology. She's a very talented person, I never doubted that she would find success there as well. But I can't imagine myself not playing chess; maybe I loved it more. My gift was less, but I loved chess more.

After retiring from tournament play, I started playing correspondence chess. I also work as a chess coach. I think that my life would have lacked something important if I'd worked with the same children, but taught them mathematics, for instance. By the way, I worked as a part-time independent tutor when I studied at university. It wasn't like modern cramming, when you prepare talented kids for college exams; I had to work with D-grade students, proving to them that any section of a sphere is a circle. You can't imagine how many apples I had to cut as an example!..

I worked as an 11th grade schoolteacher [for 17-18 year old pupils] for my in-house practice, and it was quite a challenge. I was small and thin, and didn't resemble a typical teacher. Some boys and girls were quite tall. I can't say that my new pupils met me with open arms. And so, before my second lesson with them, I wore my Master of Sports badge on my jacket. The kids started guessing what sport it was, and they became more restrained.

A teacher should love their subject — then the children will feel that and become interested in it themselves. I didn't have such feelings towards mathematics. But I love chess. I think I could teach some other subject, but if you took chess away from my life, it would've been much poorer. But I can do without math!

It's always strange for me to see people quitting chess easily. They set a challenge for themselves and say, "If I don't succeed in my task, I'll quit." Chess pervades you, you can't just throw it away — you can't throw a part of your soul away, right? Chess is actually jealous: if you forget about it for a while, if you cheat on it, it will take vengeance. If you quit and then return, chess might not accept you back. When Yurkov got angry, he would say, "Your Kushnir (so, now she's 'mine'!) doesn't like chess!" Perhaps he was right... I think that we both loved chess, but when chess turned into a full-time job for her, when she had to study seriously and play constantly... At first, we were simple amateurs: just 2–3 tournaments per year that didn't bring in any money. Only a few players received stipends, and all others had a full-time job. Perhaps this necessity was what killed Alla's love for chess.

I often see the following situation when working with children: first successes often come easy – enthusiasm and passion are enough at first. The child is glad, the parents are glad. But to climb the next step, you have to work, and I doubt anybody loves to work. When it's fun to study something, you never think about it as work, but sometimes you have to force yourself to do something. Then it becomes work, and the child slows down and tries to find ways to avoid lessons, but the parents pile on the pressure. The child has to force themselves, and this slowly kills the joy of playing... After that, quitting chess becomes much easier.

Dutch Impressions

In 1976, the Interzonals were held in Georgia and Netherlands. I asked to be sent to the Netherlands tournament. Not that I especially wanted to go abroad (even though it was alluring – we weren't exactly allowed to go abroad every day). I had to jump through some hoops, even though, seriously, what could have happened if two grown women who were friends for 20 years just met? But back then, because of Korchnoi's defection, the higher-ups had to increase their "vigilance". Still, I was sent to the Netherlands, while the young Maia Chiburdanidze was included in the Georgian group, even though she had no right to play in the Interzonal besides the fact that she was a local player. But Maia won that cycle, and, in the Candidates' final, she defeated Kushnir.

The Dutch, of course, lived very differently from us. You go into the most ordinary of shops, which would have been called "Fruit and Vegetables" in the Soviet Union. What could you usually see on the counter of a Soviet shop? Canned peas, some more cans, dubious-looking potatoes... But they had literally everything: green grapes, gray grapes, white grapes, pink grapes, blue grapes, really, grapes of any color!.. Other fruit I'd never seen in my life: such as avocados and kiwis – which were strange, furry...

Another thing that impressed me was their attitude towards children. We were dining in the restaurant. A Dutch family sat at a nearby table. A toddler was sitting in a chair, then he was let down on the floor. He crawled under the table, licked its leg, then got up and walked around the dining hall. A waiter with a tray of food stopped, smiled, let him pass and went on his way. In our restaurant, the waiter would've immediately said, "Take the child away, what if I drop hot tea on him!" But the Dutch kid did whatever he pleased, he was totally free. His mother slowly got up, smiled, went up to him and took him away. I saw similar scenes numerous times in the Netherlands, I liked it. But I didn't see much difference between Romania or East Germany and the Soviet Union. Yes, they had slightly more stuff in the shops. But if you don't have money to buy it, it's still quite unpleasant. Thankfully, now our shops have everything too, I can buy whatever I want.

Chess School TV

When I joined the Young Pioneers Stadium, I was absolutely unfit for a coaching job. Further, Yurkov didn't have a concrete program – he just loved chess and shared his knowledge in every way he could.

I replaced master Boris Nisman, who emigrated to Israel. Yurkov was the only chess coach for a while, paired with a checkers coach (it was a chess and checkers circle). But soon, the checkers coach left as well, and the circle focused exclusively on chess. I actually like Russian checkers, the crisis in the game arrives quite quickly in it. In chess, you can give a hundred checks, prolonging the game almost indefinitely. Vyacheslav Shchyogolev, a former world checkers champion, once told me that international checkers were more difficult than chess, and he was a decent chess player too, earning the candidate master title.

In 1974, I became a host for a chess educational TV program. The shows ran only once per month, but still, they made me concentrate and systematize my knowledge. I had half an hour to explain a chess subject in an interesting way. A very good artist, Galina Amurskaya, and I came up with animation shorts. I still remember one of those shorts, it was very good. The subject was double attacks. A lonely rook was roaming over a chess field, smelling flowers. The king sat tight, hiding behind the pawns. Then the king became bored and walked out of its hiding place. The opposing queen was watching the proceedings, looking into its binoculars from the king to the rook and back. And as soon as the king left its home, the queen threw the binoculars away, grabbed two pistols and shot! And then, the caption "Double Attack" appeared immediately! Many years later, people told me that this cartoon helped them understand: an unprotected piece is a motif for a double attack!

In another animated short, two angry rooks break into the seventh rank. There was also a cartoon about a luft: the rook bursts into the room, the king runs about, then sees an open window pane [in Russian, a luft to prevent back rank mate is called a "little window"] and climbs into it. The rook grabs it by

Me on my TV show

the hem of his mantle, but it manages to break away and escape. And then I explain: "Remember, children: a luft is very important for your king safety!"

Other hosts of the show helped me of course: grandmasters Alexander Kotov and Yuri Averbakh. I read lectures for beginners, while they gave lessons for more skilled players. Averbakh's assistant was Radik Muratov, the actor who played Vasily Alibaba in the movie *Gentlemen of Fortune*. He played the fool, asking dumb questions, and Yuri answered.

Many young players who won prizes at youth tournaments appeared in our studio. I remember Sergei Dolmatov and Artur Yusupov arriving for a shoot straight from the under-20 world championship... We also invited Alexei Shirov, Jaan Ehlvest, Svetlana Matveeva... you really can't remember them all. Sometimes we would go to tournaments and record two or three shows right in the tournament halls. We tried to follow all junior tournaments, such as the White Rook (which gave its name to our TV show), and team tournaments where young pioneers clashed with grandmasters – Vasily Smyslov, Yuri Averbakh, Mark Taimanov, Anatoly Karpov and a very young Garry Kasparov all played in those tournaments.

Of course, we were paid a pittance compared with modern TV salaries, so you could say that we were doing the community a service. When we started, the shows were shot in black and white. At first, they were aired live, but later, we started recording them. The last episode aired in 1989. Afterwards, there were numerous attempts to revive Chess School TV, but they all failed. Even though I think that we need such a show now: I can't understand why there are shows about literally everything but chess on TV.

Our show was hugely popular and we received literally bags of letters. We held problem-solving competitions to help people earn categories. The correspondence was handled by women's ex-world champion Elizaveta Bykova. She checked everything, corresponded with people, and analyzed whether the solutions were correct. Together with a helper, she went through all this sea of letters. It's thought that only one viewer out of 100 wrote in, so, by this estimate, a lot of people watched the show, it was very popular. But then new executives came to TV, and they wanted the programming to be "prettier". Arrows and other gimmicks on diagrams quickly lose their novelty, and only the inner beauty of chess remains, the beauty that has kept the game alive for so many years.

I slowly grew into liking my coaching job. I love chess, I like working with children. My husband told me, "I wouldn't be able to bear that – haven't you repeated this lesson for the fifth time or so?" I answered, "Well, Genochka, this is a teacher's job." You explain that the knight should head towards the center, and then you see half of the knights on the a-file, and the second half on the h-file. It seemed excruciating for my husband, but I wasn't bothered in any way. And I'm still doing that. For instance, you show smothered mate to a kid for the first time, and you see his eyes light up! And I'm glad as much as he is. There are many more beautiful things in chess.

The Young Pioneers Stadium provided two big rooms for chess players, one across the hall from the other. A lot of children came to study. In the late 1980s, however, they started to push us away – they took away the best room and gave us another, small one. And then they took away all the rooms and told the kids to leave...

Over the years, I have given a start in chess life to many children. Not all of them became masters and grandmasters, and many quit chess pretty soon, but most of them, after falling in love with chess, remained loyal to this great game for their entire life, even if they had other jobs. Vladimir Barsky became an international master and a great journalist. There are lots of talented children, but not everybody can fully realize their potential: it depends both on them and their coach. Still, true talents are rare and require utmost care. I think that the most talented pupils of our school were Alexey Vyzmanavin (sadly, he died way too soon, aged 40), Andrei Sokolov and Alexander Morozevich. I believe that Morozevich hadn't said his last word yet, and that he can achieve even more.

At the Soviet Championship in Tbilisi, 1976

Women's World Correspondence Champion

I gradually retired from over-the-board play in the late 1970s. When you have a steady job, it's hard to travel to tournaments too often. To play well, you have to prepare well, and if you can't prepare well, then you can't expect good performances. My last USSR women's championship was in 1979; on 22nd December, my husband's birthday, I defeated the young women's world champion, Maia Chiburdanidze: what a gift that was for Gennadi!

I was almost 40 years old, mostly playing in team tournaments. Correspondence chess became a great outlet for me, it helped me to maintain form. The situation has now changed, but back then, the attitude towards chess-playing women was mostly ironic and condescending. You constantly had to prove that you could do something, and for that, you had to keep your thoughts in order. I also simply liked correspondence chess. The demonstration board I used for correspondence chess is still hanging on my wall. I could set up some problematic position on it, which deprived me of eating and sleeping. We had no computers, we could only use our heads.

People sometimes say, "What good is correspondence chess? You can consult anybody on each move!" Of course you can, but nobody's going to play instead of you. You can show a game, boast something; the other person might look at the position, give you a bit of their time, but then you still remain one-on-one with the position. Sometimes I did ask someone else's opinion, I was curious what others would say, but still, I found all the main ideas on my own. Sometimes someone gives you an idea, and you look at it from all sides; sometimes it works, and sometimes you have to admit that it doesn't.

I remember one incident. Master Nikolai Kopilov from Voronezh liked to reply to moves very quickly when he played correspondence chess. We were at a training camp in Novogorsk, and David Bronstein was also there. He once came to our training session, and Kopilov showed him one of his games. Bronstein asked, "Maybe you could sacrifice a knight on e6 there?" We looked through the position a bit and decided that the move worked. Bronstein then left, Kopilov left too, but we continued to study the position. And found an unexpected Zwischenzug that refuted the combination. When we met Kopilov, we told him, "Oh, such a pity – we found an intermediate move, such a beautiful combination, but it doesn't work." He answered, "Really? And I've already sent my move..."

So, nobody is going to think for you. I don't consider the cases when a husband helps his wife – then it becomes a joint family effort; but in all other cases, it's just not feasible. Some of my positions were analyzed by master Rudolf Kimelfeld, he loved analyzing games. Rudik was an inconspicuous man, but he, for instance, helped Karpov a lot. In chess, he was concerned with the truth; sometimes he would call me and ask, "So, what was the reply to your move?"

I officially became world correspondence champion in 1992, once all the results were counted, although by 1990 I had completed all my games and nobody could catch me. I was awarded a diploma and a dish with the tournament table engraved on it. All world champions get these dishes. Of course, it was a lovely moment in my chess career. The first such moment occurred in 1975 in Frunze (now Bishkek, the capital of Kyrgyzstan), when I stood on stage and the USSR champion's medal was placed around my neck. A lot of people gathered in the hall: the chess tournament was a big event for Frunze. And in 1992, I was sent to the ICCF congress in Graz, Austria. I remember being constantly asked who my husband was (the subtext is clear: they thought he was the one who actually played for me). I answered that he was an engineer, but he played a bit of chess; everyone nodded in understanding. And then we held a blitz tournament for the congress attendees, and I won it. After that, there were no more questions in the vein of "Who's your husband? Who's been playing for you?" I was slightly offended by them, even though my husband did like to take part in analysis. Back then, Grigory Sanakoev, world correspondence chess champion, would often stay at our apartment. Gennadi loved it when he showed us his positions. A couple of times, my husband managed to baffle our guest with his questions, "What if we play this move?" Grigory would freeze, and next morning, he grumbled, "Gennadi should mind his own business! I didn't sleep for three hours afterwards, trying to refute this nonsense!"

Correspondence chess made life more interesting and vivid. I should say that our family life became a bit more interesting, too; when Gennadi made the bed, he would occasionally find a pawn in the sheets and say, "Why the hell am I sleeping with a pawn? I'd hoped for a queen!" I sometimes fell asleep with a pocket chess set in hand. Someone might say that correspondence players are slightly daft, but, on the other hand, this is not the worst type of madness. Chess players are slightly crazy in general, but I think that correspondence players are a bit crazier...

It's a pity that correspondence chess is dying out, but I remember this stage of my life quite fondly. In the early 1990s, when I was women's world champion, and Sanakoev was overall world champion, someone asked me, "Do you think that computers will kill chess?" I replied vaguely that computers will not kill chess immediately, but if they do, sadly, they'll start with correspondence chess. I think that's what is happening. I discussed this with Sanakoev recently. He said that he's still playing, but I don't understand it. You constantly have to correct your moves: I have a computer, he has a computer... This wasn't what attracted me to correspondence chess. Maybe I'm a bit of an old-timer, and I'll freely admit it.

When I retired from correspondence play, coaching became the main part of my life. I must admit that I was never as anxious about my own games as I was about my pupils' games! Sometimes you can't find words to describe what you see your student doing!.. Kimelfeld

Fernschach, a magazine for correspondence chess fans. July 1990 issue

once suggested, "Count the major pieces, make sure that their number is roughly equal, and then leave the hall!"

Small children come to study, at eight years old or so, then you blink a couple of times, and they're already sixteen; indeed, life goes so fast, it's very inconsiderate of it. But even when you replay some old events in your head and remember what you've lost forever, it still makes you happy.

Recently, there was a funny episode at the children's championship in Turkey. I went to a restaurant to eat, and then somebody cried out, "Oh my god, it's Lyuska! Lyuska Belavenets!" I thought, whoa, who's calling me Lyuska? I turned around and then heard myself exclaim, "Oh my god, it's Lyubka Kristol!" She was from Leningrad, emigrated to Israel a long time ago and came for a sightseeing

With my husband Gennadi Anatolevich Dorf (1929-1998) in Smolensk

tour. By the way, she was also a women's world correspondence chess champion, we used to play each other. And so, a very excited conversation started. She asked, "What are you doing here?" I said, "There's a world championship, I came with the kids." "Ah yes! I think Berkovich is the head of our delegation." And then, like in a bad vaudeville, the door opened, and Berkovich entered the restaurant! They hadn't seen each other in years in Israel, and then met in Turkey!

My Friends

I've always felt that the chess world was populated with incredibly interesting people, and now, when I bring order to my thoughts and memories, I'm constantly amazed at how lucky I was. I've met a lot of outstanding personalities in my life; I think I can write a three-volume book just listing their surnames! Many of them became my friends for life. I've already told you about Alla Kushnir: we had the same tastes and interests; we both loved opera, bought LPs when we had some spare money, knew a lot of arias by heart. One woman chess player wrote a poem that started with, "Two friends, two sisters – Lyuska and Alenka. Same braids, same thoughts...", and so on.

I remember my first big tournament – the Soviet championship, my first encounter with great chess players. For Alla, it was already the second championship, and she introduced me to my opponents. I knew Olga Rubtsova, but Larisa Volpert, already a well-known player by then, was a completely new figure for me. She's almost 15 years older than me, and, of course, we thought of her as an adult, a mature lady. Alla said, "She's really cool!" I've never seen another person so eager to share their thoughts and knowledge, on a very positive note, too. First of all, she started teaching us French poetry. I still remember one of Verlaine's poems in the original French. We didn't know the language at the time, but we were entranced by the melody of the words and even started studying French after that.

Then she started giving us lectures on literature – all that happened during the Soviet championship, when we were out on walks. Our friendship started at that championship and still continues. She lived in Leningrad with her husband, then they moved to Tartu. At a certain moment, Volpert decided to retire and work as a teacher, even though she enjoyed great success in chess – she won several Soviet women's championships and finished as a runner-up at a Candidates Tournament.

With Larisa Volpert and her husband Professor Pavel Reifman, 1978

Larisa defended her thesis, wrote lots of books, and worked as a students' theater director. Students in Tartu adored her. Together with her husband, Professor Pavel Semyonovich Reifman, she worked at the Russian language and literature department in the local university. I visited them frequently over the years, and met Yuri Mikhailovich Lotman and many other people who taught there. It's another facet of life, another world, but still, chess opened the door for me. Sadly, time waits for nobody, and Pavel died in 2012... Larisa will probably have to move from Tartu to another place – her son lives in the United States. Life disconnects people. But Larisa Volpert is a really fun person! I think everybody who knows her would agree with me.

Recently, a tournament was held in Chelyabinsk to mark Kira Alexeyevna Zvorykina's 85th birthday. Quite a few elderly ladies showed up to play: ex-world champion Nona Gaprindashvili, Vera Tikhomirova, Larisa Volpert, Valentina Kozlovskaya, Rimma Bilunova, Ludmila Lyubarskaya, and me. You might have wondered who would be interested in seeing some old women playing? But the organizers held a meet and greet, and one of the spectators confessed to me later, "I never thought that woman chess players (and he also 'delicately' reminded us of our age!) could be so interesting!"

So, the chess world is indeed populated with interesting people. But I write about only a few of them in this book, because you can write a whole book on each of them. I've played Zvorykina, Volpert and Bilunova, and we're still friends. As I said before, correspondence chess players are a special sort. This is a fine and pure art, the players don't expect much money or honors – basically, they're doing it for the soul. And a lot of correspondence players had a full-time job and usually were quite successful at it. Vladimir Zagorovsky is a professor of history, Vsevolod Kosenkov worked in the field of nuclear power, and Sergei Korolev is a Doctor of Sciences and taught at an institute. Grigory Sanakoev has a Ph.D. in chemistry. After Perestroika, he became a chess professional, a club director. By the way, he's still playing correspondence chess, which surprises me a bit. Abram Khasin, Yakov Neishtadt, Oleg Moiseev... Olga Rubtsova won both over-the-board and correspondence world championships.

I captained our correspondence chess national team, and we won two Olympiads under my stewardship. Our team included Rubtsova, Marta Litinskaya (she took part in women's Candidates matches), Merike Rotova from Estonia – players who achieved great over-the-board success as well. The men's team also consisted of strong players who could do much more than send a move on a post card. For instance, Tonu Oim, the two-time correspondence chess world champion from Estonia. Since his surname was very unusual to a Russian ear, he constantly had to explain over the phone: "It's Tonu Oim calling. Oim. Three letters." I once came home, and my mom said to me, perplexed, "You had a call from some 'three letters'..." Of course, it became a permanent source of jokes [in Russian, "three letters" is a euphemism similar to a "four-letter word" in English].

I can't remember another collective that was as diverse as our national correspondence team. Sometimes we would go to training camps together; there were no computers, and so we looked through our positions for days. At first, we were led by Alexander Konstantinopolsky – a great coach and wonderful man, one of those who made chess life better. We reported to him one by one. He would say, "First board – Vladimir, your turn, please!" Zagorovsky would show his positions, we would give some recommendations, then separated into small groups and studied the more difficult positions. Most often some player would say, "Here, my position is better, and I'm counting on a win." And then, for instance, Khasin would inevitably interject, "Have you analyzed ♘d5?" And there we would go – endless analysis begins, often quite emotional. Then somebody would say at lunch, "I refuted that move of yours, ♘d5. Stop talking nonsense!" But the refutation was always met with a counter-refutation, then a counter-counter-refutation, and so on... I again digress, recalling my correspondence chess days, but it's truly immense. A whole gallery of portraits, so many people whom I was lucky enough to meet and still think about with gratitude and happiness!

In general, people don't usually keep many friends. They can establish a lot of friendly relationships, but it's rare for these relationships to become really long-term. At some moment, when people work together or do something together, they get closer, establish a friendly rapport. And then fate separates them, and they drift apart. But I was lucky: I still maintain relationships with a lot of friends I made at the start of my chess career. I've already mentioned Ludmila Lyubarskaya. She's a bit younger, so I was a bit protective of her: I'm an adult, and she's still a girl. When you're 20, and she's 15, it feels like you're a whole generation ahead of her. Of course, now five years is not a real difference. Fate separated us, Lyubarskaya has been living in Germany for many years. But if there is any trouble, I'm always ready to come to her aid, and she will come to mine. For instance, in autumn 2011, we held a women's champions tournament in honor of Nona Gaprindashvili's round birthday. I gave my word that I'd play, but I had certain problems with mobility. And then Ludmila came over and helped me with domestic matters. It's a touchstone that tests your relationships, but I've never doubted any of my friends.

When I started working as a coach, I of course found new friends in fellow coaches. As I've already mentioned, Vladimir Yurkov was the person who offered me the job. We met when I was 14 years old, and he was a grown 18 year-old. We worked together for years. Vladimir was Alla Kushnir's coach, and we trained many pupils at the Young Pioneers Stadium together. He is one of the people whom I remember with gratitude, and it's very unfortunate that he died so soon...

Yurkov married very early. He had to provide for his family, so he dropped out of university and went to work at an aircraft factory. But he had coaching talent, and soon he started work at the Young Pioneers Stadium. He was a master at that point. He never received any formal coaching education, but he loved chess and could instill that love in others. He

With Vladimir Yurkov, 1989

taught children and learned a lot in the process. Love for chess is probably the most essential requirement. He taught many players, and they remember Vladimir with gratitude. He became a highly-qualified coach, working with truly talented pupils. In truth, he only achieved great things when he lit up, only when he encountered talent. Routine work was a chore for him, he usually asked me to do it. But that's beside the point: we always worked together and never separated our laurels. We had a small and tight team at the Young Pioneers Stadium – Vladimir Yurkov, Vladimir Sergeev (he worked with the smallest kids) and me.

In the early 1980s, we got an opportunity to invite another coach. Yurkov and I were in our forties at the time. We thought that we were getting on a bit, so we decided to find a young master, because children like young adults. And one day, at the chess club on Gogolevsky Boulevard, we were introduced to Sergey Yanovsky. Serezha had only recently graduated from university, worked for a year in his main profession but wanted to find a job in chess. That's how he joined our chess life. The children adored him: he was young and sporty, played football with them, and spoke the same language. I knew clearly that I could ramble on for long on some moral or ethical topic, and they would half listen to me, but Yanovsky could explain why something was wrong in a couple of words. So, all in all, we made a great choice!

We're still friends, Sergey helps me greatly in many situations. And he does all this gladly and joyfully, as though nothing will make him happier. He always treated me a bit patronizingly, because he thought that I knew too little about mundane life and my head was constantly in the clouds. All in all, he was right in most cases. When I face difficulties of any sort, the first thing I do is call Sergey and ask, "Serezha, what do you think I should do?" And it sometimes seems like no problems exist for him! He says, "You can do this or that", or, "Do nothing, I'll come over and help."

Of course, I'm thankful to him beyond words. He's another friend that chess helped me gain. Maybe there are similar people in other spheres as well, but I was especially lucky in the chess world. My current collective is also outstanding: Ludmila Zaitseva, Artem Akhmetov, director Natasha Chukhrova – my former student, Zhenya Reshetnikov, Zhenya Kuchumova, and other colleagues. We are all very different – in age, in upbringing, in worldviews – but we all love chess, and this helps us quickly smooth out any disagreements that occasionally arise.

Another category of friends is grown-up pupils and their parents. Of course, I've seen a huge number of kids and their parents, but some of them became my friends. Lately, I've been talking a lot with two former students – Lena Gutkina and Timur Khvalko. They often call me, asking "How can we help?" It's very moving.

Even if the children have left the chess school long ago, their parents still don't disappear, they try to make themselves useful. Three boys of the same age studied at my school – Alesha Dvoretsky, Ilyusha Razdolsky and Sasha Inodin. They have all graduated from university by now, one of them defended his thesis at the age of 26. All of them are successful adults. But still, their parents call me, come and visit, ask me how can they help – all in all, we enjoy a good chinwag. Igor Lobanov grew up long ago, but his mother Vera still takes part in all our affairs. She was the chairwoman of our parents' council. Parents would go with us to summer camps and try to make our life easier, maintaining some

With Sergey Yanovsky and Grigoriy Oparin at the "Chess Hopes of Russia" school training session. Ognikovo, March 2012

Sergei Perman

semblance of order among the throng. What feeling can I have towards such people, besides gratitude?

Of course, I have to thank specially the father of one of our boys, Zhenya (Evgeny) Perman – Sergei. A decent chess player himself, he often played with the kids and helped us immensely. He thought that our work was very valuable, educating children, and he was really glad to have his son study under such a great coach as Ludmila Zaitseva. He thought that it was he who should be grateful to us, not vice versa. Sergei Perman did a lot of good for everyone. He helped at our chess club and many other talented players, especially Ian Nepomniachtchi, Ildar Khairullin and Valentina Gunina, who have now become strong grandmasters. Nevertheless, Sergei was always really modest and didn't publicize himself. But we know and remember everything! Now Zhenya has a younger brother, Denis – also a chess player, he recently became Swiss U10 champion. Their little sister Anya is growing up, maybe she will become a chess player, too?

The children in our school can transfer from one group to another: all in all, they are all our common kids, and the successes are ours to share, too. Everybody who played a part in them shares the common joy. It's very important for the collective. Someone works with small kids, someone else with older kids. But we all understand that we pursue a common goal.

Kostroma – Loo – Eforie Nord

About ten years ago, Andrei Beletsky, a chess coach from Kostroma, decided to open a school for children from other regions in his hometown. He came to Moscow and asked Igor Zaitsev to work in the school. They needed a household name, and Igor was a great choice. But Igor couldn't go. And then Beletsky asked me, "Would you like to take part?" I saw his great enthusiasm, his selfless desire to help the kids from Kostroma Oblast, so I agreed. Two or three times per year, we get together and continue this valuable work: for a relatively small price, the kids, many of whom have no permanent coach or even no coach at all, can acquire important knowledge and take a rest from school life for a bit.

Many Moscow schoolchildren, including our pupils, gladly travel to Kostroma. The schedule of chess lessons is very tight, but they still somehow manage to play football and table tennis, to squabble, fight and make peace. In other words, they live a full life! There are other coaches in the training camp, too – including Konstantin Chernyshov and Vladimir Belikov, one of Kramnik's coaches. The parents are quite surprised: "Will he really teach our children?" Yes, he does teach them – he liked the first session, so he took part in four or five more. Belikov analyzes openings with the strongest kids. Local coaches from Kostroma are also there – Beletsky, Lebedev and others.

I have traveled a lot with children to chess competitions – to the Russian championships and to festivals. For instance, I enjoy the traditional tournament at Eforie Nord, Romania, at the seaside. The children play with great enthusiasm there, earning new categories. Everyone can play there – the smallest children, the older kids, even their parents and coaches. All this is complemented with swimming in the sea, sightseeing, etc. I love going to such tournaments; the lessons are much more fun and emotional there – the kids show the games they just played, fresh off the board.

Of course, official competitions are very important for improvement. The Russian championship had been held in Loo (near Sochi) for the last few years. All tournaments, from U10 to U20, are held in the same place. This is a

At a chess festival in Romania, summer 2012

special event, with lots of people. And it gets bigger and bigger because of the first league, and the highest league is growing too, as many players pay their own entrance fees. Even though the initial idea was different: only those who qualified through other tournaments were able to play. But what can you do if you share 4th–5th place, and only four players are admitted? Something is always lacking in life...

Actually, the job of coaching has changed significantly, because the importance of opening preparation has risen sharply. Coaches put a lot of effort into... I don't want to say "cramming", but let it be searching for opportunities in openings, ways to win the game at the very start. Whether it's the right or wrong approach, I think that you should always have a sense of proportion: children are sometimes so tired of this multi-hour preparation that they don't have any energy left for the game itself. Yes, they can gain a significant advantage, and the satisfied coach will say, "We had this position at home!" Yes, that is true, but there is no opening that can immediately win the game, no magic variation...

Sometimes I meet a fellow coach at the end of the tournament and say, "Hi, you're here as well? Why didn't I see you earlier?" "Well, I'm mostly sitting in my room, working: preparing one player, then a second, a third, and then it begins anew." Times are changing, it's not intrinsically good or bad – they simply are. But these tournaments make it possible to see many people from other cities whom aren't easy to meet otherwise. Traveling to world and European championships is especially interesting. We are scattered all around the world. We lived in one country, played in Spartakiads and Soviet championships, we were bonded. But now we come from different republics, people work as coaches in different countries. I'm not even surprised to see Guus Hiddink and Dick Advocaat as our national soccer team managers. When I was young, though, something like that was completely unthinkable.

I think that there are many enthusiastic young coaches in chess,

With my talented pupil, European champion Liza Kisteneva

and they have achieved some success. They work in difficult conditions: I know well how hard it is to get money for trips. Of course, Moscow is a special city, there are more opportunities, more people who can finance their kids' travels. And there can be some real talents among those kids. There's no strict formula, such as "talented equals poor, rich equals mediocre". Different situations happen.

I can't fully agree with those who claim that only the richest can rise to the very top. Recently, for instance, a boy named Urii Eliseev returned to our school, to his coach Evgeny Reshetnikov. Just an ordinary lad from an unassuming family, his parents weren't at all wealthy. Still, he loves chess, works a lot and has achieved a high level. He was under-16 Russian champion and earned the international master title.

I don't think that sheer talent is insufficient to rise to the top. Of course, it's easier with support, but if the player is talented and determined, they will make it. There's a huge choice of competitions where you can prove yourself. And if you play well in an important tournament, you get an invitation to a training camp and an opportunity to get coaches noticing you.

My Lineage

I would also like to talk a bit about my grandfather and my father's family.

All my forefathers from my father's line served in the navy. Our most famous ancestor was Ivan Petrovich Belavenets, a renowned scientist, the head of the Kronstadt Observatory, Captain 1st Rank. He invented a device that prevented magnetic deviation of the compass caused by iron in the ship's hull. His portrait hung in the Naval Museum in St. Petersburg for a long time, but after the upheavals, it was replaced by photos of revolutionary sailors.

Nikolai Petrovich Belavenets was a hero of the Sevastopol campaign; he was buried in Crimea, and his grave is still intact.

My grandfather, Vsevolod Pavlovich Belavenets, told me all about that. I remember him, but I was still a little girl and didn't understand much, otherwise I would have asked him a lot of questions about the whole family. Still, he was very cautious when he told me about it. He once mentioned the name of his mother, Nadezhda Nikanorovna Potemkina (my sister was named after her), but said that it would better not to mention this to anyone.

I asked, "Grandpa, why didn't you become a naval officer?" Like all boys in his family, he was sent to the naval corps during Tsarist times, but he was expelled for bad behavior. He told me his story, it was rather funny. But when I expressed my regret, saying "But you could have become a naval officer too," he laughed, "Well, what can I say? Perhaps then I would have perished at Tsushima, like

This photo was taken before the revolution, in 1916 or 1917. The three Belavenets brothers: Vladimir, Kirill and Sergei (my father)

many of my classmates. And then I wouldn't have met your grandmother, and you wouldn't exist, silly!"

This made quite an impression on me! Every child thinks that the whole world revolves around them – how can it be that he wouldn't have existed?! I often think that we consider some events in our lives as tragic, but then we realize that it was meant to be this way, and it's all right. In this case, some boyish antics changed my grandfather's entire life.

He learned a civilian profession and became a renowned constructor, specializing in bridges. Towards the end of his life, he moved from Smolensk to Moscow and worked in the Highway State Department. He encouraged me to play chess: he loved it, and it was no accident that my father also got interested in chess. Even my grandmother Natalia Evlampievna, his wife, played correspondence chess, although I suspect that my grandfather played for her. By the way, my other grandmother was called Agrippina Kharlampievna – there's some old-time Russian names for you.

When my father was a child, he lived with the family of his aunt Sofia Pavlovna Belavenets, the sister of Vsevolod Pavlovich, for a time. Her husband Konstantin Alexeevich Vygodchikov was a famous chess player as well, and he competed in several Russian SFSR championships. They studied chess a lot. My grandmother said that it was impossible to talk to them: as soon as they

Late 1930s. My father observes a friendly game in the park

were out in the street, they started playing blindfold chess. One says "e4", the other says "e5", then "knight to f3", "knight to c6", and this dialogue, very "interesting" for her, continued the whole way!

My father was friends with Mikhail Yudovich since childhood – the humorous poem about "the twins from Smolensk" didn't appear out of thin air. I met Mikhail when I started playing chess, he always treated me very well. When I joined the chess world, many people who respected my father projected their goodwill onto me as well. Nobody ever spoke ill of him; I always felt that aura of friendliness, the desire to help. Those who remember Sergei said that I looked like him. Sometimes, when Alla and I went to some tournament together, we were asked, "I'm sorry, which of you two is Sergei Belavenets's daughter? You? Glad to meet you, I knew your dad!" These words, "I knew your dad!", accompanied me often.

My father died on 6th March 1942, when I was just a year old. I don't remember him; my sister did, and she told me a lot about him. He couldn't do anything for me, since he died so soon. But, on the other hand, he did a lot: somehow, I inherited his love for chess. As a parting gift, he left me a huge world populated with diverse people, and I'm sure that most of them are good! I'm convinced that if you love chess, you can't be a bad person.

I remember how I once came home, proud of some victory of mine. My aunt said, "Serezha would be so glad that Milochka plays chess!" And mother replied thoughtfully, "Well, I don't know, he didn't think that this game was for women..." Vera Chudova once cried openly in his presence; he became very upset and said, "At the end of the day, this brutal game is not for girls!" If only he saw the brutal games modern girls take part in... But still, I want to believe that my father would indeed be glad that I play chess.

Chess Lessons

Sergei Belavenets

Evgeny Sveshnikov, grandmaster:

Master Sergei Belavenets [1963, written by Ludmila Belavenets and incorporated into the current book] was the first chess book that I read, and I really enjoyed it. Before that, I had never read any chess literature, except for the illustrated book *Shakhmaty cherez veka i strany (Chess Through the Ages and Countries)*, my mother's gift for my tenth birthday (however, I mostly looked at the stamp reproductions in it).

Interestingly, my opening repertoire was largely formed by Sergei Belavenets. I rather liked his idea – the move ♘d5 in the Botvinnik system (white then plays ♘xf7, black plays ♕xh4, etc.). I started building my opening repertoire based on his games in this line. Only many years later, in 1995, did I come to the conclusion that this idea, which I'd lived with most of my chess life, had been finally refuted. But that is beside the point! Thanks to the book on Sergei Belavenets, I learned to analyze. I was attracted by its bright ideas and depth of analysis, and this is much more important! That's what I value in chess the most.

Mark Dvoretsky, Distinguished Coach of the USSR (from an interview):

Mikhail Shereshevsky wrote a great book called *Endgame Strategy*. Do you know how it was created?

In 1976, I played in the First League of the Soviet Championship in Minsk, and Mikhail helped me. We discussed various subjects, but he was especially interested in methods for improving chess technique. Later, he came to Moscow and studied my notes, in particular, the notebook which I had labeled "General Principles of Endgame Play". When he returned to Minsk, he applied these principles in his work with the Belorussian youth team. The results were impressive: his team won the USSR team championship, which was previously only won by the "giants": Moscow, Ukraine, or Russia. Based on ideas derived from my notes and newly-acquired experience, he wrote that book, handpicking all the examples himself. I was very flattered.

But I was first prompted to work on this subject after reading the book *Master Sergei Belavenets*, specifically, the part where Belavenets discusses endgames. His thoughts seemed clever and interesting.

Ludmila Belavenets:

The following work is only a fraction of the materials my father prepared for his textbook. Sadly, most of them were lost during the war and in the early post-war years.

GENERAL PRINCIPLES OF MIDDLEGAME PLAY

The game of chess is divided into three general parts: the opening, middlegame and endgame. The goal of the opening is to mobilize your forces. The middlegame is the time for a pitched battle: mutual attacks, maneuvers, and tactical skirmishes often end with one player gaining a material or positional advantage. Conversion of this advantage often happens at the third stage, the endgame.

Chess games don't always include all three parts. Sometimes they don't even reach the endgame. This happens when the middlegame battle leads to a quick and unfortunate result for one side: their king gets checkmated, or they lose so much material that further prolonging the game is useless.

There is also another kind of chess game, where tactical middlegame-like complications already occur in the opening. Even before all the pieces are developed, we see dazzling fights on the board of which any middlegame would be envious. Often, such games don't have a middlegame at all. After the furious opening fight, most pieces get exchanged, and the game, skipping the most romantic stage – the middlegame – goes straight into a prosaic endgame.

Let's look, for instance, at the game **Belavenets – Lisitsin** *(game i)* from the 10th Soviet championship (1937). Here's how it went:

1.d2-d4	♘g8-f6
2.♘g1-f3	d7-d5
3.c2-c4	♗c8-f5

Black obviously intends to sharpen the game right out of the opening. With his next move, white decides to cooperate. If he wanted a quieter game, he would have played 4.cxd5 ♘xd5 5.♘bd2.

4.♕d1-b3	♘b8-c6
5.♘b1-c3	...

Not 5.♕xb7 ♗d7 6.♘c3? ♖b8 7.♕a6 ♘b4, but 6.♕b3 gives White an edge.

5... e7-e5

6.c4xd5! ♘c6-b4?

Black should have accepted an equal position after 6...♘xd4 7.♘xd4 exd4 8.♕a4+ c6 9.♕xd4 cxd4, but his approach is "complicate things, no matter what".

7.e2-e4!	♘f6xe4
8.♗f1-b5+	c7-c6
9.d5xc6	b7xc6
10.♘f3xe5	...

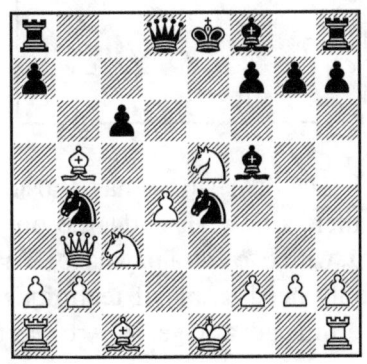

Look at this position. It doesn't resemble an opening at all. Usually, it's all quiet on the board after ten moves, but this is a tense middlegame already. Such dazzling complications always lead to sudden simplifications, and the board becomes very calm after the storm. Black's position is already lost.

10...	♗f5-e6
11.♘e5xc6!	...

A fascinating subtlety. It now turns out that, after 11...♗xb3, white can first grab the knight along the way, 12.♘xb4+, and only then, after 12...♔e7 13.♘c6+, come back for the queen. Black's reply is forced.

12...♕d7 13.♗xd7+ ♔xd7 was relatively better. 11.d5! would also win.

11...	♕d8-b6
12.♘c6xb4+	♕b6xb5
13.♕b3xe6+	f7xe6
14.♘c3xb5	♗f8xb4+
15.♔e1-e2	♔e8-d7

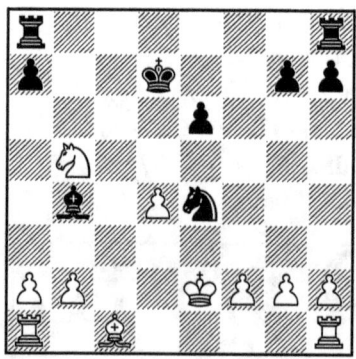

The tactical storm has subsided, and there's now an endgame on the board, with two extra pawns for white. He only needs a bit of technique to convert the advantage. Where was the middlegame in this encounter? The common concept of three stages of the game was turned on its head: there were middlegame-like complications in the opening, and then the players went straight to the endgame, essentially skipping the middlegame. [Note this game is analyzed in full as No. 11 later in this book.]

There are two types of position in the middlegame. One is characterized by an abundance of tactical blows, complications, and intricate piece interactions. Let's call this kind of middlegame "tactical". It has no solid strategic ideas and no series of purposeful maneuvers. What decides the outcome here is tactics, calculation of lines, the ability to find tactical blows. Such positions usually have no pawn chains and the game is open. Pieces of both sides easily come into contact with each other, creating a branching net of lines. In such positions, you need precise calculation first and foremost, while the other side of chess struggle, strategy, plays only a secondary role.

Let's look at an example of a tactical middlegame.

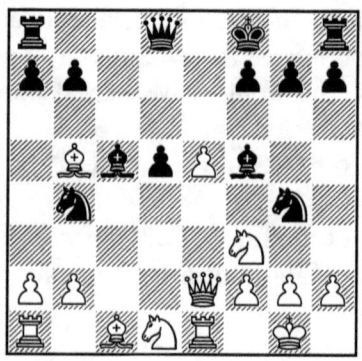

This position is taken from game 19 of the **Euwe – Alekhine** return match, 1937 *(game ii)*. The game is very open, and it enters the stage of wild complications. After

1. h2-h3   h7-h5!

Alekhine sacrificed his g4 knight, hoping to get an attack on the white king's position in exchange. There followed:

2. ♗c1-g5   ♕d8-b6
3. ♘f3-h4   ♗f5-e4
4. h3xg4   ♘b4-c2

There is no general strategy behind either sides' play. The fight boils down to creating and fending off single tactical threats. Now, black both threatens to capture the a1 rook and play 5...♘d4, so white's reply is more or less forced.

5. ♘d1-c3   ♘c2-d4!

Capturing the rook doesn't do much good, since after 5...♘xa1 6.♘xe4 dxe4 7.♖xa1 hxg4 8.♗c4, white retains an overwhelming position.

However, black has the resource 8...♖h5!, and the situation remains unclear.

6. ♕e2-f1!?   ...

This move still wins, but it is not the best. Analysis shows that white could easily win if he gave back the sacrificed piece and launched a counter-attack on the opposing king – 6.♕d2. However, it's hard to navigate such complications, and Euwe's desire to keep the material advantage is understandable.

6...   h5xg4

7. ♘c3-a4   ♕b6-c7
8. ♖e1xe4?   ...

White probably thinks that he has to give back some material, because the hanging g5 bishop and h4 knight ensure an initiative for black (he threatened both 8...♖h5 and 8...♕xe5).

White could retain his advantage with 8.♘xc5! ♕xc5 9.♗d3.

8...   d5xe4
9. ♕f1-c4   ...

9.♕f1-c1! would clearly be more precise, as on 9...♕xe5 10.♗f4 would give him a clear advantage.

9...   ♖a8-c8?

A bad move. White can now win with 10.♘xc5. Black should have played 9...♕xe5 10.♕xc5+ ♕xc5 11.♘xc5 ♘xb5 with a somewhat worse endgame.

10. ♖a1-c1?   b7-b6?

The sudden 10...♕xe5 11.♘xc5 ♔g8! gave black a decent position.

11. ♘a4xc5   b6xc5

The position has simplified a bit. Had Euwe played 12.e6! now, he would have easily won, since 12...♘xe6 is decisively met with 13.♘g6+.

To avoid making things too difficult, we won't show all the complicated lines here. The reader can find them in the match game collection. We'll only point out that in this position, white played **12.♗b5-a6?**, which gave Alekhine an opportunity to play **12...♕c7xe5!** and launch a counter-attack that led to a draw.

We can draw some conclusions. There are no general strategic ideas in a tactical middlegame, only concrete lines.

The ways to expose the flaws in one's opponent's position in such cases depend on the chess player's ingenuity, their skill and experience. Playing such a tactical middlegame is very difficult. The previous example shows that even the best players in the world were unable to resolve the situation correctly.

Play is very different in the other kind of middlegame position, where both players have certain strategic goals and pawn chains are present on the board, making the game more closed and relatively quiet. Let's call such middlegames "strategic". We should warn the reader that this distinction is more or less hypothetical: in some cases, a quiet strategic middlegame can turn into a very complicated tactical one, and vice versa. But still, in most cases, the distinction between tactical and strategic middlegames is fully correct. As an example of a strategic middlegame, let's look at the following position from the game **Flohr — Sultan Khan** (match, 1932) *(game iii)*.

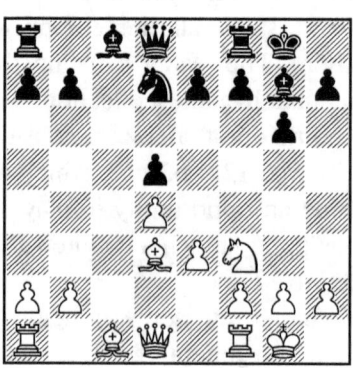

The position is almost closed. The center is solid enough for both players, and they aren't preparing any central operations on their next moves. White executes his plan: seize the c-file and exert pressure along it. The following play mostly consists of quiet positional maneuvers.

1. ♕d1-b3   ♘d7-b8

The knight is transferred to c6. It would look awkward on b6, and white would threaten to kick it back with a2-a4-a5.

2. ♗c1-d2   ♘b8-c6
3. ♖f1-c1   ♗g7-f6
4. ♖c1-c5   e7-e6
5. ♖a1-c1   a7-a6
6. ♗d3-e2!   ...

White transfers his knight to d3, intending to put it on c5 or e5. Black's only try is to organize some kingside counterplay.

6...   ♔g8-g7
7. ♘f3-e1   ♗f6-e7
8. ♖c5-c2   ♗e7-d6
9. f2-f4   ...

In conjunction with the queenside operations, white prevents his opponent's potential activity in the center and on the kingside. Placing the knight on d3 at once is a bit better, though.

9...   ♕d8-e7?!

9...a5 then placing the knight on e7 would fully equalize.

10. ♘e1-d3   ♗c8-d7
11. ♘d3-c5   ...

Not 11.♕xb7 ♖fb8, winning the queen.

11...   ♗d6xc5?!

Black unnecessarily gives up the bishop pair. Defending the b7-pawn with the rook on the f-file would keep the balance.

12.♖c2xc5   ♖a8-b8
13.♗d2-e1   f7-f5?!

Black should play 13...♖fc8 with a slight advantage for White. Black thinks that white threatened f4-f5 and ♗g3, and that's why he played 13...f5. Now, white executes another deep idea, typical for such positions. White's advantage on the queenside is obvious, the black pieces are passive and tied to protecting their weak squares. Flohr uses a typical strategic technique: he keeps the pressure on the queenside, but launches an attack on the kingside as well. White's pieces are much more mobile and can create threats on both sides of the board. Black can't maneuver as much, and so it's hard for him to organize defense on both flanks at once. A catastrophe is coming.

14.a2-a3   ♖f8-c8
15.♕b3-d1   ♕e7-e8
16.g2-g4?! ...

16.♗h4! would keep white's advantage

16...   ♘c6-e7

Black resorts to the most powerful defensive technique – piece trades.

It was better to play 16...fxg4, to use f5 as an outpost.

17.g4-g5   ♖c8-c6
18.h2-h4   ♖b8-a8

Defending the a6 pawn and intending b7-b6.

19.h4-h5   ♖c6-c8

20.♗e2-f3   b7-b6
21.♖c5-c3   ♖c8xc3
22.♗e1xc3   ...

Of course, it's not beneficial for white to trade the second rook as well after 22.♖xc3 ♖c8, since he's using it for his two-pronged attack.

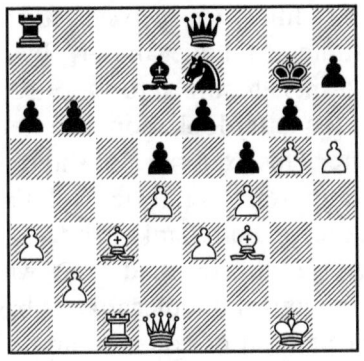

22...   ♗d7-b5?

After 22...a5! white had only a small advantage. Now, his advantage is obvious both on the queenside, where his opponent has several weaknesses, and on the kingside, where he's currently attacking. The final stage begins.

23.♗c3-b4   ♕e8-d7?

White threatened to transfer the bishop to e5 through d6. Black could resist better with 23...♔g8!.

24.♔g1-f2   ...

24. ♗xe7! ♕xe7 25.♕c2! would win.

24...   a6-a5?

24...♘c6 would not equalize, but would keep the position playable.

25.♗b4xe7   ♕d7xe7
26.♕d1-h1! ...

The winning move. White

threatens 27.hxg6 hxg6 28.♕h6+. Black can defend from that, but this only leads to new trouble.

26...   ♔g7-g8

26...♗e8! was more tenacious.

27.♗f3xd5   ♖a8-d8

28.♗d5-a2, and white soon won.

The difference between tactical and strategic middlegames is obvious. The former are similar to a sword duel, while the latter look more like trench warfare. This example also showed us one important strategic technique: attacking on both flanks at once.

As we already said, the whole play in tactical middlegames is based on calculation of concrete lines. It's likely impossible to find any general considerations in such middlegames, because you need different approaches for every position. Thus, in the following sections, we shall mostly consider the issues in strategic middlegames.

The most important factor in every middlegame is position evaluation and, consequently, the choice of plan and area of struggle.

The main part of evaluation is analyzing the advantages and flaws of both your own and opponent's structures and considering mutual chances. After we identify all the main features of the position, it will become clear what we should do next. You should never spare time and effort to answer this all-important question during the game. Otherwise, we'll be making moves without understanding clearly why they are selected. It's better to execute a plan – even if it's not the strongest one possible, perhaps even if it's wrong – than to move pieces aimlessly.

However, the correct plan and correct choice of the immediate goal is only a part of the whole, albeit a big part. Another, equally important question is how to achieve the goal you set.

But no textbook can help you here – a chess player can only count on their own skills. The correct answer to this second question largely depends on one's playing ability. Below, we shall examine the various elements of a strategic middlegame.

THE CENTER

The first strategic concept you learn when studying chess is the role and importance of the center. The necessity of seizing the center of the board for the upcoming piece battles is so obvious that we don't think it necessary to encourage that specifically. It's clear to everyone that centralized pieces are the most active, and they can be quickly transferred to either flank to support the upcoming attack. We would only highlight one very important factor. Usually, chess players instinctively feel that fighting for the center is necessary. But often, a player gets too carried away with events in other areas of the board and totally forgets about the center, allowing the opponent to seize it and undermine all their previous efforts. Thus, we should advise every over-the-board chess player to keep the center in mind for the whole game and not forget the importance of central squares even if events on the flanks are exciting.

The center of the board is the area comprised of four squares, d4, d5, e4 and e5; their neighboring squares form the so-called "extended center", a 16-square area. With the very first opening moves, 1.d4 or 1.e4, white and black try to seize the central area. The opening of the game is a fierce fight for the center. Sometimes, you have to sacrifice material to gain a solid pawn or piece position in the center. The first 8–10 moves decide the outcome of the initial fight for the center and define the subsequent middlegame fight. The value of any opening line is usually determined by how successfully it helps to win the battle for the center. There are two ways of seizing the central squares. You can put your pawns on those squares – create a pawn center or, at the very least, attack these central squares with pawns. The other way is to put pieces onto the central squares or organize piece pressure on the center. In the first case, we're talking about building a pawn center, and in the second case, it's a piece center. The nature of the resulting position is different in these cases; the ways to convert the advantage of seizing the center are also different.

Pawn centers

When we put our white pawns on d4 and e4, or, conversely, our black pawns on d5 and e5, and the opponent has no pawns of their own to challenge our center, this means that, all other things being equal, we have an advantage. Of course, we can only speak of an advantage if our pawns aren't in danger of being captured or neutralized, i.e. if our pieces provide enough support for them. The most important goal for the player who controls the center is to strengthen the position of their central pawns and prevent possible attacks from the opponent. If you manage that, the next goal is to increase the pressure in the center, and only then should you think of ways to convert your advantage of controlling the center. Of course, your opponent doesn't sit down at the board to resign, and they will search for ways to destroy our attractive pawn position.

How should you use a strong pawn center? Obviously, we're talking about a center that's well-protected by pieces, otherwise the question is different: how to *protect* that center. Of course, the simplest way is to try and advance the central pawns and create confusion among your opponent's pieces. However, this way of converting the central advantage is rare. First of all, your central advantage would need to be enormous in this case – only if your opponent has no central pawns.

Thus, in practice, the method of central pawn advantage conversion is different. Using the strong pawn position as a foundation, the more active side switches play to a flank. The role of central pawns in such flank attacks is very important: they take central squares away from the opponent's pieces, making defensive maneuvers more difficult. Sometimes, you can combine a flank attack with central pawn advancement. This makes your attack even more formidable.

Let's look at the following example from the game **Budo – V. Makogonov**, Tbilisi 1937 *(game iv)*.

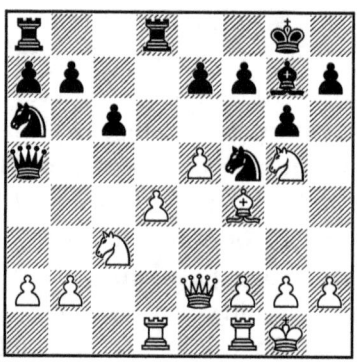

It's clear that this position arose from Grunfeld Defense. By the way, this opening always gives white a pawn advantage in the center, and the question of whether these pawns are going to be strong or weak gets resolved in the middlegame.

In this position, black has already forced white to advance his pawn from e4 to e5. In general, the best position for these pawns is to be side-by-side, which allows them to attack the most squares. Since the pawn has moved to e5, this frees up the important central squares d5 and f5 for black, and his pieces aim to seize them. One black knight is already on f5, and the other one needs just two moves to jump to d5 and completely paralyze the white central pawns. Thus, white has to play energetically to use his center advantage. How should he do that? It's hard to advance the d- and e-pawns, and it won't do much good anyway. Budo decides to launch a kingside attack, and to do that, he first needs to weaken the black king's pawn cover. There followed:

1.g2-g4! ...

The knight has only two escape squares – h4 and h6, which are equally bad. White's central pawns have already done their first good deed: they have taken good central squares away from the black pieces. It's bad to capture on d4 due to 1...♘xd4 2.♕c4 ♘e6 3.♘xe6 fxe6 4.♕xe6+ ♔h8 5.♕xe7 ♖e8 6.♕g5 *(6.♕xb7 is simpler)*, and now 6...♗xe5 is bad for black, since after 7.♖d7 white gets a strong attack. Now we see the other important role of central pawns: the black pieces are divided into two separate groups, and it's hard to get the a6 knight or the a5 queen involved in kingside defense.

1...   **♘f5-h6**

The best defense was 1...♖xd4 but then 2.♘ce4! should win.

2.h2-h3   **f7-f6**

This is almost forced. White threatened to win the knight after 3.♘ge4 and 4.♕e3. Now that the black king's position is compromised, white can launch a direct attack.

**3.♘g5-e6   ♖d8-e8
4.♘e6xg7   ♔g8xg7
5.♕e2-e3   ...**

5.d5! ♘f7 6.e6 would win more convincingly.

**5...   ♘h6-f7
6.d4-d5!   ...**

Opening the way for the d1 rook and seizing the d5 square for the knight. Black doesn't dare to capture on d5 — he's scrambling to get the queenside pieces involved in defense.

6...   ♘a6-b4?

Only 6...fxe5! would give black a slight chance to survive.

7.e5-e6   ♘f7-d8

7...♘d6 lost a pawn: 8.dxc6 ♘xc6 9.♗xd6 exd6 10.♖xd6.

8.♗f4-h6+   ♔g7-h8

8...♔g8 9.d6 exd6 10.♖xd6 with the strong threat 11.♘e4 was even worse.

9.d5-d6!   ...

The white pawns do their heroic deed: by sacrificing their lives, they blow up the opponent's defenses.

**9...   e7xd6
10.♕e3-f4   ♖e8xe6**

The black queen has no time to join the defense of the f6 square, since the b4 knight is hanging.

11.♖f1-e1   ...

Threatening 12.♕xf6+! ♖xf6 13.♖e8+ with mate next move. Black is now defenseless.

**11...   ♔h8-g8
12.♖e1xe6   ♘d8xe6
13.♕f4xd6!   ...**

The final subtlety. Capturing on f6 was bad due to 13...♕e5. Now, 13...♕e5 is impossible on account of 14.♕xb4.

**13...   ♖a8-e8
14.♖d1-e1   ♔g8-f7
15.♖e1xe6.**

Black resigned, since he gets checkmated after 15...♖xe6.

The role of central pawns in this game was most instructive. First, they drove a wedge between the black pieces, hindering their coordination. Then they moved, leading to the decisive weakening of the f6 square. And even though both pawns fell, they played key roles in white's attacking plan.

The importance of the pawn center is not limited to attack. A strong pawn cover can make even an uncastled king's position impregnable; even the most formidable attacks were often stopped by a strong pawn center. The following position occurred in the game **Bondarevsky — Botvinnik** from the 1941 six-player match tournament *(game v)*.

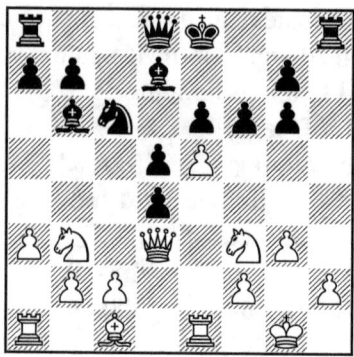

Black failed to castle in time, so his king's position in the center of the board looks quite precarious. But black has a strong pawn center, so Botvinnik boldly played

1... ♔e8-f7!

Now it's hard for white to find attacking opportunities: his piece activity is restricted by the black pawns. In such positions, the attack is usually resumed with great effort after a sacrifice that breaks the pawn barrier, but sometimes it's not possible to find a tactic in such positions. Bondarevsky didn't want to allow the black pawns to move as they would after 2.exf6 gxf6 3.♘bxd4 ♘xd4 4.♘xd4 e5, with the two black bishops seizing important diagonals.

Hence, there followed:

2.h2-h4 ♕d8-g8!

Botvinnik plays a deep idea, an outstanding maneuver. Black transfers his queen to h7, to force subsequent exchanges after g6-g5. This will make his king's position less dangerous, and his pawn center will become even more important. However, black has an instantly winning move 2...♖h5!.

3.♗c1-d2 ...

White could still show some activity with 3.a4, and he would have a playable position after 3...a6 4.♘bxd4, 3...♖h5 4.♗f4 or 3...a5 4.c3

3... ♕g8-h7
4.♗d2-b4? ...

4.a4! would give white hopes to survive.

4... g6-g5

Botvinnik gives the pawn back, hoping to use his pawn center. Preparing to advance the g-pawn with 4...♕h5! would win quickly.

5.♕d3xh7 ♖h8xh7
6.e5xf6? ...

This is a clearly losing move. 6.hxg5 fxe5 7.♖xe5 ♖ah8 8.g6+ would give white slight hopes to survive.

6... g7xf6
7.h4xg5 e6-e5
8.g5xf6 ♔f7xf6

Black's center is now playing a different role. Earlier, the central pawns served as a simple barrier, stopping the opponent's pieces in their tracks, but now they're becoming a strong factor in the unfolding attack on the white king. Bondarevsky's last hope is to try and stop his opponent's pawns.

9.♗b4-d6 ♖a8-e8
10.♘f3-h4 ...

Hoping to play f2-f3, stopping the e5 pawn.

10...	♖e8-g8
11.♔g1-h2	♗d7-f5
12.♖e1-e2	d4-d3!

The d4 pawn is tired of its long inactivity and now moves forward energetically. White can't capture it because of 13.c2xd3 ♗xd3 14.♖d2 ♗c4, and the black knight gets to f3 through d4.

13.♖e2-d2	d3xc2
14.f2-f4	...

The last desperate attempt to get the d6 bishop involved in the defense of his kingside. But it's too late.

14...	♗b6-e3
15.♗d6xe5+	♘c6xe5
16.f4xe5+	♔f6-e7
17.♖a1-f1	...

If the d2 rook moved, black would win with 17...♖xh4+ and subsequent bishop checks.

17...	c2-c1=♕

White resigned.

Now we know about the advantages of a pawn center. It's useful for both attack and defense. The reader should pay attention to the fact that, in all the examples above, the center had excellent piece protection — that's what made it so strong. When we have an opportunity to create a pawn center, we should always consider the question: are we able to provide sufficient protection? The lack of necessary piece support can lead to a catastrophe: your opponent will concentrate the attacks of their pieces on our pawns, and our pawns will be weakened, traded away or simply captured. There are many cases when a formidable-looking pawn center crumbled under blows of the opponent's pieces.

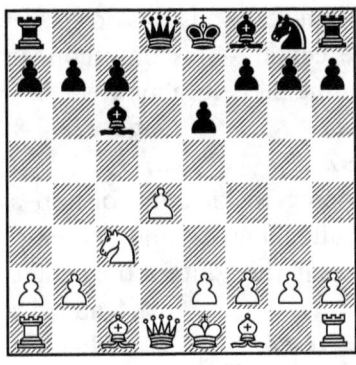

This position occurred in the game **Pillsbury — Chigorin**, St. Petersburg 1895 *(game vi)*. White played **1.e2-e4**, seizing the center with his pawns. But it later turned out that these pawns can't get enough support from pieces, and Chigorin prepares a devastating attack against the center.

1...	♗f8-b4
2.f2-f3	f7-f5!

What should white do?

If he captures on f5, there might follow 3.exf5 exf5 4.♗c4 ♕h4+ 5.g3 ♕e7+ 6.♔f2 0-0-0 with a good position for black. Pillsbury decided against going for this sharp line.

The position on the diagram is one of the tabiyas of the Chigorin Defense, occurring after 1.d4 d5 2.c4 ♘c6 3.♘f3 ♗g4 4.cxd5 ♗xf3 5.dxc6 ♗xc6 6.♘c3 e6. After 7.e4 ♗b4 8.f3, modern theory considers the immediate 8...f5 break too risky because of 9.♗c4. Black usually searches for chances after 8...♕h4+ 9.g3 ♕h5.

3.e4-e5 ...

Now the d4 pawn is weak, and black has a strong outpost for his knight on d5. White has no advantage in the center – his only concern is defending his central pawns.

3... ♘g8-e7
4.a2-a3 ...

Hoping to kick the bishop away from attacking c3 and increase his chances in the fight for the center.

4... ♗b4-a5
5.♗f1-c4 ♗c6-d5
6.♕d1-a4+ ...

6.♗xd5 ♘xd5 7.♗d2 is bad due to 7...♕h4+ and 8...♕xd4. The best resource was 6.♕b3.

6... c7-c6
7.♗c4-d3 ...

7.♗xd5 ♘xd5 8.♗d2 again didn't work because of 8...b5 9.♕c2 ♕h4+.

7... ♕d8-b6!
8.♗d3-c2 ...

Black threatened 8...♗b3, winning the queen. White is now forced to find only moves to defend his ill-fated d4 pawn, but he still can't hold it.

8... ♕b6-a6!

Again threatening to win the queen after 9...b5. White would be somewhat worse after 9.b4 ♕c4 10.♗b2 ♗b6 11.♘xd5 ♘xd5 12.♗b3.

9.♗c2-d1 ♗d5-c4

9...b5 10.♕c2 ♖d8 would give black a bigger advantage.

10.f3-f4? ...

10.b4 ♗b6 11.♕xa6 ♗xa6 12.♗e3 leads to an equal game.

10... 0-0-0?!

10...b5! would have won for black but he is still clearly better.

11.♗c1-e3? ...

11.b4 is the only move that doesn't immediately lead to defeat.

11... ♘e7-d5
12.♗e3-d2 ♘d5-b6
13.♕a4-c2 ♖d8xd4

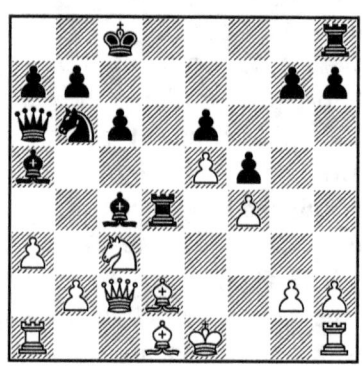

The d4 pawn has fallen. In addition to a material advantage, black's position is also significantly better. He won the game a few moves later with a direct attack on the king.

All in all, an unprotected pawn center is vulnerable to many threats. The opponent can capture these pawns, exchange them or, like in the last example, force a weakness and then launch a systematic siege. One way or another, a pawn center without sufficient protection only brings trouble to its owner.

We should also consider another case. When the pawns of one opponent move forward, the squares behind them are weakened. You often have to advance the c- and f-pawns to protect the pawn center, but this weakens the flanks and thus the king's position. This allows the opponent to explode the position with a sacrifice and then forcibly attack the exposed weaknesses.

The following example is taken from the game **Ilyin-Zhenevsky – Botvinnik**, 7th Soviet Championship, 1931 *(game vii)*.

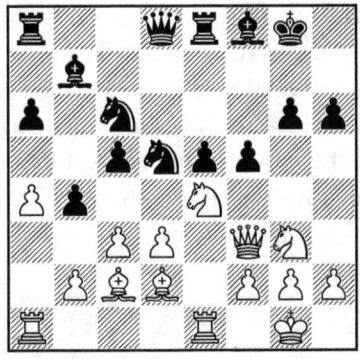

Black's advantage in the center is obvious. His c5 and e5 pawns control the d4 square, constraining white's mobility. With his last move, f7-f5, black hoped to increase his advantage even more. He thought that white was now forced to play 1.♗b3, and after 1...♘a5 2.♗xd5+ ♗xd5 3.♘xf5 gxf5 4.♕xf5 ♗g7 5.♗xh6 ♗xe4 6.♕g4 ♗g6 black has a slight edge. However, the move f7-f5 created numerous weaknesses in the black king's position, and Ilyin-Zhenevsky boldly blows up black's pawn barricades by sacrificing a knight.

1.♘g3xf5   g6xf5
2.♕f3xf5   ♗f8-g7?
2...♔h8! 3.d4! ♕c7 4.♘xc5! with an advantage for white, but it would not be sufficient to win.

3.♘e4xc5?!   ...
Black's pawn center is nonexistent now. White has three pawns for the piece and a strong kingside attack. He has seized the initiative. Nevertheless, white could have won here with 3.♕g6! as taking on h6 would be decisive.

3...   ♗b7-c8
4.♕f5-g6?!   ♘c6-e7
Black constantly has to keep the threat ♗b3 in mind.

5.♕g6-h5   ♘e7-f5??
White should have played ♕h5 back on move 4, since now black could have used the tempo gifted to him: 5...♗f5! 6.♗xh6 ♕d6, consolidating the defense.

6.d3-d4!   ♖e8-f8
7.d4xe5   ...
White now has four pawns for the piece, and his attack is still going strong. Interestingly, all black's central pawns have fallen, and now it's white who has a strong pawn on e5, causing black a lot of trouble.

7...   b4xc3
8.b2xc3   ♕d8-e7
9.e5-e6!   ...
The central pawn goes forward, causing even more confusion in the opponent's ranks. Black is defenseless against the devastating power of the c2 and d2 bishops.

9...   ♕e7xc5
10.♗c2xf5   ♕c5-e7
Not 10...♘e7 due to 11.♗h7+, winning the queen.

11. ♗d2xh6   ♖f8xf5
12. ♕h5xf5   ♗g7xh6
13. ♕f5xd5   ♗c8-b7
14. ♕d5-d7   ♗h6-g5
15. ♖a1-b1   ♗b7-c8
16. ♕d7-c6. Black resigned.

Indeed, having a well-defended pawn center gives you an indisputable advantage and is useful both in attack and defense.

Sometimes, you can even sacrifice material to obtain such a center, for instance, in the Evans Gambit, King's Gambit, etc. But you always have to remember that it's necessary to defend these central pawns well, or else they'll cause you a lot of trouble.

Piece centers

If the central pawns are gone, or they don't play a decisive role in the fight over the central squares, then both sides try to seize the center with pieces. Putting our pieces on central squares brings a number of benefits. They can be relocated to a flank for an attack or directly decide the outcome with their movements in the center. Still, we shouldn't forget that the pieces' position in the center may be only temporary, the opponent can drive them away or exchange them. Thus, you have to be quick and energetic in converting your centralized piece advantage. The most rational method is to launch a flank attack.

Piece fights for the center are usually fierce. To obtain a central advantage and then use it, you need to do some clever maneuvering. There are no universal principles in the struggle for a piece center – everything depends on the concrete position. We can only advise you to try and drive away the opponent's pieces from the center with various maneuvers and then transfer your own pieces to the central squares. This is one of the hardest tasks in chess, and experience plays a crucial role here.

Let's look at the following position from the game **Botvinnik – Lilienthal** from the 1941 six-player match tournament *(game viii)*.

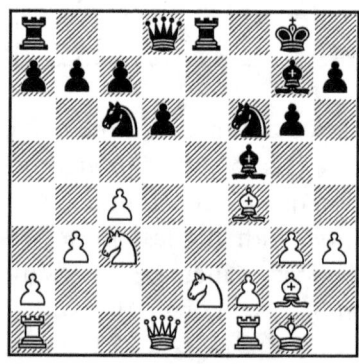

There is rough equality in the center. White controls the d5 square, while black holds the e5 square. Nobody can create a pawn center, so the opponents try to seize the central squares with pieces. Black's pieces are well-centralized, so his position looks solid enough. However, it's actually not so. White is able to use his kingside pawns in the fight for the center, driving away the well-placed black pieces. And this brings him the central advantage.

1.♕d1-d2   h7-h5

Such weakening moves are always very unpleasant to make. But there's no other way to prevent g3-g4 and maybe the subsequent g4-g5, disrupting the piece balance in the center.

2.♖a1-e1   ♕d8-d7
3.♔g1-h2   ♔g8-h7
4.♗f4-g5   ...

White intends to play 5.♘f4, involving the e2 knight in the battle for the center as well. Black decides to protect the d5 square in a radical way

4...   ♘c6-e5
5.♘e2-f4   ...

Not falling for the trap: 5.♗xb7? c6 with the threat 6...♘f3+.

5...   c7-c6
6.♗g5xf6   ♗g7xf6
7.♘c3-e4   ...

White's maneuvers are quite poisonous. He's piling on the pressure in the center and planning to attack the weakened kingside.

7...   ♗f6-e7
8.♕d2-c3   ♕d7-c7

White threatened 9.c5. Black can't trade on e4, because it would be hard to defend the g6 square without the light-squared bishop.

9.♘f4-e2!   ...

A great maneuver. Botvinnik drives the opponent's pieces away from the center, and this quickly decides the game.

9...   ♖a8-d8

10.f2-f4   ♘e5-f7
11.♘e2-d4   ♘f7-h6??

This move loses. The f5 bishop couldn't retreat because of f4-f5. However, 11...♕d7 would keep black alive in a bad position.

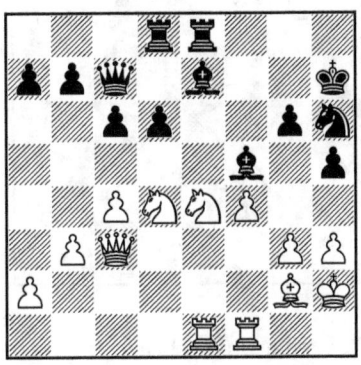

Let's compare this position with the initial diagram. Instead of a roughly equal position, white has gained a huge advantage with difficult maneuvering. His d4 and e4 knights are brilliantly positioned, and black has nothing to counter the pressure in the center. Now that white has such a strong piece center, no wonder he managed to find a decisive flank blow.

12.♘e4-g5+. Black resigned.

After the forced 12...♗xg5 13.fxg5 ♘g8, there follows 14.♘xf5 gxf5 15.♖xf5, crushing.

In that example, white got a huge piece advantage in the center. All of his pieces were centralized, and this fact led to the quick winning solution. Of course, you can't always centralize all your pieces in such a way. Often, you have to settle for just one good central square for a minor piece. But even such a modest gain can give you an advantage if your opponent doesn't get enough compensation.

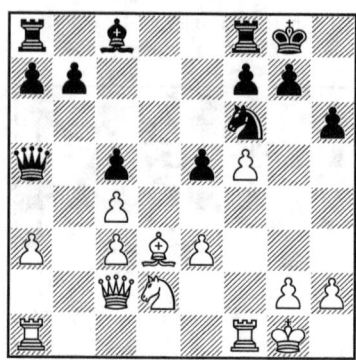

The diagram shows a position from the game **Botvinnik – Kan**, 11th Soviet Championship, 1939 *(game ix)*. White has no central advantage. An obvious idea is to seize the d5 square with the bishop or knight. One possible way is to put the d2 knight on d5. However, this is hard to achieve; besides, as soon as white puts his knight on d5, black will trade it for the c8 bishop and then put his own knight on d6, getting a defensible position. Botvinnik implements a different plan: he trades the knights and seizes the d5 square with the bishop.

| 1.♘d2-e4! | ♕a5-d8 |
| 2.♘e4xf6+ | ... |

It was bad to take on c5 due to 2...♕b6.

2...	♕d8xf6
3.♗d3-e4	♖a8-b8
4.♖a1-d1	b7-b6
5.h2-h3	♗c8-a6
6.♗e4-d5	b6-b5
7.c4xb5	♖b8xb5?

By playing 7...♗xb5 8.c4 ♗c6 black could live with a small disadvantage. After 9.♕e4 ♗xd5 10.♖xd5 ♖b3 he has great drawing chances in the major-piece endgame.

| 8.c3-c4 | ♖b5-b6 |
| 9.♖d1-b1 | ... |

Preventing 9...♗b7.

| 9... | ♖f8-d8 |

9...♖fb8! 10.♖xb6 ♕xb6 is met with 11.f6!, destroying the king's defenses, but white's advantage would be small after 10...♖xb6!.

| 10.♖b1xb6 | a7xb6 |
| 11.e3-e4 | ... |

The bishop on d5 is the harbinger of white's impending victory. Thanks to its activity, white focuses his attack on the kingside, and this quickly leads to success.

| 11... | ♗a6-c8? |

This is a serious mistake. Black should play 11...♖b8!, as if 12.♕a4 then 12...b5! could be played with a playable position.

| 12.♕c2-a4 | ♗c8-d7?! |

This passive move makes a very difficult position lost, as the white queen invades. After 12...♕e7! black would be worse, but still had reasonable chances to hold.

13.♕a4-a7	♗d7-e8
14.♖f1-b1	♖d8-d6
15.a3-a4	...

All black pieces are immobilized. This is the result of the immovable, formidable d5 bishop.

| 15... | ♔g8-h7 |
| 16.a4-a5 | b6xa5 |

17.♕a7xa5   ♖d6-a6

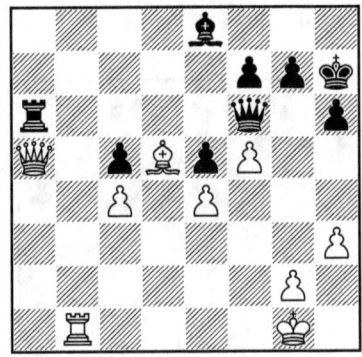

18.♕a5xc5   ...

White has won a pawn. Black tries to find his last chance in tactical complications.

18...   ♖a6-a2
19.♕c5-e3   ...

Black threatened 19...♕g5.

19...   ♕f6–a6
20.♖b1-b8   ♕a6-a4
21.♔g1-h2   ...

Preventing 21...♕c2 thanks to 22.♕g3 ♖a1 23.♖xe8 ♕d1 24.♕g6+! fxg6 25.♗g8+ ♔h8 26.♗f7+ and 27.♗xg6#.

21...   ♖a2-a3

22.♕e3-c5   ♖a3-a2
23.♖b8-a8   ♕a4xa8
24.♗d5xa8   ♖a2xa8
25.♕c5xe5   ♗e8-c6
26.♕e5-c7. Black resigned.

This game is a good illustration of the strength of a centralized piece and its influence on flank attacks. If the reader wants to study similar positions in more detail, they might analyze the games Botvinnik – Sorokin and Kirillov – Botvinnik from the 7th Soviet Championship, Botvinnik – Panov (11th Soviet Championship), and Botvinnik – Chekhover (11th Soviet Championship semi-final, 1938). In all these games, a minor piece that seized an important central square decided matters.

The above examples illustrate the importance of the center very well. The possibility of a direct attack through the center is not even as important as support for a flank attack. A strong center ensures the success of flank operations – this rule works 99 times out of 100.

GENERAL PRINCIPLES OF ENDGAME PLAY

In fierce middlegame battles, the atmosphere might become quite heated. There are sacrifices and beautiful combinations everywhere, both players watch out for tactical blows, devious traps, and subtle unexpected moves. And suddenly, several piece trades follow, the poetry of the frantic tactical battles disappears, and a prosaic endgame appears on the board. The transition to the endgame is sometimes forced by one of the players who thinks that it's the easiest way to convert an advantage. But often, the endgame occurs because both players want it.

Technique is the most important skill in endgames. The first thing a player should do is to restructure their thinking, their approach. You should forget about "brilliancies", about tactics. I advise every player to take a few minutes and just calm down, "get rid of your burning passions" — of course, if the clock allows it. This time investment will definitely pay off later, allowing the player to look at the position in the correct, "endgame-like" way. What does this mean?

We should consider this question more thoroughly, because all the multi-volume endgame textbooks throw endless examples and positions at you without paying necessary attention to the thought process in the endgame.

During the middlegame, your mind is mostly busy with calculating the lines that pursue a certain goal. The main occupation of a player in the middlegame is checking for numerous tactical blows, calculating the combinations and lines. In the endgame, it's all different. Only in rare tactical endgames you should concentrate on calculations. In the overwhelming majority of endgames, you should be thinking in terms of plans. The concrete lines play only a secondary role. The main approach here is thinking in set-ups. We plan the positioning of our pieces — of course, taking the opponent's plans into account. And only then do we calculate whether we can get this position. For instance, in the following position from the game

Capablanca — Ragozin, Moscow 1936 *(game x)*, white was quite laconic in formulating his goals.

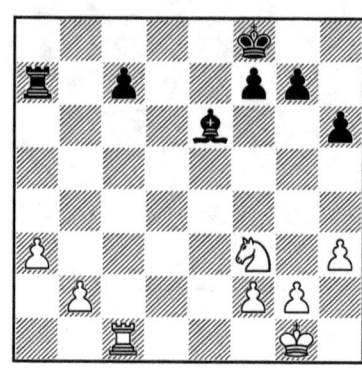

Capablanca wrote about his thoughts during the game: "The essence of white's plan is to stop the c-pawn from moving (otherwise, the b-pawn might become too weak) and control the whole board up to the 5th rank. This can be achieved by moving the king to e3, putting the rook on c3, the knight on d4, and pawns on b4 and f4. After getting that position, white will push the queenside pawns."

As you see, Capablanca wasn't concerned with lines or even with time — the amount of moves necessary to achieve the intended position. The main thing is done: he drew up the intended position and now makes moves according to these blueprints.

1.♘f3-d4	♖a7-b7
2.b2-b4	♗e6-d7
3.f2-f4	♔f8-e7
4.♔g1-f2	♖b7-a7
5.♖c1-c3	♔e7-d6
6.♖c3-d3	♔d6-e7
7.♔f2-e3	♖a7-a4

8.♖d3-c3   ♚e7-d6

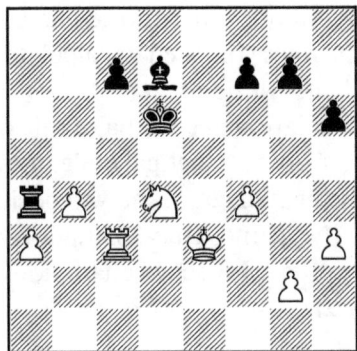

White has achieved his intended structure. Now he has a new task ahead of him: push the queenside pawns. To do this, he first needs to get his king to help the pawns.

9.♖c3-d3   ♚d6-e7
10.♖d3-c3   ♚e7-d6

Now we are here, let's discuss move repetitions. The main rule of the endgame is *do not hurry*! If you have a choice between moving the pawn one or two squares ahead, push it first to the adjacent square, look carefully at the board, and then push it further. Of course, the advice don't hurry only applies to quiet endgames, tactical endgames are another thing entirely. The "do not hurry" rule may seem counter-intuitive to some, but it's seen very clearly in most endings of the great endgame masters. Look carefully through the endgames of Capablanca or Flohr, and you'll see how slow, even boring their advantage conversion is.

Move repetitions play an important role in endgames. Even besides the fact that it saves time for thinking, we must point out that, by repeating moves, the active side gains a certain psychological advantage. The defender, whose position is worse, often can't stand the pressure, creates new weaknesses and makes the attacker's task easier. Also, repetition helps to clarify the position. Of course, we know that some advocates of "pure" chess art will criticize us for this advice. But still, we can't help but advise chess players: do occasionally repeat moves in endgames! You have to use all your chances in battle, and there's nothing unbecoming or unethical in move repetitions.

11.♘d4-e2   g7-g6
12.♖c3-d3+   ♚d6-e6
13.♔e3-d4   ♖a4-a6

Instead of 13.♔d4?, white had to play 13.g4 or even 13.f5+!? ♚e7 (13...gxf5 14.♘f4+ ♚e7 15.♘d5+) 14.♘c3!, because in the game, black could have replied 13...♗b5! 14.♘c3 (14.♖e3+ ♚d6, intending 15...c5+) 14...♗xd3 15.♘xa4 ♗f1 (M. Dvoretsky).

14.♖d3-e3+   ♚e6-d6
15.♘e2-c3   f7-f5
16.b4-b5   ...

The pawns start moving, and the white pieces are there to support them. We should point out that Capablanca only started pushing his pawns when his pieces had assumed the strongest possible positions. Of course, black can't capture on a3 due to 17.♘e4+.

16...   ♖a6-a8
17.♔d4-c4   ♗d7-e6+
18.♔c4-b4   c7-c5+

19.b5xc6	♗e6-g8
20.♘c3-b5+	♔d6xc6
21.♖e3-d3	...

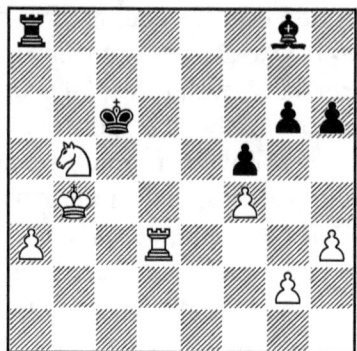

Now it's not even necessary to push the a-pawn. Black's kingside pawns are weakened, and one of them falls.

21...	g6-g5
22.♖d3-d6+	♔c6-b7
23.f4xg5	h6xg5
24.♖d6-g6	♖a8-f8
25.♖g6xg5	f5-f4
26.♘b5-d4	...

A very important move. Capablanca deprives his opponent of any chances connected with f4-f3.

26...	♖f8-c8
27.♖g5-g7+	♔b7-b6
28.♖g7-g6+	♔b6-b7
29.♘d4-b5	♖c8-f8
30.♘b5-d6+	♔b7-b8
31.h3-h4. Black resigned.	

Thinking in setups is a characteristic feature of endgames. Here's how you need to play them. First, you plan the positioning of your pieces and look for the most important measures your opponent might take to stop our plan. Afterwards, it's easy to find the move order in the endgame, and the lines you need to calculate are usually not difficult.

Calculation plays a major role only in relatively rare tactical endgames.

The next diagram shows a position from the game **Duz-Khotimirsky — Kotov**, 1941 Moscow championship *(game xi)*.

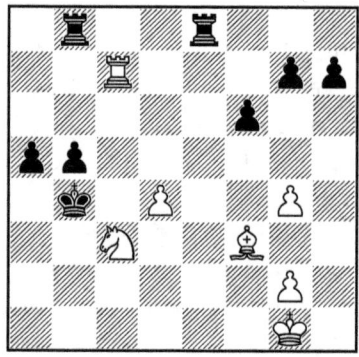

Here, it's obvious that thinking in setups is simply not enough. Suffice is to say that white has two moves here that look more or less sensible: 1.♘d5+ and 1.♖c5. But still, the role of setups-thinking in the endgame is so great that even here, white could achieve a draw had he planned the correct defensive position. The right defensive structure here is the following: the white rook goes to c5, the king to f2, and the bishop to d5 or, if black plays ♖ec8, to c6. There could follow: 1.♖c5! a4 2.♔f2! ♖ec8 3.♗c6, then 4.♔e3 and 5.♔d3, and the most probable result here is a draw. White, however, missed this line and played

1. ♗f3-e2   ♖b8-c8!

Now the game enters the stage of tactical complications. We can even say that this looks more like a middlegame than an endgame.

2. ♘c3-d5+   ...

2.♗xb5? ♖xc7 3.♘d5+ ♔xb5 4.♘xc7+ ♔c6 5.♘xe8 a4 lost: the a-pawn is unstoppable.

2...   ♔b4-b3
3. ♗e2xb5   ♖c8xc7
4. ♗b5xe8   ♖c7-c4

In this position, each tempo is valuable. The play is forced, and setups-thinking has no place here.

5. ♗e8-f7   ♖c4xd4
6. ♘d5xf6+   ♔b3-b2
7. ♘f6xh7   ♖d4xg4
8. ♗f7-g8   ...

This loses immediately. 8.♗e8 a4 9.♗xa4 ♖xa4 also led to a lost endgame for white, although the tablebase indicates that it would take 62 moves to win.

8...   a5-a4
9. ♔g1-f2   a4-a3
10. ♔f2-f3   ♖g4-b4
11. ♘h7-g5   ♖b4-b3+
12. ♗g8xb3   ♔b2xb3

White resigned, because the a-pawn is unstoppable. Here, after 1.♗e2, we saw an example of a forced, tactical endgame which was essentially not that different from a middlegame. On the other hand, this example shows how important setups-thinking is both for converting the advantage and defense. Indeed, had white found the defensive structure shown above, he would have saved the game.

So, the first distinctive feature of the endgame is the struggle between attacking and defensive setups. The second feature, equally important, is the king's active role. This all-important piece is rather problematic in the middlegame — other pieces constantly have to defend it. However, when only a few pieces are left on the board, the king becomes emboldened and exacts revenge. It bravely charges forward and, in many cases, decides the outcome of the fight. Every chess player should know about the king's important role in the endgame. It's often underestimated, some players play the endgame without getting the king into battle, and this always brings only trouble. In the previous example, we already saw how important the king's activity in the endgame is. The black king supported the kingside pawn movement, while its white counterpart passively watched events unfold.

In the very beginning of the endgame, you have to move the king quickly to the center or another important area. Look through the endgames of Capablanca or Flohr, and you'll see how carefully they improve their king's position even when it doesn't look that necessary. And it always turns out that their king takes an active part in the fight when it's needed most. The principle might seem simple — centralize the king in the endgame. But this principle often gets overlooked even by experienced players – perhaps precisely because of its simplicity.

The next diagram shows a position from the game **Bogatyrchuk – Mazel**, 7th Soviet Championship, 1931 *(game xii)*.

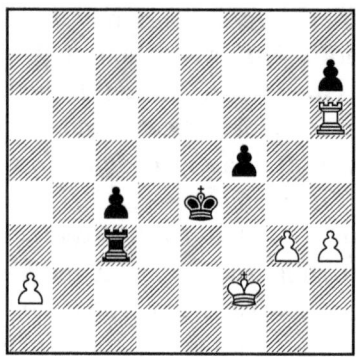

It was perfectly clear that white would have to sacrifice his rook for the c4 pawn. Thus, his only hope to save the game was capturing the black kingside pawns. So, white's first goal should have been to secure an active central position for his king. This could have been done with 1.♖h4+ ♔d3 2.♖xh7 ♖c2+ 3.♔f3!, and white draws easily. Instead, Bogatyrchuk played **1.♖h6xh7?**, and after **1... ♖c3-c2+**, the king had to retreat to e1.

2.♔f2-e1 ...

And this makes a huge difference. White cannot support the movement of his h-pawn with the king and in practice loses because of that, even though there was a much harder way to draw later.

2... ♖c2xa2
3.♖h7-e7+ ♔e4-d3
4.♖e7-d7+ ♔d3-c2
5.♖d7-d5?? ...
5.g4 still drew.
5... c4-c3
6.♖d5xf5 ♔c2-b1!
7.♖f5-f1 ♖a2-h2

White resigned.

So, you should always ensure that your king takes an active, centralized position in the endgame.

Besides the king, there's another piece that sharply increases its value in the endgame: the pawn. While they mostly play auxiliary roles in the middlegame, they become much more important in the endgame. Let's recall the Duz-Khotimirsky – Kotov game on the previous page. It's known that two minor pieces are as strong as a rook and two pawns in the middlegame. But it's different in the endgame, as pawns are precious material at that stage. Thus, at the finishing stage of the game, a rook and two pawns are almost always stronger than two minor pieces. Especially if these pawns, as in the aforementioned example, are passed. The strength of passed pawns is well-known. We don't think it necessary to examine the question of passed pawns and methods of their creation in great detail here. In the vast majority of examples, both above and below, passed pawns played the decisive role in endgame fights.

Finally, the last question we would like to examine in this section is the value and role of individual minor pieces in the endgame. In complicated multi-piece endgames, you often have to answer the question: which piece to trade and which to retain? It's a difficult question, and sometimes the correct answer is quite elusive. Let's explain that with an example.

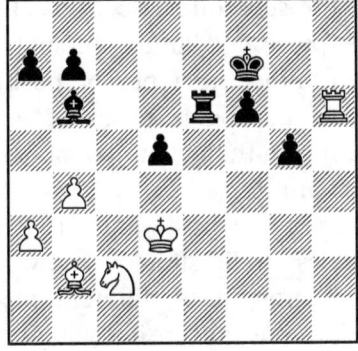

This position was taken from the game **Alatortsev – Levenfish** (match, 1940) *(game xiii)*. Obviously, only white has winning chances here. He has a piece for three pawns, but the d5 pawn is weak and should fall soon. White's desire to simplify play by trading the b6 bishop is clear. So, Alatortsev played

1.♗b2-d4 ...

Here's what Levenfish wrote about this move: "White should have preserved his bishop like the apple of his eye, because the knight is not a good piece in the fight against passed pawns. The correct move was 1.♗c1 and then, after 1...g4 – 2.♗f4". Indeed, the knight couldn't stop the kingside pawns from moving and defend its own queenside pawns at the same time. By retaining the bishop, white could still have hoped to win the game.

Black could counter the proposed moves by pushing the passed pawns – 2...♖e4 and 3...f5 with sufficient counterplay.

1...	♔f7-g7
2.♖h6-h1	♔g7-g6
3.♗d4xb6	♖e6xb6
4.♘c2-e3	♖b6-a6
5.♖h1-a1	f6-f5
6.♘e3xd5	f5-f4
7.b4-b5	...

It was necessary to activate the rook.

7...	♖a6-e6
8.♖a1-c1	♖e6-e5!
9.♖c1-c5	...

Or 9.♔d4 ♖e2 10.♖c7 f3, and black draws.

9...	f4-f3
10.♘d5-f4+	♔g6-f5
11.♖c5xe5+	♔f5xe5
12.♘f4-h5	♔e5-d5

A draw was agreed after three more moves. It's useful to remember that the knight is not a good piece in the fight against passed pawns.

Here's another typical example.

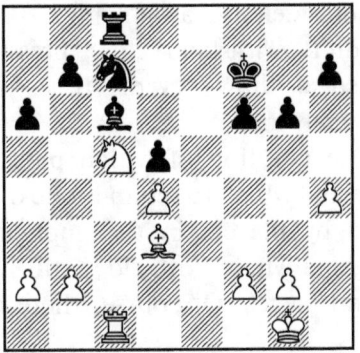

This position occurred in the game **Levenfish – Kotov**, 11th Soviet Championship, 1939 *(game xiv)*. After a difficult defense, black has almost managed to equalize. Now he has to find the correct continuation. Had he played 1...♘e6, for instance, he could have easily saved the game. However, black couldn't answer the question of which minor piece he should retain – his next move isn't an error, but it makes the draw harder to find.

1... ♘c7-b5
2.♗d3xb5

Levenfish immediately trades his bishop for the knight.

2... ♗c6xb5
3.♖c1-c3   b7-b6

Black should have kept the rooks on the board, increasing his chances to defend. 3...♖e8! would draw with ease.

4.♘c5-a4   ♖c8xc3
5.♘a4xc3   ♗b5-c6

A typical endgame has now occurred – a knight versus a bishop with a weak black d5 pawn, which we shall study later. Black's position is not exactly lost, but now a long and arduous defense awaits him. Black couldn't withstand the pressure, missed a draw several times and ultimately lost.

The question of which piece to trade and which to retain is one often faced by players in a complicated endgame where both sides still have several pieces. Of course, there can be no one answer that fits every situation.

The correct decision in each concrete case is found after the thorough consideration of all specifics of the position. To find the right move, you have to know various types of minor-piece endgames very well.

In the subsequent sections about minor-piece endgames, we shall try to determine the types of position where a particular piece of yours is stronger than your opponent's particular piece.

Everyone who wants to play endgames well should know the relative strength of different pieces in various positions. After you master this important skill, it won't be hard to answer the question which pieces to trade and which to retain.

Some words on our approach in the subsequent sections. It's not necessary for us to study all the matters associated with endgames. There are a number of full-fledged endgame textbooks in chess literature, with comprehensive analysis of many endgame matters and the most important endgame positions. We think that our duty here is just to give some practical advice for each type of endgame and study some especially characteristic positions. We give the most general formulation of known rules and principles necessary to play each type of endgame. We think that if you internalize all that's said in the subsequent sections on the endgame, you will be well-prepared for practical struggle in the final stage of a chess game.

First of all, let's study pawn endgames — the base of bases, the main endgame that any other type of endgame can boil down to. Here, we shall figure out the most important, principled moments, and characterize the main types of positional advantage: outside passed pawn, protected passed pawn, and king activity. After studying this materially simplest endgame, the reader may proceed to endgames with other pieces.

PAWN ENDGAMES

In pawn endgames, kings play the decisive role. The king is the main active piece, and its position largely determines the outcome of the fight. Playing pawn endgames requires precise and detailed calculation. You should remember that pawns do not move backwards, and one careless move can permanently damage the position.

The main goal in the pawn endgame is to queen a pawn. Thus, analysis of such endgames usually begins with ways of queening a pawn with the help of the king or without it, providing there is at least one pawn on the board. Of course, all this is true and important, but we do not want to repeat well-known examples from textbooks, so we'll jump straight into the practically important questions of material and positional advantage in pawn endings.

In the subsequent sections, we assume that the reader knows the basics of pawn endgames: opposition, zugzwang play, and rule of the square.

Material advantage

Because of limited remaining material and the complete lack of opportunities to create mating threats to the opposing king, a material advantage in pawn endgames both has a decisive importance and is usually easily converted. The method of converting an extra pawn is not difficult. We push pawns on the flank where we have a material advantage and create a passed pawn. This passed pawn diverts the attention of the opponent's king, and our king moves to the other flank, capturing the pawns there.

Let's look, for instance, at this position:

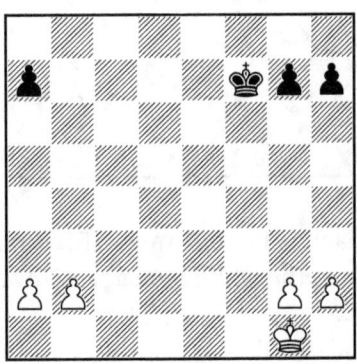

White has an extra pawn, which can easily become passed. The win is not difficult.

1.♔g1-f2   ♚f7-e6

2.♔f2-e3 ...

First of all, we should centralize the king.

2... ♚e6-e5
3.b2-b4 ...

Intending to create a passed pawn. It's more sensible to move first the unopposed pawn — a "candidate passed pawn", in Nimzowitsch's terminology. 3.a4 is weaker due to 3...a5, and the white pawns are stopped. In this particular example, this still doesn't miss the win, but makes it more difficult. We should point out that the best method of defense for the weaker side is to put his king into opposition.

3... ♚e5-d5
4.♔e3-d3 ...

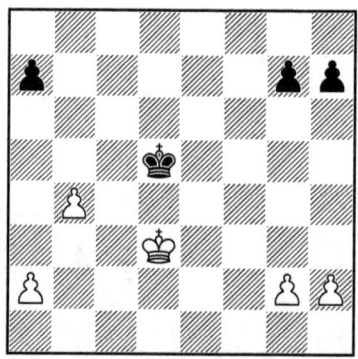

Black is in zugzwang. If he moves his king, the white king goes forward.

4... g7-g6
5.a2-a4 h7-h6
6.g2-g4 ...

It's not the only way to win. But in such cases, it's useful to stop the pawns on one flank to narrow the opponent's choice of moves.

6... g6-g5
7.h2-h3 ...

We recommend you pay attention to the following consideration. It doesn't play an important role in this particular endgame, but sometimes can become very significant. White puts his pawns on g4 and h3. It's better than to put them on h4 and g3, because if the black king moves in to attack the pawns, it has to take a longer route. You have to place your pawns in such a way that requires the maximum amount of moves for the opponent's king to capture them. In this particular case, to capture the g4 pawn, the black king would first have to attack the h3 pawn, losing a tempo.

7... a7-a6
8.b4-b5 a6xb5
9.a4xb5 ♚d5-c5
10.♔d3-e4 ♚c5xb5
11.♔e4-f5 ...

Even though the black king has captured white's extra pawn, it has fallen hopelessly behind in the race towards the kingside. Both black pawns fall, and the win is elementary.

When you think about transposing into a pawn endgame with an extra pawn, you should always check if you can create a passed pawn and push it forward. There are some positions where you can't move your extra passed pawn, and the game ends in a draw.

The next drawn position has been known since the times of Philidor.

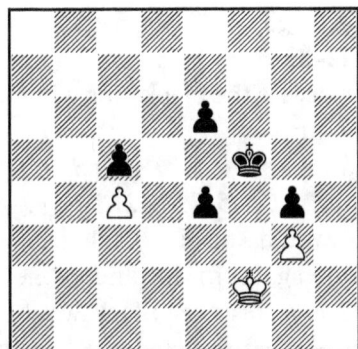

to the side with an outside passed pawn.

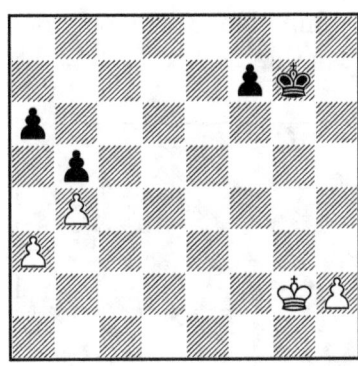

Black has two extra pawns, but he cannot win because he cannot push the e-pawn. White should be careful to always put his king on e3 in reply to black's move ♚e5. For instance:

1... ♚f5-f6
2.♔f2-e2! ♚f6-e5
3.♔e2-e3, and black will never be able to break through to d4 and support the movement of the e-pawn. We must point out that it's necessary to choose the maneuvering squares for the white king carefully. This matter lies in the heart of theory of corresponding squares, developed by N. D. Grigoriev and outlined in endgame textbooks. We will not examine it here.

Let's now look at the three main types of positional advantage in pawn endgames: outside passer, protected passer, and active king.

Outside passed pawns

The route of the kings is determined by the passed pawns. As a rule, this gives a decisive advantage

Material is equal, but the white passed h-pawn is two files farther from the queenside pawns than the black passed f-pawn. As a result, when the white king captures the f-pawn and the black king captures the h-pawn, white will be two tempi closer to the queenside. The game may continue as follows:

1... ♚g7-g6
2.♔g2-g3 ♚g6-g5
3.h2-h4+ ♚g5-h5
4.♔g3-h3 ...

4.♔f4 is too premature, since white will need too much time to capture the f-pawn. He first has to wait for the pawn to come closer.

4... f7-f6
If 4...♚g6, then 5.♔g4.
5.♔h3-g3 f6-f5
6.♔g3-f4 ...
And now it's time.
6... ♚h5xh4
7.♔f4xf5 ♚h4-g3
8.♔f5-e5, and white gets to the queenside pawns faster than black.

Protected passed pawns

A protected passed pawn is even more important than an outside passed pawn.

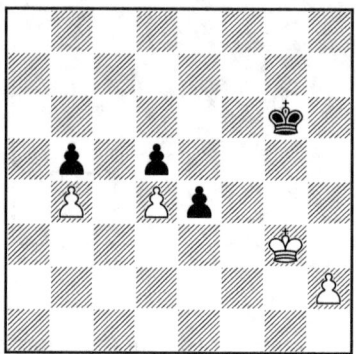

Black has a protected passed pawn on e4, which restricts the white king's mobility. The latter can never advance to the fifth rank, otherwise the e4 pawn queens. White's outside passed pawn, which could give him a decisive advantage in other positions, can't help here because the e4 pawn cannot be captured.

The game might continue:

**1.♔g3-g4   ♚g6-f6
2.♔g4-f4   ♚f6-g7**

Black calmly retreats with his king to get into opposition. The white king, on the other hand, is tied to the e4 pawn and cannot move to the fifth rank.

**3.♔f4-g4   ♚g7-g6
4.♔g4-f4   ...**

Moving the h-pawn will only make black's task easier, getting it closer to the black king.

4...   ♚g6-h5

**5.♔f4-g3   ♚h5-g5
6.h2-h3   ...**

Otherwise the black king will move in even further.

6...   ♚g5-h5

After 6...♚f5 7.♔g2 ♚f4 8.♔f2, black would have to change the structure again; for instance, 8...e3+? 9.♔e2 is a mistake. Black would no longer have a protected passed pawn, and white's outside passed pawn becomes dangerous. For instance: 9...♚e4 10.h4 ♚xd4 11.h5 ♚e5 12.♔xe3, and white wins.

7.♔g3-h2   ♚h5-h4

Again, 7...e3 is bad. All in all, you can only part with a protected passed pawn if you have a clear way to win.

8.♔h2-g2   e4-e3

Now is the time.

**9.♔g2-f3   ♚h4xh3
10.♔f3xe3   ♚h3-g3**

Black wins by pushing the white king away from the d4 pawn.

**11.♔e3-e2   ♚g3-f4
12.♔e2-d3   ♚f4-f3
13.♔d3-d2   ♚f3-e4
14.♔d2-c3   ♚e4-e3**

Winning both white pawns.

The above examples provide only a basic understanding. The reader can learn more about the details of pawn endgames and their various subtleties in existing endgame textbooks.

King activity

We've already said that the king in a pawn endgame is the main attacking piece. By getting our king to an active position, we limit the mobility of our opponent and, in the majority of cases, get an opportunity to put our pawns on the best squares.

The next position arose in the game **E. Cohn – Rubinstein**, St. Petersburg 1909 *(game xv)*.

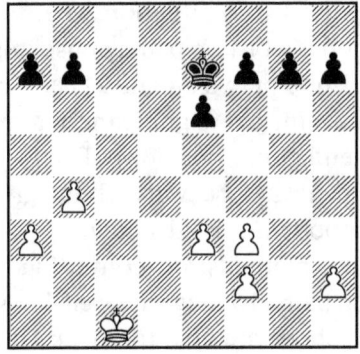

White has just traded rooks, not realizing that the pawn endgame is lost for him. There followed:

1... ♚e7-f6

The black king heads for h3.

2.♔c1-d2 ♚f6-g5
3.♔d2-e2 ♚g5-h4
4.♔e2-f1 ♚h4-h3
5.♔f1-g1 e6-e5

Now white cannot do anything. He can only move his king from h1 to g1 and back, while black launches a pawn assault.

6.♔g1-h1 b7-b5

Fixing the white pawns just in case. Black still has the waiting move a7-a6 at his disposal.

7.♔h1-g1 f7-f5
8.♔g1-h1 g7-g5
9.♔h1-g1 h7-h5

10.♔g1-h1 g5-g4
11.e3-e4 ...

White can't save the game. After 11.fxg4, black plays 11...fxg4, then e4, h4, g3, and after the trades on g3, the e3 pawn falls.

11... f5xe4
12.f3xe4 h5-h4
13.♔h1-g1 g4-g3
14.h2xg3 h4xg3

White resigned – he loses the e4 pawn after 15.fxg3 ♚xg3. Neither can he save the game with 15.f4 exf4 16.e5 f3 17.e6 f2+ 18.♔f1 g2+ 19.♔xf2 ♚h2 etc.

We have shown some simple positions to illustrate the three main types of positional advantage in pawn endgames. In more complicated cases, these advantages are intertwined, sometimes canceling each other out. For instance, an extra pawn or a protected passer are sometimes not enough for a win because of the opposing king's active position; in other cases, an outside passed pawn does not give you a win because of the bad position of your other pawns.

The resources of many positions are immeasurable. Nevertheless, you should calculate precisely all the lines of the endgame and, before starting any maneuvers, identify the character of the subsequent struggle. In pawn endgames, the concrete calculation of lines is all-important. The lines can be quite long, but calculating them is not particularly hard. The ability to evaluate a simple pawn endgame is an elementary basis of endgame technique. Before studying endgames with pieces, any player should first try their hand at simple pawn endings. There should be no unclear paths, no "blank spots".

Assuming that the reader has enough knowledge of pawn endings, let's look at endings with pieces next. First of all, let's consider minor-piece endgames. Here, we shall look at all possible piece combinations: bishop versus knight, knight versus knight, and same-colored and opposite-colored bishops. The following sections will be structured in the same way: the main techniques for playing each type of endgame and the most important types of positional advantage.

SOME CONSIDERATIONS ON ENDGAMES WITH MULTIPLE MINOR PIECES

Two bishops

Sometimes, both opponents have three or four minor pieces in the endgame. Play with such material balance is quite complicated and similar to the middlegame in many ways. However, the material does not stay the same until the very end – pieces get traded. You have to be especially careful here. It's necessary to weigh your options and decide which piece – knight or bishop – to retain. Before going for trades, you have to consider the character of the position and decide which piece would be more beneficial for you. If you come to a conclusion that any trade is unfavorable, it's better to avoid trades altogether and look for chances in a multi-piece endgame. The player should learn to solve the problem of piece trades in each individual case.

You should also remember another important consideration. Sometimes, trades lead to a situation where one player has a bishop pair against knight and bishop or two knights. The bishop pair advantage is significant in almost any endgame position. Thus, you should always be wary about giving the opponent this advantage.

The methods of converting the bishop pair advantage are well-known. The bishops are able to attack all the squares on the board; two bishops are especially dangerous if you have at least one passed pawn. The player who has the two bishops usually plans to limit the mobility of his opponent's knights and create a passed pawn. Having a passed pawn with two bishops usually means "the beginning of the end".

Even if the opponent manages to block this passed pawn, the long-range bishops can still wreak havoc in other areas of the board. The reader can find a lot of examples in tournament books where the simple fact of having a bishop pair, without any additional positional advantages, was enough for a win. It's enough to mention the great example of systematic utilization of the bishop pair advantages by Flohr in the sixth game of his 1933 match against Botvinnik. Here, we'll show just one example where obtaining the bishop pair immediately decided the outcome of the game. The diagram shows a position from the game **Yudovich – Bondarevsky**, Tbilisi 1937 *(game xvi)*.

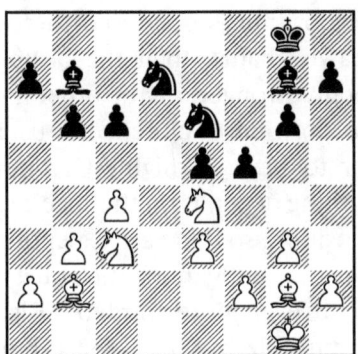

The white pieces are very active. The black c6 pawn is weak, which allows white to trade his knight for a bishop.

1. ♘e4-d6   ♗b7-a8
2. e3-e4!   ...

A strong move that further improves the position of the white pieces. Black's reply is forced, since he can't play 2...f4 due to 3.♗h3 ♘df8 4.♘c8, winning a pawn.

Still, 2...f4 was the most resilient defense, since after 3.♗h3, instead of 3...♘df8, black can play the active 3...♘dc5, and if 4.b4, then 4...♘g5.

2. ...   f5xe4?
3. ♘c3xe4   a7-a5

White again threatened 4.♘c8 and 5.♗h3.

4. ♘d6-e8!   ...

This move has a concrete objective – to trade the g7 bishop. Black can't avoid it, because 4...♗h8 is met with 5.♗h3 ♘df8 6.♘8f6+ and then 7.♗xe5. The black bishop on a8 is bad, so he can't play 4...♘d4 due to 5.♘c7 ♗b7 6.♘d6, and wins.

4. ...   ♔g8-f8
5. ♘e8xg7   ♘e6xg7
6. ♗b2-a3+!   ♔f8-g8

Not 6...c5? 7.♘xc5 ♗xg2 8.♘xd7+.

7. ♘e4-d6   ♘g7-e6
8. ♘d6-e8

[According to some sources white played ♘c8 here but the essence of the game is the same.]

8. ...   ♔g8-f7
9. ♘e8-d6+   ...

The next moves were made in time trouble to buy some time, they don't spoil anything.

9. ...   ♔f7-f6
10. ♘d6-e8+   ♔f6-f7
11. ♘e8-d6+   ♔f7-f6
12. ♘d6-e4+   ♔f6-f7
13. ♔g1-f1?   ...

Allowing black to play c6-c5 and trade the a8 bishop. The simplest way to convert the advantage was to launch a pawn attack on the queenside with 13.h4. Black would have had to fend it off while being essentially a piece down, because his a8 bishop cannot enter the play.

13. ...   c6-c5
14. ♘e4-d6+   ...

Not 14.♘xc5? ♗xg2+.

14. ...   ♔f7-e7
15. ♘d6-c8+!   ...

The king should be pushed as far away from the center and kingside as possible.

15...	♚e7-d8
16.♗g2xa8	♚d8xc8
17.♗a3-c1	♞e6-d4?

White's advantage is obvious. But this move loses more quickly, because the black king cannot defend the weak pawns on h7 and g6. He had to play 17...♞f6 with decent chances to hold.

18.h2-h4	♞d7-f6?

Another delay. 18...♚d8 was still necessary.

19.♗c1-g5	...

The black knights are driven away. They cannot protect the kingside pawns.

19...	♞f6-e8
20.♗a8-d5!	♞e8-d6
21.♗d5-g8	h7-h5
22.♗g8-h7	...

After losing the g- and h-pawns, black is defenseless. His queenside counterplay comes too late.

22...	a5-a4
23.b3xa4	♞d6xc4
24.♗h7xg6	♞c4-b2
25.♗g6xh5	c5-c4
26.♗h5-g4+	♚c8-c7
27.h4-h5.	

Black resigned. The h5 pawn is unstoppable.

Black's quick demise was caused by his errors on moves 17 and 18.

But even without these mistakes, his position was hard to hold. White could launch attacks on both flanks at once, and in this combined play, the advantage of long-range bishops would have decided matters.

Bishop versus knight

The difficult question – which piece is stronger, bishop or knight – usually arises in the middlegame and is resolved in the following way: if the position is open and there are no pawn chains, then the bishop is generally stronger; on the other hand, if the position is closed, it's usually better to have a knight. Of course, everything depends on the specifics of the position, so there are exceptions.

In the endgame, the question becomes even more pointed. "Bishop and multiple pawns versus knight and multiple pawns" endgames occur often, perhaps even more often than any other minor-piece endgame. Space constraints won't allow us to examine all the specifics of that endgame. Thus, our goal is to determine the main essence of bishop versus knight endings and give some practical advice. Let's first answer the question: when is the knight stronger?

Above all, the knight prevails in blocked endgame positions where there is no danger of pawn breakthroughs. It's especially pronounced when the bishop's owner's pawn chains are positioned on squares of the same color as the bishop. In this case, the bishop's activity is greatly limited, and the knight becomes very dangerous. Let's look at an example from the game **Alekhine – Yates**, Hastings 1925 *(game xvii)*.

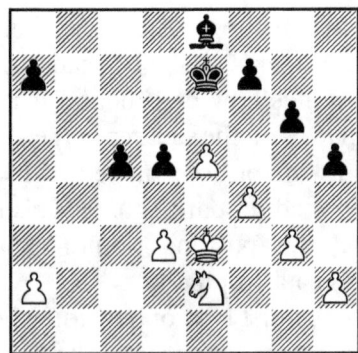

White's advantage is not obvious yet. After 1...d4+ and 2...♗c6, the black bishop gets a couple of good diagonals and can become very active. However, white is to move, and his move changes the position drastically.

1.d3-d4! ...

What can black do? He can't capture on d4, since this will cost him the d5 pawn. For instance: 1...cxd4+ 2.♔xd4 ♗c6 3.♔c5 ♗b7 4.♘d4, and the d5 pawn falls soon. Alternatively, after 2.♘xd4 f6 black would have a passive ending, but white may not have a forced win. Thus, black should push the pawn forward.

1... c5-c4

Now the bishop is severely limited by its own pawns, almost all of which stand on light squares. In addition, the black d5 pawn is weak. White only needs to create a second weakness in black's position, and the combined attack on two weaknesses will lead to a material gain.

2.f4-f5! g6-g5

2...gxf5 3.♘f4 is obviously bad.

3.h2-h4! ...

White is concentrating his efforts on fixing the h5 pawn on the weak light square. If now 3...gxh4 4.gxh4 f6, then 5.♘f4 ♗f7 6.e6, winning.

3... f7-f6
4.h4xg5! ...

This move required precise consideration of all the factors. White allows black to create a second passed pawn, which might become dangerous if supported by the bishop.

4... f6xg5
5.♘e2-g1 ♗e8-d7

After this, the advance g5-g4 is forced, and the h5 pawn becomes hopelessly weak. White took into account all of black's attempts to create counterplay when he played 5.♘g1. After 5...h4, there's 6.g4 ♗a4 and on 7.♘h3 ♗d1! holds. 7.♔e2 with the subsequent 8.♘h3, capturing the g5 pawn, looks winning, however, 7...♔e8!! 8.♘h3 c3 9.♘xg5 ♗b5+ 10.♔d1 c2+! 11.♔xc2 ♗e2 and black holds.

6.f5-f6+ ♔e7-e8

The attempt to avoid g5-g4 did not work: 6...♔f7 7.♘f3 ♔g6 8.♘xg5 and then 9.f7.

7.♘g1-f3 g5-g4

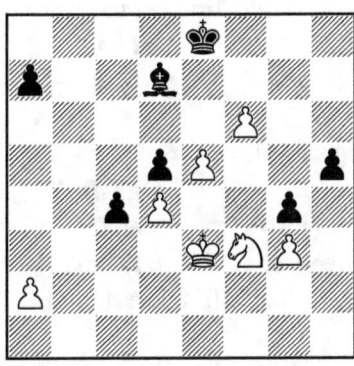

White has achieved his goal — he has weakened the backward h5

pawn. His new task is to attack two weaknesses at once — the d5 and h5 pawns. Obviously, he needs to transfer his knight to f4 to do that.

8.♘f3-h4   ♗d7-e6
9.♘h4-g6   ♗e6-f7
10.♘g6-f4   ♔e8-d7
11.♔e3-e2   a7—a5
12.♔e2-e3   ...

A typical zugzwang in this type of endgame. Black runs out of pawn moves and is forced to move his pieces, which leads to material losses.

12...   ♗f7-g8

12...♗e8 13.♘xd5 or 12...♔d8 13.e6 is even worse.

13.♘f4xh5   ♗g8-f7
14.♘h5-f4   ♗f7-g8

The conversion stage begins. White moves his king to support the pawn push, and the knight goes to e2 to guard the c4 pawn.

15.♘f4-e2   ♗g8-e6
16.♔e3-f4   ♔d7-e8
17.♔f4-g5   ♔e8-f7
18.♘e2-c3   ...

Another zugzwang. Black is forced to let the white king get to g6.

18...   ♔f7-f8
19.♔g5-g6   ♔f8-g8
20.f6-f7+   ...

The simplest.

20...   ♔g8-f8
21.♔g6-f6   ♗e6xf7
22.e5-e6   ♗f7-h5
23.♘c3xd5. Black resigned.

In this example, white's maneuvers to create weaknesses in black's camp were quite typical, as were the methods of exploitation of the said weaknesses. The reader now understands how detrimental it is to have pawns on the squares of the same color as the bishop. Indeed, if black had owned a dark-squared bishop instead, his position wouldn't have been as catastrophic.

So, the first type of position where the knight is stronger than the bishop is a closed position where the bishop's activity is limited, and the struggle commences in a confined space. The practical conclusions from this fact should be obvious.

The presence of pawns on the squares of the same color as the bishop can be a liability in a non-closed position as well. Open positions where the bishop's owner has pawns that are ostensibly protected by the bishop are the second type of position where the knight is stronger than the bishop. A typical example is a position with an isolated black d5 pawn and a light-squared bishop versus knight. The following position occurred in the game **Capablanca — Reshevsky**, Nottingham 1936 *(game xviii)*.

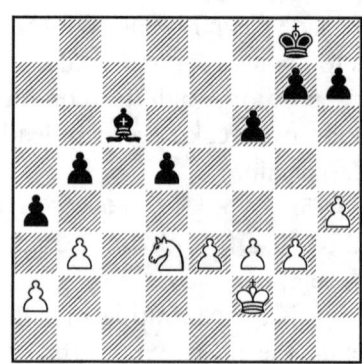

The pawns' positions on b5 and d5 are very poor, as they limit their own bishop and create "holes" on c5, d4 and b4. It's obvious that white will get his king to d4 and c5, and the pawns will become indefensible.

Many years later, this endgame was reanalyzed by grandmaster Igor Bondarevsky, who published his conclusions in the Shakhmatniy Bulletin *magazine (No. 1, 1973). Here's what he wrote in particular: "The above considerations would have been enough to evaluate black's position as strategically lost if white didn't have some weaknesses as well.*

Looking carefully at white's pawn configuration, we see some weaknesses on the kingside. The f3 pawn may require attention, and the advanced rook pawn is a 'hook' that black can grab onto to create some counterchances. If the pawn were on h2, we would say that white's position was won. But in this situation, concrete analysis might help clarify if black can really create some counterplay."

There followed:

1... g7-g5

Black's only chance is to try to create an outside passed pawn. Passive play will quickly lead to his demise. Still, 1...♔f7 would hold objectively.

2.h4xg5 ...

"*Capablanca chooses the simplest continuation. 2.h5 deserved serious consideration – I think it gave more winning chances.*" (Bondarevsky)

2... f6xg5
3.♘d3-b4 ...

Bondarevsky proposed a strong move 3.f4! (getting rid of the f3 weakness which he pointed out), but came to an erroneous conclusion that after 3...gxf4 4.exf4 d4 black can activate his bishop and draw the game. Let's continue the line: 5.b4 a3 6.♘e1 ♗e4 (6...♗d5 7.♘c2 ♗xa2 8.♘xa3, and black can't protect his pawn with 8...♗c4?, because the pawn endgame is won for white – his passed pawns will queen) 7.♘f3 d3 8.♘d2! ♗d5 9.♘b1, winning.

3... a4xb3
4.a2xb3 ♗c6-b7
5.g3-g4 ...

It's necessary to prevent h7-h5-h4.

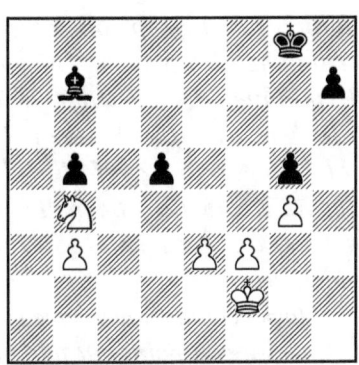

"*In his time, Capablanca came up with a rule: 'When your opponent has a bishop, put your pawns on the squares of the same color as that bishop.' However, in this case, his opponent's 'bad' bishop is already restricted enough by its own pawns. So, the main point of 5.g4 is to prevent the advance of the h-pawn. Still, the pawns on f3 and g4 give black a good foundation to create counterchances.*

Black has two possible active plans:

1) Get the king to support the h7-h5 push.

2) Put the king in the center to protect the d5 and b5 pawns and support the h7-h5 push with the bishop.

Reshevsky executed the first of the two plans. As we shall see, his kingside operation failed.

To see the main flaw in Reshevsky's plan, let's look at the second plan: 5...♔f7 6.♔e2 ♔f6 7.♔d3 ♔e5 (not 7...d4 due to 8.e4). Now white can't move his king to c3 because of 8...d4+ 9.exd4 ♔f4. Thus, the most logical way for him to go is to put his knight on d4. Black counters this maneuver by putting his bishop on e8 and supporting the h7-h5 push. The game could continue: 8.♘c2 ♗c6 9.♘d4 ♗e8 10.♔c3 (if 10.f4+, then 10...gxf4 11.♘f3+ ♔f6 12.exf4 h5) 10...h5 11.gxh5 ♗xh5 12.♘b4 g4 13.fxg4 ♗xg4 14.♔xb5 ♔e4 15.♔c5 ♔xe3, and black draws.

So, black could have saved the game. Now we can point out the main flaw of the plan chosen by Reshevsky. By organizing the h7-h5 break with his king, black moves it too far away from the center." (Bondarevsky)

5...   **♔g8-g7**
6.♔f2-e2   **♔g7-g6?**

6...♔f6! 7.♔d3 ♔e5 8.♘c2 ♗c6 and black seems to hold with ♗e8 and h5.

7.♔e2-d3   **h7-h5**

Of course, not 7...d4 8.e4.

8.g4xh5+   **♔g6xh5**

9.♔d3-d4   **♔h5-h4**
10.♘b4xd5   **♔h4-g3**
11.f3-f4   **g5-g4**

While black had to settle for passive defense in the previous example, here he chose the correct way, organizing active counterplay. However, the forced pawn sacrifice led black to a lost position. The pawn endgame 11...♗xd5 12.♔xd5 is lost both after capturing on f4 or 12...g4. In the second case, after 13.f5, black is forced to either put his king on the f-file (and the f-pawn queens with a check in this case) or on the h-file, which forces the immediate trade of the new queens. Therefore, black avoids trading pieces

12.f4-f5   **♗b7-c8**
13.♔d4-e5   **♗c8-d7**
14.e3-e4   **♗d7-e8**

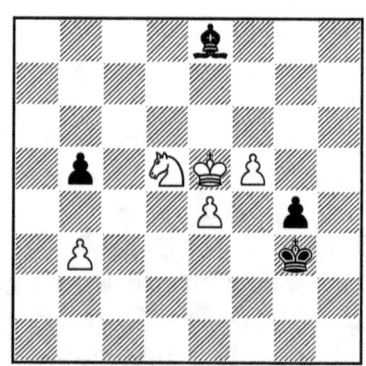

15.♔e5-d4

White would win with 15.f6! ♔f3 16.♘f4 g3 17.♔f5 ♗d7+ (the most resilient; white's task was easier after 17...♗f7 18.e5 ♗xb3 19.e6 ♗xe6+ 20.♔xe6 ♔xf4 21.f7 g2 22.f8=♕+, and he has enough time to drive the black king to g1 and then reach the b5 pawn's square with his king: 22...♔g3 23.♕d6+ ♔h3 24.♕d4 ♔h2 25.♕h4+ ♔g1 26.♔d5 etc.) 18.♔g5 ♗e6 19.♘xe6! g2 20.f7 g1=♕+ 21.♔f6, and black can't stop two white pawns at once, for instance: 21...♔xe4 22.f8=♕ ♕f2+ 23.♔e7 ♕a7+ 24.♔d6 ♕a6+ 25.♔d7 ♕b7+ 26.♘c7 etc.

15...	♔g3-f3
16.e4-e5	g4-g3
17.♘d5-e3	...

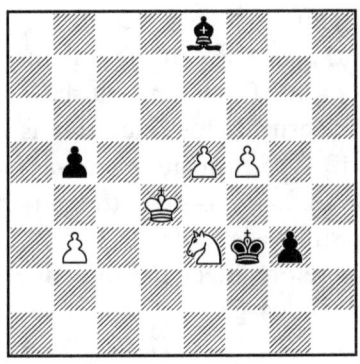

17...	♔f3-f4?

Black also loses after 17...♗d7 18.e6 ♗c8 19.e7 ♗d7 20.f6 ♗e8 21.♘f5 g2 22.♘h4+ and then 23.♘xg2 and ♔e5.

However, he could have saved the game with 17...♗h5! 18.e6 ♗g4 19.e7 (or 19.♔d3 g2) 19...♗h5 20.f6 ♔f4 etc. Now, black's position is hopeless again.

Even 17...♗f7! 18.e6 ♗g8 19.b4 ♔f4 was enough. "The bishop holds the pawns, the knight can't help them because he guards the passer, and the white king plays the humble role of his knight's defender." (Bondarevsky)

18.e5-e6	g3-g2
19.♘e3xg2+	♔f4xf5
20.♔d4-d5	♔f5-g4
21.♘g2-e3+	♔g4-f4
22.♔d5-d4.	

Black resigned. White will play 23.e7 and 24.♘d5 with the subsequent 25.♘c7.

Therefore, even a single pawn on the square of the same color as the bishop can cause big trouble in defense. Of course, it does not always lead to a loss, but it condemns the bishop owner to a long, passive defense in most cases.

So, considering the above, it wouldn't be hard for the reader to determine the methods of converting the knight's advantage over the bishop in each particular position.

Now let's look at positions where the bishop is stronger than the knight. As a rule, it happens when there are opportunities to create passed pawns on both flanks. In the previous example, we've already seen how monstrously strong a passed pawn supported by a bishop can become. When there are passed pawns on both flanks, the long-range bishop easily supports their movement, while the less-mobile, clumsy knight cannot hold both flanks at once.

Let's look at the following position from the game **Rubinstein – P. Johner**, Carlsbad 1929 *(game xix)*.

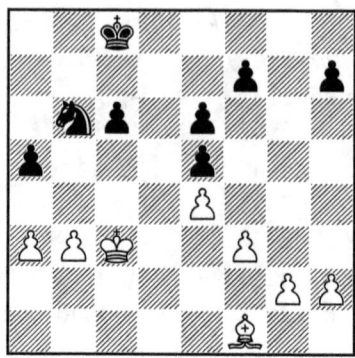

White played **1.b3-b4**, and black's reply **1...a5xb4+?** immediately led to a lost position. Black had to try and close the position at all costs by playing 1...a4 and meeting 2.b5 with 2...c5. White has no opportunities to break through, and the game should end in a draw. Instead, play continued:

2.♔c3xb4   ♚c8-c7
3.a3-a4   ...

White has a strong outside passed pawn that restricts the mobility of black's pieces. However, one passed pawn is not enough: white has to prepare a kingside breakthrough to win.

3...   ♞b6-d7
4.a4-a5   h7-h6
5.♗f1-d3   ♚c7-b7
6.♗d3-c2   ♞d7-b8
7.♗c2-d3   ...

Waiting move; we've already mentioned it in the introductory article.

7...   ♞b8-d7
8.g2-g4   ♚b7-c7
9.h2-h4   ♞d7-f8
10.♗d3-f1   ♞f8-d7
11.♗f1-h3   ♞d7-f8

12.h4-h5   ...

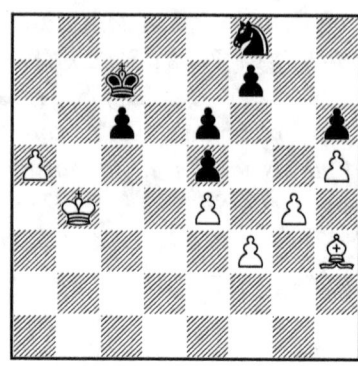

A critical position. White is threatening 13.g5! hxg5 14.h6, with the decisive bishop maneuver ♗h3-g4-h5xf7-g8 and h6-h7. 12...♞h7 doesn't help, since this is met with 13.♔c5, threatening a5-a6. The reply 13...♞f8 is forced, and then white still plays 14.g5.

Therefore, black has only one way to prevent g4-g5:

12...   f7-f6

Now, there's a new weakness in black's camp, the e6 pawn, and Rubinstein immediately attacks it.

13.♗h3-f1   ♞f8-d7
14.♗f1-c4   ♞d7-f8
15.♗c4-b3   ♞f8-h7
16.♔b4-c5   ...

Not 16.♗xe6 ♞g5, losing the f3 pawn and allowing the black knight to activate.

16...   ♞h7-f8
17.♗b3-a2   ♞f8-d7+
18.♔c5-b4   ♞d7-f8
19.a5-a6!   ...

The decisive breakthrough. White sacrifices a pawn on one

flank to clear the way for his king on the other one. A typical strategy for such endgames.

19...	♔c7-b6
20.a6-a7	♔b6xa7
21.♔b4-c5	♔a7-b7
22.♔c5-d6	♔b7-b6
23.♔d6-e7	♘f8-h7
24.♗a2xe6	♔b6-c7
25.♗e6-c4	♘h7-g5
26.♔e7xf6	♔c7-d6
27.♔f6-g6.	

Black resigned. The kingside pawns are unstoppable.

So, positions where the bishop is stronger than the knight best feature active play on both flanks, with opportunities to create passed pawns. Sometimes, however, the bishop's advantage shows even in positions with the play concentrated on one flank. Here, we're talking about positions where the bishop can totally paralyze the knight. For instance, in the following position from the game **Sergei Belavenets – Ilyin-Zhenevsky**, Tbilisi 1937 *(game xx)*, white played

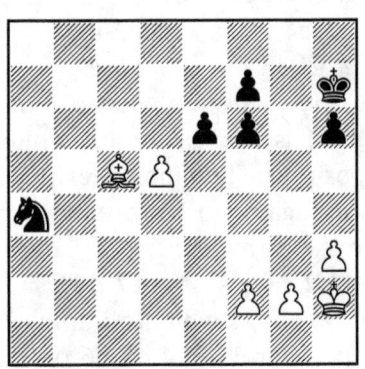

1.♗c5-d4! ...

The black knight has no moves, and this decides the game. After 1...e5 2.d6, the white pawn is unstoppable, while after 1...exd5 2.♔g3, the white king just calmly moves to the queenside and captures the a4 knight. Black's reply is forced

1...	♔h7-g7
2.d5-d6	♔g7-f8
3.♗d4xf6	♘a4-b6

3...♘c5 was not really better. It prevents 4.♔g3 due to ♘e4+, but 4.f3 would win easily.

4.♔h2-g3	♘b6-d7
5.♗f6-b2	♔f8-g8
6.♔g3-g4	...

The white king goes to h5 to attack the h6 pawn.

6...	♔g8-h7
7.♔g4-h5	♘d7-f8
8.g2-g4	♘f8-d7
9.g4-g5	h6xg5
10.♔h5xg5	...

Now white has a second passed pawn on the h-file, and further resistance is futile.

10...	♔h7-g8
11.♗b2-d4	♔g8-h7
12.h3-h4	♘d7-f8?

Loses quickly. However, black's position is already hopeless. White has a simple winning plan: get the pawn to h6, put his bishop on g7 and then get the king to d7, winning the knight.

13.♔g5-f6. Black resigned. [This game is analyzed in full later in this book, No. 13.]

Now we can finally answer the question: in which positions is the bishop stronger than the knight, and when should the knight be preferred to the bishop? If the position is closed, with blocked pawn chains, it's better to have a knight. If the opponent has pawns on squares of the same color as his bishop, the knight is again stronger.

On the other hand, in positions with two-flank play and strong passed pawns, the bishop will definitely show its superior strength.

We have only listed the positional advantages specific for bishop versus knight endgames. Of course, general positional advantages are also important here: king activity, better pawn structure, pawn weaknesses, etc. Often, for instance, it's impossible to exploit the pawns' position on the squares of the same color as the bishop because we have too many weaknesses in our own camp, or our king's position is too bad.

In the examples above, we talked about the advantages of a special sort, characteristic only for this distinctive type of endgame. However, you should also keep general advantages in mind – which, of course, also play an important role in the struggle.

Bishop and rook versus knight and rook

All the above positional advantages are still applicable in cases where rooks are still on the board. If the position is closed, play is concentrated on one flank, and the bishop's owner's pawns are on the squares of the same color as that bishop, then the knight and rook will have an advantage. However, if the position is open, play is on both flanks, and there are passed pawns on the board, the rook and bishop are stronger.

The next diagram shows a position from the 2nd game of the 1937 **Alekhine – Euwe** return match *(game xxi)*.

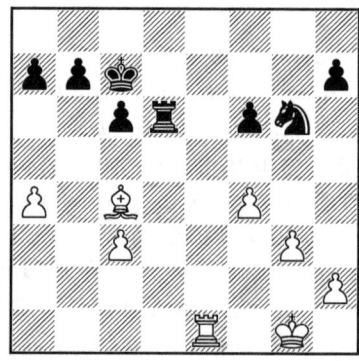

White has an opportunity to push the kingside pawns and create a passed pawn. Thus, the bishop and rook are much stronger than the knight and rook in this position.

1.h2-h4 ♔c7-d7
2.♔g1-f2 ♘g6-e7

A pure bishop versus knight endgame is also better for white in this position. Therefore, Alekhine has nothing against a rook trade, while Euwe tries to avoid it.

3.♔f2-f3 ♘e7-d5?

Euwe allows white to improve the bishop. After 3...f5 4.h5 h6 or 3...h6

4.♖b1 b6 white's advantage would be symbolic.

4.♗c4-d3! ...

Of course not 4.♗xd5? – white would have immediately lost all his advantage.

4... h7-h6?

After 4...h5 5.♗f5 ♔d8 6.g4 white would probably win.

5.♗d3-f5+ ♔d7-d8
6.♔f3-g4! ...

Paying no heed to possible losses on the queenside, white diverts all his efforts to the creation of a passed pawn. It's bad now for black to take on c3, since after 7.♔h5 and ♔xh6, the h4 pawn wins the game.

6... ♘d5-e7
7.♗f5-b1?! ...

7.♗e6! would win effortlessly.

7... ♔d8-e8

Scrambling to get the king to defend the kingside weaknesses.

The text move loses immediately because it deprives black of the resource f6-f5 in reply to ♔h5. 7...♖d5! 8.f5 ♖a5 was better than queenside pawn moves, preventing the white king from going forward. Black had decent drawing chances.

8.♔g4-h5 ♔e8-f7
9.♗b1-a2+ ♔f7-f8
10.♔h5xh6 ♖d6-d2

After the h6 pawn falls, black's position is hopeless. White wins quickly by pushing his kingside pawns.

11.♗a2-e6 ♖d2-d3
12.g3-g4 ♖d3xc3
13.g4-g5.

Black resigned. He can't even sacrifice his knight for the formidable white pawns.

That example perfectly illustrated the strength of the bishop. The following position from the game **Botvinnik – Chekhover** (Leningrad 1934) paints a very different picture *(game xxii)*.

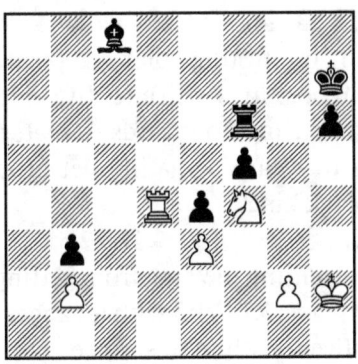

Almost all black pawns are on squares of the same color as the bishop. This doesn't just decrease his chances of converting his material advantage – it actually makes his position worse. Despite being a pawn down, white can play for a win.

1.♖d4-b4 ♖f6-c6

Not 1...♗e6 2.♖b6, and wins.

2.♖b4xb3 ♗c8-a6?!

Black would be only slightly worse after starting to centralize the king with 2...♔g7.

3.♔h2-g3 ♖c6-c2?

Black should still bring the king towards the center.

4.♖b3-b6 ♗a6-f1
5.♖b6-b7+ ♔h7-g8

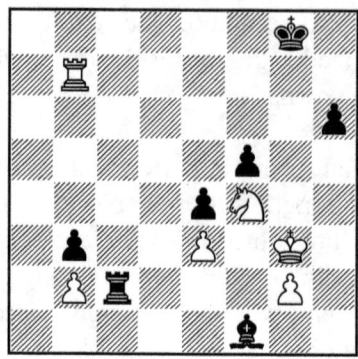

6.♔g3-h4! ...

An interesting plan, typical of similar positions with an active knight. White, paying no regards to material, starts to weave a mating net around the black king.

6... **♗f1-e2**

Preventing the king from getting to h5. 6...♗xg2 7.♔h5 with a dangerous initiative for white was worse.

7.♘f4-e6 ...

7.b4! would be stronger.

7... **♖c2-d2**

If 7...♗f1 then 8.♘f4! wins (8...♗xg2 9.♔h5).

8.b2-b4 **♖d2-b2**
9.♔h4-g3! ...

The king still breaks into the enemy camp via the f4 square.

9... **♗e2-a6**
10.♖b7-b6?! ...

10.♖g7! ♔h8 11.♖g6 would win quickly.

10... **♗a6-f1**

10...♗c4! 11.♘d4 ♗f1 would give black slight drawing chances.

11.♔g3-f4 **♗f1-c4**
12.♘e6-d4 **♖b2-f2+**

Or 12...♖xg2 13.♘xf5, attacking the h6 and e4 pawns at the same time.

It happens all the time: you think that putting the pawns on squares of the same color as your bishop makes defending them easier. Actually, they're much more vulnerable to attack this way. This is explained by the fact that your opponent can exploit the holes around your pawns and attack them with the strongest piece of the endgame, his king. In our example, the white king attacked the weak f5 and e4 pawns through the holes on f4 and e5 and helped to capture them.

13.♔f4-g3 ...

Moving the king to e5 is not good due to 13.♔e5 f4 14.♔xe4 fxe3 15.♔xe3 ♖xg2, and black draws after sacrificing his bishop for the b4 pawn.

13... **♖f2-f1**
14.♖b6-c6 **f5-f4+**

Or else the b-pawn becomes a monster after b4-b5-b6.

15.e3xf4 **♗c4-d3**
16.♖c6xh6 **♖f1-b1**

Black prevented the mating attack, but lost two pawns in the process. Now white's material advantage decides matters.

17.♘d4-f5 **♖b1xb4**
18.♘f5-e3.

Black resigned. His e4 pawn also falls. After f4-f5, ♔f4 and g2-g4, white creates a strong attacking position, and black will have to involve his bishop in the defense, leaving the e4 pawn unprotected. Finally, converting two extra pawns is rather easy.

Same-colored bishops

Same-colored bishop endgames don't occur in tournament practice as often as bishop versus knight endings, but still often enough. Playing such endings requires great skill, as they contain various study-like subtleties more often than any other type of ending. Like in other sections, we will not examine elementary endgames – bishop and pawn versus bishop – too thoroughly. We shall only point out that if the opponent's king is far from the pawn, and our pawn is advanced and supported by the king, we can prevent our opponent from sacrificing the bishop for the pawn and then promote it. It would be useful to remember this method of pawn promotion, since this technique of pushing away the bishop can also be used in more complicated endgames.

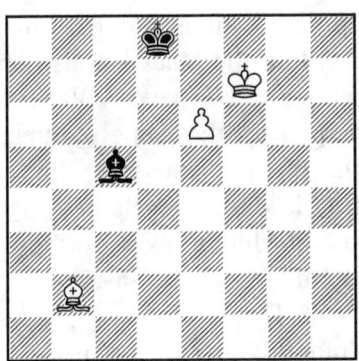

In this position, white managed to promote the pawn with the following maneuver:.

1.♗b2-f6+   ♚d8-c8

Not 1...♚c7 2.♗e7 ♝f2 3.♗d6+ and 4.e7, winning.

2.♗f6-e7   ♝c5-f2
3.♗e7-a3   ♝f2-h4

The e7 square is a junction of the two diagonals useful for the opponent's bishop. It's important for white to neutralize its checks on the e7 square. With the maneuver ♗f6-e7-a3, white drove it away from one diagonal, and now he pushes the pawn to e7 by putting his bishop on f6, closing off the h4 bishop.

4.♗a3-b2 and then **5.♗b2-f6**, winning easily.

We should point out how important white's domination over the f6 square is (and, in similar cases, the d6 square). Had the black king managed to get to f5, white wouldn't have had available the interference move ♗f6, and the game would have ended in a draw. The above method of driving away the bishop is very important for more complicated bishop endgames as well, so we recommend our readers to learn it. You also need to remember the only correct defensive resource for the weaker side: a king march to a square adjacent to the pawn and behind it. Of course, another way to make the draw is to get the king to the pawn promotion square.

In most cases, an extra pawn in a same-colored bishop endgame is enough for a win. Only in rare cases when they can't advance the pawn or have no play against other pawn weaknesses is the stronger side unable to force a win and the game ends in a draw. The methods of converting the extra pawn are relatively simple. By looking through tournament games or multiple fragments in endgame textbooks, the reader will definitely find many examples where an extra pawn was enough to win. A thorough examination of such endgames is not our goal, so we'll only limit ourselves to practical advice — first of all, we shall look through types of positional advantage in bishop endgames and show how to convert these advantages.

In our analysis of bishop versus knight endgames, we have already seen how detrimental having pawns on squares of the same color as our bishop was. Such a pawn position is equally detrimental in same-colored bishop endgames. If material on the board is equal, but your opponent's pawns are positioned on squares of the same color as their bishop, then this means that, firstly, there are "holes" on the adjacent squares, and the king can attack the pawns, and, secondly, the pawns become targets for your own bishop. Such an advantage is very significant and is often enough to win the game. The following position occurred in the correspondence game **Kamyshev — Shamaev** *(game xxiii).*

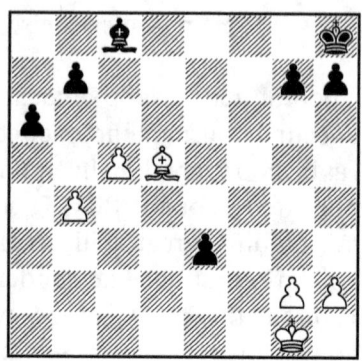

Black's extra pawn on e3 will obviously fall soon, but the position will not be equal after that. The black pawns on b7 and a6 are placed on light squares, limiting the black bishop's mobility and becoming an easy target. White wins without much difficulty.

**1.♔g1-f1   g7-g5
2.♔f1-e2   ♔h8-g7
3.♔e2xe3   ♔g7-f6
4.♔e3-d4   h7-h5**

White's goal is to break through to the black queenside pawns. It's achieved easily, because the white bishop takes an active part in the game, while the black one is tied to its backward b7 pawn. Black tries to sharpen up the game by creating threats on the kingside, but this attempt is easily repelled — again, because of white's "extra" bishop.

**5.h2-h3   ♔f6-f5
6.♗d5-f7   ...**

White has also put pawns on light squares, but this is tied to a concrete threat ♗d5-f7-h5 and then ♗g4, transposing into an easily won pawn endgame, or ♗f3, like in the game.

6...   h5-h4

7.♗f7-h5   ♚f5-f4
8.♗h5-f3   ♚f4-g3

This simplifies matters for white. It would be harder for him to win after 8...g4! 9.hxg4 h3. However, a piece sacrifice decides matters here: 10.gxh3 ♚xf3 11.♔e5 ♚g3 12.♔d6 ♚xh3 13.♔c7 ♗xg4 14.♔xb7. The reader can easily prove that white wins in other lines as well after sacrificing his bishop.

9.♔d4-e3!   ...

Unexpected and very strong. Black gets into zugzwang on his next move.

9...   ♚g3-h2
10.♔e3-f2.

Black resigned. He either has to give away his pawns, which is tantamount to resignation, or play 10...♚h1, and white easily wins after 11.g3+ ♚h2 12.gxh4 gxh4 13.♗g4.

In this example, the black pawns were especially badly positioned. We have purposely chosen this extreme example to discourage the reader from putting pawns on squares of their bishop's color.

Another type of positional advantage in same-colored bishop endgames is better piece activity. This type of advantage is common for any endgame, so we won't discuss its conversion in detail.

The third important type of positional advantage in same-colored bishop endgames is having passed pawns. The threat of pushing them immobilizes your opponent's pieces and allows us to launch a strong attack in other areas of the board. The position on the diagram occurred in the game **Eliskases — Capablanca**, Semmering-Baden 1937 *(game xxiv)*.

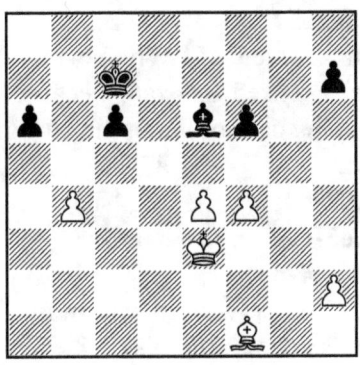

White to move. The a6 pawn is under attack, but if white captures it, there would follow 1...♚b6 2.♗f1 c5, exchanging the b4 pawn. This increases black's drawing chances: after the inevitable e4-e5, he can trade on e5 and then sacrifice his bishop for the e-pawn. As we know, you cannot win if you have a pawn on h2 and a light-squared bishop. However, white wasn't tempted by the a6 pawn. He decided to exploit his positional advantages. Firstly, his pieces, especially the king, are more active, and, secondly, he can create a strong passed pawn on e5, which gives him good winning chances.

1.♔e3-d4!   ♚c7-b6

Now white really did threaten to capture the a6 pawn after his first move, because this did not force further pawn trades. The black king remains tied down to the weak a6 pawn. Exploiting that circumstance, white creates a dangerous passed pawn.

2.♗f1-c4   ♗e6-g4
3.e4-e5   f6xe5+
4.f4xe5   ...

Or 4.♔xe5 c5. White wins after 5.bxc5+ ♔xc5 6.♗xa6, because the black king cannot reach the kingside.

4...   h7-h6
5.h2-h4   ♗g4-h5
6.e5-e6   ♗h5-e8
7.♗c4-d3   ...

A simpler way to win was 7.e7. After 7...♔c7, there's 8.♔e5 ♔d7 9.♔f6 and 10.♗f7. If 7...♗d7, then 8.♔e5 c5 9.♔d6.

After this inaccuracy, white gave black some chances to save the game, but he didn't use them. A series of mutual blunders followed — this shows, by the way, how difficult it is to play a bishop endgame, even for the strongest players — but white eventually won. The ending of the game is not relevant for our subject matter, so we have omitted it. The reader has seen how even a single passed pawn can influence the outcome of the game.

Knight endgames

An extra pawn in a knight endgame is usually enough for a win. We shall only examine the conversion of positional advantages, since converting a material advantage is easy.

The biggest advantage directly follows from the knight's main property as a low-mobility piece that cannot support play on both flanks at once. This advantage is when you have an outside passed pawn. The weaker side is forced to keep their knight or king on the flank with the outside passed pawn. Meanwhile, their opponent unleashes their pieces on the other flank and gains material or creates another, unstoppable passed pawn. Therefore, an outside passed pawn is a serious advantage in a knight endgame, often sufficient for a win by itself.

The next diagram shows a position from the game **Duz-Khotimirsky – Kan**, Leningrad 1933 *(game xxv)*.

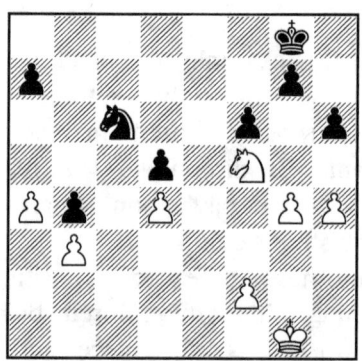

White's pawns on d4 and b3 are weak. With a forced combination, black creates an outside passed pawn on b4.

1...   g7-g6!
2.♘f5-e3   ...

2.♘xh6+ ♔g7 3.g5 f5 loses immediately.

2...	♘c6xd4
3.♘e3xd5	a7-a5!

Now the b3 pawn falls, clearing the way for the b4 passed pawn. White's reply is forced.

4.♘d5xf6+	♚g8-f7
5.♘f6-e4	♘d4xb3

We haven't discussed the role of pawn weaknesses in a knight endgame in great detail. Of course, they are important, as in any other endgame. However, there is nothing specific in pawn weaknesses that occur in knight endgames.

6.f2-f4	♘b3-d4
7.♔g1-f2	b4-b3

The pawn moves to b2, and white is forced to block it with his piece. Meanwhile, black prepares a blow on another flank.

8.♔f2-e3	b3-b2
9.♘e4-d2	...

Or 9.♘c3 ♘c2+ 10.♔d2 ♘a3, and then, instead of the immediate 11...b1=♕, black first plays ♔f6 and h6-h5.

9...	♘d4-b3
10.♘d2-b1	♘b3-c5

The a4 pawn falls too. Now, white is forced to keep both his king and knight on the queenside, which makes black's kingside blow even stronger.

11.♔e3-d4	♘c5xa4
12.♔d4-c4	♘a4-b6+
13.♔c4-c5	♘b6-d7+
14.♔c5-c4	...

14.♔b5 ♘f6 15.g5 h5! 16.gxf6 ♔xf6 17.♔xa5 ♔f5 18.♔b4 ♔g4 19.♔b3 ♔xh4 20.♔xb2 ♔g3 also loses.

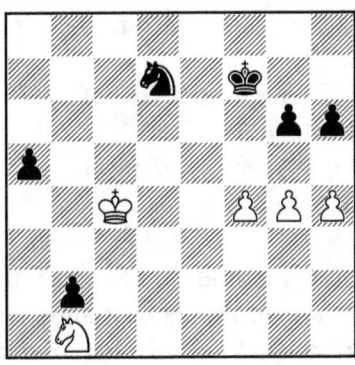

14...   **h6-h5!**

A standard blow in such positions, disrupting white's kingside. It allows the black king and knight to swoop on the newly-created weaknesses.

15.g4xh5	g6xh5
16.♔c4-b3	♔f7-f6
17.♔b3xb2	♔f6-f5
18.♔b2-c3	♔f5xf4
19.♔c3-c4	♔f4-g4
20.♔c4-b5	...

The white king first has to go to a5 and capture black's last queenside pawn. But this requires too much time, and the h5 pawn gets promoted.

20...	♔g4xh4
21.♘b1-c3	...

The knight is finally free. But now it's too late.

21...	♔h4-g4
22.♘c3-d5	...

Or 22.♘e4 h4 23.♘f2+ ♔f3 24.♘h3 ♘f8! 25.♘g5+ (otherwise 25...♘e6 and 26...♔g2) 25...♔g4 26.♘e4 ♘e6! 27.♔xa5 ♔f3 28.♘d2+ ♔g2, and wins.

22...   **♔g4-f3!**

The best position for the king is

two squares away from the knight diagonally.

23.♘d5-c7   ♘d7-f8
24.♔b5xa5   h5-h4
25.♘c7-b5   ♘f8-e6

White resigned.

The methods of advantage conversion in the game **Kamyshev — Zagoriansky**, VTsSPS championship 1938 *(game xxvi)*, are highly instructive.

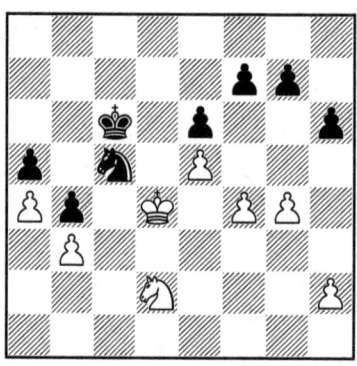

White has the advantage: his pieces are more active, and he has better resources to mount a kingside attack. Both sides have pawn weaknesses: a5 for black and b3 for white. However, if we consider the positioning of the pieces, these two weaknesses are not equal. The white king is highly active: it can defend the b3 square and free up the knight for kingside raids, but the black king can't defend the a5 pawn in a satisfactory way. Because of that, the black pieces are tied down to defending the queenside and cannot prevent a breakthrough on the other flank. There followed:

1.h2-h4   ♘c5-b7
2.h4-h5   ...

2.♘c4 ♔d7 doesn't lead to anything.

2...   ♘b7-c5

Black constantly has to reckon with the threat 3.♘c4, which prevents his knight from going to defend the kingside.

3.g4-g5   ♘c5-b7
4.♘d2-e4   ...

White's goal is to create an outside passed h-pawn on the kingside. This is achieved with a spectacular maneuver.

4...   ♔c6-b6
5.♔d4-c4!   ...

Not 5.♘d6? ♘xd6 6.exd6 f6!, and it's now black who wins.

5...   ♔b6-c6
6.♘e4-f6!   ...

This ensures the creation of a passed h-pawn for white. The knight obviously cannot be captured because of 7.gxh6; meanwhile, white threatens 7.♘e8.

6...   ♘b7-c5
7.♘f6-e8   h6xg5
8.f4xg5   ♘c5-e4
9.h5-h6   g7xh6
10.g5xh6   ♘e4-g5

The first part of white's winning plan is completed. He has created an outside passed pawn on h6, intending to win the black knight for it. However, the defensive resources haven't been exhausted yet. Black finds a way to stop the formidable h6 pawn.

11.♘e8-f6   ♘g5-f3
12.♘f6-g4   ♘f3-g5

13.♔c4-d4   f7-f5!

Only this move gives black hope for a successful defense. White is obviously forced to take on f6, but this frees the way to the h6 pawn for the black king.

14.e5xf6   ♔c6-d6
15.♘g4-e5   ♘g5-h7
16.♘e5-c4+   ♔d6-d7
17.f6-f7   ♔d7-e7
18.♘c4xa5   ...

As soon as black sends his knight and king to stop the outside passed pawn on h6, the white pieces destroy the black queenside pawns.

18...   ♔e7xf7
19.♘a5-c6   ♔f7-g6

Instead of running to defend the queenside, the black king has to capture the h6 pawn first, to free up his knight. Of course, after that, it will never make it to the queenside in time.

20.a4-a5   ♘h7-f6
21.a5-a6   ♘f6-d5
22.a6-a7   ♘d5-c7
23.♘c6xb4?   ...

White grabs another pawn, "just to be sure". 23.♔c5 won immediately.

23...   ♘c7-b5+
24.♔d4-c5   ♘b5xa7
25.♘b4-c6   ♘a7-c8
26.b3-b4   ...

White still has a win, but now it's study-like.

26...   ♔g6xh6
27.b4-b5   e6-e5

Or else white played 28.♘e7 ♘xe7 29.b6, promoting the b-pawn.

28.♘c6xe5   ♔h6-g7

29.♘e5-c6   ♔g7-f7
30.♘c6-a7!   ...

It's all over. The b6 pawn promotes.

30...   ♘c8-e7
31.b5-b6   ♘e7-g6
32.♔c5-d6. Black resigned.

Multi-piece endgames

The main distinctive feature of an endgame is not the absence of queens, but rather the increased activity of the king. For instance, the position from the game Bondarevsky – Botvinnik that we examined in the section about the center cannot be considered an endgame. Indeed, the game ended with a mating attack.

In the endgame, opportunities for mating attacks are rare, and the game becomes quieter.

Of course, this does not mean that endgames have no tactical possibilities and you don't have to calculate lines precisely. When there's a pawn race for promotion or one player is trying to stop the other's pawns, you can only choose the correct continuation if you calculate the possible moves. In such cases, general positional evaluations don't work. Indeed, why talk about any weaknesses if your opponent promotes a pawn and immediately gets an overwhelming advantage?

We will not examine endgames where precise calculations are necessary to decide the outcome, because no general principles apply in such positions, and every chess player has to rely on their own skills.

Play is very different in quiet endgames. Positional factors take the front stage here. Pawn weaknesses, open lines, strong squares for pieces, etc. — all this is at least as important as in the middlegame, if not more.

However, the play is not like in middlegames. The kings' participation in the fight expands the defensive resources, since the king can be used to guard weak squares, and, at the same time, the king provides more attacking resources, too. We've already seen many endgames where king activity became the main winning factor.

One of the greatest masters of multi-piece endgames is grandmaster Flohr. Playing through his games and analyzing them will definitely benefit any player who wants to improve their endgame technique. It's possible that, as they play through Flohr's games, many would think it's strange how slowly play unravels. Instead of taking action immediately, Flohr executes a series of preparatory maneuvers, and then it turns out that all his pieces are positioned exactly as they should be.

Do not hurry to force matters, first improve your position as much as you can – this is perhaps the main rule for the endgame. Flohr's evaluation of the following position from the game **Boleslavsky – Smyslov**, Moscow 1940, is rather interesting *(game xxvii)*.

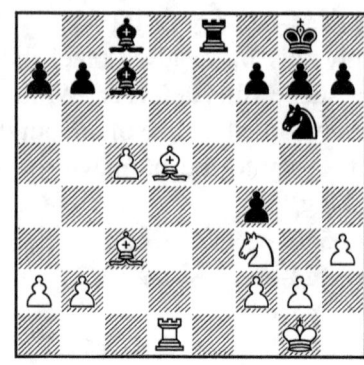

"Boleslavsky's positional advantage is perfectly clear. First of all, he has a pawn majority on the queenside. This fact is especially important because black has doubled pawns. They appeared way back in the opening (Caro-Kann Defense, 1.e4 c6 2.d4 d5 3.♘c3 dxe4 4.♘xe4 ♘f6 5.♘xf6+ exf6) and weren't a liability while they served as a defense for the king's position, creating outposts for the black pieces and preventing his opponent's pieces from invading e5 and g5. However, in the endgame, these doubled pawns may give white a decisive advantage.

In the diagram position, the doubled pawn is also a liability because it's already advanced to f4, taking an important square from the black knight. Additionally, all white pieces are more active than their black counterparts. All that should have led to black's defeat.

Thinking logically, white's task is quite simple: he has to position his pieces in the most beneficial way. Except for the knight, all his pieces are already well-placed. Boleslavsky's evaluation was the same, and he played 1.♘g5. However, this move allowed Smyslov to defend the seventh rank with 1...♖e7, then play h7-h6, opening a luft for his king and achieving a defensible position.

In my opinion, the correct knight move in this position was 1.♘f3-d4, centralizing it. Now white threatens ♘b5. If black plays 1...♗e5, white still plays 2.♘b5, and he can meet 2...♗xc3 with 3.bxc3!. On the other hand, if black plays 1...a6, white only needs to put his pawns on a4 and b4, greatly restricting his opponent's mobility, because, after 1...a6, black's position becomes even more cramped."

Flohr's thought process in the evaluation of this position is very characteristic. After 1.♘d4 a6, white only needs to put his pawns on a4 and b4. Flohr doesn't even consider what happens afterwards, but this is not necessary. It's clear that the moves a4 and b4 restrict his opponent's mobility and improve white's position, and, if that's indeed so, then these moves are correct. This is the most economical way of calculation. Of course, you need certain experience to find the correct way, but you can only gain it by analyzing quite a few of your own mistakes.

To illustrate the course of play, let's look through the game. Boleslavsky hurried to force matters and, as already pointed out above, played

1.♘f3-g5   ♖e8-e7
2.b2-b4   h7-h6
3.♘g5-e4   b7-b6

4.♘e4-d6   ...

The knight has reached d6, but has lost several tempi in the process. Black has managed to consolidate.

4...   ♗c8-e6
5.♗d5xe6   ♖e7xe6
6.♘d6-b5   ♗c7-e5
7.♗c3xe5   ♘g6xe5
8.♖d1-d8+   ♔g8-h7
9.♘b5-d4   ...

9.♘xa7 would have been met with 9...bxc5 10.bxc5 ♖a6.

White still has some advantage, but the position has greatly simplified, and black has obtained some counterplay.

9...   ♖e6-g6

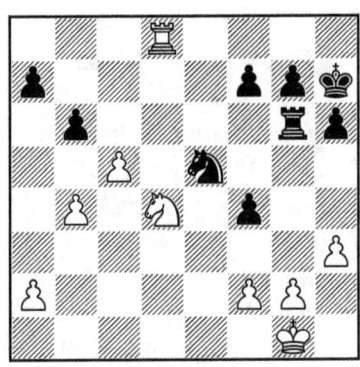

10.♔g1-f1?   ...

After 10.♖c8!, black would have to give up a piece for the c-pawn.

10...   b6xc5
11.b4xc5   ♖g6-a6
12.c5-c6   ...

Counting on the resulting knight endgame, where the passed a-pawn gives white some chances. However, his hopes don't materialize, since the black king manages to take up a strong position in time.

12...	♘e5xc6
13.♖d8-d6	♘c6-b4
14.♖d6xa6	♘b4xa6
15.♘d4-c6	♚h7-g6
16.♔f1-e2	♚g6-f5
17.♘c6xa7	♚f5-e4
18.♘a7-b5	f7-f5

Black tries to activate his pawns as quickly as possible to exchange them.

19.h3-h4	g7-g5
20.♘b5-d6+	♚e4-e5
21.♘d6-f7+	♚e5-f6
22.♘f7xh6	g5xh4
23.♔e2-f3	...

White has driven the black king away and weakened his pawns, but the white knight's position is very awkward.

23...	♘a6-b4
24.♔f3xf4	♘b4-d3+

After 24...♘xa2 25.♘xf5, black loses the h-pawn and the game.

25.♔f4-e3	♘d3-e1
26.g2-g4	h4xg3
27.f2xg3	♚f6-g6
28.♘h6-g8	♚g6-f7
29.♔e3-d4	...

The last attempt. After 29...♚xg8 30.a4, the pawn promotes.

International Master Maxim Notkin found a study-like draw in this position:

30...♘f3+ 31.♔d5 f4! 32.gxf4 ♘h4!!, and the knight manages to stop the a-pawn in time in a roundabout way (for instance, through f5 and e7), while the king stops the f-pawn.

29...	♘e1-c2+
30.♔d4-c5	♘c2-a3

Draw.

The next example is good learning material: how to play an endgame with a positional advantage. White's play is exemplary for a chess player of any level.

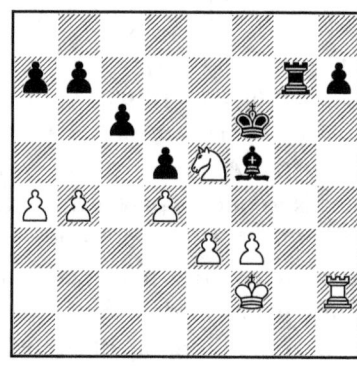

The diagram shows the position from a game **Flohr — Bondarevsky**, Moscow 1939 *(game xxviii)*.

White's position is clearly better. His strong e5 knight is very well-positioned and dominates the black bishop. Black controls the open file, but it's not important in this position, since all the possible invasion squares — g1, g2 and g3 — are controlled by the white king. The black passed pawn on h7 cannot move currently and poses no danger for white. White also has a passed pawn, on f3, but it's not time to push it forward yet. Moreover, the immediate f3-f4 would have been a grave error, ceding the important e4 square to the black bishop. All in all, the strong knight is the most important component of white's advantage.

However, the knight alone is not enough for a win. White first needs to weaken his opponent's position somehow. Black's structure looks very solid, but Flohr manages to prove that his queenside is not completely problem-free.

1.a4-a5 ...

Threatening a5-a6 with complete destruction of black's kingside.

1... ♖g7-c7?

Black prepares b7-b6 with the subsequent c6-c5 and protects the c6 pawn at the same time. However, he should stop the white rook from getting to h6 or else neutralize its effect and hence play either 1...♔g5 or 1...a6.

2.♖h2-h6+ ...

Forcing black to close the open file, just in case. However, improving the king with 2.♔g3! would give white a clearly bigger advantage after 2...♖g7+ 3.♔f4 or 2...♔g5 3.f4+.

2... ♗f5-g6
3.♖h6-h1 ♗g6-f5

After 3...b6, white would have played 4.♖c1, forcing 4...♗e8 and putting pressure on the c6 pawn. Still, this was a lesser evil than the game move. With the bishop on e8, black could activate his pawn with h7-h5. White also had to reckon with the possible c6-c5. When one of the opponents is piling on the pressure, passive defense is rarely successful.

4.♖h1-c1! ...

Now white's plan is completely clear. He finally wants to play a5-a6, disrupting black's pawn structure. Black, of course, can easily prevent this, but at the price of a serious positional concession.

4... a7-a6

The whole operation was about this move. It's a great achievement for white. Now, black's entire pawn chain — a6, b7, c6, d5 — risks getting doomed. The white knight will occupy a strong position on c5 and will constantly target the b7 pawn.

Such moves, of course, need to be avoided, because they condemn you to a tough and tedious defense, but in this case, black didn't have much choice. For instance, 4...♔e6 is met with 5.a6 bxa6 6.♖a1, and black can't avoid material losses.

5.♖c1-h1 ...

There's nothing more to do on the queenside, so now the white rook goes back to the kingside:

5... ♖c7-g7
6.♖h1-h2 ♖g7-c7?

Black should play 6...♔g5! with good chances to survive.

7.♖h2-h6+ ♗f5-g6
8.♖h6-h4! ...

White needs to put his knight on c5. With this in mind, he prepares e3-e4, which makes ♘d3 possible.

8... ♗g6-f5

After 8...♔g5, there's 9.♖g4+ and then e3-e4.

9.e3-e4	d5xe4
10.f3xe4	♗f5-g6
11.♖h4-f4+	♔f6-e6
12.♔f2-e3	...

White will seize the c5 pawn sooner or later, and it's always useful to improve the king's position in the meantime.

12...	♖c7-g7
13.♘e5-d3	♔e6-d6
14.♘d3-c5	♖g7-e7
15.♖f4-f8	...

Threatening 16.♖b8.

15...	♔d6-c7
16.e4-e5	♖e7-e8

Black is tired of waiting passively for white to improve his position, and he offers to trade rooks. White readily agrees, because his knight ties the black king to the queenside pawns. In the subsequent struggle, white essentially has an extra piece – the king. After 16...b6, white would have played 17.♘a4! and then, after the trade on a5, put his knight back on c5.

17.♖f8xe8	♗g6xe8

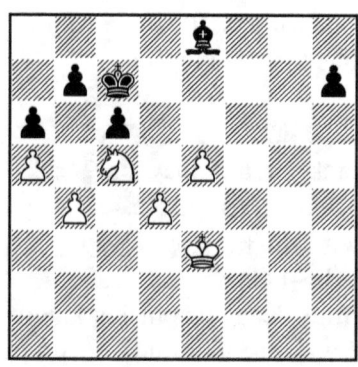

This is a typical endgame where a knight is stronger than a bishop. White controls all the important dark squares, and he can stop the dangerous h7 passed pawn in time.

There followed:

18.♔e3-f4	b7-b6
19.♘c5-a4!	b6xa5
20.b4xa5	♗e8-f7
21.♘a4-c5	...

Now the a6 pawn is weak.

21...	♗f7-c4
22.♔f4-g5	♗c4-e2
23.♔g5-h6	♔c7-d8
24.♔h6xh7	♔d8-e7
25.♔h7-g6	♗e2-f1
26.♔g6-f5	♗f1-h3+
27.♔f5-e4	♗h3-g2+
28.♔e4-e3	♗g2-f1
29.♔e3-d2	...

The white king heads for c5.

29...	♔e7-f7
30.♔d2-c3	♔f7-g6
31.♔c3-b4	♔g6-f5
32.♘c5-b7.	

Black resigned – he can't avoid further loss of material after ♔c5. A very instructive game.

White put in a lot of effort to weaken his opponent's position, but his effort led to brilliant results. The main challenge in such endgames is to set a goal. In this case, white had two tasks: to force a7-a6 and then to put his knight on c5. Afterwards, he simply improved the position of his pieces bit by bit: put the rook on f8, pushed the pawn to e5 and prepared to send his king to f4. As a result, black's position became so cramped that he had to offer the rook exchange himself, which was beneficial for white.

The next position looks roughly equal.

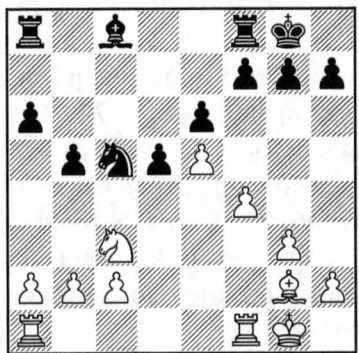

This is the ending of the game **Tarrasch — Teichmann**, San Sebastian 1912 *(game xxix)*.

Indeed, neither white nor black has any pawn weaknesses. All files are closed. In this regard, black even has a small advantage because he can seize the semi-open c-file. Still, it would be wrong say that this position is equal. The main flaw of black's structure is that his bishop is restricted by its own pawns: a "bad" bishop. The d4 square also plays a very important role. It's a great outpost for the white knight. There followed:

1. ♘c3-e2   ♗c8-d7
2. ♘e2-d4   ♖a8-c8

It's hard to find an active plan for black. If he plays 2...f6, intending to get his bishop to g6 through e8, white can execute a typical maneuver for this type of position: 3.exf6 gxf6 4.f5!, breaking up black's center.

3. ♔g1-f2   ...

The king is an active piece in the endgame. You always have to remember that.

3...   ♖c8-c7
4. ♔f2-e3   ♖f8-e8

It's not clear why black made this move. He probably should have played more energetically — 4...♘a4, and if 5.b3, then 5...♘c3 with the subsequent a6-a5 or b5-b4, creating complications on the queenside. Finally, 4...♖fc8 looked much more natural. 4...f6 is still unacceptable because of 5.exf6 gxf6 6.f5!.

5. ♖f1-f2   ...

The white knight and king are positioned great, now he prepares to put his bishop on the good d3 square.

5...   ♘c5-b7

Black has finally formulated a plan. He wants to put his knight on a5 and then offer to trade the knights on c6. However, this worsens his position.

6. ♗g2-f1   ♘b7-a5
7. b2-b3   ...

The c2 pawn is now backward, but it's well-defended.

7...   h7-h6?

A waste of time; besides, this move weakens the position, as it turned out later. Black should have played 7...h5.

8. ♗f1-d3   ...

White is playing simply and purposefully.

8...   ♘a5-c6
9. ♘d4xc6   ♗d7xc6
10. ♔e3-d4   ...

The knight is replaced by the king. Black now has to reckon with the threat of invasion on c5.

10...   ♗c6-d7
11. g3-g4   ...

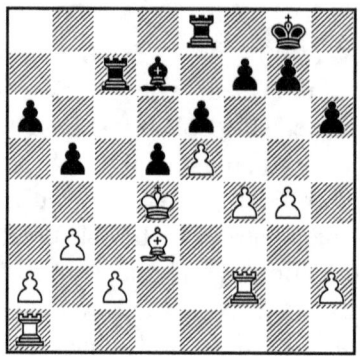

White has positioned his pieces in the best possible way and now launches a pawn attack on the kingside to open files. Black's move 7...h6 only makes it easier for white.

11...　　　　♗d7-c8

You can't save the game with such insipid moves. Black still needed to double rooks and play b4.

12.h2-h4　　　g7-g6
13.♖a1-h1　　...

Preparing 14.h5.

13...　　　　♔g8-g7
14.h4-h5　　　♖e8-h8
15.♖f2-h2　　　♗c8-d7
16.g4-g5!　　...

Forcibly opening files for his rooks.

16...　　　　h6xg5

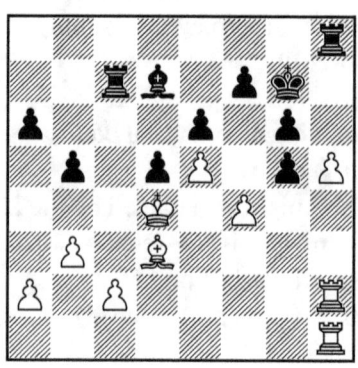

17.f4xg5　　　...

White wants to execute his plan of a kingside breakthrough no matter what. However, it's not necessary to follow one idea until the end. It was much simpler to play 17.h6+ ♔h7 18.fxg5. Black is now essentially playing without his king, which is tied to the h6 pawn. White could open files on the queenside without much difficulty and then force trades or invade black's camp.

Still, the text move doesn't miss the win completely, though it complicates it, because there's not much material left on the kingside now.

17...　　　　♖h8xh5
18.♖h2xh5　　　g6xh5
19.♖h1xh5　　　♔g7-f8

Or else white would have won with ♖h7+ and g6. The main trouble for black is that he cannot trade rooks, as the white king would invade c5 with decisive effect.

20.♖h5-h8+　　♔f8-e7
21.g5-g6　　　...

This move could have greatly complicated the win. There was no need to help black get rid of his weak f7 pawn. He should have played 21.♖h7, threatening g6. After 21...♔e8 white can continue 22.c3, then ♗e2 and ♗h5, attacking the f7 pawn. Still, white's task would have been harder than after 17.h6+.

21...　　　　f7xg6
22.♗d3xg6　　　b5-b4
23.♖h8-h7+　　♔e7-d8
24.♗g6-d3　　　...

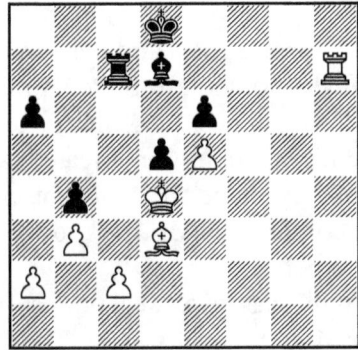

24... ♖c7-c3?

Black could still resist with 24...♖c6. All weak black pawns are now defended, and the limited material gave him some chances to draw. White would have most probably had to reply 25.♕h1 with the subsequent a3, trying to attack the a6 pawn. It seems that black was too tired of difficult defense and already thought that the game was lost.

25.a2-a3   a6-a5
26.♖h7-h8+   ♔d8-e7

Black resigned: after 27.♖a8, he can't avoid material losses.

We could show you many more endgames with various positional advantages. But in all cases, the game goes essentially the same way. The player who has the advantage uses the strengths in his position to create more advantages in another area of the board. The main difficulty here is evaluating the position correctly, taking mutual chances into account and choosing the next target to attack.

These targets can be very different, depending on the concrete features of the position. When you play a complicated endgame, you should never lose sight of what might happen next. Trading a few pieces may quickly turn a complicated endgame into a simple one.

For instance, in the game Flohr – Bondarevsky, white put a lot of effort into forcing black to play a7-a6, weakening the black queenside pawns. After that, the knight versus bishop endgame was easily won for white, and this made play much simpler. His opponent tried to avoid the trade of rooks but couldn't stop the white rook from invading as a result.

The previous examples showed us how difficult it is to maneuver correctly in a complicated endgame. Every chess player who wants to improve should learn the art of precise and focused maneuvering. In every position, you need to formulate the goal of your subsequent play and then take actions that get you closer to the goal.

The importance of purposeful maneuvers was already mentioned in the section on the middlegame. These maneuvers become even more important in the endgame. The thought process in complicated endings should be along the following lines. First, we point out the opponent's weaknesses, of course, not forgetting about our own weak points as well. Then we plan ways to exploit those weaknesses and the optimal positioning of our pieces. You should always take your opponent's activity into account and carefully consider all the measures you need to take to restrict their activity. Both attack and defense in a complicated endgame should follow a consistent plan! Therefore, the main quality necessary for a chess player to play endgames well is the ability to maneuver.

This art of maneuvering comes with long game experience. Every chess student should pay special attention to this aspect of endgame play. When maneuvering in the endgame, you should take the subtlest nuances of the position into account and be able to discover the most hidden features in the pieces' and pawns' positions.

Let's look at a position from the game **Factor – Rubinstein**, Lodz 1916 *(game xxx).*

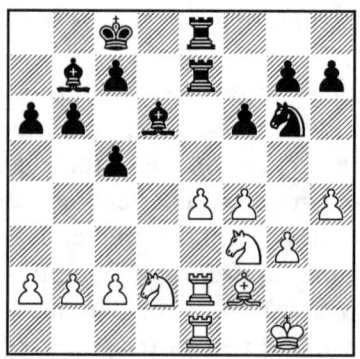

It's hard to say that any side has an advantage here, and the position should be evaluated as roughly equal. In such a complicated endgame position, it's especially important to set the correct goals and play precise maneuvers to achieve them. Aimless play in such positions always leads to demise. Rubinstein created and skillfully executed the following plan in accordance with the position's requirements.

White has two weaknesses: the e4 pawn and the g4 square. The first goal for black is to lock up these weaknesses. The e4 pawn is already locked up on a weak square, so black has to prevent it from escaping at all costs. To do that, it's necessary to force the move c2-c4, preventing the threat ♘c4 and e4-e5.

The weakness of the g4 square is locked up with h7-h5. The subsequent goal of the maneuvers (after white is forced to play c2-c4) is to put the knight on g4. This will significantly improve the position of black's pieces. This initial plan should be enough; the subsequent possibilities will come up by themselves after the preparatory maneuvers. So, black targets the weak e4 and g4 squares with his maneuvers.

 1...   **h7-h5!**

Interestingly 1...♘h8! was also very strong.

 2.c2-c4?   **...**

White hasn't created a similar plan for his own maneuvers. Otherwise, he would have refrained from this move until the last possible moment – it only makes his opponent's task easier.

 2...   **a6-a5**

Before starting his kingside operation, Rubinstein wants to close off the position on the other side of the board and protect himself from unexpected threats. White's thinking is again very primitive – he's playing right into his opponent's hands.

3.a2-a4   ♔c8-d7
4.♔g1-f1 ♗b7-c6
5.b2-b3   ♔d7-c8

As we see, black doesn't hurry with executing his plan. Such slowness is often very useful, because it prevents the opponent from understanding the purpose of our maneuvers. Later, we shall see similar "secrecy" numerous times.

6.♖e2-e3 ♗c6-d7
7.♔f1-g2 c7-c6

Preventing the attempt to put the knight on d5 and preparing an escape square for the d6 bishop in case of e4-e5.

8.♘d2-b1 ♗d6-c7
9.♘b1-c3 ♘g6-h8

Black is finally slowly showing his intentions: transfer the knight to h6 and then to g4. This move has another purpose as well: after retreating to d7 with the bishop, black weakened the pressure on the e4 square. Rubinstein doesn't leave the e4 pawn unattended and wants to put his bishop on g6.

10.♖e3-d3 ...

The knight maneuver was timely. Now, 10.e5 fxe5 just loses a pawn.

10...   ♘h8-f7
11.♖e1-d1 ♗d7-g4
12.♖d1-d2 ♘f7-h6
13.♗f2-g1 ...

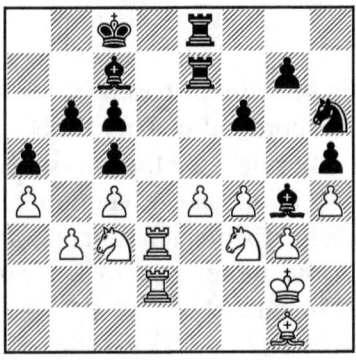

13...   ♗c7-b8!

In any position, you should prevent attempts by your opponent to create activity. Black needs to transfer the g4 bishop to g6 through e6-f7. However, the immediate 13...♗e6 is met with 14.♘d5!, and black loses his advantage. Rubinstein prevents the ♘d5 threat.

This combination doesn't work due to 14...cxd5 15.cxd5 (15.exd5 ♗f5) 15...♗d7 16.d6 ♖xe4 17.dxc7 ♗c6 and then ♔xc7 with an extra pawn. Still, perhaps neither player had noticed this at the time.

14.♗g1-f2 ♗g4-e6
15.♖d2-d1 ♗e6-f7
16.♗f2-g1?! ...

After 16.♖3d2 ♗g6 17.♖e2 white's disadvantage was small.

16...   ♗f7-g6!
17.♘f3-d2 ♘h6-f7

The same tactical trick we mentioned before. Black intends to put his knight on g4 and play g7-g5. But first, he makes some waiting moves to conceal the plan from his opponent and make it more difficult to understand.

18.♖d1-e1 ♗g6-h7
19.♔g2-f3 ♘f7-h6

Black could have immediately played 19...g5!, but he prefers to keep his opponent in the dark.

You should always remember the important rule: "the threat is stronger than its immediate execution". It's often better to threaten your opponent with some move than to make this move immediately.

20.♗g1-f2   ♘h6-g4
21.♗f2-g1   g7-g5!

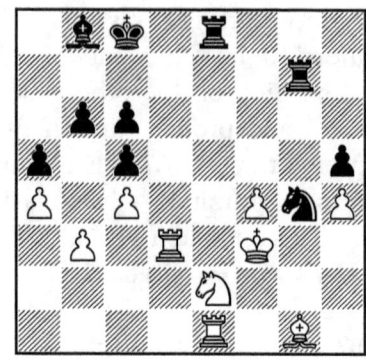

Black has fully executed his entire plan. The white king's position opens up, pawn weaknesses are created in white's camp, and a real attack is launched on the white king's position.

22.♖e1-e2?   ...

White should have played 22.♘f1! gxh4 23.gxh4 ♖g8 24.♗h2 and he seems to hold.

22...   g5xf4
23.g3xf4   ♖e8-g8
24.♖e2-e1?   ...

This move loses. White should play 24.♗h2! to avoid losing instantly.

24...   ♖e7-g7

The incredible 24...♗e5!! followed by f5 would win more convincingly.

25.♘c3-e2   ...

Black threatened 25...♘h6 and 26...♖g4, but this defensive move allows him to blow open the position.

25...   f6-f5!
26.e4xf5   ...

Not 26.e5 ♗xe5 27.fxe5 ♘xe5+ 28.♔e3 f4+, and black wins.

26...   ♗h7xf5
27.♘d2-e4   ♗f5xe4+
28.♔f3xe4   ♖g8-e8+
29.♔e4-f3   ...

29...   ♖g7-f7

White can't save the f4 pawn. After it falls, black gets a minor piece endgame which is easily won.

Even more resolute and effective was 29...♗xf4! 30.♔xf4 ♖f8+, and white either loses the d3 rook (31.♔g3 ♘e5+) or gets checkmated in the center of the board — 31.♔e4 ♖e7#.

30.♖d3-d1   ♖e8-f8
31.♖e1-f1   ...

This leads to a series of trades. Keeping the rooks on the board is even worse for white, because, in addition to his material advantage, black will also have an attack.

31...   ♗b8xf4
32.♘e2xf4   ♖f7xf4+
33.♔f3-g2   ♖f4xf1
34.♖d1xf1   ♖f8xf1
35.♔g2xf1   ♘g4-h6

With an extra pawn, black won after several more moves.

The endgame maneuvering skills shown by Rubinstein in this game are most impressive. We think that such subtle usage of the smallest advantages is much more important and difficult than playing spectacular combinations with sacrifices. Any chess student should strive to develop this maneuvering technique.

MATERIAL ADVANTAGE IN A ROOK ENDGAME

Pawn majority on the flank

An extra pawn in rook endgames does, of course, give you an advantage, but doesn't always guarantee a win. If you go into a rook endgame with a material advantage, you should try to obtain an overwhelming advantage on the flank. For instance, we have four pawns, and the opponent has three. If all those seven pawns are on the same flank, our advantage is minimal. It's much better, for instance, to have four pawns against two on one flank, and give the opponent a lonely passed pawn on another flank. It's much easier to win in the latter position than in the former.

The following position occurred in the game **Stahlberg — Lasker**, Zurich 1934 *(game xxxi)*.

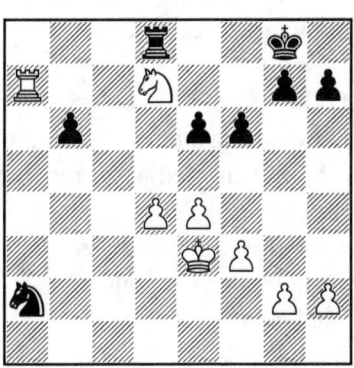

White to move. He has a choice between 1.♘xb6 and 1.♘xf6+. In the first case, all pawns will be on the same flank, and winning will be much more difficult, even though the presence of the knights on the board is more beneficial to the stronger side. However, the second move is much more technical.

1.♘d7xf6+ ...

Black retains the b-pawn, but five kingside white pawns provide an overwhelming advantage over the three black ones. There followed:

1...	g7xf6
2.♖a7xa2	♔g8-f7
3.♖a2-a7+	♔f7-g6
4.♖a7-b7	♖d8-d6

The b6 pawn becomes a liability for black.

5.♖b7-c7 ...

Preparing f3-f4 and e4-e5, leaving the b6 pawn defenseless. Black vainly tries to get some counterplay.

5...	b6-b5
6.♖c7-b7	♖d6-a6

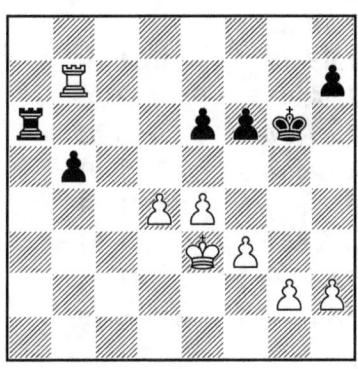

7.d4-d5 ...

In case of 7.♖xb5 ♖a2, black would capture one of the kingside pawns, making the win much harder. White creates a strong passed pawn without wasting time on capturing the b-pawn. A typical technique in rook endings.

White can still retain two extra pawns after 8.♖b8 ♔f7 9.♖b7+ ♔g6 10.g4 ♖xh2 11.♖e7. Again, maybe neither player saw this. Other winning lines are also available.

7. ... ♖a6-a3+

7...e5 8.♔f2 ♖a5 9.♔g3 was no better, with the black rook tied to the defense of the b5 pawn.

In this line, black has a much stronger reply 8...♖a2+ 9.♔g3 ♖b2. White can instead capture on b5: 8.♖xb5 ♖a2 9.♖b8 ♔f7 10.♖b7+ ♔g6 11.d6, and black cannot capture on g2, as otherwise the d-pawn promotes.

8.♔e3-d4   e6xd5
9.e4xd5   ♖a3-a2
10.g2-g4   ♖a2xh2

Black has got the pawn back, but this doesn't matter. The white passer is too strong.

11.d5-d6   h7-h5
12.g4xh5+   ♖h2xh5
13.d6-d7   ♖h5-h1
14.♔d4-d5   ♖h1-d1+
15.♔d5-e6   ♖d1-e1+
16.♔e6-d6   ♖e1-d1+
17.♔d6-c7   ♖d1-c1+
18.♔c7-b8. Black resigned.

Here's another example on the same theme.

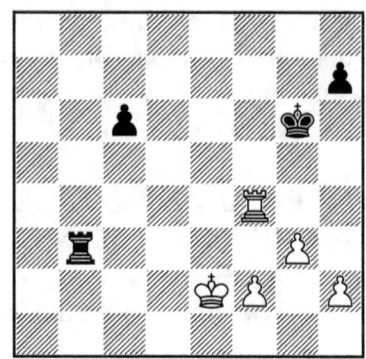

The position is taken from the first game of the **Euwe – Alekhine** return match, 1937 *(game xxxii)*. White has an extra pawn, with three pawns versus one on the kingside. This ensures an easy win for him. But had the c6 pawn stood on f6 or g7, black could have drawn, even though the material balance was the same. There followed:

1.♖f4-c4   ...

Forcing the black rook to assume a passive position.

1. ...   ♖b3-b6
2.♔e2-e3   ♔g6-f5
3.g3-g4+   ...

The pawns start moving. If 3...♔g5, then 4.f3 ♔h4 (or else 5.♖c5+) 5.♔f4 ♔h3 6.♔g5 ♖xh2 7.f4, and the f-pawn goes forward.

3. ...   ♔f5-e6
4.f2-f4   ♔e6-d5

Trying to activate the black passed pawn. White immediately repels this attempt.

5.♖c4-d4+   ♔d5-e6
6.f4-f5+   ♔e6-e7
7.♖d4-e4+   ♔e7-f7
8.h2-h4   ...

The white pawns are moving without any trouble.

8... ♖b6-b1
9.♔e3-f4 ♖b1-c1
10.♖e4-a4 ...

Making horizontal checks possible.

10... h7-h6
11.♖a4-a7+ ♔f7-g8
12.g4-g5 ♖c1-f1+
13.♔f4-e5. Black resigned.

Of course, the idea of the importance of an overwhelming advantage on one flank cannot be correct in all cases. If, for instance, your opponent's passed pawn on the other flank is too dangerous, it's of course better to get rid of it, even at the cost of some of your own advantage. Or another example: you have four connected passed pawns on one flank, and your opponent has three on the other flank. In this case, it's totally unclear who has the advantage. The most important factor here is how quickly the pawns can promote, not the material advantage itself. All in all, the main decisive factor is evaluation of the concrete position.

You can't always gain a significant pawn advantage on one flank. In the absence of a tangible flank advantage, the task of converting an extra pawn becomes much more difficult. It's not possible to formulate any general playing methods in such positions. Thus, we shall resort to examining several types of frequently occurring positions. The most important of these are positions with equal forces on one flank and one player having a passed pawn on the other.

The other matter we shall consider is the advantages and disadvantages of various rook positions. There's a great rule formulated by Tarrasch: "Put your rook behind passed pawns, regardless of whether they're yours or your opponent's." It's not always possible to follow this advice – in that case, you have to protect the passed pawn from the front or laterally.

Let's examine the specific features of each case.

Rook positions: behind the passed pawn

It's easiest to convert your passed pawn if it's supported by a rook from behind. In this case, your opponent has to block your passed pawn, and their pieces lose mobility.

A classic example of converting such a passed pawn was shown by **Alekhine** in the 34th game of his 1927 match with **Capablanca** *(game xxxiii)*.

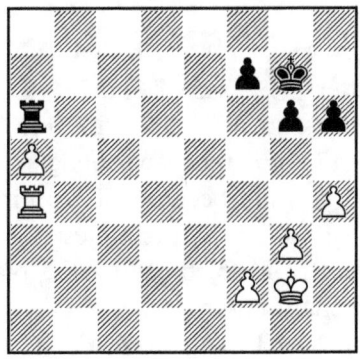

1...	♚g7-f6
2.♔g2-f3	♚f6-e5
3.♔f3-e3	h6-h5
4.♔e3-d3	♚e5-d5
5.♔d3-c3	♚d5-c5
6.♖a4-a2	...

This is black's main problem. White has as many waiting moves as he pleases, while the black rook has to block the passed pawn. Black can't allow the white king to get to b4, therefore, his next move is forced.

6...	♚c5-b5
7.♔c3-b3	...

The immediate 7.♔d4 was also possible, but white repeats moves, according to the well-known endgame principle – do not hurry!

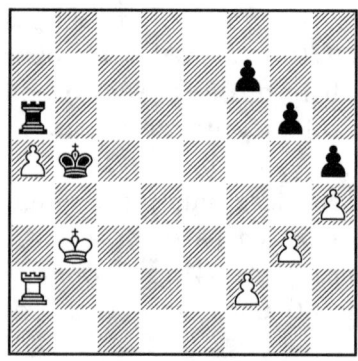

7...   ♚b5-c5

After 7...♖xa5 8.♖xa5+ ♚xa5 9.♔c4 ♚b6 10.♔d5 ♚c7 11.♔e5 ♚d7 12.♔f6, the pawn endgame is won for white because of his king's active position. The simplest way is to push f2-f4-f5, breaking the black pawn chain.

8.♔b3-c3	♚c5-b5
9.♔c3-d4	...

Black can't defend both flanks at once.

9...	♖a6-d6+
10.♔d4-e5	♖d6-e6+
11.♔e5-f4	♚b5-a6
12.♔f4-g5	♖e6-e5+
13.♔g5-h6	♖e5-f5

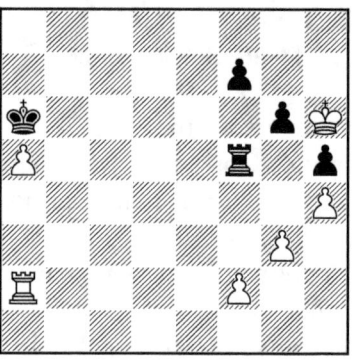

Black has neutralized the a-pawn, but he can't defend his pawns using only his rook from the coordinated assault of the white king and rook.

14.f2-f4	♖f5-c5
15.♖a2-a3	...

Protecting the g3 pawn.

15...	♖c5-c7
16.♔h6-g7	♖c7-d7
17.f4-f5	...

Destroying the black pawn chain. But the preliminary 17.♔f6 was more precise.

17...	g6xf5
18.♔g7-h6	f5-f4
19.g3xf4	♖d7-d5
20.♔h6-g7	♖d5-f5

Black again protects everything, but now the white rook joins the fray.

21.♖a3-a4	♚a6-b5
22.♖a4-e4	♚b5-a6

Capturing the pawn is obviously bad because of the rook trade.

23.♔g7-h6	♖f5xa5

Waiting moves didn't help black either. After 23...♚b7 24.♖e5 ♖xf4 25.♔g5 ♖f1 26.♔xh5 f6 27.♖e4, the h-pawn easily decides the outcome.

24.♖e4-e5	♖a5-a1
25.♔h6xh5	♖a1-g1
26.♖e5-g5	♖g1-h1
27.♖g5-f5	...

It's over.

27...	♚a6-b6
28.♖f5xf7	♚b6-c6

29.♖f7-e7. Black resigned.

In short, the winning idea is this: the threat of pushing the passed pawn distracts the black pieces from defending their pawns. Eventually, these pawns become targets. Like in the middlegame, playing on both flanks at once is the decisive factor. This plan became possible because the passed pawn was far enough from the kingside. If it were on the d-file, it would be much easier for black to defend both flanks. Generally, an extra central pawn is not enough for a win.

Rook positions:
lateral to the passed pawn

If you can't get the rook behind your passed pawn, then you'll have to settle for defending it from the side or from the front. In either case, it's very hard to win. Your opponent holds the passed pawn with his rook and attacks your pawns on the other flank at the same time. In this case, a king walk may be fraught with material losses and other risk.

The player who has an extra passed pawn should position the rook in such a way that it protects both the passed pawn and the pawns on the other flank.

The following example is quite instructive, demonstrating the methods of attack and defense in positions where the stronger side's rook is forced to defend its pawns horizontally.

The next diagram shows a position from the game **Lisitsin – Kan**, Moscow 1935 *(game xxxiv)*.

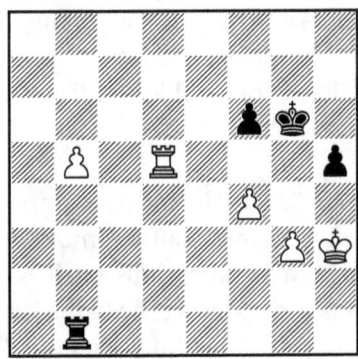

White has an extra pawn that's defended laterally by his rook. He can't send his over king to defend the pawn, because black will capture the g3 pawn and obtain a strong passed h-pawn. To win, it's necessary for white to trade the g3

pawn and advance the f4 pawn to f5. If he manages to do that, his rook will protect everything, and the king will be able to support the passed b-pawn. However, the most straightforward execution of this plan leads to serious trouble. If white immediately plays 1.g4, then 1...hxg4+ 2.♔xg4 f5+. White can't capture the pawn because of ♖g1+, and after 3.♔f3, black plays 3...♖b3+ 4.♔f2 ♖b4, attacking the f4 pawn – now the king can't get away from it. In the game, white made a waiting move.

1.♖d5-c5   ♖b1-b2

Black could have played 1...♖b3, preventing g4. After that, he would have drawn the game more easily.

2.g3-g4!   h5xg4+
3.♔h3xg4   ♖b2-b4!

After 3...f5+, white simply plays 4.♖xf5 ♖g2+ 5.♔f3, attacking the rook. Thus, black tries to prevent f4-f5. The rook could do it from f2 as well.

4.♖c5-d5   ...

Black has defended from all threats, but this waiting move puts him in a very precarious position. If the rook moves along the b-file, then, after 5.f5+, white fully executes his plan and wins easily by getting his king to the b-pawn. Further, 4...♔f7 is met with 5.♔f5, and now black also has to think about defending the f6 pawn.

4...   ♖b4-a4

Allowing white to push the passed pawn further.

5.♖d5-d6   ♖a4-c4
6.b5-b6   ♖c4-b4
7.♔g4-f3   ♔g6-f5??

Black has to hurry with the king to approach the white rook, but the king should do it via the f7 square. 7...♔f7! 8.f5 (8.♔e3 ♔e7 9.♖c6 f5 10.♔d3 ♔d7) 8...♔g7!! 9.♔e3 ♔h6! 10.♖xf6 ♔g5 11.♖c6 ♔xf5 12.♔d3 ♔d5 13.♔c3 ♔d5! and black draws.

8.♔f3-e3   ♖b4-e4+
9.♔e3-d3   ...

It turns out that the f-pawn is indirectly protected. 9...♖xf4 loses immediately to 10.♖d5+ and ♖b5. Or 9...♔xf4 10.♖d4.

9...   ♖e4-b4
10.♔d3-c3   ♖b4-b1
11.♔c3-d4   ...

The d6 rook protects both the b6 and f4 pawns.

11...   ♖b1-d1+
12.♔d4-c5   ♖d1-c1+
13.♔c5-d5   ♖c1-b1+
14.♔d5-c6   ♖d1-c1+
15.♔c6-d7, and white won after a few more moves.

When defending the passed pawn from the side, you can win most easily if the pawn has already reached the seventh rank. The opposing rook is tied down to stopping the pawn from promoting, which allows your king the freedom to go and support it without worrying about the pawns on the other flank.

Rook positions: ahead of the passed pawn

The rook's position ahead of its own passed pawn is deservedly considered the least beneficial. However, it still has its advantages. When the rook is on the last rank, and the pawn is on the next-to-last, the opponent has to constantly watch out for the threat of a rook check. This greatly limits the maneuverability of the opposing pieces. For instance, in the following position:

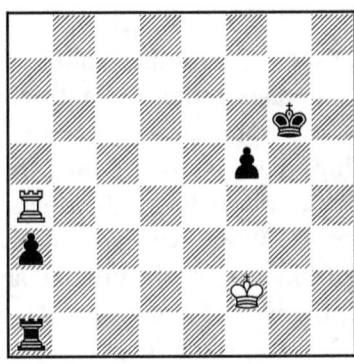

The simplest way for black to win is

1... a3-a2

Now he threatens 2...♖h1, and after 3.♖xa2 he can play 3...♖h2+, winning the rook. White has only one defense.

2.♔f2-g2 ...

It's worth noting that the white king has only two safe squares: g2 and h2. It can't move to the third rank because of the rook check with subsequent pawn promotion, and it can't remain on f2 or go to e2 because of the aforementioned threat ♖h1.

2... f5-f4

Now black, regardless of his opponent's moves, just pushes the f-pawn. White cannot capture it either with the rook or the king, because the a-pawn will then promote.

We recommend paying serious attention to this way of winning. The result wouldn't have changed at all if, for instance, white had a pawn on g5, protected by the rook from a5. Black promotes the f-pawn without the help of his king.

Of course, we should also consider the downsides of the rook and pawn's position on a1 and a2. The black king can't hide from checks anywhere. If it gets to b2, white gives checks from behind until the king moves away from the pawn, and then puts the rook back onto the a-file again.

This way of winning wouldn't have worked had the black pawn been on g5 instead of f5. In this case, the white king would have been quite comfortable on g2. If black had a g-pawn, then 1...a3-a2 would have been a blunder. Black couldn't have won without a hiding place for the king. The right way in this case was not a3-a2, but, rather, getting the king to the queenside to support the a-pawn.

The rook and pawn positioned on a1 and a2 is sometimes a good defensive structure, too.

For instance, in the following position

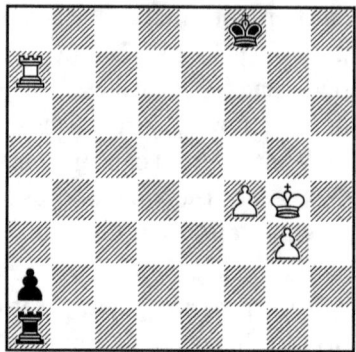

white cannot win, despite having two connected passed pawns.

Indeed, 1.♔g5 or 1.♔f5 is met with 1...♖g1, and black then captures the g3 pawn with an obvious draw. If 1.f5, then black plays the waiting move 1...♔g8, and white can't meaningfully improve the position because 2.f6 is met with 2...♖f1.

However, if we place the white king and pawns one rank higher, a draw is impossible. Consider the following position.

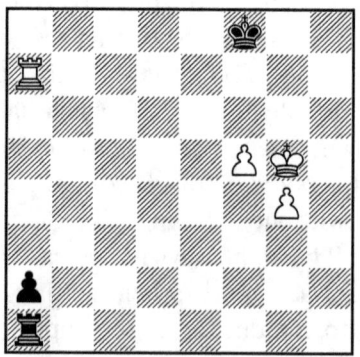

Here white plays 1.♔f6, or, if the black king is on g8, 1.♔g6, immediately creating a mate threat, and now black can't play 1...♖g1 and capture the g4 pawn.

In conclusion, we'll show you the following position, with a rather interesting way to win.

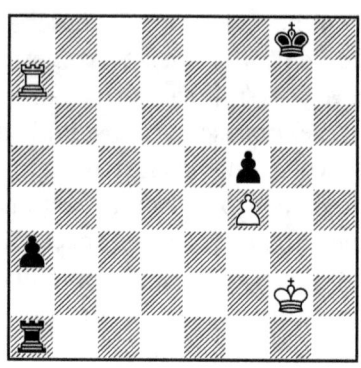

Black to move

In such positions, you should devise a plan rather than think in terms of individual moves. The winning plan is as follows: black moves the pawn to a2 then gets his king to e4. White will have to give a check from a4 to protect the f4 pawn. Then, the black king goes to e3, and white is in zugzwang. The rook cannot move from a4 because white loses the f4 pawn, and the only remaining move, ♔h2, is met with ♔f3, and the f4 pawn still falls. And after winning the f4 pawn, black promotes the f5 pawn. The reader will easily find the concrete moves that allow him to execute this plan.

Still, in general, the rook's position in front of the passed pawn is the least advantageous. If the forces on the other flank are equal, converting the material advantage is only possible in rare cases.

Maneuvering in rook endgames

In positions without passed pawns, winning is usually even more difficult. The plan for the stronger side usually consists of an attack on the flank with the pawn majority. However, you shouldn't always be blunt with executing your plans in rook endgames.

As we have already seen, piece activity usually plays the decisive role in the majority of cases. Thus, it's advisable to try and weaken the opponent's position first.

The following game from a Moscow tournament is quite instructive in this regard *(game xxxv)*.

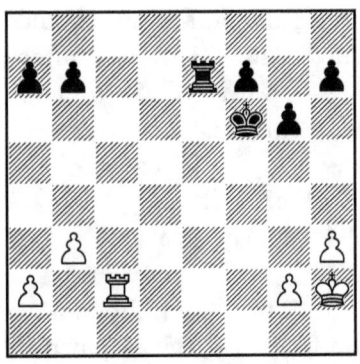

White to move

Black has an extra pawn. There are no passed pawns, and it's hard to create them. The simplest plan for black is to push the kingside pawns. However, the consequences of such a plan are far from clear. Black may be able to create a passed pawn, but, as we have already seen, this does not always give him a decisive advantage. Black preferred another way. He correctly noticed that white's queenside was somewhat weakened because of b2-b3. Therefore, he preferred to create pressure on this flank and eventually tied down the white pieces to defense.

1.♔h2-g3   ♔f6-e6?

1...♔e5! would shoulder the white king and probably wins.

2.♔g3-f4   f7-f6
3.♖c2-d2   ...

White had better chances to hold after 3.♖c8! g5+ 4.g4 or 3.h4! followed by g4.

3...   ♖e7-d7
4.♖d2-c2   ...

After 4.♖e2+ ♔f7 5.h4 (5.♖c2 g5) 5...♖d4+ 6.♔g3 h5 black wins.

4...   ♔e6-d6
5.h3-h4   ...

White could consider improving his rook with 5.♖c8!, and he would have chances to hold.

5...   ♖d7-e7

5...♖c7 6.♖d2+ ♔e6 (6...♔c6 7.♖d8!) 7.♖e2+ ♔f7 8.♖d2 would resist.

6.g2-g3   ...

6.♖c8 or 6.g4 could be tried.

6...   ♔d6-d5?!

6...♖c7! is clearly stronger.

7.♖c2-d2+   ...

It seems that white didn't understand black's idea, which made the latter's task easier. Of course, he shouldn't have let the black king get onto the c-file. 7.♖c8! would probably hold.

7...   ♔d5-c5
8.a2-a3?!   ...

White thinks that if he doesn't play this move, the black king will go to b4 and a3. However, the white pawns have now become even weaker. 8.♖c2+ would resist, as on 8...♔b6 9.♖c8 or on 8...♔b4 9.♖c4+ could be played.

8... b7-b5?

8...a5! would win.

9.♖d2-d3?! ...

This is not the best move. 9.b4+! ♔c4 10.♖d6 and white holds.

9... a7-a5
10.g3-g4 b5-b4?

Black could press with 10...♖e5!.

11.a3-a4? ...

11.axb4+! ♔xb4 (11...axb4 12.♖d8 would hold for white) 12.h5! ♖b7 (12...♖e1 13.♖d7) 13.h6! ♔a3 14.♖d5 and he would draw.

Black has created a target to be attacked, the b3 pawn, and could now win easily with the bold 11...♖e1 and the subsequent ♖b1 or ♖c1. The b4 passed pawn would have played the decisive role. Instead, he made a cautious move 11...♔c6 and only won because of his opponent's mistakes. In the decisive moment of a rook endgame, you often have to play boldly, not fearing to sacrifice. It's not always possible to convert the extra pawn without any hassle and worries.

Still, despite the mistake, black's plan was quite interesting. The extra pawn forced white to avoid trading rooks and to allow the black king to reach the center.

In conclusion, let's show an example of an excellent, systematic conversion of an extra pawn in a rather difficult endgame.

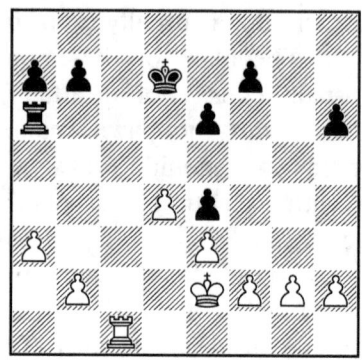

This position occurred in the game **Flohr – Mikenas**, Kemeri 1939 *(game xxxvi)*.

1.f2-f3 ...

The e4 pawn limits white's mobility, therefore, it should be exchanged away. However, after first forcing f5 with 1.♖c5! white's win would be simpler.

1... ♖a6-b6
2.♖c1-c2 ...

2.b4 would be stronger.

2... e4xf3+

If black plays 2...f5, then after the trade 3.fxe4 fxe4, the e4 pawn might become too weak.

3.♔e2xf3 ♖b6-b3!

Black puts his rook on a strong square, complicating white's task.

4.g2-g4 ...

First of all, white gets his kingside pawns away from the second rank and creates a possible threat of a kingside breakthrough. If 4.♔f4 then 4...♖d3! would resist.

4... ♔d7-e7?

Black would have reasonable drawing chances after 4...b5! He would then aim to swap the queenside pawns with a5-a4 and b4, and if 5.h4 then 5...f6.

5.h2-h4   ♔e7-f6?!

5...a5 is preferable.

6.♔f3-f4   ♔f6-g6

Black has defended very carefully so far, but now the fact that he's a pawn down finally starts to tell. White threatens to create a passed pawn and defend it with the rook from behind. Black allows that, but drives the white king away.

7.♖c2-d2!   f7-f6
8.e3-e4   ♖b3-b5

If the rook were still on b3, then white, of course, couldn't play d4-d5 due to e6-e5#. However, black also has to reckon with the possibility of the white rook transferring to c7 through c2.

In hindsight, knowing the game's outcome, it's easy to advise black to stick to a passive strategy and play 8...a5. However, it's much harder to find a relatively better continuation in the practical struggle.

With 8...♖b5, black threatens e5+ and forces white to play d5, precisely calculating that he would be able to hold that pawn.

9.d4-d5   e6-e5+
10.♔f4-e3   ♔g6-f7

10...♖b3+ gives black nothing due to 11.♖d3, and the b2 pawn cannot be captured because the d-pawn promotes. But now, 11.d6 doesn't lead to a clear result on account of 11...♖b3+ 12.♔e2 ♔e8, and black's position is rather solid.

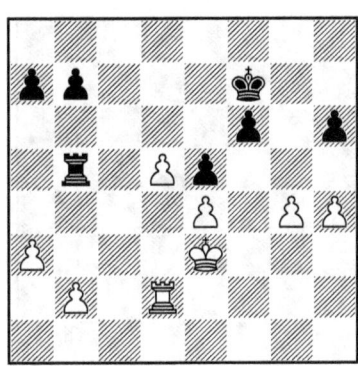

11.b2-b4   ...

Before going for decisive operations, white wants to deprive black of any chances on the queenside.

11...   ♖b5-b6
12.♔e3-d3   ♖b6-a6
13.♖d2-a2   ...

The rook's position is not particularly good, but it's only here temporarily.

13...   ♔f7-e7

13...♖a4 is useless due to 14.♔c4 and ♔b5 or ♔b3.

14.a3-a4   ♖a6-d6

Trying to get the rook to the g-file. White immediately prevents that. While executing your plan, you should never forget about your opponent's resources.

15.♖a2-c2!   ♔e7-d8
16.♖c2-f2   ...

The rook moves to the kingside to attack the weak h6 pawn. Since the f6 pawn is undefended, black doesn't have time to relocate his rook to g7. Now we see how important the quiet Zwischenzug 15.♖c2 was.

16...	♔d8-e7
17.♖f2-f5	♖d6-a6

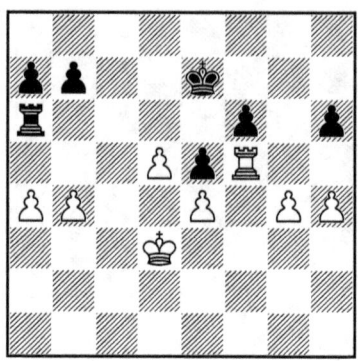

Trying to create chances on the queenside. However, white is prepared for that as well, as all his forces are well-positioned. Were the white pawn still on a3, then after 18.♖h5 ♖xa3+ 19.♔c4 ♖e3, it would have been hard to predict the consequences of the mass pawn destruction.

18.a4-a5	b7-b6
19.♔d3-c4!	...

Leaving no chances for his opponent.

19...	b6xa5
20.♔c4-b5	♖a6-b6+
21.♔b5xa5	♖b6-b8

Hoping for 22.♖h5 ♖g8.

| 22.g4-g5! | ... |

Again, the clearest way to victory. Black loses another pawn. The moves h4 and g4, made by white at the very beginning of the endgame, also proved useful.

22...	h6xg5
23.h4xg5	f6xg5
24.♖f5xg5	...

The e5 pawn will fall anyway. There's no sense in letting the g5 pawn stay on the board.

24...	♔e7-d6
25.♖g5-g6+	♔d6-d7
26.♖g6-e6	♖b8-c8

The only way to save the e5 pawn is to trade rooks, but this leads to a pawn endgame with an extra pawn for white.

27.♖e6xe5	♖c8-c1

28.♖e5-e6, and black resigned several moves later. White sent his king to e5 and pushed his passed pawns.

When you look at this endgame, it seems very simple and clear. However, there aren't many chess players, even strong ones, who can convert their advantage so logically. If you have an obvious advantage, then, right after formulating your plan, you should consider various defensive efforts of your opponent. Resolute actions only lead to quick and sure success after thorough preparation.

The selected way of converting the material advantage in a rook endgame is determined by experience. In each position, there may be several ways to win, and it's not easy to find the best and most reliable one. Every chess player who wants to improve their technique should practice such endgames. This will make them more sure of themselves when converting the material advantage and also allow them to increase their playing ability in other types of rook ending. The chess player who can play a rook ending well can always assess other kinds of endgame best.

Serezha Belavenets

Mikhail Yudovich

This story happened in 1925. The team of our Smolensk school #2 played a match against school #3. I was very anxious, and for a good reason. First of all, I'd never played as a champion before, and secondly... I had to face Serezha Belavenets, who was known to all Smolensk chess-playing boys.

And so, the game started. My opponent, fair-haired, below-average height, played very calmly and confidently. I chose my favorite King's Gambit. Serezha easily repelled my attack, which was not very sound, then traded queens and skillfully converted his positional advantage in the endgame.

After I lost, Serezha saw that I was very upset and started consoling me.

"You should learn to play endgames first and foremost," he told me. "Come to my home, let's look through interesting positions..."

That was the start of our friendship that lasted for years. Some chess wits even called us the "Smolensk twins", because we usually analyzed games together, and wrote annotations and articles together.

Sergei's chess talent became apparent in early childhood. Without a doubt, this happened because he grew up in a "chess atmosphere". His father played in correspondence tournaments, and his uncle, the well-known Russian player Konstantin Alexeevich Vygodchikov, was a multiple Smolensk champion and achieved success in All-Union competitions.

In 1924, when Serezha was just 14, he had already won the Belorussian championship and earned first category.

In 1925, Vygodchikov went to Moscow to watch the international tournament. He took Sergei along. The Smolensk schoolboy defeated Em. Lasker and R. Reti in simultaneous displays. On the sidelines of the tournament, Sergei played several friendly games with C. Torre. His result was quite respectable.

I'll never forget our Smolensk chess "academy". We would go to Vygodchikov's flat, play home tournaments, check opening lines, and analyze the games of famous players.

I was Sergei's close friend, and soon my play improved considerably, I almost became his equal. Evaluating what we were doing back then, I want to pay tribute to the dear K. A. Vygodchikov. He would always correct us, watch our creative growth, teach us to choose independent research and investigation.

"In chess, you can and should help those who want to learn. The basis of bases is your willingness to learn, your own work," Konstantin Alexeevich liked to say.

And we worked on chess together, with love and passion for the game.

Even back then, Sergei showed his characteristic impartiality in analysis, belief in defensive resources in difficult positions, maneuvering skills, and subtle endgame understanding.

It's hard to say how many games we played against each other in those years, in tournaments and matches. Probably several hundred. Sometimes we would check opening lines and systems in these games, but sometimes we would play thematic matches, starting our games from middlegame positions we evaluated differently.

I remember how we amazed the spectators of one first-category tournament. We had a disagreement over advantages and disadvantages of a rare King's Gambit defense, 1.e4 e5 2.f4 f5. Serezha thought that this move was viable, while I was quite skeptical about it.

We decided to check this line in our next tournament game, and, as luck would have it, S. Belavenets had White. What could we do? With his characteristic ingenuity, Serezha immediately found the way.

Our game started the following way: 1.e3 e5 2.e4 f5 3.f4, boiling down to the line we'd disagreed about. After a fierce struggle, the game was ultimately drawn.

That's how we went forward, down the hard road of chess mastery.

In 1926, we both moved to Moscow to study at university. I read my favorite occupation, journalism, while Serezha enrolled in a technical institute. After that, we started playing in adult tournaments more and more often.

I earned the master's title earlier than him, in 1931. But I knew perfectly well that "still-not-master" Serezha Belavenets was already a formidable opponent for the best chess players in the country.

Sergei Belavenets won his master's title in 1933, and his subsequent sporting successes quickly brought him deserved fame among a broad audience of chess fans.

Belavenets's greatest sporting achievements were his wins in the 1937 and 1938 Moscow championships, sixth place in the 10th Soviet Championship (1937), and third place in the 11th Soviet Championship (1939).

Even when Serezha became one of the country's most prominent masters, he still remained a humble, hard-working, kindhearted man, always ready to help his friends, both near and far. Being around him was so easy and comfortable. He could support you when needed, give you advice, or even scold you when you deserved it, impartially, in a true friendly way.

That's why he was so beloved and respected by everyone who met him and asked him anything.

For several years, we worked together on the editorial board of the *64* newspaper and *Shakhmaty v SSSR* magazine. He set a great example for all of us with his caring attitude towards amateur chess fans; he corresponded with a lot of readers, always eager to pass his knowledge on.

We also worked together in the chess club of the Pioneers House. We created training programs and developed study plans. Our main goal was to impart lively interest and love for chess – we both knew how important this was from our own experience.

"If we teach them to love and respect chess," S. Belavenets told me numerous times, "then our mission is complete. The other things will come in time, the kids will find themselves in chess."

I think that it was this approach to chess education that helped the Pioneers House club to train such great chess players as grandmaster Y. Averbakh, masters P. Kondratiev, O. Moiseyev, Y. Estrin, Y. Solntsev, Y. Neistadt, and many others.

Sergei Belavenets, as I said already, was a great master of maneuvering, positional play. His advantage conversion and endgame technique were most skillful. Further, he also had a good eye for spectacular combinations, and tricky and unexpected tactical blows.

S. Belavenets's favorite players were Emanuel Lasker and Jose Raul Capablanca. He always analyzed their games with great interest, and he learned from these renowned chess artists throughout his entire life.

Belavenets was a great expert in theory. Many times, his deep research clarified the most complicated questions of chess strategy and tactics. He wrote many articles and annotations. For our chess encyclopedia *Modern Openings*, he wrote a very important chapter on the problems of the Ruy Lopez.

S. Belavenets successfully combined his chess career and main job. As an electrical engineer, he studied the prospects of electrification in agriculture. His latest constructions for kolkhoz animal farms were demonstrated at the 1939 All-Union Agricultural Exhibition.

In the frightening year 1941, engineer and chess master Sergei Belavenets followed the call of his heart and became a warrior in the people's militia. A loyal patriot of his Motherland, he bravely fought the Nazi invaders at the approaches of our capital city. Commanding a mortar unit, S. Belavenets died the death of the brave near Leningrad.

The small book *Master Sergei Belavenets*, written by S. V. Belavenets's daughter Ludmila Belavenets, one of the strongest Moscow woman chess players, contains only a small part of the great contribution of S. Belavenets's generous and immense talent. But even this small part shows us how great was our loss, how much this man could have done for our art. We'll never forget our dear, our beloved Serezha Belavenets!

Duet of the Smolensk Twins

Yudovich:
I'm the master of the opening.

Belavenets:
I'm the master of the ending.

Twins together:
Everyone knows
Yudovich—Belavenets.

Yudovich:
Every line created
By us together
Is an amazing diamond
In the frame of theory.

Belavenets:
And we work selflessly
For the sake of openings:
Our secrets grow into
Points on the table.

Twins together:
There's a fire of chivalry
In our chests:
I'll give him the glory,
And I'll take the royalties.
Ah, but there's a doubt in the heart:
Yes, he's my brother indeed,
But is there any way
To count our result together?..

Cartoon by Y. Yuzepchuk (USSR Chess Premiership, No. 6, 1938).

The Triumph of Logic

Alexander Iglitsky

When you play through the games of Sergei Vsevolodovich Belavenets or re-read his chess works, you can't help but remember with great sadness that he's no longer among us. He died a glorious death during the Great Patriotic War at the age of just 31.

The most distinct feature of Sergei Belavenets's personality was his love for clarity. This feature clearly showed in everything he did, be that a new engineering construction (he was an electrical engineer), chess game or any work he'd done. Chess players of the older generation, those who got to meet Belavenets, a very versatile and original man, probably remember well one of his favorite sayings, "The logic does not add up!" He, a great commentator and relentless editor, spared no effort in analyzing some interesting positions, and woe betide the annotation author if he found any inconsistencies or deviations from the correct way, however small. Belavenets tirelessly persisted in his search for the sources of these deviations from logic and common sense. After Belavenets conducted his analysis, with characteristic integrity and thoroughness, everything fell into place. Inevitable disputes with masters after they brought their games to the editor's office of *64*, where Belavenets headed the game department, usually ended up with Belavenets's point of view prevailing. The readers got thoroughly checked material where logic always "added up". It's no coincidence that it was Belavenets who was asked to write a most important chapter in the book *Modern Openings*.

During the course of his short life, Belavenets didn't have time to systematize a lot of things he'd written on the topic of chess. But even those articles that were published under his name attract a lot of chess art fans, revealing new aspects of chess creativity for them.

Belavenets's passionate love for chess and loyalty to chess art combined with intolerance towards everything superficial, ostentatious, and short-term. He only recognized the beauty of chess truth. That's where his constant striving for clarity, his almost scientific approach to playing stems from. The constructions should be solid! And doesn't being solid mean being correct?

In his book *Diary of a Chess Player*, grandmaster A. Kotov remembered Belavenets quite warmly, and I think he painted a correct picture of his playing style. "I once sat at the table where Belavenets played against Chistiakov. Belavenets got into severe time trouble, and the position on the board was really complicated. While Chistiakov, who had quite a lot of time, thought on his move, I also decided to calculate some possible lines. When the game ended, and we started to analyze the possibilities of this position, Belavenets showed me mind-boggling tactics, subtleties I hadn't even thought about."

These words reminded me of the faraway days when Moscow held its first international tournament. I once walked into the players' room after a round ended. Capablanca had just defeated Marshall and he analyzed the game, showing a number of beautiful and complicated combinations that were never played out. When he was asked why didn't he play them, he answered, "I wasn't absolutely sure that I wouldn't overlook something, so I decided to win the game in a simple, but safe way."

To understand how much Belavenets saw at the board, it's best to look at his numerous analyses, which often included beautiful tactical blows. His article "The Immortal Game", published in *64* (10th July 1938), is highly characteristic of Belavenets. In his thorough analysis of this masterpiece of chess art, Belavenets used Reti's annotations, but he was quite critical of them. In one important question, he took Anderssen's side, defending him from Reti's criticism – the latter doubted that the great German player's idea was correct. Strict impartiality was a very organic feature of Belavenets!

Belavenets's successes grew from tournament to tournament. He spent a lot of time on chess and almost always was in good playing form. He calculated far ahead and precisely, but if there was an opportunity, he preferred to win "simply", reducing the number of possible mistakes to a minimum. The games of Belavenets look more like an austere engineering drawing than a colorful work of art. But, on the other hand, chess is so malleable that the old French proverb, "Style is the man", sometimes shows very clearly.

You can get some understanding of Belavenets's playing style from the quotes of Botvinnik and the arbiter of the 11th Soviet championship, Zubarev. "The success of Belavenets and Chekhover," the future world champion wrote, "was well-deserved. The former is a fully-fledged master, who perhaps played more accurately than any other championship participant in terms of lack of blunders and miscalculations." Master Zubarev wrote, "The Moscow champion master Belavenets took third place, achieving his greatest success to date. The distinctive features of Belavenets's play are the incredibly strong, almost grandmaster-like technique and defensive skills, in particular the ability to calculate clearly and precisely any complicated and difficult line. In addition, this talented master almost never blunders, despite getting into severe time trouble from time to time."

This book offers the readers more than thirty games played by Belavenets in various competitions and quotes from his articles on teaching chess. Belavenets was a brilliant teacher. He was always able to get his audience interested and, using his great erudition, reinforced the study material with examples from games of outstanding chess players. No question was left without an answer, clear and lucid. Belavenets's sense of humor — benevolent, not nasty — also helped make studying chess "secrets" that much easier.

Now let me show you an example of Belavenets's unconventional way of outlining complicated chess problems. After describing the advantages of seizing the center, he makes an observation that's very important for a practical player that will send many students the right way: "When we have an opportunity to create a pawn center, we should always consider the question: are we able to provide sufficient protection? The lack of necessary piece support can lead to a catastrophe: your opponent will concentrate the attacks of their pieces on our pawns, and our pawns will be weakened, traded away or simply captured." Such a remark about the well-learned concept of the center will make the student approach the problem more thoughtfully rather than mechanically, looking somewhat ahead. We're sure that careful study of Belavenets's lectures will be beneficial for chess players of any level.

This feature of Belavenets's chess thinking helps explain a strange-looking paradox. While Belavenets masterfully played friendly games and was almost always among the winners in blitz tournaments, even when the line-up was very strong, he would often get into time trouble in serious games. This may sound counter-intuitive, but it happened because he saw so much at the board and was very demanding on himself. And even though not all combinations and complicated maneuvers which he considered were implemented at the board, they were still thoroughly analyzed. And this required precious chess time.

The games compiled for the book were mostly published back in his time, but even 25–30 years later, they still look fresh and interesting as part of a collection, revealing the ways of chess thinking of one of the greatest Soviet masters.

The idea of publishing the chess legacy of Belavenets had been discussed by Moscow chess players for quite a while — many of them remember that charismatic man very well. Now this idea has finally been realized, even if quite late. Our chess players will get a valuable book which will serve as a monument to a late master who made a great contribution to the Soviet chess school, the strongest in the world.

Two Chess Ajaxes
Vasily Panov, from the book Forty Years at the Chessboard

I didn't know much about the "two chess Ajaxes" — Sergei Belavenets and Mikhail Yudovich — before they moved from Smolensk to the capital in 1930. Friends since school, they grew together as chess players as well, collaborating on chess theory and training each other. Both were masters of an elegant positional, maneuvering style; the only difference was that Belavenets was mainly a strategist, while Yudovich was more of a tactician. Their personalities were different as well. Belavenets was very tenacious and stubborn in both attack and defense, relentlessly "squeezing" the win out of the smallest advantages. He had a philosopher's mind. I remember two of his sporting adages quite well: "Chess is a tragedy of one tempo!" (meaning, you often lack just one tempo to execute some combination or maneuver) and "You can't win a game without heavy stress!" I think that any experienced player will agree with these adages, they are not just jokes.

Yudovich, on the other hand, is an exceptionally cunning, tricky tournament psychologist, able to find the key to any player and provoke him into some dubious activity that draws him into deeply-hidden traps. As a fighter, he's not as persistent as Belavenets, but he never avoided complicated, sharp struggle and eagerly went for it, while Belavenets preferred purely maneuvering play. In the 1930s, they both developed many interesting novelties in various openings, and the detailed analysis of the French Defense which they published in the 1938 *Yearbook* is a classic that's still relevant even in our days. Such a pity that this creative symbiosis ended after Belavenets perished on the front lines at the beginning of the war.

The Training Camp at Koktebel
Grigory Levenfish, from the book Selected Games and Memories

The Zenit sports society gave me a lot of help *(to prepare for the 1937 Soviet championship match against M. Botvinnik – auth.)*. I was able to rest and prepare for two months, and even had a coach for a month. I invited the young talented master Serezha Belavenets, whose style was somewhat similar to Botvinnik's. The Leningrad Writers' Union kindly provided two package trips to their holiday center in Koktebel, and soon we headed off to Crimea.

The wonderful Koktebel beach consisted of fine, pretty shingle of bizarre shapes, polished by the sea. There were even some agates and cornelians there. Tourists avidly collected them. This "stone fever" is at first quite acute, but it slowly subsides towards the end of the trip. Suitcases can't hold the heavy load, so you reluctantly have to choose only the best specimens.

This picturesque corner of Crimea was once "discovered" by the poet Maximilian Voloshin. The museum in his house is still intact. Koktebel is the best place for swimming and bathing on the entire Crimean coast. The holiday center was in decent shape, and the writers' company was interesting and funny: Zoshchenko, Lavrenev, Marvich, Chukovsky-junior, Rakhmanov and others. Belavenets soon won the hearts of everyone.

During the day, we would go to the beach and work on analysis, and then swim during breaks. Of course, in such an environment, analysis couldn't just be "dry" and boring. My main goal was to find a defense for black against the Queen's Gambit – Botvinnik's main weapon. Of course, it was hard to patch all the numerous holes in my play in a month, but our collaboration was beneficial both for me and my coach. Without a doubt, Belavenets would have grown into a strong grandmaster, but, sadly, Belavenets died heroically in the first months of the Great Patriotic War, defending the Motherland.

Sergei Belavenets

2nd category chess lessons. Sverdlovsk, April 1938

First All-Union Chess Tournament for employees of the Higher School and scientific institutions of the USSR. Minsk, 30 October – 15 November 1935

Sergei Belavenets (left) and Grigory Levenfish (right) at the training camp in Koktebel, September 1937

A friendly game at a holiday center in the south of the Soviet Union

Lilienthal versus Belavenets, Moscow Championship, 1937. Photo from V. Eremeev's archive

A meeting of club players and USSR Master of Sport Sergei Belavenets

Training tournament table, Leningrad-Moscow, January 1939, which Sergei Belavenets had started to fill in. Photos (from left, then down, then left-to-right, then up): Levenfish, Lilienthal, Romanovsky, Konstantinopolsky, Panov, Alatortsev, Bondarevsky, Smyslov, I. Rabinovich, Ragozin, Tolush, V. Makagonov, Kan, Goglidze, Belavenets, Flohr, Reshevsky, Keres

Ludmila Belavenets, Central Chess Club, 1957

Moscow Junior Team, winners of the 1955 USSR Cup.
First row: Svetlana Smekalova, Ludmila Belavenets, Valeria Alfeeva, Irina Ubert.
Second row: Valentin Chernykh, Alexei Garin, Grigory Abramovich Podolny, Grigory Ionovich Ravinsky, Vladimir Liberzon, Vladimir Zelevinsky, Igor Zakharov, Boris Shashin, Iosif Krichevsky, Viktor Lvovich Khenkin, Anatoly Grishanin

Game against Nina Voitsik, Moscow Championship, 1956

With Alla Kushnir, Central Chess Club, 1957

Nina Borisovna Voitsik, Alla Kushnir, Ludmila Belavenets, Alexander Markovich Konstantinopolsky, Bronislava Goikhenberg (Mosionzhik), Nonna Avanesova (Karakshyan), Marina Statnikova, Vera Nikolaevna Tikhomirova. Moscow, 1957

With Alla Kushnir and Yuri Averbakh at the Moscow team's training camp in the Moscow region, 1962

Leningrad 1962

25th Soviet Championship, Beltsy, 1965
First row: Tamara Golovei, Elena Kesselman, Elena Rubtsova (Fatalibekova), Boris Aronovich Bogatin, Olga Nikolaevna Rubtsova, S. Ivanova. Second row: Tamara Archakova, Eliso Kakabadze, Elena Mikhailova, Kira Zvorykina, Inna Poprukailo, Valentina Kozlovskaya (tournament winner), Klara Skegina, Natalia Konopleva. Third row: Tatiana Zatulovskaya, Natalia Kolotii, Ludmila Belavenets, Lubov Idelchik, Maaja Ranniku, Olga Ignateva

Moscow champion, 1962

Leningrad 1970

Moscow. Pioneers House on Stopani Lane. Opening of the Sergei Belavenets memorial tournament. Ludmila Belavenets, Viktor Kott, Boris Krapil, Yakov Neishtadt. Late 1980s

Meeting with military servicemen from the railway forces. Yaroslavl, 1986

Moscow, Spartak Club, 1980s

With her most famous pupil Alexander Morozevich, Moscow 2005

With David Bronstein

Chat at the Bolshoi Theater with its director, the famous dancer Vladimir Vasiliev. 1997

Former pupils celebrating Ludmila's 60th birthday. Vladislav Oreshkin, Evgeny Chernyakov, Anton Aleferenko, Alexander Tsvetkov, Elena Gutkina, Natalia Chukhrova and Vladimir Barsky. Moscow, 2000

The latest pupils are growing up

With colleagues at the Petrosian Club. Sitting: Natalia Chukhrova, Lev Berezov, Ludmila Zaitseva. Standing: Artem Akhmetov, Valery Kedrov, Ludmila Belavenets, Evgeny Reshetnikov and Nikolai Kurenkov

Announcing the results at a junior tournament. Vadim Karpov, Ludmila Belavenets, Artem Akhmetov and Evgenia Kuchumova

Selection of Photos

Chelyabinsk 2004 at a tournament marking Kira Zvorykina's 85th birthday – participants and their young pupils

With a prize at the Victory Day handicap tournament, Moscow 2012

Interview with Anna Zakharova and Konstantin Savenkov

With winners of the Petrosian Memorial tournament, Moscow, January 2012

With the Sparrow Hills Chess Club director Alexander Mazia

Konstantin Savenkov – world under 8 champion, Turkey, 2007

Celebrating Alexander Nikitin's 70^h birthday

With Mark Dvoretsky and Alexander Nikitin

The post-mortem

With Maxim Vavulin, one of our club's students, a winner and prize-winner of Russian junior championships

Tournament of champions to mark Nona Gaprindashvili's 70th birthday. Elena Fatalibekova, Ludmila Saunina, Valentina Kozlovskaya, Tamara Khmadashvili, Nona Gaprindashvili, Marta Litinskaya, Ludmila Belavenets, Tamara Vilerte and Hanna Erenska-Barlo. Moscow, November 2011

Celebrating Alexander Nikitin's 85th birthday, January 2020

At a big birthday celebration in the Dvorkovich chess lounge. Nina Medyanikova, Alexander Orlov, Olga Katskova and Evgeny Vasiukov

Congratulating Yuri Averbakh on his 90th birthday

With winners of the Young Stars of Moscow tournament

The cup is ours!

Declaring the tournament results

Ex-pupils pay a visit

With Sergey Yankovsky and Mark Dvoretsky at a session of the Chess Hopes of Russia school. Ognikovo, 2012

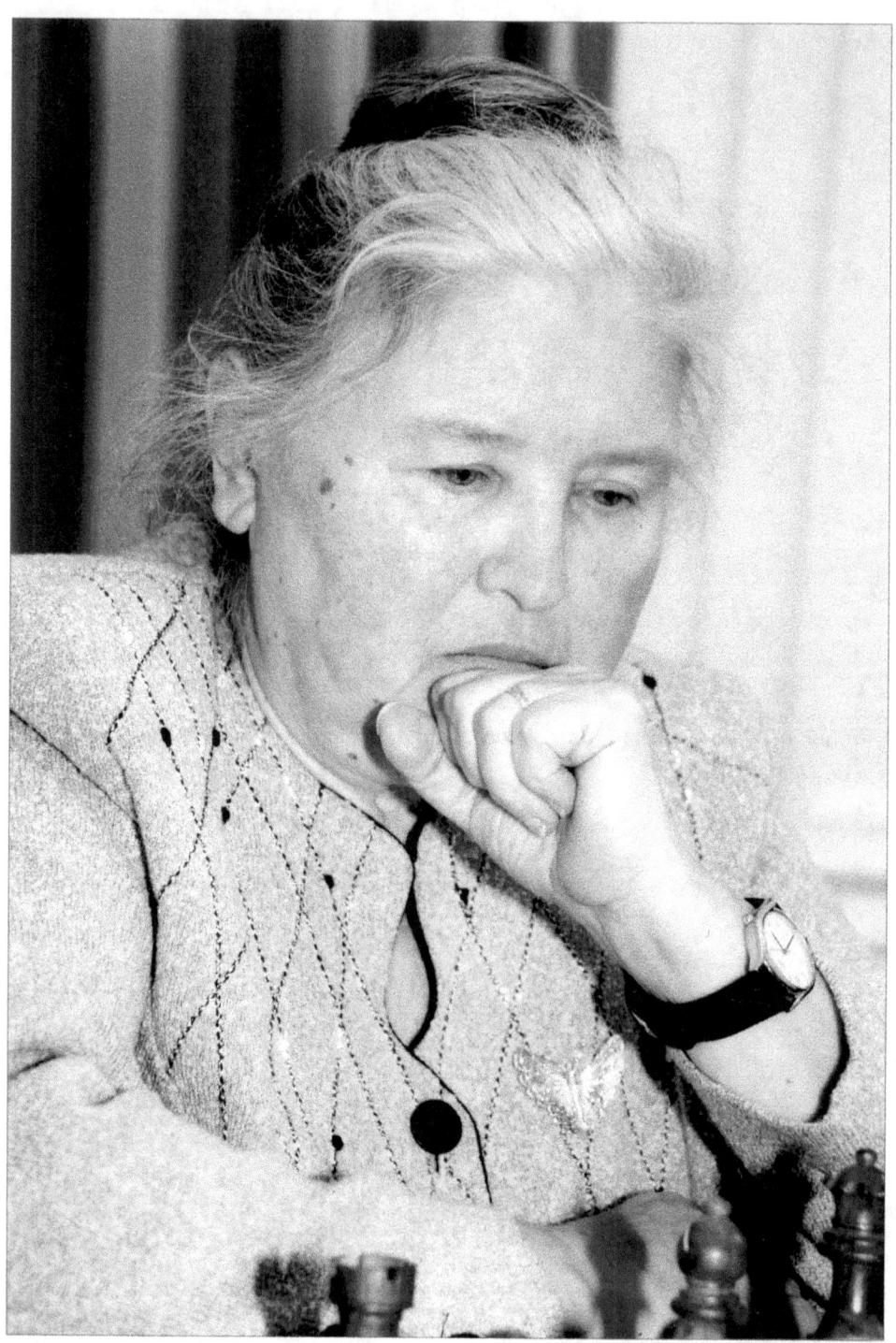

Interest in chess doesn't wane

Selected Games of Sergei Belavenets

Ludmila Belavenets

The annotations below are based on the analyses of Sergei Vsevolodovich himself, who was rightfully considered one of the best Soviet analysts in the pre-war years: he always strove for depth and impartiality, never trying to "adjust" the solution to the task. Of course, all lines have been checked with a computer, and corrections were made where needed [computer corrections for the 2012 edition are highlighted in italics but we have not highlighted additional corrections made for the 2024 edition].

Now it's probably impossible to determine the dates of his games against Vygodchikov and L. Grigoriev (games 1 and 2). They were likely played when Sergei still lived in Smolensk.

No. 1. Sergei Belavenets – Konstantin Vygodchikov
Queen's Gambit D30

1.d2-d4	d7-d5
2.c2-c4	c7-c6
3.♘g1-f3	♘g8-f6
4.e2-e3	e7-e6
5.♗f1-d3	♘b8-d7

Inviting white to go for the sharp Meran Variation, which occurs after 6.♘c3 dxc4 7.♗xc4 b5 8.♗d3 a6 9.e4 c5 etc. White avoids the theoretical lines, planning for the core battle in the middlegame.

6.♘b1-d2	♗f8-e7
7.0-0	0-0
8.e3-e4	d5xe4
9.♘d2xe4	b7-b6

Perhaps it was simpler to play 9...♘xe4 10.♗xe4 ♘f6 11.♗c2 c5 with good chances to equalize.

10.♗c1-f4	♗c8-b7
11.♘e4-c3	♘f6-h5

This knight move is a mistake. Black should have played 11...c5. The line 12.d5 exd5 13.♘xd5 ♘xd5 14.cxd5 ♗xd5 15.♗xh7+ ♔xh7 16.♕xd5 ♘f6 leads to equality. Now white, using the lack of control over the d5 square, achieves what he wanted.

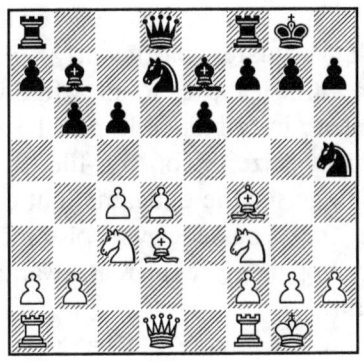

12.♗f4-e3	c6-c5
13.d4-d5	e6xd5
14.♘c3xd5	♗b7xd5?!

14...♘df6! would equalize.

15.c4xd5 g7-g6?
15...♗d6! should be played.
16.♕d1-d2 ...
16.d6! would win.
16... ♗e7-d6
17.♖a1-d1 ♕d8-c7
18.g2-g3 ♖f8-e8
19.♖f1-e1 a7-a6
20.a2-a4 ...

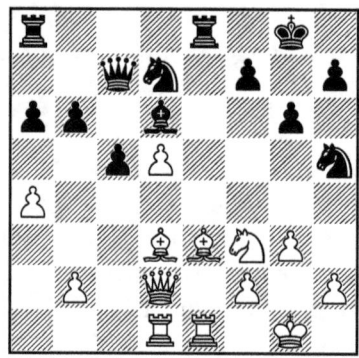

White has managed to obtain strong pressure in a simple way, combining developing moves and prophylaxis (18.g3 and 20.a4). His new plan is to increase pressure along the light squares, particularly on the a6 pawn: if it moves to a5, white will be able to install his bishop on b5 and gradually seize the open e-file. Black tries to go for the endgame, but even there, the d5 passed pawn bolstered by the bishop pair gives a great advantage to white.

20... ♘d7-e5
21.♘f3xe5 ♖e8xe5
22.♗d3-c4 ♘h5-f6
23.♕d2-d3 ♕c7-d7
24.b2-b3 ♕d7-h3
25.♕d3-f1 ♕h3xf1+
26.♖e1xf1 ♖e5-e7
27.♗e3-g5 ♔g8-g7
28.♖f1-e1 ♖e7xe1+
29.♖d1xe1 h7-h6
30.♗g5-d2 ♘f6-g8
31.♗d2-c3+ ♔g7-f8
32.♔g1-g2 a6-a5?!
Black should play 32...♘g8.
33.f2-f4 ♘g8-e7
34.♗c3-e5 ♖a8-d8
35.♔g2-f3? ...
35.♗f6! ♖b8 36.g4 would paralyze black and win.
35... ♘e7-g8?
Black should play 35...♘f5! with decent chances to hold.

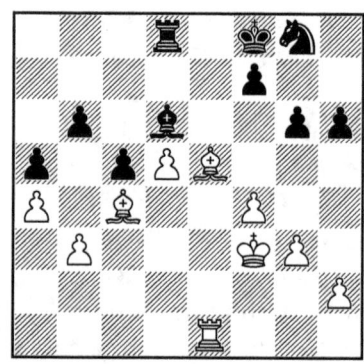

White's advantage becomes increasingly tangible. He's threatening to storm the kingside and up-end black's defense. Thus, black is forced to concede new weaknesses in his camp.

36.g3-g4 f7-f6
37.♗e5-c3 ♖d8-e8
38.♖e1-e6 ...

Getting the passed pawn one step closer to promotion and obtaining the d5 square for the king – black has to patch up this "hole" immediately. Keeping the rooks on would win as well.

38...	♖e8xe6
39.d5xe6	g6-g5

39...f5 would be more practical.

40.f4xg5	h6xg5
41.h2-h3	♔f8-g7
42.♔f3-e4	♘g8-e7
43.♗c4-a6	...

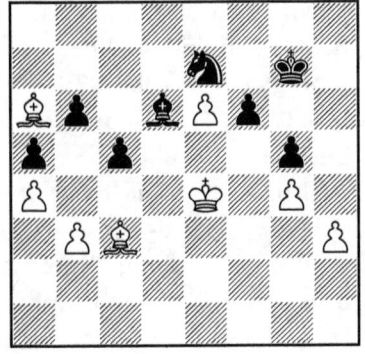

Freeing up the route d3-c4-b5 towards the queenside for the king. Black can't do anything to stop that plan. The endgame moves to its final phase.

43...	♔g7-g6
44.♗a6-b7	♗d6-c7
45.♔e4-d3	f6-f5
46.♔d3-c4	♗c7-g3
47.♔c4-b5	♗g3-f2
48.♔b5xb6	...

The trap is illusory: 48...c4+ 49.♔xa5 cxb3 50.♔b4.

48...	♗f2-d4
49.♗c3xd4	c5xd4
50.♔b6xa5	d4-d3
51.♔a5-b4	d3-d2
52.♗b7-f3	♘e7-d5+
53.♔b4-c5	f5xg4
54.h3xg4	♘d5-c3
55.♔c5-d6	♔g6-f6
56.e6-e7	♘c3-e4+
57.♔d6-d7.	Black resigned.

"The game is highly illustrative for understanding Belavenets's style: unassuming opening play, where he's ready to settle for a minimal advantage, logical increasing of this advantage based on his opponent's small positional mistakes in the middlegame, and, finally, calm and clear endgame play, reaping the fruits of skillful strategy." (A. Iglitsky)

No. 2. Sergei Belavenets – L. Grigoriev
Queen's Gambit D63

1.d2-d4	d7-d5
2.c2-c4	e7-e6
3.♘b1-c3	♘g8-f6
4.♗c1-g5	♗f8-e7
5.e2-e3	0-0
6.♘g1-f3	♘b8-d7
7.♖a1-c1	d5xc4

Too premature. This move is usually made only after white loses a tempo to move his light-squared bishop. No wonder white gets a great position out of the opening.

8.♗f1xc4	a7-a6
9.a2-a4	b7-b6
10.0-0	♗c8-b7
11.♕d1-e2	c7-c5

Black has reached his goal and... a very difficult position! It was probably better to try and simplify with trades after 11...♘d5.

12.♖f1-d1	♕d8-c7
13.e3-e4	c5xd4
14.♘f3xd4	♘d7-c5?

A gross mistake that leads to defeat. After 14...♗c5, the whole fight was still ahead, and white was only slightly better.

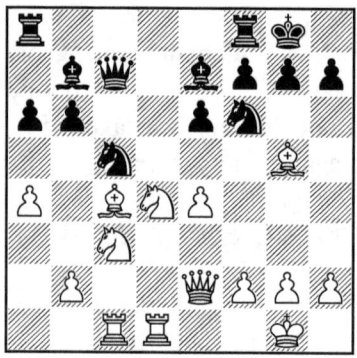

15.b2-b4! ...

The blow that immediately decides the game. Alas, black can't just go back: 15...♘cd7 16.♘xe6 fxe6 17.♗xe6+ ♔h8 18.♗xd7, and so he is forced to close his eyes and jump into the abyss.

15...	♘c5xe4
16.♘c3xe4	♘f6xe4
17.♘d4xe6	♘e4-c3

This attempt to muddy the waters is easily refuted by white.

18.♖c1xc3	♕c7-c6
19.♕e2-g4	♗e7xb4
20.♗g5-f6	♕c6xg2+
21.♕g4xg2	♗b7xg2
22.♖c3-g3	g7-g6
23.♘e6xf8	♗g2-c6
24.♘f8xg6	h7xg6
25.♖g3-h3.	Black resigned.

No. 3. Sergei Belavenets – Boris Yuriev
Moscow vs. Leningrad metalworkers team match, 1929
Queen's Gambit D52

1.d2-d4	♘g8-f6
2.c2-c4	e7-e6
3.♘b1-c3	d7-d5

After "scaring" his opponent with the Nimzo-Indian Defense, black goes down the well-beaten route of the Queen's Gambit Declined.

4.♗c1-g5	♘b8-d7
5.e2-e3	c7-c6
6.♘g1-f3	♕d8-a5
7.♘f3-d2	♗f8-b4
8.♕d1-c2	0-0

The old simplifying Rubinstein system in this line of the Cambridge Springs Defense – 8...dxc4 9.♗xf6 ♘xf6 10.♘xc4 ♕c7 – suffered a strong blow in the mid-1930s when A. Alekhine played 11.g3! 0-0 12.♗g2 ♗d7 13.a3 ♗e7 14.b4. White employs a similar system in this game.

9.♗f1-e2 ...

Capablanca's move 9.♗h4 leads to more complicated play. This move was successfully used by him in the match against Alekhine; its purpose is to prevent the simplifications arising from the eventual blow along the fifth rank.

9...	d5xc4

Another known continuation is 9...e5. 9...b6 with the subsequent ♗a6 is also interesting.

10.♗g5xf6	♘d7xf6
11.♘d2xc4	♕a5-c7

11...♗xc3+ 12.♕xc3 ♕xc3+ 13.bxc4 ♗d7 14.♗f3 ♖fd8 15.a4 and 16.♔d2 leads to a clear advantage in the endgame.

For instance: 15...♖ac8 16.♔d2 ♖c7 17.♖hb1 ♗c8 18.a5 ♘d7 19.♔c2 ♔f8 20.♘b6 axb6 21.axb6 ♘xb6 22.♖xb6 with better chances for white, Alekhine – Bogoljubov, Germany/ Netherlands 1929.

12.a2-a3　　　　♗b4xc3+

It was probably better to play 12...♗d6 and try to break free with e6-e5. Now black's position is difficult.

13.♕c2xc3　　　　♗c8-d7

13...♘d5 14.♕c2 c5 was stronger, preventing white from clamping down.

14.b2-b4　　　　♖f8-d8
15.0-0　　　　♗d7-e8
16.♖f1-d1　　　　♖a8-c8
17.♖a1-c1　　　　♕c7-e7
18.♗e2-f3　　　　...

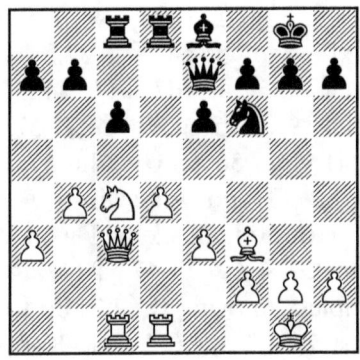

The Alekhine system shown in the annotation to black's 8th move has now occurred on the board. White has a big space advantage, control over the center, queenside pressure and a clear plan – a pawn minority attack with a3-a4 and b4-b5. Black's difficulties are exacerbated by weak dark squares in his camp – the consequences of the erroneous trade 12...♗xc3+.

18...　　　　♘f6-d5
19.♕c3-b3　　　　♕e7-g5
20.g2-g3　　　　f7-f5?
21.♘c4-e5　　　　...

A couple of prophylactic moves are enough to prevent black's activity on the kingside.

21...　　　　♕g5-e7

21...♗h5 was worthy of consideration, trying to trade the "dumb" bishop. White would have most probably played 22.♗xd5 ♖xd5 23.♖e1 with an obvious advantage.

22.♖c1-c2　　　　a7-a6
23.♖d1-c1　　　　♖c8-a8

White threatened 24.a4 with the subsequent b5. He immediately thwarts the attempt to free up the position with 24...a5.

24.♖c1-c5　　　　♘d5-f6
25.a3-a4　　　　♘f6-d7?

Black sacrifices a pawn, trying to get at least some freedom in a very difficult position. However, it worsens his position a lot.

26.♘e5xd7　　　　♗e8xd7
27.♖c5xf5　　　　♖d8-f8
28.♖f5xf8+　　　　♖a8xf8
29.♗f3-g2　　　　♔g8-h8
30.f2-f4　　　　♕e7-f6
31.♖c1-c5　　　　g7-g6
32.♖c5-e5　　　　♔h8-g7
33.♕b3-c4　　　　♖f8-e8
34.♗g2-h3　　　　♕f6-f7
35.♕c4-c5　　　　...

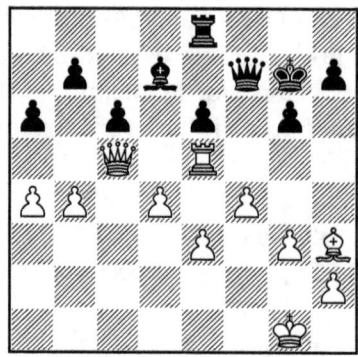

White pieces are invading the catastrophically weak dark squares. The agony is short.

35...	♛f7-f8
36.e3-e4	♛f8xc5
37.b4xc5	♚g7-f6
38.d4-d5	c6xd5
39.e4xd5	♝d7xa4
40.♖e5xe6+?	...

40.♝xe6 would win easily.

40...	♖e8xe6
41.♝h3xe6	

Black's position seems hopeless. A win was adjudicated to white.

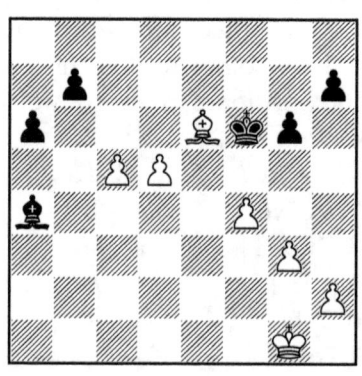

Belavenets stops his annotations here. So was the adjudication correct? Let's see:

41...♝b3 42.♔f2 a5 43.♔e3 a4 44.♔d3 a3 45.♔c3 a2 46.♔b2. The king is tied to the passed a-pawn, and now black has a choice: either try to create some kingside activity or just wait.

1) 46...h5 47.♝g8 ♝c4 (47...♚g7 48.c6 bxc6 49.d6) 48.h3 h4 49.g4 ♝f1 50.g5+ ♚g7

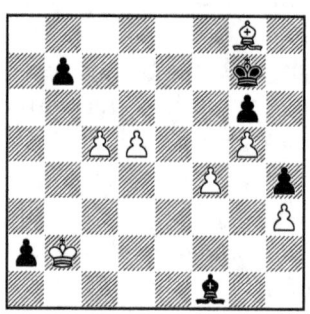

51.d6! ♝xh3 52.♝xa2 ♚f8 53.♝d5 ♝c8 54.♚c3 – black's position is hopeless;

2) 46...♚e7 47.♝g8 ♚f8 48.♝xh7 ♚g7 49.f5 gxf5 (49...♚xh7 50.c6) 50.♝xf5 ♝xd5 51.g4 ♚h6 52.h4 ♝c4 53.♝c8 ♝d5 54.♝d7 ♝f7 (54...♝c4 55.♝e8 ♝d5 56.g5+ ♚g7 57.h5) 55.♚a1 ♚g6 56.♝f5+ ♚h6 57.♝e4 ♝e6 58.♝f3, and white wins.

3) However, black had a hidden defence!: 46...♚g7!! 47.g4 (47.h4 h6 is simplest, moving the bishop to b3 and back) 47...h6 (47...h5 48.g5 h4! works as well) 48.h3 ♝c4 49.h4 ♝b3! and black holds.

No. 4. Sergei Belavenets – Gavriil Veresov
9th Soviet Championship
Leningrad 1934
Slav Defense D19

1.d2-d4	d7-d5
2.c2-c4	c7-c6
3.♘g1-f3	♘g8-f6
4.♘b1-c3	d5xc4
5.a2-a4	♗c8-f5
6.e2-e3	e7-e6
7.♗f1xc4	♗f8-b4
8.0-0	0-0
9.♕d1-e2	c6-c5
10.♖f1-d1	♘b8-c6

Black is playing a system recommended by Kmoch. Now, white gains nothing with 11.dxc5 ♕e7 or 11.d5 exd5 12.♘xd5 ♘xd5 13.♖xd5 ♕f6 with equality (I. Rabinovich – Kmoch, Leningrad 1934)

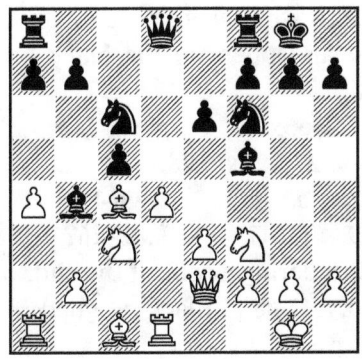

11.♘c3-a2! ...

Intending to gain at least the bishop pair. Black should have probably accepted that, playing 11...♕b6 or 11...♕a5, because after the game move, he immediately gets into trouble.

"One of the lines that Belavenets and I prepared together. We spent a lot of time working on this position, but Sergei was the first one to test this novelty in practice." (M. Yudovich)

11...	♗b4-a5?
12.d4xc5	♕d8-e7
13.♘f3-d4!	♕e7xc5

There's nothing else: otherwise, white plays 14.♘xc6 and b2-b4, holding onto the pawn.

"Flohr played 13...♖fd8 against Ragozin at the 1936 Moscow tournament (it turned out that it was Euwe's move, prepared for his match with Alekhine), but after 14.b4! ♗c7 *(14...♘xb4 15.♗d2! ♕xc5 16.♘b3)* 15.h3 ♘e5 16.♗b2 a5 17.♖ac1! he lost as well. Ragozin was well-prepared, because before that championship he had worked on the lines after ♘a2 together with Belavenets and Yudovich..." (S. Voronkov)

However, Black could try 13...♖ab8!, which would not equalize but would be playable.

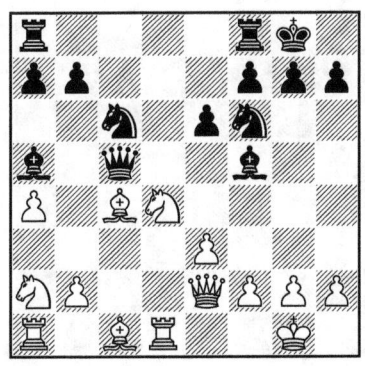

14.b2-b4! ...

This combination, based on pinning the black pieces, wins by force.

14... ♘c6xb4

The only move; black can't play 14...♗xb4 due to 15.♘xc6 bxc6 16.♘xb4 and ♗a3, winning an exchange.

15.♗c1-a3! ...

15.♘b3 ♕e5! 16.♗b2 ♕c7 17.♘xa5 ♘xa2! doesn't work.

Here, after 18.♘xb7! ♕xb7 19.♖xa2, white is actually better. 15...♕b6 is more precise; after 16.♘xa5 ♘xa2 white doesn't have time to capture the b7 pawn because of the threat ♘c3, and the game is equal. 15...♕c7! 16.♘xa5 ♘g4 would give black an equal position.

15... ♖f8-c8
16.♖d1-c1 ♕c5-b6
17.♘d4xf5! e6xf5
18.♖a1-b1 ♘b4xa2

Hoping to get two rooks for the queen after 19.♖xb6 ♘xc1. However, white has another continuation that gives him a decisive material advantage.

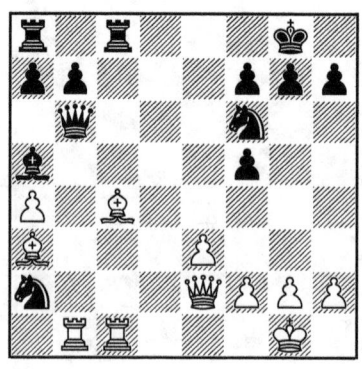

19.♗c4xf7+! ...

The simple 19.♕xa2 ♕d8 20.♖xb7 or 19...♕c7 20.♗e6 was good as well.

19... ♔g8xf7

19...♔h8? 20.♖xc8+ ♖xc8 21.♖xb6.

20.♕e2xa2+ ♔f7-g6

20...♕e6 is bad due to 21.♖xb7+ ♘d7 22.♖xd7+ ♔f6 23.♗b2+ ♗c3 24.♖xc3 ♕xa2 25.♖c6+ ♔g5 26.♖xg7+ ♔h5 27.♖xh7+, with a mate in two.

21.♖b1xb6 ♗a5xb6

"After the great combination started on move 11, white won the queen for rook and knight." (G. Levenfish)

22.h2-h3 ♖c8xc1+
23.♗a3xc1 ♖a8-d8
24.♕a2-b3 ♖d8-d7
25.♗c1-b2 ♖d7-d6
26.♗b2-e5 ♖d6-d2

Accelerates the loss, but the game is already hopeless. For instance, after 26...♖c6 white would eventually play g2-g4 and open up the black king's position.

27.♗e5xf6 g7xf6

Not 27...♔xf6 28.♕c3+.

28.♕b3-g8+ ♔g6-h6
29.♕g8-f7 ♖d2-d6?

Blundering a rook at the end.

30.♕f7-f8+! Black resigned.

No. 5. Sergei Belavenets – Alexander Kotov
Moscow Championship, 1935
Nimzo-Indian Defense E23

1.d2-d4 ♘g8-f6
2.c2-c4 e7-e6

3.♘b1-c3	♗f8-b4
4.♕d1-b3	c7-c5
5.d4xc5	♘b8-c6
6.♘g1-f3	♘f6-e4
7.♗c1-d2	♘e4xc5
8.♕b3-c2	0-0
9.a2-a3	♗b4xc3
10.♗d2xc3	f7-f5
11.b2-b4	♘c5-e4
12.♗c3-b2	b7-b6
13.g2-g4	...

A sharp move first tried by Botvinnik in his game against Myasoedov (Leningrad championship, 1933).

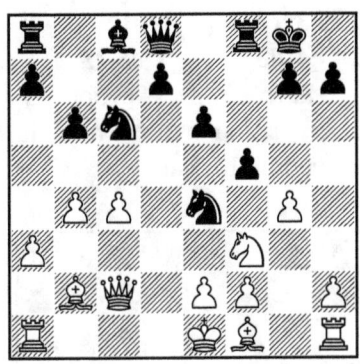

13...	♘e4xf2

Otherwise, white opens up the g-file and gets an obvious advantage

14.♔e1xf2	f5xg4
15.♖h1-g1	♕d8-h4+
16.♔f2-e3	♕h4-h6+
17.♔e3-d3	...

17.♔f2 is risky, because, in addition to the simple 17...♕h4+ with repetition, black can play 17...♕xh2+ 18.♖g2 ♕f4, with three pawns for the piece and the white king placed awkwardly.

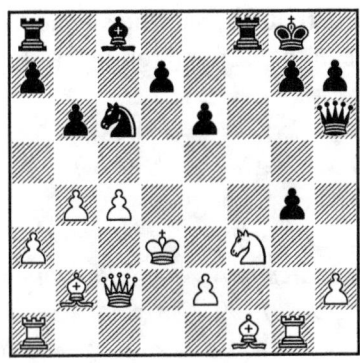

This position occurred in the game Botvinnik – Myasoedov as well. Black played 17...d5 and managed to draw the game after a complicated struggle with a number of sacrifices. A simpler continuation is also interesting: 17...♕g6+ 18.♔d2 ♕xc2+ 19.♔xc2 gxf3 20.♖xg7+ ♔h8 21.♖xd7+ e5 22.♖d6, and white only has a slightly better endgame.

There's a stronger move: 21.♖f7+ ♔g8 22.♖xf8+ ♔xf8 23.exf3, with an obvious advantage.

Thus, black has to put up quite a fight for the draw after 13.g4. We can conclude that this move seemingly refutes this entire line in the Nimzo-Indian Defense. The main drawback of 13.g4 is that this move is too forced and can be easily analyzed, which means that it won't exist for much longer.

17...	g4xf3

Black played this sacrifice because he unquestionably relied on the authority of master Riumin, who used this move in one of his living piece games against Botvinnik. Black drew that game from a position of strength.

Despite that, the sacrifice is incorrect and can be refuted quite easily by white.

18.♖g1xg7+ ♕h6xg7
19.♗b2xg7 ♔g8xg7
20.♕c2-b2+ ...

20.exf3? ♖xf3+ 21.♔e4 d5+! loses, Stepanov – Romanovsky, Leningrad 1929. 22.cxd5 (22.♔xf3 ♘d4+) 22...exd5+ 23.♔xd5 ♗e6+! 24.♔d6 ♖d8+ 25.♔c7 ♖f7+ 26.♔xc6 ♖c8+.

20... ♔g7-g8

Unfortunately, black can't play 20...e5, because after 21.b5 ♘d4 22.e3, white wins a pawn.

21.e2xf3! ...

Necessary to prevent f3-f2 with a dangerous passed pawn for black.

21... ♖f8xf3+
22.♔d3-e2 ♖f3-f7

After 22...♖b3, white quickly wins with 23.♕f6.

23.♗f1-g2 ♖f7-g7
24.♖a1-g1 ...

Threatening both ♕xg7+ with the subsequent ♗xc6 and the immediate ♗xc6.

24... ♖a8-b8

There is no defense anyway. After 24...d5, there's simply 25.♗xd5 ♖xg1 26.♗xc6 ♖b8 27.♕e5, winning. And if 24...♖g6, then after 25.♗xc6 dxc6 26.♖xg6+ hxg6 27.♕f6, the endgame is hopeless for white.

25.♗g2xc6

Black resigned. After 25...♖xg1, white wins a rook with 26.♕e5.

A curious game that has a certain theoretical interest.

No. 6. Evgeny Zagoriansky – Sergei Belavenets
VTsSPS Championship
Moscow 1936
Grunfeld Defense D81

1.d2-d4	**♘g8-f6**
2.c2-c4	**g7-g6**
3.♘b1-c3	**d7-d5**
4.♕d1-b3	**c7-c6**
5.♗c1-g5	**...**

This line was fashionable for a while. It's probably more precise for white to first play 5.cxd5 cxd5 and only then 6.♗g5.

5...	**d5xc4**
6.♕b3xc4	**b7-b5**
7.♕c4-d3	**♗c8-f5**

A sharp move proposed by Yudovich; as far as we know, it was first played in this game.

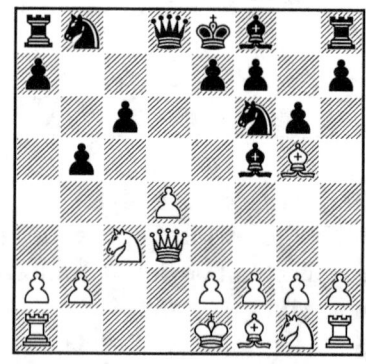

8.♕d3-d1? ...

Now black gets an active position. 8.e4 ♘xe4 9.♘xe4 ♕d5 with mutual tactical possibilities was more interesting and principled.

8...	**b5-b4**
9.♘c3-a4	**♘f6-e4**

10.♘g1-f3	♗f8-g7
11.♗g5-d2	♕d8-a5
12.e2-e3	c6-c5
13.a2-a3?	...

13.b3 was better here: white would have enough defensive resources to manage the weakness of the a1-h8 diagonal. The game move was refuted by black's energetic play. 13.♖c1 or 13.♘xc5 should be played with a small disadvantage for white.

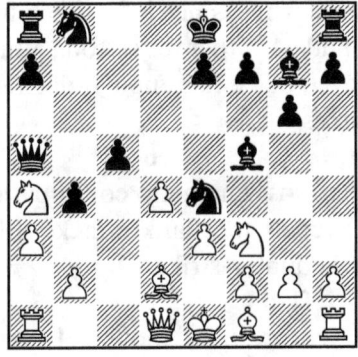

13...	♘e4xd2
14.♘f3xd2	c5xd4
15.♕d1-f3	d4xe3
16.♘d2-c4	...

Of course, 16.♕xa8 exd2+ 17.♔xd2, for instance, is bad because of 17...0-0 with an unstoppable attack.

16...	e3xf2+
17.♔e1xf2	♗g7-d4+
18.♔f2-e1	♕a5xa4
19.♕f3xa8	0-0

In this position, despite being an exchange up, white is doomed: his position is a shambles, the king is stuck in the center, and the black bishops are on the rampage...

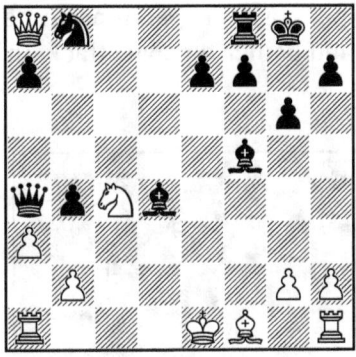

20.♕a8-f3	b4xa3
21.♖a1xa3	♕a4-b4+
22.♔e1-d1	♖f8-d8
23.♘c4-d2	♗d4xb2

White resigned.

No. 7. Sergei Belavenets – Alexander Chistiakov
Qualification match
Moscow 1937
Queen's Gambit D61

1.d2-d4	♘g8-f6
2.c2-c4	e7-e6
3.♘b1-c3	d7-d5
4.♗c1-g5	♘b8-d7
5.e2-e3	c7-c6
6.♕d1-c2	♗f8-e7

As we know from the Alekhine – Capablanca match, the Cambridge Springs Defense is not particularly advantageous for black, because after 6...♕a5 7.cxd5 ♘xd5 there's 8.e4 ♘xc3 9.♗d2!, and white is somewhat better.

7.♘g1-f3	0-0
8.h2-h4	...

A double-edged move proposed by Rubinstein. White strengthens the g5 bishop's position, planning to castle long and launch a pawn attack on the kingside.

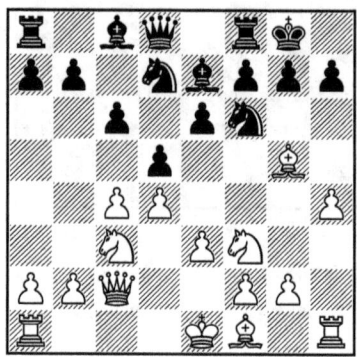

8... a7-a6

A useful move, preparing counterplay with b5 if given the opportunity.

9.0-0-0 h7-h6

This weakening of the king's defenses wasn't necessary. The calm defensive plan with ♖e8, ♘f8 and (after necessary preparation) f6, with subsequent counterplay along the e-file, looks more solid.

10.♗g5xf6 ...

This straightforward attempt to exploit black's move h6 ultimately gives white nothing. 10.♗f4 with the subsequent ♘e5 or even 10.♗d3 looked better.

10...	♘d7xf6
11.e3-e4	d5xe4
12.♘c3xe4	♕d8-c7
13.♘e4xf6+	♗e7xf6
14.♕c2-e4	...

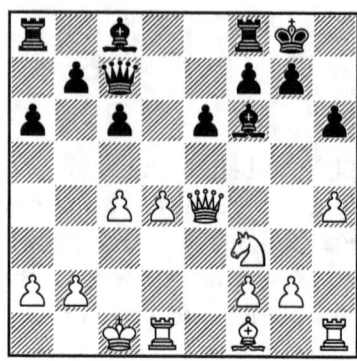

At first glance, this position seems better for white, since he's threatening ♗d3 and g4 with a very strong attack. However, black has enough defensive resources.

14... c6-c5

The most energetic continuation. Black repels the flank attack with a central counter-strike.

15.♗f1-d3 ...

A venturesome move. However, it's not clear how white can play for the advantage. For instance, after 15.g4 ♗xd4 16.g5 f5, or 15.dxc5 ♕xc5 16.g4 ♗e7, threatening f5, black has sufficient counterplay in both cases.

15...	♖f8-d8
16.g2-g4	♗f6xd4
17.g4-g5	...

White is forced to attack, because after 17.♘xd4 ♖xd4 18.♕h7+ ♔f8 19.♕h8+ ♔e7 20.♕xg7 ♕f4+, black gets an advantage.

17... h6xg5

17...f5 was dangerous, since after 18.gxf6 ♗xf6 the kingside light squares are too weak.

Still, the computer thinks that this

move was strong and gave black the initiative.

**18.hxg5   g7-g6
19.♘f3xd4   ...**

It's necessary to trade the bishop away, or else white won't have any semblance of an attack after 19...♗g7.

**19...   ♖d8xd4
20.♕e4-e3   e6-e5?**

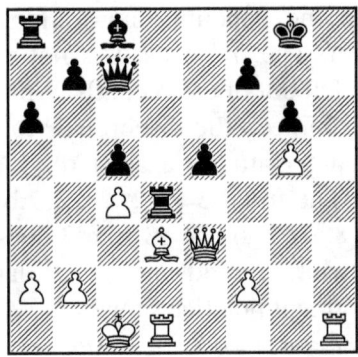

Black has kept the extra pawn, but his king's position looks dangerous. With this move, he prepares to transfer his bishop to h5, defending against various threats along the h-file. If black traded queens with 20...♕f4, then white could at least force a draw with 21.♗e4! ♕xe4 (21...♖xc4+ loses to 22.♗c2!) 22.♕xe4 ♖xe4 23.♖d8+ ♔g7 24.♖hh8 (unfortunately, 24.♖dh8 doesn't work on account of 24...♖e1+) 24...f5!, and white has to give perpetual check. Black could develop the queenside by pushing the b pawn one or two squares, for example 20...b5 21.♕h3 ♕e5! 22.f4 ♕g7! and the position would be equal.

21.♕e3-g3?   ...

White shouldn't have allowed the bishop to get to h5, therefore, it was better to play 21.f3, intending to double the rooks along the h-file. Now black can fully repel the attack.

After 21.f3 ♗e6, the king will hide on e7, with an advantage for black. 21.♖h6! was stronger, for instance: 21...♔f8 (after 21...♗g4 22.♖dh1 ♗h5 23.♕f3! ♖d6 24.♕e4!, black has no good defense against the threats ♕xe5 and ♖1xh5) 22.♖dh1 ♕d6 (or 22...♔e7 23.♗xg6! ♖xc4+ 24.♔b1) 23.♗xg6! ♖xc4+ 24.♔b1, and white's attack is winning.

**21...   ♗e8-g4
22.♕g3-h2   ♗g4-h5
23.♗d3-e2   ♖d4xd1+**

An unnecessary trade. The simplest was 23...♔g7!, and if 24.♗xh5, then 24...♖h8! with a clear winning advantage for black.

24.♗e2xd1   ♕c7-e7

Even now, black still retained some advantage after 24...♔g7 25.♗xh5 ♖h8 26.♖e1 gxh5!, and he has a better endgame.

25.♕h2-h4   ♕e7-f8?

And now white finally gets a decisive attack. Of course, it was necessary to play 25...♔g7 26.♗xh5 ♖h8 27.♕g4 ♖xh5 28.♖xh5 gxh5 29.♕xh5, and the queen endgame should end in a draw, even though it's slightly better for black.

**26.♗d1xh5   g6xh5
27.♕h4xh5   ♕f8-g7**

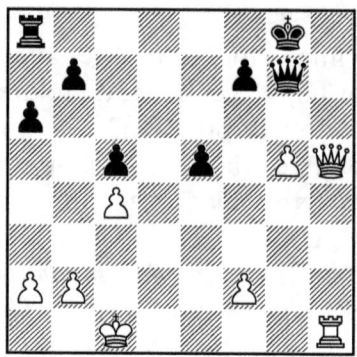

28.♖h1-d1 ...

The invasion of the d-file is good, but it was not the best move. 28.f4 exf4 29.g6! fxg6 30.♕d5 would win quickly.

28... b7-b5

A futile attempt to create counterplay, which is simply ignored by white. After 28...♕f8 (protecting the d6 square), white could play 29.g6.

29.♖d1-d6 b5xc4
30.g5-g6 f7-f6
31.♕h5-f5 ♖a8-e8

White threatened ♖d7 and ♕e6+.

32.♖d6xf6 e5-e4

There's still no defense. The pawn endgame after 32...♖f8 is lost.

It's not even necessary to go for the pawn endgame; there's a quicker win after 32...♖f8 33.♕e6+ ♔h8 34.♕h3+ ♔g8 35.♕h7+!

33.♕f5-d5+ ♔g8-h8
34.♕d5-h5+ ♔h8-g8
35.♕h5-d5+ ♔g8-h8
36.♖f6-f5 ♕g7xg6
37.♖f5-h5+ ♔h8-g7
38.♖h5-g5. Black resigned.

No. 8. Vsevolod Rauzer – Sergei Belavenets
Moscow – Leningrad match, 1937
French Defense C12

1.e2-e4	e7-e6
2.d2-d4	d7-d5
3.♘b1-c3	♘g8-f6
4.♗c1-g5	♗f8-b4
5.e4-e5	h7-h6
6.♗g5-c1!?	...

Another opening innovation by Rauzer. The move itself is not new, but it fell out of use recently. White is trying to keep the bishop pair to use it for later attacks against the black king. The usual 6.♗d2 ♗xc3 7.bxc3 ♘e4 8.♕g4 g6 9.♗d3 ♘xd2 doesn't give white an advantage, as latest tournament practice shows.

The move 6.♗c1 never became popular, and now white usually tries to play for an advantage with 6.♗e3 or 6.♗d2.

6... ♘f6-e4

Probably the best move, since 6...♘fd7 7.♕g4 is not pleasant.

7.♕d1-g4 ♔e8-f8

Black didn't want to weaken his kingside with 7...g6, considering that white still has his c1 bishop.

Nevertheless, 7...g6 is played more often than 7...♔f8 in modern times.

8.♘g1-e2 c7-c5
9.a2-a3 ♗b4-a5

9...♗xc3+ 10.bxc3 is obviously bad: white has the two bishops and a solid center, and the knight's position on e4 is very precarious.

Still, this position remains unclear.

9...♕a5 looks interesting, but white can play 10.axb4 ♕xa1 11.♘xe4 dxe4 12.bxc5 and then win the e4 pawn as well, getting two pawns for the exchange.

9...cxd4 10.axb4 dxc3 11.♘xc3 (11.f3?! ♘d2) is not particularly good either.

10.b2-b4 ...

There's no other promising continuation for white, since black threatens 10...cxd4.

Later, white would successfully deploy 10.dxc5 as well. The fresh idea 10.♗e3!? is interesting, too.

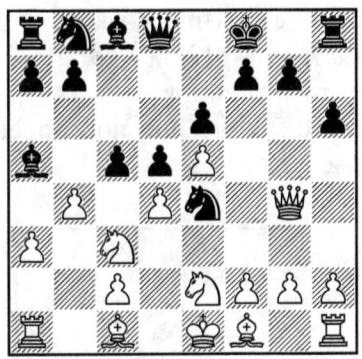

10... f7-f5?

An over-eager and poor move, seriously weakening black's kingside. Black is trying to strengthen the e4 knight's position, which ultimately didn't do him any good. It was better to play 10...♘xc3 11.♘xc3 cxd4! (worse was 11...cxb4 12.♘e2 bxa3+ 13.c3, and white has a solid center and good kingside attacking chances for the pawn; *12...b3+ was worth considering*) 12.♘b5 ♗b6 with a complicated and unclear position.

11.♕g4-h3 ...

Now 11...♘xc3 gives black nothing because of 12.♕xc3, so black accepts the pawn sacrifice, even though the situation is now less beneficial than on the previous move.

11... c5xb4?

Black should play 11...♗c7, accepting a worse position.

12.♘c3xe4 d5xe4
13.a3xb4 ♗a5xb4+
14.c2-c3 ♗b4-e7

14...♗a5 was probably better, tying the opponent down with defense of the c3 and d4 squares.

15.♘e2-f4 ...

The weakness of the e6 and g6 squares gives white an overwhelming advantage.

15... ♕d8-e8
16.♗f1-c4 ♕e8-f7
17.d4-d5 ...

White destroys black's position with simple moves.

17... g7-g5

The only chance. 17...exd5 18.♗xd5 ♕e8 19.♘e6+ ♗xe6 20.♗xe6 is hopeless for black.

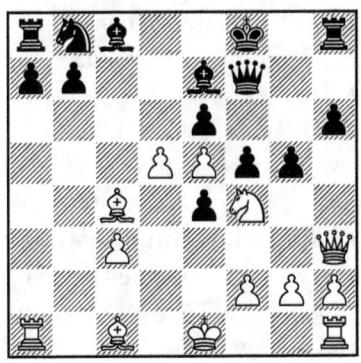

18.♘f4xe6+ ...

Or 18.dxe6 ♕h7 19.♘d5 ♗xe6 20.♘xe7 ♗xc4 21.♗a3 and white wins.

**18... ♗c8xe6
19.d5xe6 ♕f7-g6
20.♖a1-b1 ...**

A sluggish move that allows black to extricate himself and get counterplay. After 20.0-0 ♘c6 21.f4, white would have most probably won. In fact, 20.f4 looks like white's strongest move.

**20... ♘b8-c6
21.♖b1xb7 ♘c6xe5**

After 21...♘a5, white could play 22.♖xe7.

22.♕h3-e3! ...

The best. In case of 22.♗d5 f4 with the threat g5-g4, white's position is not particularly pleasant.

22... ♕g6-f6

It was bad to play 22...♘xc4 23.♕d4!

23.♗c4-a2? ...

As it turned out later, 23.♗b3 was better, with complicated play and equal chances for black. Now it's black who gets an advantage.

23.♗e2 ♕xe6 24.0-0 with complicated play was better.

**23... ♘e5-d3+
24.♔e1-e2 ...**

24.♔f1 ♕xc3 25.♗b2 ♕c2 26.♕e2 was more resilient.

24... ♘d3-f4+

Black gained nothing with 24...f4 25.♕d4! (not 25.♕xe4 ♘c5) 25...f3+ 26.gxf3 ♕xf3+ 27.♔d2, and his position is now bad.

White could meet 24...♕xc3 with 25.♖d1, getting the rook into play, so black prefers to capture the e6 pawn and make it harder for white to develop the h1 rook.

24...♖d8 looks very strong.

25.♔e2-f1 ♖a8-d8

Had white played 23.♗b3, black wouldn't have this important tempo.

26.♗a2-b3 ...

Not 26.♖d7 ♖xd7 27.exd7 ♕a6+, winning the a2 bishop.

**26... ♘f4xe6
27.g2-g3 ...**

White's position is difficult. Black threatens f4, which is quite unpleasant. If 27.♕xa7, then 27...♕xc3. The best move was probably 27.♖xa7 ♖d3 (27...♗c5 28.♗a3) 28.♕e1, protecting the c3 pawn, with a difficult, but not hopeless defense.

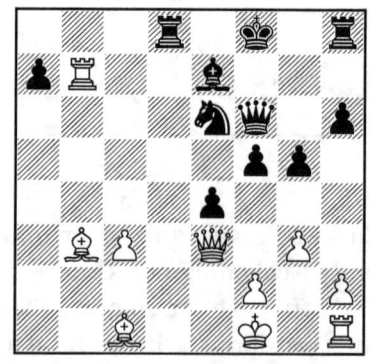

27... f5-f4!

Winning the exchange after 27...♘c5 28.♖xe7 ♕xe7 29.♗a3 ♖c8 30.♕d4 would be quite dubious for black. Now, on the other hand, the choice is difficult for white, because any queen retreat is met with ♘c5.

28.g3xf4	g5xf4
29.♕e3xe4	♘e6-c5
30.♖b7xe7	...

White sacrifices his queen, trying to exploit the compromised position of his opponent's king and queen. Sacrificing the exchange with 30.♕xe7+ ♕xe7 31.♖xe7 ♔xe7 was equally hopeless.

30.♕c4 ♘xb7 31.♖g1 ♗d6 32.♖g8+ ♖xg8 33.♕xg8+ ♔e7 34.♕h7+ ♔e8 35.♕xb7 ♕f5 didn't save white either.

30...	♘c5xe4
31.♖e7xe4	♕f6-a6+

In time trouble, black didn't have enough time to calculate all the bishop checks, so he chose the simplest continuation and gave back the queen. Another possibility was 31...♕xc3 32.♖xf4+ ♔e7 33.♗a3+ ♔d7, or 32.♗a3+ ♔g7 33.♖g1+ ♔f6 34.♗e7+ ♔f5 etc.

32.♗b3-c4	♖d8-d1+
33.♔f1-e2	♖d1xh1
34.♗c4xa6	♖h1xc1
35.♖e4xf4+	♔f8-g7

Black should gradually win the endgame.

36.♖f4-c4	♖c1-c2+
37.♔e2-d3	♖c2xf2
38.♖c4-c7+	♖f2-f7
39.♖c7-c4	♖h8-d8+
40.♖c4-d4	♖d8xd4+
41.♔d3xd4	♔g7-f6
42.♔d4-d5	♖f7-c7
43.c3-c4	♔f6-e7
44.c4-c5	♔e7-d8
45.♔d5-d6	♖c7-g7

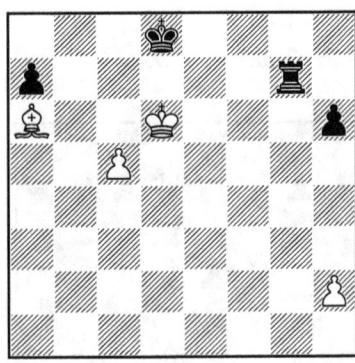

The game was stopped here and adjudicated as won for black. The rest is simple. For instance: 46.♗c4 ♖g6+ 47.♗e6 a5 48.c6 ♖xe6+ 49.♔xe6 a4! and wins.

A difficult and interesting game that convincingly proves that good opening play alone is not enough for a win.

No. 9. Sergei Belavenets – Vsevolod Rauzer
Moscow – Leningrad match, 1937
Queens' Gambit D62

1.d2-d4	d7-d5
2.c2-c4	e7-e6
3.♘b1-c3	♘g8-f6
4.♗c1-g5	♗f8-e7
5.e2-e3	0-0
6.♘g1-f3	♘b8-d7
7.♕d1-c2	c7-c5
8.c4xd5	♘f6xd5
9.♗g5xe7	♕d8xe7
10.♘c3xd5	e6xd5
11.♗f1-d3	g7-g6
12.d4xc5	♘d7xc5
13.0-0	♗c8-e6
14.♖a1-c1	♖a8-c8

15.♘f3-d4	♘c5xd3
16.♕c2xd3	...

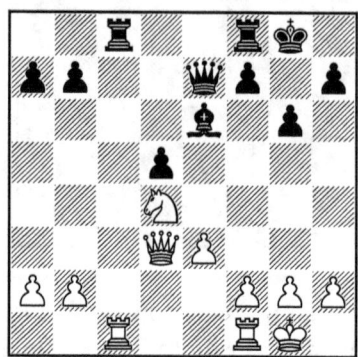

16...	♖c8xc1

16...♕d7 17.♖cd1 ♖fd8 18.f4 ♗f5 19.♘xf5 ♕xf5 20.♕xf5 gxf5 21.♖d2 with somewhat better chances for white, Flohr – Stahlberg, Prague 1931.

17.♖f1xc1	♖f8-c8
18.♖c1xc8+	♗e6xc8
19.♕d3-b5	♗c8-e6
20.♕b5-a5	b7-b6
21.♕a5-b5	♕e7-d7
22.a2-a3	♕d7xb5
23.♘d4xb5	♗e6-d7
24.♘b5-c3	...

24.♘xa7 is no good for white, since the knight won't have any moves, and freeing it with b3 and a4 will waste too much time, giving black an opportunity to get closer with his king.

24...	♗d7-c6
25.♔g1-f1	♔g8-f8

25...♔g7 was more precise, getting to e5 one move earlier.

26.f2-f3	...

But not 26.♔e2 in view of 26...d4!

26...	♔f8-e7
27.♔f1-e2	♔e7-e6
28.♔e2-d3	♔e6-e5
29.f3-f4+	♔e5-e6
30.♔d3-d4	♔e6-d6

Black could have played 30...a5, and if 31.b4 axb4 32.axb4 followed by white playing b5, then the b5-pawn would be vulnerable.

31.b2-b4	♔d6-e6

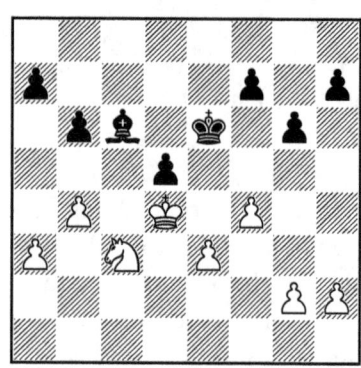

This is an often-occurring type of position: knight versus bishop with an isolated d5 pawn. Without a doubt, white is better, but he can only win if he creates new weaknesses in black's position, in addition to the d5 pawn.

32.b4-b5	...

This is necessary. Before starting knight maneuvers, white should prevent the black bishop's invasion. If black manages to force g2-g3 after transferring his bishop to f1, he will have some counterchances – his king will move to h3.

32...	♗c6-b7
33.♘c3-a2	♔e6-d6
34.♘a2-b4	♔d6-e6?

Black moves passively, allowing white to improve his position. As it turns out later, he had to play f7-f6 or h7-h6.

35.g2-g4   ...

The immediate 35.♘c6 ♗xc6 36.bxc6 ♔d6 37.c7 ♔xc7 38.♘xd5 led to nothing because of 38...f5!, and white can't win. Now, however, he threatens ♘c6, and black can't play 35...f6 or 35...h6, because the pawn endgame after, for instance, 35...h6 36.♘c6 ♗xc6 37.bxc6 ♔d6 38.c7 ♔xc7 39.♔xd5 is lost due to the white king's strong position. The game might continue: 39...♔d7 40.e4 ♔c7 41.e5 ♔d7 42.f5 gxf5 43.gxf5 ♔c7 44.e6 f6 45.h3 h5 46.h4 a6 47.a4 a5 48.♔c4 ♔c6 49.e7 ♔d7 50.♔b5, and wins.

In this line, black draws with 43... h5!, for instance: 44.h4 ♔c7 45.e6 f6 46.a4 a6 47.e7 ♔d7 48.e8=♕+ ♔xe8 49.♔c6 b5 50.axb5 axb5 51.♔xb5 ♔d7 52.♔c5 ♔c7, or 46.e7 ♔d7 47.e8=♕+ ♔xe8 48.♔c6 ♔e7 49.♔b7 ♔d6 50.♔xa7 ♔c6.

But white's play can be improved as well: 41.♔e5! (instead of 41.e5) 41...g5 42.f5 ♔d7 43.♔f6 ♔e8 44.e5, or 41... ♔d7 42.♔f6 ♔e8 43.e5 b5 44.e6 fxe6 45.♔xe6, and wins.

35...   **f7-f5**

Since f6 or h6 are impossible, this move is relatively better, as 35... ♔d6 is met with 36.g5, and the black queenside pawns are totally paralyzed. In this case, white has an opportunity to transfer the knight to f6 and win the h7 pawn.

36.g4-g5   ...

This restricts the black bishop's movement even more. White's plan is to push the h-pawn to h6 and threaten to sacrifice the knight on f5 or g6, making black's defense even more difficult. And if black trades on h5, white can attack black's second weakness, the h7 pawn, with the knight from f6.

36...   **♔e6-d6**

37.h2-h3!   ...

The more natural 37.h4 was weaker because of 37...♔e6 38.♘a2 ♔d6 39.♘c3 ♔e6 40.♘e2 ♗c8 41.♘g3 ♗d7 42.a4 ♗e8, and black manages to stop h4-h5.

37...	**♔d6-e6**
38.♘b4-a2	**♔e6-d6**
39.♘a2-c3	**♔d6-e6**
40.h3-h4	**♔e6-d6**
41.♘c3-e2	...

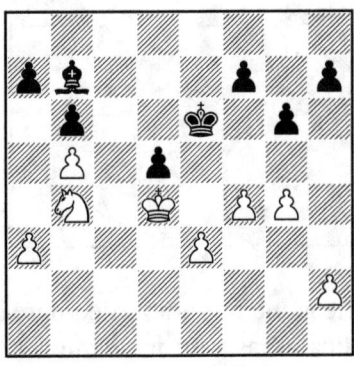
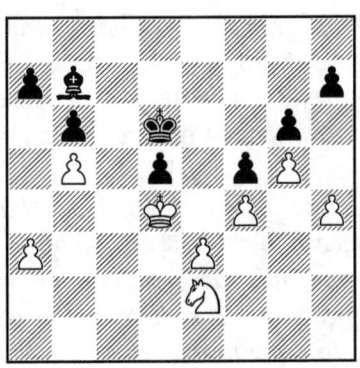

41... ♗b7-c8?

The last chance to save the game was 41...a6 (but not 41...a5, because the white knight will threaten the b6 pawn from a4), but still, after 42.♘c3 axb5 43.♘xb5+ ♔c6! (if 43...♔e6, then 44.♘c7+ ♔d6 45.♘e8+ ♔e6 46.h5! ♗c6 47.♘f6! gxh5 48.♘xh5 ♗d7 49.♘f6 wins) 44.♘c3 ♔d6 45.♘a4 ♔c6 46.♔e5 ♔b5 47.♘b2 ♔c5 48.♔f6 d4 49.exd4+ ♔xd4 50.♔g7 ♔e4 51.♔xh7 ♔xf4 52.♔xg6 ♔g4 53.h5 f4 54.♔h6, white wins. However, if he plays 42.a4 instead of 42.♘c3, then 42...a5! Now it's possible, because the a4 square is occupied by the pawn, and white, losing all the chances on the queenside, cannot win.

Instead of 50...♔e4, black has the much more resilient 50...♗f3 51.♔xh7 ♗h5, but it seems that even here white has a way to win: 52.♘a4 ♔e4 (or 52...b5 53.♘b6 ♔e4 54.♘d7 ♔xf4 55.♘f6 ♗d1 56.♔xg6) 53.♘xb6 ♔xf4 54.a4 ♔e5 (54...♔g3 55.a5 f4 (55...♔xh4 56.♔h6 ♗e2 57.♘d7 f4 58.♘e5) 56.a6 f3 57.♘c4 f2 58.♘d2 ♗f3 59.a7 ♗c6 60.♔xg6) 55.a5 ♗e2 56.♔xg6 f4 57.♘d7+ ♔d4 58.♘f6 f3 59.♘g4 ♔e4 60.♘f2+ ♔e3 61.♘h1, winning.

42.♘e2-g3   ♗c8-d7

Now 42...a6 is too late because of 43.bxa6 ♗xa6 44.h5 ♔e6 45.h6 with the deadly threat ♘h5.

Instead of 44...♔e6, black has a stronger reply 44...♗c8! 45.h6 ♗e6, and the h5 sacrifice doesn't work now because the bishop gets to g8 in time. In reply to 42...a6, white should

play 43.♘e2! with the idea 43...axb5 44.♘c3 ♗e6 45.♘xb5+ ♔c6 46.a4, and then the white king invades through dark squares.

43.a3-a4   ♔d6-e6

After 43...♗e8, white still plays 44.h5 gxh5 45.♘xf5+, and there's no 45...♔e6 due to 46.♘g7+, trading the knight for the bishop and then winning the d5 pawn.

44.h4-h5   ♗d7-e8

Black still loses after 44...gxh5 45.♘xh5 ♗c8 (the only move, otherwise ♘f6) 46.♔c3! (black is in zugzwang) 46...♔f7 47.♔d3 (stronger than the immediate 47.♘f6 h6 48.♘xd5 h5 with some counterchances for black) 47...♔e7 (if 47...♔e6, then 48.♔d4, and black has no moves, because 48...♗b7 is met with 49.♘g7+; the same happens after 47...♔g6 48.♘g3 ♔f7 49.♔d4 ♔e6 50.♘h5) 48.♘f6, and black loses the pawn.

45.h5-h6   ♔e6-d6
46.♘g3-e2   ...

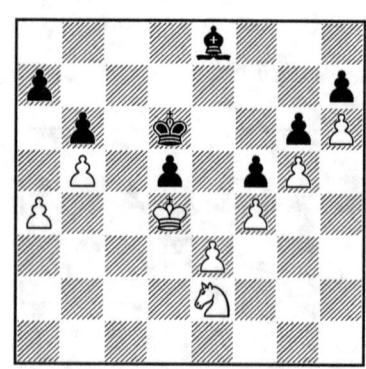

The game was adjourned here and adjudicated as won for white. White managed to fully implement his plan, and black, who has three weak pawns — a7, d5 and h7, is defenseless. For instance:

46... ♗e8-d7

Black's attempt to get the knight stuck on a7 wouldn't have worked: 46...♗f7 47.♘c3 ♗e6 48.♘a2 ♗g8 49.♘b4 ♗f7 50.♘c6 ♗e8 51.♘xa7 ♗d7 52.♔d3 (black is in zugzwang) 52...♔c7 53.♔c3 ♔b7 (if 53...♔d6, then 54.♔d4, and black is forced to free the knight) 54.♔d4! ♔xa7 55.♔e5, and white wins.

47.♘e2-c3 ♗d7-e6
48.♘c3-a2 ♗e6-f7

Black can't protect the d5 pawn with the bishop from b7, because after, say, 48...♗c8 49.♘b4 ♗b7, white wins with 50.♘d3 ♗c8 51.♘e5, and there's no defense to 52.♘xg6.

49.♘a2-b4 ♗f7-e6
50.♘b4-c6 a7-a5
51.b5xa6! ...

Now it's clear that if black had managed to play a5 earlier, white wouldn't have this move.

51... ♔d6xc6

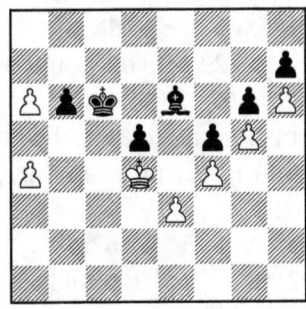

52.a6-a7! ...

Necessary, because if 52.♔e5, then 52...♗c8! 53.a7 ♗b7 54.♔f6 ♔d6 55.♔g7 ♔e7 56.♔xh7 ♔f7, and white can't win.

52...♔c6-b7 53.♔d4-e5 ♗e6-d7 54.♔e5-f6 ♗d7xa4 55.♔f6-g7 b6-b5 56.♔g7xh7 b5-b4 57.♔h7xg6 b4-b3 58.h6-h7 ♗a4-e8+ 59.♔g6-f6 b3-b2 60.h7-h8=♕ b2-b1=♕ 61.a7-a8=♕+ ♔b7xa8 62.♕h8xe8+, and the queen endgame is easily won for white.

This whole endgame is a good example of a knight's battle against a bishop.

No. 10. Vitaly Chekhover – Sergei Belavenets
10th Soviet Championship
Tbilisi 1937
Grunfeld Defense D95

1.d2-d4	d7-d5
2.c2-c4	c7-c6
3.♘g1-f3	♘g8-f6
4.e2-e3	g7-g6
5.♘b1-c3	♗f8-g7

A typical Grunfeld Defense position has occurred. The purpose of this change in move order is to avoid 4.♕b3! after the usual 1.d4 ♘f6 2.c4 g6 3.♘c3 d5.

6.♕d1-b3	0-0
7.♗c1-d2	e7-e6
8.♗f1-d3	♘b8-d7
9.0-0	b7-b6
10.c4xd5	...

Both 10.♖fd1 ♗b7 11.a4 and even 10.e4 were worthy of consideration.

10... e6xd5

11.e3-e4   c6-c5

Probably the only move. After 11...dxe4 12.♘xe4 c5, white has quite an unpleasant reply in 13.♘xf6+ ♕xf6 14.♗g5 ♕d6 15.♖fe1.

12.♘c3xd5   c5xd4
13.♘d5xf6+   ♗g7xf6

In case of 13...♘xf6, white has a good continuation 14.e5 ♘d5 15.♗c4 ♗b7 16.♗g5 ♕d7 17.♖fd1, attacking the d4 pawn.

14.♗d2-b4   ♘d7-c5

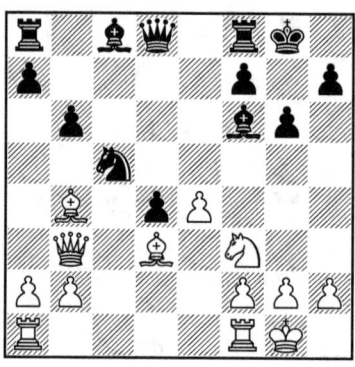

15.♕b3-c2   ...

White could have kept his advantage with the simple 15.♗xc5 bxc5 16.♗c4 and the subsequent transfer of the knight to d3. In this case, black's bishops have no prospects, and the d4 and c5 pawns are blocked and weak.

It's hard to achieve this ideal structure, because after 16...♕c7, black will put his rook on b8, then his bishop on b7, putting pressure on the b2 and e4 pawns... After trading on c5, it's better to play 16.♕c2!? ♗e7 17.♘d2 with the subsequent f2-f4 and ♘c4. In this case, white's chances would have been at least equal.

15...   ♗f6-e7
16.♗b4-d2   ...

An attempt to exploit the weak dark squares on the kingside that doesn't work. 16.♗xc5 ♗xc5 17.♖ad1 still offered white a decent game.

16...   ♕d8-d6

White threatened ♗h6 and ♗b5. 16...♕d7 would have been met with 17.♗h6 ♖d8 18.♗c4 and the threat of ♗xf7+.

17.♗d2-h6   ♖f8-d8
18.e4-e5?!   ...

This gives black some advantage.

18...   ♕d6-d7
19.♗h6-g5?   ...

This leads to a worse endgame for white. However, his position is already difficult, because after ♗b7, all black pieces will be placed very nicely, which, together with the strong d4 passed pawn, gives him a clear advantage. Therefore, the whole bishop maneuver to h6 was wrong and gave black the advantage.

19...   ♗c8-b7
20.♗d3-b5   ♕d7xb5
21.♗g5xe7   ♖d8-d7?

21...♗xf3 22.gxf3 d3 would win.

22.♗e7-f6?   ...

The bishop should take the knight, as it would give white some hope of surviving.

22...   ♗b7xf3
23.g2xf3   ♕b5-d3

White could still create some threats against the black king, so the queen trade is sensible, especially since the endgame is favorable for black.

24.♕c2-d1 ...

The best. 24.♕c1 ♕xf3 25.♕h6 ♘e6 is bad for white.

24... ♖d7-d5

The computer promises a big advantage after 24...♕f5, but a human would be wary of avoiding the queen trade when the g7 square is so weak.

25.f3-f4 ...

Black threatened to trade queens and play ♘d7.

The alternative 25.b4 ♕xd1 26.♖fxd1 ♘d7 27.♖ac1 brought good drawing chances.

25... ♕d3xd1
26.♖f1xd1 ♔g8-f8

In addition to black's plan in the game, he could instead play the calm 26...♘d7 27.♗h4 ♖c8 28.♖d2 ♔g7 with the subsequent f6.

Here, 29.♖ad1 ♖c4 30.b3 ♖b4 31.♗e7 ♘c5 32.♔g2 is rather unpleasant for black – he cannot play f7-f6. The game move is obviously stronger.

Black could instead play 26...♘e6! 27.♖ac1 ♖c5 winning a pawn for nothing.

27.♔g1-g2 ♘c5-e6

To seize the c-file.

28.♔g2-f3 ♖a8-c8
29.♖a1-c1 ...

29.♔e4! ♖dxc5 30.♖d2 would give white some chances to hold.

29... ♖d5-c5
30.♖c1xc5 ♖c8xc5

31.♖d1-d2 ♔f8-e8
32.♔f3-e4 ♔e8-d7?

32...♖c1 would win as if 33.f5 then 33...♖e1+.

33.f4-f5 g6xf5+
34.♔e4xf5 ♔d7-c6

Black intended to get this position when he played 27...♘e6; now he threatens to put his king on d5 and prepare to push the d-pawn.

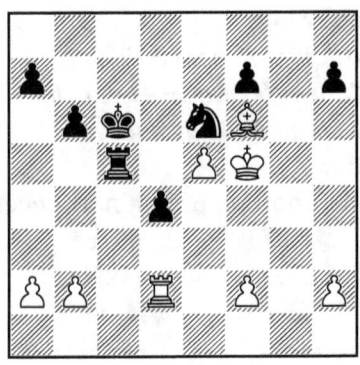

35.♔f5-e4? ...

White goes for calm defense. He could cause some complications instead, which were unclear but still better for black: 35.♗e7 ♖c1 36.♔f6 ♔d5 37.♗xf7 ♖e1 38.♗f6 (38.♗d6 ♘g5+ loses) 38...♘c5, and the d-pawn is more dangerous than the e-pawn. 35.♗h4 ♔d5 36.f3 ♖c8 37.♔f6 with real counterchances for white was best.

35... ♖c5-c1

An important maneuver that deflects the white rook to e2 because of the threat ♖e1+.

36.♖d2-e2 ♖c1-c4?

36...♖d1! would win.

37.♗f6-e7 ...

Black threatened ♘c5+ and ♔d5. 37.f4 ♘xf4 38.♔xf4 d3+ loses immediately.

37... ♘e6-f4!

The only way to improve the position.

38.♖e2-d2 ...

Of course, the knight cannot be captured.

38... d4-d3+
39.♔e4-e3 ♔c6-d5
40.♗e7-g5? ...

40.♗f6 was more resilient, but even here, after 40...♖e4+ 41.♔f3 b5 black has a substantial advantage.

40... ♖c4-e4+!

An important preliminary check.

41.♔e3-f3 ♔d5xe5
42.♗g5xf4+ ♖e4xf4+
43.♔f3-e3 ♖f4-e4+
44.♔e3xd3 ♖e4-d4+
45.♔d3-e3 ♖d4xd2
46.♔e3xd2 ♔e5-f4

The pawn endgame is easily won.

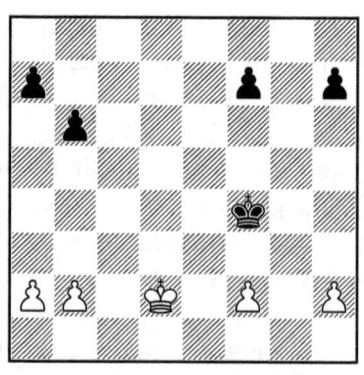

47.♔d2-e2 ♔f4-g4
48.♔e2-f1 ♔g4-f3

White resigned. His position is hopeless. For instance: 49.♔g1 b5 50.♔f1 b4 51.♔g1 ♔e2, and black scoops up the a- and b-pawns.

No. 11. Sergei Belavenets – Georgy Lisitsin
10th Soviet Championship
Tbilisi 1937
Queen's Gambit D00

1.d2-d4 ♘g8-f6
2.♘g1-f3 d7-d5
3.c2-c4 ♗c8-f5

A rare move, rejected by theory.

4.♕d1-b3 ...

The simplest way for white to gain an advantage is 4.cxd5 ♘xd5 5.♕b3 ♘c6 6.♘bd2, threatening e2-e4.

4... ♘b8-c6!
5.♘b1-c3 ...

5.♕xb7 ♗d7 6.♕b3 would give white some advantage.

5... e7-e5

Black goes for complications, avoiding the quiet 5...e6 6.c5 ♖b8 etc.

6.c4xd5! ...

The only move. After 6.dxe5 dxc4 7.♕a4 (otherwise ♘b4-d5) black is better.

6... ♘c6-b4?

Black should have stopped in time and transitioned the game onto positional rails with 6...♘xd4 7.♘xd4 exd4 8.♕a4+ c6, with roughly equal chances.

7.e2-e4! ♘f6xe4
8.♗f1-b5+ c7-c6
9.d5xc6 b7xc6

All of black's moves are forced.

10.♘f3xe5! ...

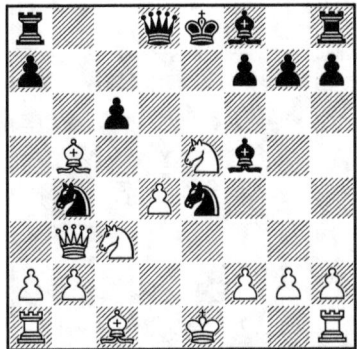

It's hard to believe that such a wild position could occur in the Queen's Gambit after just 10 moves. Black's pawns on f7 and c6 are under attack, and he can't adequately defend both.

10... ♗f5-e6

Admitting his helplessness. However, there's nothing better. If 10...♕xd4, then 11.♗xc6+ ♔d8 12.0-0!, and black inevitably loses something. 10...♕e7 11.♘xc6, or 10...♕c7 11.♘d5 (11.♘xc6 ♘xc6 12.♕d5! is also good) 11...♕a5 12.0-0 ♗e6 13.♘xc6 ♕xb5 14.♘c7+ ♔d7 15.♘xb5 ♗xb3 16.♘e5+ ♔e6 17.axb3; or, finally, 10...♕f6 11.♘d5!

11.♘e5xc6   ♕d8-b6

11...♗xb3 12.♘xb4+! ♔d7 (or 12...♔e7 13.♘c6+, regaining the queen) 13.♗xd7+ ♔xd7 14.♘d3 is no better.

12.♘c6xb4+   ♕b6xb5
13.♕b3xe6+   ...

The simplest — now black has no hope of drawing with opposite-colored bishops.

13...   f7xe6

14.♘c3xb5   ♗f8xb4+
15.♔e1-e2   ♔e8-d7

15...♖c8 is met with 16.f3! and ♔d3 with full consolidation; black gains nothing.

16.f2-f3   ♘e4-f6
17.♘b5-c3   ...

White is two pawns up, and black has no serious counterplay; only the ensuing time trouble complicates things.

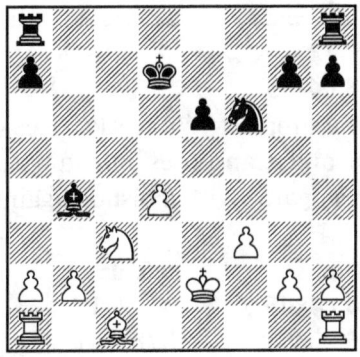

17...	♗b4xc3
18.b2xc3	♖a8-b8
19.♔e2-d3	♖b8-b6
20.♗c1-d2	♖h8-b8
21.c3-c4	♖b6-b2
22.♖h1-c1	♘f6-e8
23.♖c1-c2	♖b2-b6
24.♖a1-e1	♖b6-a6
25.♖e1-e5	...

Preparing to trade a pair of rooks.

25...	♖a6-a3+
26.♔d3-e2	♖b8-b1
27.♖e5-a5	♖a3xa5
28.♗d2xa5	♘e8-d6
29.♗a5-e1	♘d6-f5
30.♗e1-f2	a7-a6

31.g2-g4	♘f5-e7
32.♔e2-e3	♘e7-c6

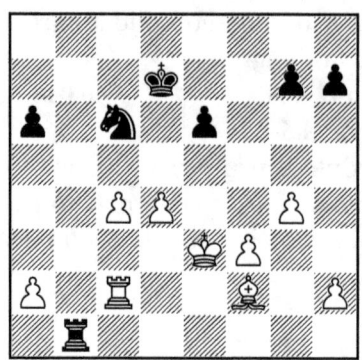

33.d4-d5 ...

The simplest. White sacrifices one pawn and transposes into an easily won endgame with a bishop against a knight.

33...	e6xd5
34.c4xd5	♘c6-b4
35.♖c2-d2	♖b1-a1
36.♔e3-e4	♖a1xa2

After 36...♘xa2, there's 37.♗d4 ♖e1+ 38.♔f4, and black loses a pawn.

37.♖d2xa2	♘b4xa2
38.♗f2-e1	♘a2-c1
39.♗e1-c3	g7-g6
40.♔e4-e5	♘c1-b3
41.h2-h4	♔d7-e7
42.♗c3-b4+	♔e7-d7
43.♗b4-c3	♔d7-e7
44.♗c3-b4+	♔e7-d7
45.♗b4-c3	♔d7-e7
46.f3-f4	a6-a5
47.♗c3-b2	♘b3-d2
48.♗b2-a3+	♔e7-f7
49.♗a3-c1	...

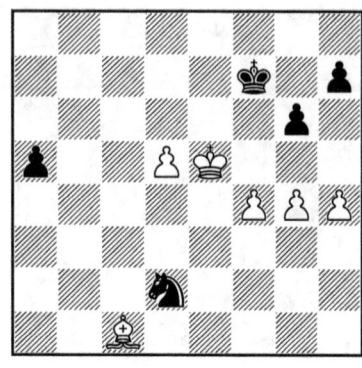

49... ♘d2-b3

Loses quickly. Black had better chances after 49...♘f3+ 50.♔d6 h5! 51.gxh5 gxh5 52.♔c7 ♘xh4 53.d6 ♘g6 54.f5 ♘f8 55.♗h6 a4! 56.♗xf8 a3 57.d7 a2 58.d8=♕ a1=♕ 59.♕e7+ ♔g8 60.♕c5, and white should eventually win. Not 50...♘h2 51.♔c6 ♘xg4 52.d6 ♘f6 53.♗b2, and white promotes his pawn.

50.♗c1-b2	♔f7-e7
51.♗b2-a3+	♔e7-d7
52.♔e5-f6	♘b3-d4
53.♔f6-g7	h7-h5
54.g4xh5	g6xh5
55.♔g7-g6	a5-a4
56.f4-f5	♘d4-f3
57.f5-f6	♘f3-e5+
58.♔g6-g7	

Black resigned. After 58...♔e8 59.d6 he has to give up his knight for the pawn.

No. 12. Andor Lilienthal – Sergei Belavenets
10th Soviet Championship, Tbilisi 1937
Grunfeld Defense D95

1.♘g1-f3	♘g8-f6

2.c2-c4	c7-c6
3.d2-d4	d7-d5
4.e2-e3	g7-g6
5.♘b1-c3	♗f8-g7
6.♕d1-b3	0-0
7.♗c1-d2	e7-e6
8.♗f1-d3	♘b8-d7
9.0-0	b7-b6
10.c4xd5	e6xd5
11.♖a1-c1	...

The continuation 11.e4 c5 was tested in the game Chekhover — Belavenets, Tbilisi 1937.

11...	♗c8-b7
12.♖f1-d1	c6-c5
13.d4xc5	...

Black already has a great position, and white is looking for counterplay, saddling black with an isolated d-pawn. In case of 13.♕c2 or 13.♗e2, black can calmly prepare a promising plan based on queenside pawn movement.

13...	♘d7xc5
14.♕b3-c2	♖a8-c8
15.♗d2-e1	♕d8-e7

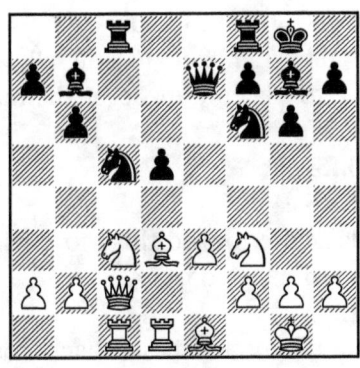

Of course, black has no reason to trade his good c5 knight for the d3 bishop; he just calmly finishes his development, intending to transfer the knight to e5 or seize the e4 square.

16.♕c2-e2	♖f8-d8
17.♘f3-d4	...

White had an interesting trap to hand: 17.♘b5 ♗a6?! (this pin looks very unpleasant for white, but...) 18.♘d6! with equality. However, after 17...a6 black is still somewhat better.

17...	♘f6-d7
18.♘d4-f3?!	...

18.♕d2 ♘e5 19.♗e2 would keep the position balanced.

18...	♘d7-e5!

Black weakens white's position a bit by this exchange.

19.♘f3xe5	♕e7xe5
20.♗d3-b1	♕e5-g5!

The immediate 20...d4 gave black nothing, but now it's a threat.

21.b2-b4	...

After getting a worse position, white doesn't settle for passive defense, for instance, 21.f4 ♕f6 22.♗f2, but tries to create complications; however, they are not dangerous for black.

21...	♘c5-e6
22.f2-f4!	♕g5-e7

22...♕f6 is bad, since white has an interesting tactic 23.♘xd5! ♗xd5 24.♖xc8 ♖xc8 25.♖xd5, winning a pawn. Now this combination is refuted with 25...♘xf4, and black wins.

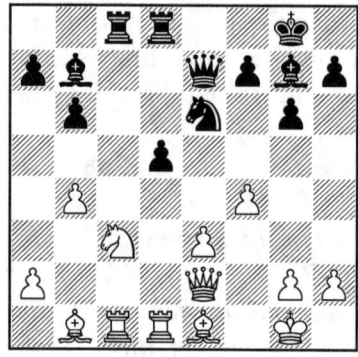

23.f4-f5   ♘e6-f8

23...♘c7 was also good, preparing for the eventual d5-d4 breakthrough or putting pressure on the e-pawn along the e-file.

Another good move was 23...gxf5 24.♗xf5 ♕g5, for instance: 25.♕g4 ♕xg4 26.♗xg4 d4 27.exd4 ♖xd4 etc.

24.♘c3-b5?   ...

24.♘xd5 still doesn't work: 24...♖xd5! 25.♖xc8 ♖xd1 26.♖xf8+ ♗xf8 27.♕xd1 ♕xe3+ 28.♔h1 (or 28.♗f2) 28...♕g5, and white loses at least a pawn in a bad position.

28...♗d6! (threatening 29...♕h3) 29.♗g3 ♗xg3 30.hxg3 ♕xg3 was even *stronger*.

White should play 24.♔h1 ♕g5 25.h4. He would be worse, but not lost.

24...   ♖c8xc1

Otherwise white will put his knight on d4, strengthening his position. The rook exchange allows black to drive away the knight and play d5-d4.

25.♖d1xc1   a7-a6

25...d4! would win more convincingly.

26.♖c1-c7   ...

With rooks on the board, d5-d4 is even more dangerous for white.

26...   ♖d8-d7
27.♖c7xd7   ♘f8xd7
28.♘b5-a3   d5-d4

28...♘e5 would be stronger as black could soon plant his knight on c4.

29.♘a3-c4?   ...

With a funny trap, which black fell for. 29.♗d2 ♘f6 30.♘c2 ♘d5 promised nothing good for white. However, after 29.♗d3 b5 30.♘c2 white would avoid losing material and had decent prospects of holding.

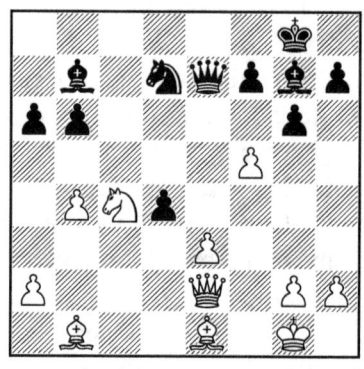

29...   ♗b7-d5?

The simple 29...b5 30.♘a5 ♗d5 or 29...dxe3 30.♘xe3 (30.♕xe3 ♗d4!) 30...♗d4 31.♗d2 ♘f6 still allowed black to keep an overwhelming advantage.

30.f5xg6   h7xg6
31.e3-e4   ...

Black overlooked this move when he played 29...♗d5.

31...   f7-f5?

Again, not the best. Black could still keep some advantage with 31...b5 32.♘d2 ♘b6 or 31...♗e6 followed by b5.

32.♘c4-d2   ♘d7-f6

Now black has nothing. 32...♗h6 is met with 33.♗f2, attacking the d4 pawn.

33.♗e1-h4   f5xe4
34.♘d2xe4   ♗d5xe4
35.♗h4xf6   ♗g7xf6
36.♕e2xe4.   Draw.

No. 13. Sergei Belavenets – Alexander Ilyin-Zhenevsky
10th Soviet Championship
Tbilisi 1937
Queen's Gambit D66

1.d2-d4   d7-d5
2.c2-c4   e7-e6
3.♘b1-c3   ♘g8-f6
4.♗c1-g5   ♗f8-e7
5.e2-e3   h7-h6
6.♗g5-h4   0-0
7.♖a1-c1   ...

White usually plays 7.♘f3 to prevent Capablanca's defense 7...b6, because after 8.cxd5 ♘xd5 9.♗xe7 ♕xe7 10.♘xd5 exd5 11.♕c2, black is forced to play c6, which is not exactly beneficial for him.

Later it turned out that instead of 11...c6, black has a much stronger move 11...c5! 12.dxc5 d4 with great counterplay, so 11.♕c2 didn't become popular, and white had to choose between several other moves. 7.♖c1, on the other hand, became the main line.

7...   ♘b8-d7
8.♘g1-f3   c7-c6
9.♗f1-d3   d5xc4
10.♗d3xc4   ♘f6-d5

Black could probably equalize more easily after 10...b5 11.♗d3 a6 12.a4 bxa4 etc. Now, because of black's move h6, white manages to avoid the simplifying bishop trade.

11.♗h4-g3   ♘d7-f6
12.♗c4-d3   ...

Black threatened (for instance, after 12.0-0) to play the unpleasant 12...♘xc3 13.♖xc3 ♘e4 with the subsequent ♘xg3, gaining the bishop pair.

12...   c6-c5
13.0-0   c5xd4
14.e3xd4   b7-b6
15.♕d1-e2   ...

It was better to play 15.♕a4 ♗b7 16.♗a6, and the weakness of black's queenside is quite noticeable.

It seems that after 16...♘xc3 17.♖xc3 ♗xa6 18.♕xa6 ♘e4, black's position is fine.

15...   ♘d5-b4
16.♗d3-c4   ♗c8-b7
17.♖f1-d1   ...

17.♖cd1 was more aggressive, intending ♘e5 and f4 with a kingside attack.

17...   ♖a8-c8
18.♘f3-e5   ♘f6-d5
19.♘c3xd5   ♗b7xd5?!

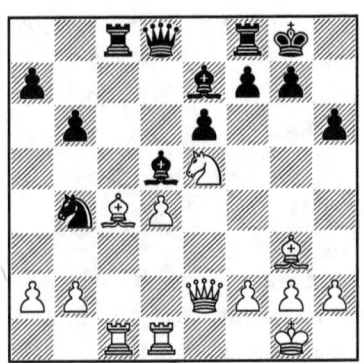

The lack of energy in white's play had allowed black to equalize, but black's last move again cedes the advantage to white. After 19...♘xd5 20.♗b3, black had an equal position.

20.a2-a3	♗d5xc4
21.♖c1xc4	♘b4-d5
22.♖d1-c1	♖c8xc4
23.♕e2xc4	a7-a5
24.♕c4-c6	...

The open c-file gives white a clear advantage, and only the strong d5 knight allows black to maintain any balance.

24...	♗e7-f6
25.♘e5-d7	♖f8-e8
26.♘d7xf6+	...

26.♘xb6 ♗xd4! gave white nothing.

26...	g7xf6
27.h2-h3	♔g8-h7
28.♗g3-c7	♕d8-c8?

A mistake that loses a pawn. After the simple 28...♘xc7 29.♕xc7 ♕xc7 30.♖xc7, white's advantage in the endgame is probably not sufficient to win.

29.♗c7xb6	♕c8xc6

Black noticed only now that he couldn't play 29...♘xb6 because of 30.♕e4+!

30.♖c1xc6	♖e8-b8
31.♗b6-c5	...

31.♗xa5 ♖xb2 was worse – the a5 bishop has no good square.

31...	♖b8xb2
32.♖c6-a6	♖b2-b5

Black wants to eliminate the dangerous passed a-pawn.

According to the engine, black could maintain equality with 32...♖b1+ 33.♔h2 ♖b2, because after 34.♖xa5 ♖xf2 35.a4 f5 it's only white who risks. However, playing such a move over the board is frightening: there might be no mate, and the a-pawn is running up the board. Therefore, black's desire to eliminate his opponent's rook pawn is understandable.

33.a3-a4	♖b5-b1+
34.♔g1-h2	♖b1-a1
35.♖a6xa5	♘d5-c3
36.♗c5-b4	♘c3-d5

Worse was 36...♘xa4 37.♗c5! ♖a2 38.d5 exd5 (38...♖c2 39.♗e3) 39.♗d4, and black will never be able to break out of the pin.

37.♗b4-c5	♘d5-c3
38.♗c5-b4	♘c3-d5
39.♗b4-c5	♘d5-c3

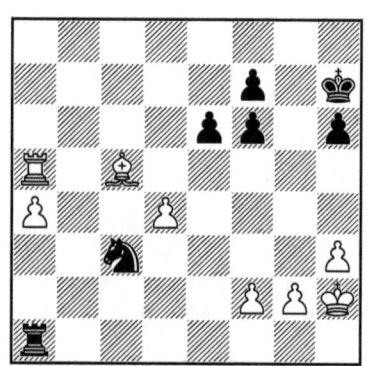

40.d4-d5! ...

The only possible way to win. 40.♖a7 ♖xa4 41.♖xf7+ ♔g6 led to a clear draw.

40... ♖a1xa4?

Still, 40...♘xd5! was better, and even though white's a-pawn is very strong, it's unlikely he'd be able to convert his advantage.

41.♖a5xa4　♘c3xa4
42.♗c5-d4!　...

The point. If now 42...exd5, then white simply plays 43.♔g3, and the endgame is hopeless for black because his knight is immobilized.

42...　♔h7-g7
43.d5-d6　♔g7-f8
44.♗d4xf6　♘a4-b6

44...♘c5 was no better. 45.f3 wins easily.

45.♔h2-g3　♘b6-d7

45...♔e8 with the subsequent ♘c4 gave black better chances to save the game, trading the h-pawn for the d-pawn. Black's passive defense now leads to a quick defeat.

46.♗f6-b2　♔f8-g8
47.♔g3-g4　♔g8-h7
48.♔g4-h5　...

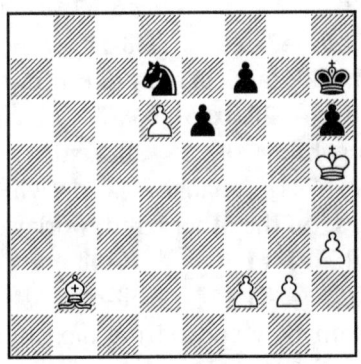

48...　♘d7-f8

The last opportunity to make things harder for white was 48...f5.

49.g2-g4　...

Now the win is very simple. With g5, white creates a passed pawn on the h-file.

49...　♘f8-d7
50.g4-g5　h6xg5
51.♔h5xg5　♔h7-g8
52.♗b2-d4　...

Preventing 52...♘c5 with the threat ♘e4+.

52...　♔g8-h7
53.h3-h4　...

White's plan is clear. He pushes his pawn to h6, puts the bishop on g7, then heads to the d-pawn with his king and wins the knight for it. Black can't do anything to prevent this — his king is tied to the h-pawn, and his knight to the d-pawn.

53...　♘d7-f8?
54.♔g5-f6. Black resigned.

No. 14. Sergei Belavenets – Grigory Levenfish
10th Soviet Championship
Tbilisi 1937
Catalan Opening E00

1.d2-d4　♘g8-f6
2.c2-c4　e7-e6
3.g2-g3　♗f8-b4+

Black doesn't want to go for the main lines of the Catalan after 3...d5.

4.♗c1-d2　♗b4xd2+

4...♕e7 was probably more precise.

5.♕d1xd2　...

Of course, white intends to develop his queen's knight on c3 – it's more active there than on d2.

5...　♘f6-e4

The unassuming 5...d5 was not a bad move here.

6.♕d2-c2　d7-d5
7.♗f1-g2　♕d8-e7

8.a2-a3 f7-f5

Black goes for the Dutch Defense structure called the "Stonewall", the c6-d5-e6-f5 pawn chain. But he doesn't have a dark-squared bishop that normally does important duty in this structure – covering the weak dark squares.

**9.♘g1-f3 0-0
10.0-0 c7-c6
11.♘b1-c3 ♘b8-d7
12.b2-b4 ...**

White is trying to attack his opponent's queenside with his own pawn chain.

12... ♘e4-d6

This maneuver forces the move c4-c5, which can make it easier for black to organize counterplay in the center (with e6-e5) and on the kingside. However, his subsequent play is not consistent.

13.c4-c5 ♘d6-c4

It was probably better to get the knight back to the e4 square, which is usual in this structure.

14.♖f1-e1 ...

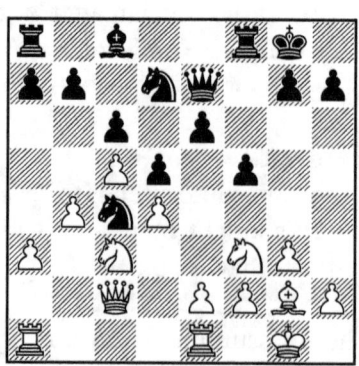

A precise move that underscores the black knight's vulnerable position on c4: 14...e5 is now powerfully met with 15.e4, opening up the position – clearly to white's advantage.

14... b7-b6?!

Not in the spirit of the position: black has to play e6-e5, and he needed to prepare for it with 14...♘f6. The black bishop's incursion to a6 is no good.

**15.♘f3-d2?! ♘c4xd2
16.♕c2xd2 ♗c8-a6
17.♕d2-c2 ...**

Now 17...e5 is met with 18.b5, and 17...♗c4 with 18.e4! fxe4 19.♘xe4.

However, instead of the game move, the natural 17...♘f6 was stronger.

**17... ♕e7-f6
18.♕c2-a4 ...**

Parrying black's positional threat 18...♗c4. Black had created a discovered attack along the f-file, and e2-e4 was now impossible.

**18... ♗a6-b7
19.e2-e3 ♖f8-b8**

Black's tactical blow doesn't work: 19...bxc5 20.bxc5 ♘xc5 21.♕b4. Meanwhile, 19...e5 20.♘xd5 cxd5 21.♕xb7 is just bad for black – white's tactics, on the other hand, work well.

**20.♖e1-c1 ♕f6-d8
21.♗g2-f1 ♖b8-c8**

Both now and on the next move, b6-b5 is too dangerous for black because of the positional piece sacrifice on b5 that will make white's queenside pawns very strong.

22.♖a1-b1 a7-a5?

Black sacrifices a pawn to consolidate his defense. It's hard to blame him – his position is already very difficult. Playing cautiously with 22...♕e7 or 22...♖c7 would be preferable.

23.b4xa5	b6-b5
24.♕a4-b4	♗b7-a6

24...♖xa5 or 24...♕xa5 is met with 25.a4, winning a pawn and immediately crushing the queenside defense.

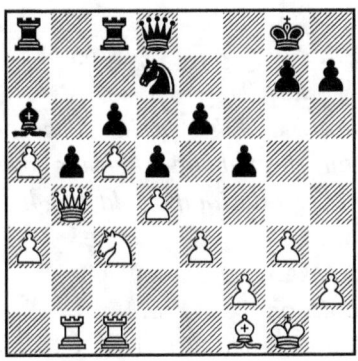

25.♖b1-a1! ...

The position has changed, so the heavy artillery should be relocated.

25...	♖c8-b8
26.♖c1-b1	e6-e5

Finally! But now, even this move doesn't bring relief: white's positional advantage is too great, and the extra pawn is quite useful too.

27.a3-a4	e5xd4
28.e3xd4	b5xa4
29.♕b4xa4	♖b8xb1
30.♘c3xb1	♕d8-c8
31.♗f1xa6	♕c8xa6
32.♘b1-c3	...

Placing the knight on d2 is more convincing.

32...	♖a8-b8?

Blundering in a difficult position. 32...♘f6 was more resilient.

33.♘c3xd5	♕a6-d3

33...♘xc5 didn't help either because of 34.♘e7+ ♔f7 35.dxc5 ♔xe7 36.♕h4+ etc.

34.♘d5-b6	f5-f4
35.♕a4-c4+	...

The simplest. Best not to give his opponent any hope to survive after 35.♘xd7 ♖b1+.

35...	♕d3xc4
36.♘b6xc4	♖b8-b7
37.g3xf4	♘d7-b8
38.♘c4-d6	♖b7-e7
39.♖a1-b1	♘b8-a6
40.♖b1-b6	♖e7-a7
41.♖b6xc6	h7-h6
42.♘d6-b5	♖a7-a8
43.♘b5-c7.	

Black resigned.

"In this game, Belavenets punished the future Soviet champion, the winner of the 10th national championship, for his inconsistent play." (A. Iglitsky)

No. 15. Ilya Rabinovich – Sergei Belavenets
10th Soviet Championship
Tbilisi 1937
French Defense C09

1.e2-e4	e7-e6
2.d2-d4	d7-d5
3.♘b1-d2	c7-c5
4.d4xc5	...

Spielmann's move, used by him in the famous 1927 New York grandmaster tournament against Alekhine and Nimzowitsch. The current main lines are 4.exd5 and 4.♘f3.

**4...   ♗f8xc5
5.♘d2-b3   ...**

In both aforementioned games, Spielmann played 5.♗d3, which is probably more promising.

**5...   ♗c5-b6
6.e4xd5**

6...   e6xd5

6...♘f6 was simpler and more natural; white can't play either 7.dxe6 or 7.♗g5 because of the tactical blow 7...♗xf2+, while 7.♗b5+ ♗d7 8.♗xd7+ ♕xd7 9.c4 exd5 10.c5 ♗c7 doesn't give white any advantage either.

Especially for the adventurous, we'll point out that after 7.♗g5 ♗xf2+!? 8.♔xf2 ♘e4+ 9.♔e3 ♘xg5 10.h4 or 9...♕xg5+ 10.♔xe4 white wins a piece and doesn't get checkmated. However, it's hard to guarantee that black would not be able to create a very strong attack here!

**7.♘g1-f3   ♘b8-c6
8.♗f1-d3   ♘g8-f6
9.0-0   0-0
10.♗c1-g5   ♗c8-g4
11.h2-h3   ...**

Perhaps 11.♗e2 was more flexible, to try and trade several minor pieces – the less material there is on the board, the weaker the isolated d5 pawn becomes.

**11...   ♗g4-h5
12.♖f1-e1   ♕d8-d6
13.♗g5-e3   ...**

Black had a rather unpleasant threat ♕g3.

**13...   ♘c6-e5
14.♗d3-e2   ...**

Now white's position becomes difficult. He could have kept the position roughly equal with the bold 14.g4!

**14...   ♗b6xe3
15.f2xe3   ♖f8-e8
16.c2-c3   ...**

The immediate 16.♘d4 made more sense.

**16...   ♘e5xf3+
17.♗e2xf3   ♗h5xf3
18.♕d1xf3   ♖e8-e5
19.♘b3-d4   ♖a8-e8
20.♖e1-e2   ♕d6-a6**

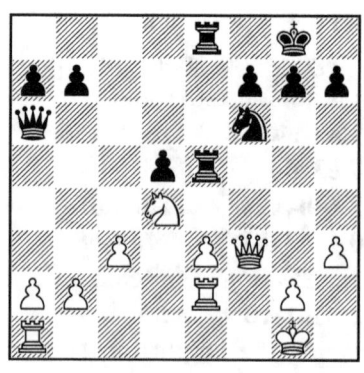

Black has gradually outplayed his opponent and gained a big positional advantage, although it's not that simple to convert it into a whole point.

21.♖a1-f1 ...

White sacrifices a pawn in search for counterplay, but he gets nothing real out of it. He should have settled for defense with 21.a3.

21... ♕a6xa2
22.♘d4-f5 ♕a2-a6

White threatened 23.♘xg7. Anyway, the queen had to come back at some point.

23.♖e2-d2? ...

23.♘h6+! would hold.

23... ♕a6-e6
24.c3-c4 ♔g8-f8

Of course, not 24...dxc4 25.♖d6 ♕c8 26.♖xf6! Soon, black manages to simplify the position, so getting the king closer to the center is not a bad decision.

25.♕f3-f4 ...

White would keep the position balanced with 25.♖d3 or 25.cxd5.

25... ♘f6-e4
26.♖d2xd5 ♖e5xd5
27.c4xd5 ♕e6xd5
28.♖f1-c1 ...

28.♕c7 would give white a slight hope of saving the game.

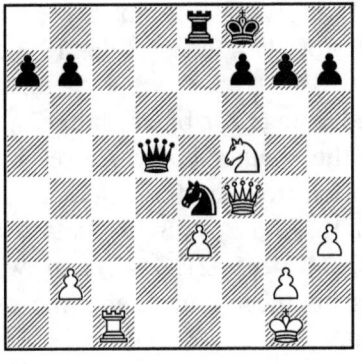

28... ♕d5-e5!

Black returns the pawn and transposes into a better knight endgame.

Still, black should have kept the pawn: 28...♕d8! And now the seemingly intimidating 29.♖c7 doesn't work due to 29...g5! 30.♘h6 ♖e7, and black wins.

29.♕f4xe5 ...

If 29.♖c7, then 29...♕xf4 30.exf6 g6, and black maintains the material advantage.

29... ♖e8xe5
30.♖c1-c8+ ♖e5-e8
31.♖c8xe8+ ♔f8xe8
32.♘f5xg7+ ♔e8-d7

Black's positional advantages are obvious: the pawn majority on the queenside eventually allows him to create an outside passed pawn that will distract his opponent's forces, and this, in turn, because of white's pawn weaknesses and black's centralized pieces, should lead to material losses for white.

33.♔g1-f1 ♔d7-c6
34.♔f1-e2 ♔c6-d5
35.♘g7-f5 ...

35.♔d3 ♘c5+ 36.♔d2 ♔e5 37.♘e8!? probably gave white better drawing chances.

35... ♔d5-c4
36.♘f5-d4 a7-a5
37.h3-h4 a5-a4
38.g2-g4 b7-b5
39.♔e2-d1 ...

39.g5 b4 40.♔d1 ♔d3 didn't save the game either.

39... ♘e4-f2+

40.♔d1-c2   ♞f2xg4

The inevitable has happened. Now black can easily convert his positional and material advantage.

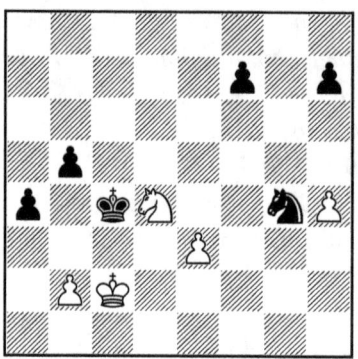

41.♘d4-f5	f7-f6
42.♘f5-d6+	♚c4-c5
43.♘d6-e4+	♚c5-b4
44.♔c2-d2	♚b4-b3
45.♔d2-c1	♚b3-c4
46.♔c1-d2	b5-b4
47.♔d2-c1	♚c4-d5

White resigned.

No. 16. Sergei Belavenets – Evgeny Zagoriansky
Moscow Championship, 1937/38
Slav Defense D49

1.♘g1-f3	d7-d5
2.c2-c4	c7-c6
3.d2-d4	♞g8-f6
4.♘b1-c3	e7-e6
5.e2-e3	♞b8-d7
6.♗f1-d3	d5xc4
7.♗d3xc4	b7-b5
8.♗c4-d3	a7-a6
9.e3-e4	c6-c5
10.e4-e5	c5xd4
11.♘c3xb5	♞d7xe5
12.♘f3xe5	a6xb5

The well-known Meran Variation is on the board. Theoreticians still argue about it.

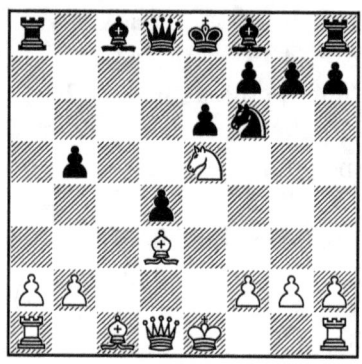

13.♕d1-f3   ...

Stahlberg's move is considered the strongest right now. The Rellstab attack is also good for white: 13.0-0 ♕d5 14.♕e2, and white gets a long-term initiative for the pawn. 13.♗xb5+, immediately regaining the pawn, gives white nothing because of 13...♗d7 14.♘xd7 ♕a5+, and black isn't any worse.

13...   ♗f8-b4+
14.♔e1-e2   ♖a8-b8

14...♕d5 is no good because of 15.♕xd5 ♘xd5 16.♗xb5+ ♔e7, and now not 17.♘c6+ ♔d6 18.♘xd4 due to 18...♔c5 19.♗e3 e5 etc. with an advantage for black, but 17.♖d1, and the weak d4 pawn gives black a lot of trouble, for instance, 17...♗c5 18.♘c6+ ♔d6 19.♘xd4 ♗xd4 20.♖xd4 ♔c5 21.♖a4!, and white saves his piece and retains the extra pawn.

After 17.♘c6+ ♚d6 18.♘xd4 ♚c5, white has a stronger move, 19.a3! In the game Foltys — Bogoljubov, Stuttgart 1939, white got a decent advantage after 19...♚xd4 20.axb4 ♗b7 21.♖d1+ ♚e5 22.♗d2. However, black's play can also be improved — 19...♗c3!, and then 20.bxc3 ♘xc3+ 21.♚d2 ♘xb5 22.♘xb5 ♚xb5 23.♗b2 f6 24.♖hc1 leads to a position with slightly better chances for white.

15.♕f3-g3   ♕d8-c7

15...♕d6 would have still been met with 16.♘c6, like in the game, while 15...♕d5 was simply bad because of 16.♘f3! with the dual threat of ♕xg7 and ♕xb8.

Modern theory thinks that, after 15...♕d6, white's most promising move is 16.♘f3, while after 15...♕d5 16.♘f3 e5! 17.♕xe5+ (17.♕xg7 e4 leads to double-edged play) 17...♕xe5+ 18.♘xe5 ♖b6 white's advantage is not too great.

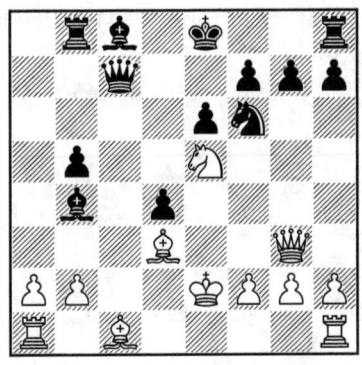

16.♘e5-c6!   ♗b4-d6?

It seems that black had to go for the exchange sacrifice: 16...♕xc6 17.♕xb8 0-0 18.f3 e5!, with a strong attack.

Almost half a century later, Eugenio Torre, the first Filipino grandmaster, came to the same conclusion. After 19.♕xb5 ♕d6 20.a3 ♗c5 21.♚d1 ♗e6 22.♗d2 e4 black got a very promising position (Meyer — Torre, Lugano 1986). However, 18...♗d7! was likely even stronger.

17.♕g3xg7   ♖h8-g8
18.♕g7xf6   ♕c7xc6
19.♗c1-g5!   ...

The best move, putting the black king in danger. After 19.♕xd4 ♗b7, the white king's position would have been too precarious.

19...   ♗c8-a6

Creating an unpleasant threat b5-b4. After 19...♗d7, white could reply 20.♗xh7, while if 19...♗b7, then 20.♖ac1 ♕d5 (20...♕b6 21.♗xh7) 21.♖c7! with a decisive advantage.

Here's how play could have continued in the last line: 21...♕e5+ 22.♕xe5 ♗xe5 23.♗xb5+ ♚f8 24.♗h6+ ♗g7 25.♗f4 with a big advantage for white, but not a decisive one.

20.♖a1-c1   ♕c6-d5

Black's only hope for activity is to push b5-b4. Therefore, 20...♕b7 was more logical, and if 21.♕xd4, then 21...♖xg5 22.♕xd6 ♖d8 23.♕f4 ♕d5 with equal chances. After 20...♕b7, the strongest move is probably 21.b4! ♗xb4 22.♗xh7 with a sharp position, but better for white.

After 20...♕b7, there's an even stronger move: 21.h4! b4 22.♕xd4 with an obvious advantage.

Black could also play 20...♕xg2, because the tempting 21.♖c7 doesn't work due to 21...♕g4+! 22.f3 ♕g2+ 23.♔d1 ♕xh1+ 24.♔c2 ♕xh2+! 25.♔b3 ♕h5 26.♖e7+ ♔f8 27.♗h6+ ♖g7 28.♗xg7+ ♔g8 29.♖xf7 ♕d5+! 30.♔c2 ♖c8+ 31.♔d1 ♕h5 etc. However, 21.♖hg1! (after 20...♕xg2) puts black in great danger.

The computer shows that in the line 20...♕xg2 21.♖c7 ♕g4+ 22.f3 ♕g2+ 23.♔d1 ♕xh1+ 24.♔c2 ♕xh2+ 25.♔b3 ♕h5 26.♗e4! (instead of 26.♖e7+), white has a mate in six. For instance: 26...♖xg5 27.♕h8+ ♗f8 28.♗c6+ ♔d8 29.♖d7+ ♔e8 30.♖a7+ ♔d8 31.♕xf8#.

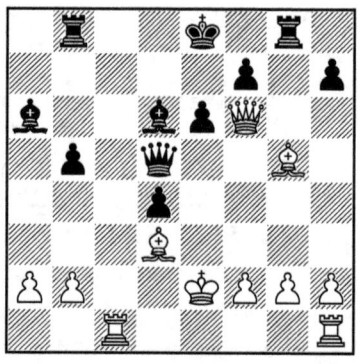

21.h2-h4 ...

After this simple move, creating the threat ♖c7, black's position becomes difficult. The immediate 21.♖c7 doesn't work because of 21...♕e5+.

21... h7-h6

Black is trying to complicate the game. If 21...♕b7, then simply 22.♕xd4 with an extra pawn and a better position, or if 21...♕e5+, then 22.♕xe5 ♗xe5 23.♖c5!, and white at the very least wins the b5 pawn.

22.♕f6xh6 ♕d5xg2

Regaining the pawn doesn't help black. It was more logical to play 22...♕e5+ 23.♔f1 ♗b7 24.♖e1 ♕d5, creating some complications.

White had a stronger reply: 23.♔d1!, immediately bringing the h1 rook into the game. After, for instance, 23...♗b7 24.♖e1 ♕d5, white delivers a pretty mate: 25.♖xe6+! fxe6 26.♗xb5+! ♕xb5 27.♕xe6+ ♔f8 28.♕xd6+ ♔g7 29.♕f6+ ♔h7 30.♕h6#.

23.♖h1-g1 ♕g2-d5

Or 23...♕b7 24.♕h7! with a decisive advantage for white (after 24...♖f8, white wins with 25.♗e4!).

24.♕h6-f6 ...

♖c7 is a threat again.

24... ♕d6-e5+

This loses by force. However, black's position is already hopeless: if, for example, 24...♗b7 (to meet 25.♖c7 with 25...♕f3+), then 25.h5 or 25.f3 (threatening ♗e4), and white should win.

25.♕f6xe5 ♗d6xe5

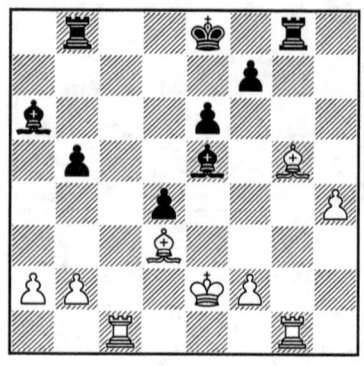

26.♗g5-f6! ...

A small combination that quickly leads to a finish.

26... ♖g8xg1
27.♖c1xg1 ♗e5-h2

Black doesn't have much choice: either lose an exchange after 27...♗xf6, or lose a piece as in the game.

28.♖g1-g8+ ♔e8-d7
29.♖g8xb8 ♗h2xb8
30.h4-h5 ♗b8-f4
31.♗f6-g7 e6-e5
32.h5-h6 ♗f4xh6
33.♗g7xh6 ♔d7-e6
34.a2-a4. Black resigned.

No. 17. Mikhail Yudovich – Sergei Belavenets
Moscow Championship, 1937/38
Ruy Lopez C71

1.e2-e4 e7-e5
2.♘g1-f3 ♘b8-c6
3.♗f1-b5 a7-a6
4.♗b5-a4 d7-d6
5.c2-c4 ...

Keres has made this move fashionable lately. White immediately strengthens the d5 square, which gives him a certain positional advantage.

5... ♗c8-d7
6.d2-d4 e5xd4

Giving up the center is too premature and leads to a worse position for black. 6...♘f6 7.♘c3 ♗e7 was stronger, with a somewhat cramped, but very solid position for black.

7.♘f3xd4 g7-g6
8.♘b1-c3 ♗f8-g7
9.♗c1-e3 ...

Another move worth considering was 9.♘xc6 bxc6 10.0-0, for instance: 10...♘e7 11.c5! ♘c8 12.♗e3 0-0 13.♖c1, with an obvious advantage for white, Zagrebelny – Nadyrkhanov, Yaroslavl 1983.

9... ♘g8-e7
10.0-0 0-0
11.♘c3-d5? ...

After this move, black deploys an interesting maneuver that doesn't just equalize, but even gains a positional advantage. White should have put his a4 bishop on c2, getting a long-term advantage because of his control over the d5 square.

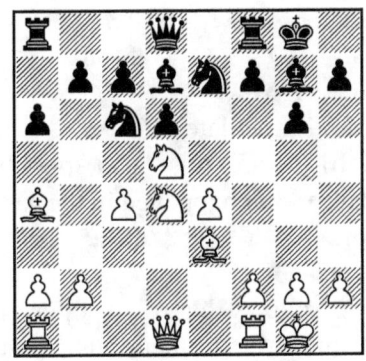

11... ♘c6xd4
12.♗a4xd7 ...

Forced, since 12.♗xd4 ♗xa4 just loses a piece.

12... c7-c5!

The point. Black gets a strong knight on d4, while the d5 knight is traded. Now it's white who has to struggle for the draw.

13.♗d7-h3 ...

Sloppy. The h3 bishop is out of play, which makes white's defense much harder. It was better to play 13.♗a4 ♘xd5 14.exd5 ♖b8 15.♗xd4 ♗xd4 16.♖b1 with great chances to draw.

But even here, black's advantage is obvious – his d4 bishop is much stronger than its counterpart.

13.♘xe7+ loses a pawn after 13...♕xe7 with the subsequent ♕xe4.

13...   ♘e7xd5
14.e4xd5   ...

After 14.cxd5, black gets a pawn majority on the queenside, and the e4 pawn becomes unexpectedly weak. For instance: 14...♕e7 15.♕d3 ♖ae8 16.f3 f5, and white can't save his pawns.

14...   b7-b5
15.♕d1-d3   ♖a8-b8
16.♖a1-b1   ...

The immediate 16.♗xd4 ♗xd4 17.♖ab1 ♕a5 was also possible, similar to what happened in the game.

16...   ♕d8-a5
17.a2-a3   ...

This allows black to open the b-file and exert tremendous pressure on the backward b-pawn. The lesser evil was to try 17.♗xd4 ♗xd4 18.b4, for example: 18...♕xa2 (if 18...bxc4, then 19.♕xd4!) 19.cxb5 axb5 20.bxc5 dxc5 21.♖xb5 ♕xd5, or 21...c4 22.♕b1 ♗xf2+ 23.♔h1, and, even though black is a pawn up, it's hard to convert it.

In the above line, instead of 19...axb5, black has a stronger reply 19...♕xd5 (threatening ♗xf2+), and white's position is still bad.

17...   b5xc4

18.♕d3xc4   ♕a5-b5
19.♕c4xb5   ...

White can't avoid the queen trade, because 19.♕c1 or 19.♖fc1 is met with 19...♘e2+.

19...   ♖b8xb5
20.♖f1-d1?   ...

After this, white's position is hopeless. Without a doubt, the best move is 20.♗xd4 *(20.♗g4!?)*, and whether black plays 20...cxd4 or 20...♗xd4, white can still breathe, for instance: 20...♗xd4 21.b4! ♖fb8 22.♖bd1; if 21...c4, then 22.♖fd1, and 22...♖xd5 is bad due to 23.♗g4!

Instead of 21...c4, black can play 21...cxb4! 22.♖xb4 ♖xd5. Now white can't pin the bishop with 23.♖d1? because of 23...♗xf2+, but otherwise black will put the bishop on c5 and invade the second rank with his rook. A difficult defense awaits white.

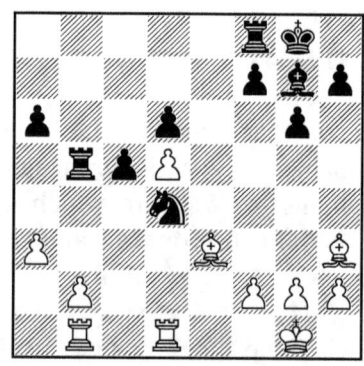

20...   ♖b5-b3!

The strongest move, since 20...♖fb8 21.♗xd4 ♗xd4 22.b4 still gave white some hope.

Even then, after 22...♖5b7! (preventing 23.♗d7) 23.g3 a5 24.♗f1 axb4 25.axb4 ♖xb4, black has good chances to convert his extra pawn.

21.♔g1-f1   ♖f8-b8
22.♗e3-f4   ...

Searching for counterplay.

22...   ♗g7-f8
23.♗f4-d2   ...

The pawn cannot be saved (if 23.♖d2, then 23...♖xa3), and white sets a small trap.

23...   ♘d4-b5

23...♖xb2 is worse because of 24.♖xb2 ♖xb2 25.♗c3.

24.♗h3-g4   ...

Or 24.a4 ♘a3 25.♖a1 ♘c4.

24...   ♗f8-g7

After 24...♘xa3 25.♖a1 ♘c4 26.♖xa6 ♘xb2, white's pieces would free up somewhat. So, black does not hurry. Now he threatens both ♘xa3 and ♗xb2.

25.♗d2-f4   ...

White's last chance is to attack the d6 pawn.

25...   ♗g7xb2

The most convincing.

26.a3-a4   ♘b5-c3
27.♗f4xd6   ♖b8-b4?

White resigned. 27...♘xb1 would indeed have won. However, the resignation is premature as black has no clear win. After 28.♖e1 ♘xb1 29.♖e8+ ♔g7 30.♗f8+ ♔f6 31.♗e7+ ♔e5 32.d6 ♘d2+ 33.♔e2 ♖xg4 34.d7 ♖e4+ 35.♔xd2 ♔f5 36.d8=♕ ♖d4+ 37.♔e2 ♖xd8 38.♖xd8 black would have an extra pawn, but it is not clear whether he can convert it.

No. 18. Boris Verlinsky – Sergei Belavenets
Soviet Championship semi-final
Kiev 1938
French Defense C19

1.e2-e4   e7-e6
2.d2-d4   d7-d5
3.♘b1-c3   ♗f8-b4
4.e4-e5   c7-c5
5.a2-a3   ♗b4xc3+
6.b2xc3   ♕d8-c7

Preventing 7.♕g4 due to f5.

7.♘g1-f3   ♘g8-e7
8.♗f1-d3   ♗c8-d7

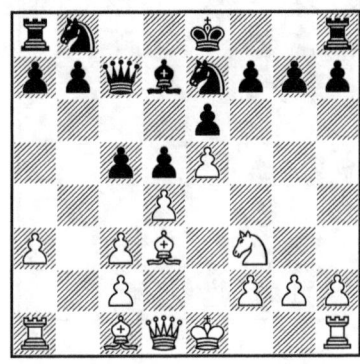

9.0-0   ...

An inaccuracy. 9.a4 was necessary here, because now black deprives white of any initiative on the queenside.

9...   c5-c4
10.♗d3-e2 ♗d7-a4!
11.♖a1-b1 ♘b8-c6
12.♘f3-e1 0-0-0
13.f2-f4   ♔c8-b8
14.g2-g3   ♔b8-a8
15.♘e1-g2 g7-g6

Black wants to close down the

kingside and slowly put pressure on the a3 and c3 pawns.

16.♘g2-e3   h7-h5
17.♘e3-g2   ...

White wants to put his knight on g5, and black wants to put his on b5.

17...   ♘e7-c8
18.♘g2-e1   ♘c8-b6
19.♘e1-f3   ♘b6-d7

Sloppy. Black first had to play 19...♕e7 and only then ♘d7-b8-a6-c7-b5 with a good position.

20.♘f3-g5   ♘d7-b8

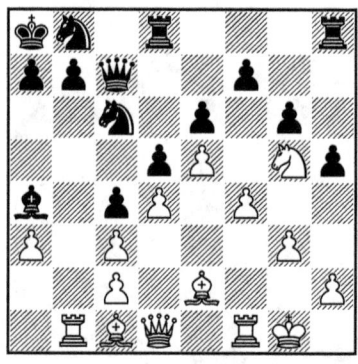

21.f4-f5   ...

Black missed this tactic, though it was later refuted. Now it looks like he can't play 21...exf5 due to 22.e6. In reality, though, after 22...f6 23.♘f7 ♖h7 24.♘xd8 ♕xd8 the position would be equal, despite white's extra exchange.

21...   g6xf5
22.♖b1-b2?   ...

22.♗xh5 is bad for white due to 22...♗xc2. However, the game move is not the best. The correct move was 22.h4, then ♖b2 and ♗xh5. White gets a clear advantage. Now the game becomes much sharper.

The computer clarifies these conclusions. After 22.♗xh5 ♗xc2 23.♕xc2 ♖xh5 24.g4! ♖h4! 25.gxf5 ♖g8, white has the initiative. Further, after 22.h4 black had several playable moves.

22...   h5-h4

Now black gets the initiative.

23.g3-g4?   ...

After 23.♗h5 white's disadvantage would be smaller.

23...   ♖d8-g8
24.♔g1-h1   ...

24.gxf5 ♕e7 would give black a nice advantage.

24...   ♕c7-e7
25.♕d1-d2   ...

25.gxf5 is met with 25...♖xg5 26.f6 ♕xa3 27.♖b4 ♕xc3, and black wins.

27.♖b3! is stronger, but even here, after 27...♕f8 28.♗xg5 cxb3 29.cxb3 ♕a3 30.bxa4 ♕xc3, black still has a winning advantage.

25...   f7-f6?

After 25...♘d8! 26.gxf5 exf5 27.♖xf5 ♖g7 white would be in big trouble.

26.e5xf6   ♕e7xf6
27.g4xf5   e6xf5
28.♘g5-h3?   ...

Black has an extra pawn, but this extra f5 pawn is weak, and white has enough compensation – the bishop pair and weak dark squares in his opponent's camp.

It seems that the strongest move was 28.♗f3 ♘e7 29.♕e3 with the subsequent ♕e5 or ♕e6 and good chances to draw. White could also play 28.♕f4.

28... ♘c6-e7
29.♗e2-f3 ♗a4-c6
30.♕d2-f2?! ...

30.♕e2! would give white some hope to get away with a draw.

30... ♘e7-c8

Intending to transfer the knight to e4.

31.♗c1-f4 ♘b8-d7
32.♖f1-e1 ♖g8-e8

Not 32...♘d6 because of 33.♗e5.

Actually black can play this, because after 33...♘e4! the complications are in black's favor. For example: 34.♖xe4 (or 34.♗xe4 dxe4 with the threat e4-e3+) 34...dxe4 35.♗xf6 ♘xf6 36.d5 ♘xd5!? (maybe 36...♗xd5 37.♘f4 ♗c6 38.♗g2 ♘g4 is even stronger, but who would want to let their opponent's knight leave h3?) 37.♗g2 e3 38.♕e1 ♖xg2! 39.♔xg2 ♘f4+ 40.♔f1 e2+, and, to avoid the worst, white has to give back the queen, after which, he has "just" a hopeless endgame.

33.♖b2-b1 ♘c8-d6
34.♖e1xe8+ ♖h8xe8

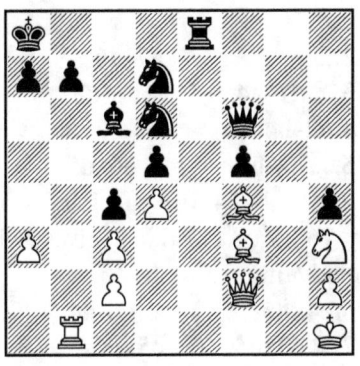

35.♗f4xd6? ...

This hands the advantage back to black. 35.♗g5 ♘e4 36.♕xh4 ♘xg5 37.♕xg5 was not bad, perhaps with slightly better chances for white. 36.♗xe4 dxe4 37.♕e3 and then ♘f4 was also possible, blocking the black pawns.

In the line 35.♗g5 ♘e4 36.♕xh4 ♕d6! black wins a pawn. While 36.♗xe4 dxe4 37.♕e3 f4 would win for black.

35... ♕f6xd6
36.♕f2xh4 ♕d6xa3
37.♖b1-e1 ♖e8xe1+
38.♕h4xe1 a7-a5

Black has managed to transpose into an endgame with an extra pawn, but winning is still difficult because the white h-pawn can become very dangerous.

39.♘h3-f4 ♕a3-d6
40.♘f4-e2! ...

Transferring the knight to c1, where it will stop the a-pawn in its tracks.

40... ♘d7-f6
41.h2-h4 ♗c6-e8

After 41...♘g4, there was 42.♕g1 ♕h6 43.♕g3, and white gets some counterchances.

42.♕e1-g1 a5-a4
43.♕g1-g5 a4-a3
44.♘e2-c1 ♘f6-e4
45.♗f3xe4 f5xe4
46.h4-h5 ♔a8-a7
47.♘c1-a2 ...

47.h6 is met with 47...♗g6.

47... e4-e3
48.♔h1-g2? ...

The last move in time trouble, and one that loses immediately. Of course, white should have played 48.♕xe3 ♗xh5 with good chances to draw.

Black would likely still have won here. He has an extra pawn that ties down the white knight, while the white king is very weak.

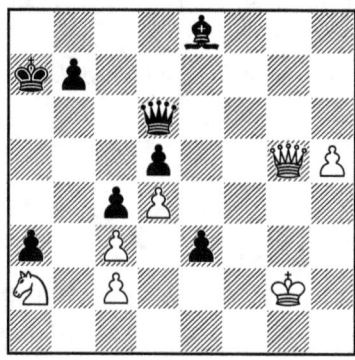

48... e3-e2!
49.♕g5-c1 ...

When playing 48.♔g2, white didn't notice that 49.♔f2 was now impossible because of 49...♕h2+.

49... ♕d6-e7
50.♔g2-f2 ♗e8xh5
51.♕c1-h1 ♕e7-g5
52.♔f2-e1 ...

Black threatened 52...♕d2.

52... ♕g5-g3+
53.♔e1-d2 ♕g3-f2

White resigned.

No. 19. Sergei Freymann – Sergei Belavenets
Soviet Championship semi-final
Kiev 1938
Sicilian Defense B50

1.e2-e4 c7-c5
2.♘g1-f3 d7-d6
3.c2-c4 ...

White tries to steer away from the theoretical paths.

3... e7-e5

Otherwise, white could get some well-known lines, but with an additional move c4. Now the game is equal.

4.♘b1-c3 ♘b8-c6
5.h2-h3 g7-g6
6.d2-d3 ♗f8-g7
7.♘c3-d5 f7-f6

7...♘ge7 is bad for black because of 8.♗g5.

8.♗c1-e3 ♘g8-h6
9.♕d1-d2 ♘h6-f7
10.♗f1-e2 ♗c8-e6

10...f5 gives black nothing, for instance, because of the simple 11.g3. Black waits for white to commit his king. If white castles short, then black doesn't need to fear a kingside attack, while if he castles long, then black gets an opportunity to start an attack with b7-b5.

11.h3-h4 h7-h5

Preventing the unpleasant h4-h5.

12.♗e2-d1 ...

Refraining from castling is a good decision.

12... a7-a6
13.♗d1-a4 ♖a8-b8
14.b2-b4 b7-b5
15.♗a4-b3 ♗e6xd5

On 15...bxc4 16.♗a4 is best and, after 16...♖c8 17.dxc4 gives white some advantage.

16.e4xd5 ♘c6-d4
17.♗e3xd4 c5xd4

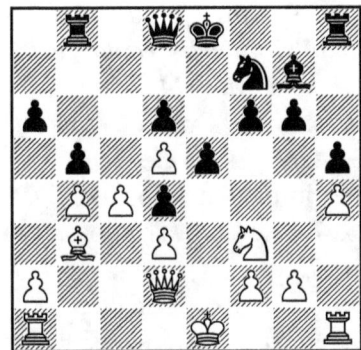

Sharpening the game. Now black has an advantage in the center and on the kingside, while white has an advantage on the queenside. 17...exd4 18.0-0 0-0 with subsequent trades on the e-file probably led to a draw.

18.a2-a4 ♗g7-h6

On 18...bxc4 19.♗c4 0-0! 20.♗xa6 f5 black had enough play for the pawn.

19.♕d2-e2 0-0

If 19...bxc4 20.♗xc4 ♖xb4, then 21.♘xd4 ♕b6 with balanced chances.

20.0-0 f6-f5?

After 20...bxc4 21.♗xc4 g5 the position would be balanced.

21.a4xb5 ...

21.cxb5 axb5 22.a5 was worse than the game continuation, because the a5 passed pawn poses no danger for black, while it's hard for white to exploit the c-file because black is controlling the c1 square.

21... a6xb5
22.c4-c5 ♖f8-e8

Black is planning e4.

23.g2-g3 ♕d8-f6
24.♖f1-d1 ...

A natural, but wrong move. White should have played 24.♗c2, and it would be very hard for black to push e5-e4. White, on the other hand, could just go for queenside operations — his chances were probably even slightly better.

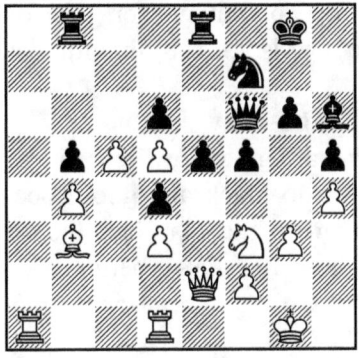

24... e5-e4
25.d3xe4? ...

Mistakes come in pairs. After 25.♘h2 or 25.♖e1, there was still a lot to fight for.

25... d4-d3!

White overlooked this resource.

26.♕e2-a2 ...

White can't play either 26.♖xd3 because of 26...♕xa1+, or 26.♕xd3 because of 26...fxe4.

26... f5xe4

White resigned.

No. 20. Sergei Belavenets – Mikhail Makogonov
Soviet Championship semi-final
Kiev 1938

Grunfeld Defense D96

1.d2-d4 ♘g8-f6
2.♘g1-f3 g7-g6
3.c2-c4 ♗f8-g7

4.♘b1-c3	d7-d5
5.♕d1-b3	c7-c6
6.e2-e3	e7-e6
7.♗f1-d3	0-0
8.0-0	♘b8-d7
9.♖f1-d1	♕d8-b6

Not a good maneuver. The correct move here is 9...♖e8, intending e5 or b6.

10.♕b3-c2	♕b6-c7

Preparing e5, which, however, doesn't do black any good, because opening up the play benefits white. Even now, 10...♖e8 is better.

11.b2-b3	e6-e5?
12.c4xd5	c6xd5
13.♗c1-a3	...

Ignoring the threat e4: it's simply met with ♘xe4.

13...	♖f8-e8
14.♖a1-c1?	...

Black's position is difficult. White threatens ♘b5 or ♘xd5.

However, white's last move was a mistake. The immediate 14.♘b5! was very strong, with material losses for black.

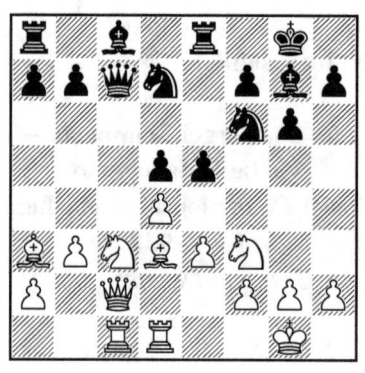

14...	a7-a6?

There's nothing better.

Actually, black could extricate himself here with 14...♕a5! 15.dxe5 ♘xe5 16.♘xe5 ♕xa3 17.♘b5 ♕f8.

15.d4xe5	...

The immediate 15.♘xd5 ♘xd5 16.♕xc7 ♘xc7 17.♖xc7 doesn't work due to 17...e4.

15...	♘d7xe5
16.♘c3xd5	♘e5xf3+?

After losing a pawn, black tries to save the game with a desperate attack that only quickens his demise. Of course, he should have played 16...♘xd5 17.♕xc7 ♘xc7 18.♖xc7 ♘xd3, getting good drawing chances because of his bishop pair.

17.g2xf3	♕c7-e5
18.♘d5-c7	♕e5-g5+

If 18...♗h3, then 19.♕c5.

It seems that there was an even stronger move, the bold 19.f4! ♕h5 20.♗e2 ♗g4 21.f3! ♗xf3 22.♗xf3 ♕xf3 23.♘xa8, and black doesn't have enough material to create real threats.

19.♔g1-h1	♕g5-h5

Black couldn't save the exchange with 19...♗h3 20.♖g1 ♕h5 due to 21.♕e2.

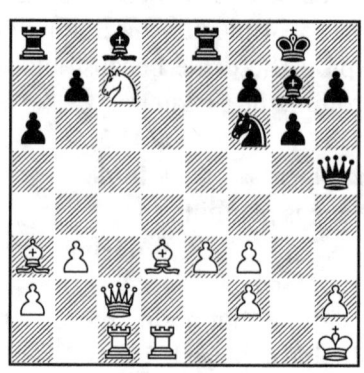

20.♘c7xe8! ...

The simplest. After 20.♗e2 ♗f5 21.e4 ♗h6 or 21.♕d2 ♘e4, the complications could become rather unpleasant. 20.♕e2 is simply bad due to 20...♘g4.

After 20.♗e2 ♗f5 21.♕d2 ♘e4 22.fxe4 ♗xe4+ 23.♔g1 ♕g5+ 24.♔f1, the computer easily parries any threats black can throw its way, but from a purely human standpoint it's a bit frightening to go there as white.

20...	♕h5xf3+
21.♔h1-g1	♕f3-g4+

21...♗h3 22.♘xf6+ and ♗e4 gave black nothing.

22.♔g1-f1	♕g4-h3+
23.♔f1-e1	♘f6xe8
24.♗d3-f1	♕h3-h4

It's necessary to prevent ♖d8.

25.♕c2-c4 ...

Forcing a queen trade that leads to an easily won endgame with an extra exchange. 25.♕xc8 ♖xc8 26.♖xc8 ♕e4 27.♖dd8 ♕b1+ 28.♗c1 ♗b2! 29.♗d3! ♕a1 30.♔d1 is not more difficult for white.

25...	♕h4-g5
26.♕c4-d5	...

After 26.♖d5 ♗f5 27.e4, black can play 27...♘f6, getting some much-needed complications.

26...	♕g5xd5

26...♗f5 is met with 27.♕xb7.

27.♖d1xd5	♗c8-e6
28.♖d5-d2	b7-b5
29.♗f1-g2	♖a8-b8
30.♗a3-e7	b5-b4
31.♖d2-d8	♖b8xd8
32.♗e7xd8	♗g7-c3+
33.♔e1-f1	♘e8-d6
34.♗d8-b6	♘d6-b5
35.♗g2-b7.	Black resigned.

No. 21. Sergei Belavenets – Fyodor Duz-Khotimirsky
USSR Championship semi-final
Kiev 1938
Dutch Defense A90

1.♘g1-f3	d7-d5
2.c2-c4	c7-c6
3.d2-d4	e7-e6
4.♘b1-c3	f7-f5
5.g2-g3	♘g8-f6
6.♗f1-g2	♘b8-d7

A typical Dutch Defense position has occurred.

7.0-0	♗f8-d6
8.♕d1-c2	a7-a6

Taking on c4 is not dangerous for white because this allows the central breakthrough e4. Black's move prevents white, after 9.cxd5 cxd5, from playing 10.♘b5.

9.a2-a4 ...

White gained nothing after 9.cxd5 cxd5, because black would have made more use of the c-file than him.

9... h7-h6

A waste of time. 9...0-0 was simpler and better.

10.b2-b3	♕d8-e7
11.♘f3-e1	...

White's plan is to transfer the knight to d3 and then prepare e4.

11...	0-0
12.♘e1-d3	d5xc4

An original plan. Black decides against the typical development of the knight to e4 and starts a pawn attack in the center on his own.

13.b3xc4   c6-c5?

This mistake opens the diagonal for the bishop on g2. After 13...e5 14.c5 ♗c7 15.d5 ♕f7 white would have a small advantage.

14.e2-e3   ♖a8-b8

Black is already on the verge of losing. If 14...e5 15.dxe5! ♘xe5 16.♘f4 black would just as equally be in a very bad shape.

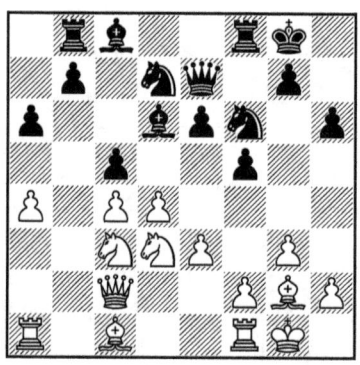

15.f2-f4!?   ...

Securing the e5 square for the knight. 15.a5 would be even stronger.

15...   ♕e7-d8

15...b6 was bad due to 16.♘e5 with threats ♘c6 and ♘g6.

16.♘d3-e5   ♕d8-b6?

A poor maneuver that only makes black's position more difficult. 16...♕c7 was better. Black's best is 16...cxd4 17.exd4 ♗b4 and white would be somewhat better.

17.♖a1-b1   ♕b6-a7
18.♗c1-a3   ...

Black overlooked this simple move. Now the pin on c5 is very unpleasant.

18...   ♘f6-e8
19.♖f1-d1   c5xd4

This move loses, but not more than any other would do.

20.♗a3xd6   ♘e8xd6
21.♘e5xd7   ♘d6xc4

21...♗xd7 22.♖xd4 ♕c5 23.♕d3 loses a piece.

22.♘d7xf8   ♘c4xe3
23.♕c2-f2   ♔g8xf8

Or 23...♘xd1 24.♖xd1! ♔xf8 25.♕xd4 with an extra piece for white.

24.♖d1-d3   ♗c8-d7
25.♘c3-e2   ♗d7-c6

If 25...♘xg2, then 26.♘xd4!

26.♘e2xd4   ♗c6xg2
27.♕f2xe3. Black resigned.

**No. 22. Sergei Belavenets –
Lev Kaiev
Soviet Championship semi-final
Kiev 1938**

Bogo-Indian Defense E11

1.d2-d4   ♘g8-f6
2.c2-c4   e7-e6
3.g2-g3   ♗f8-b4+

This leads to a slightly worse game for black. The most solid move is 3...d5 with the subsequent ♗e7, 0-0 and b6, transposing into well-known Queen's Indian lines.

4.♗c1-d2   ♗b4xd2+
5.♕d1xd2   0-0
6.♗f1-g2   ♘b8-c6
7.♘g1-f3   d7-d6
8.♘b1-c3   e6-e5
9.0-0   ♗c8-g4

After 9...exd4 10.♘xd4, white would be more mobile, so black forcibly defuses the pawn tension in the center.

10.d4-d5	♘c6-e7
11.♘f3-e1	♘f6-d7

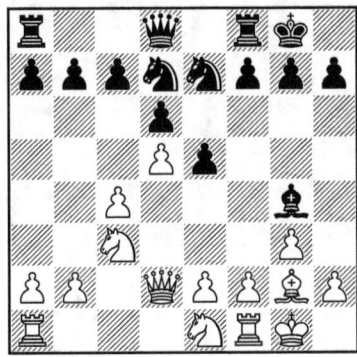

12.♘e1-d3 ...

The immediate 12.e4 was more active, preventing f5, an important move for black, because of 12...f5 13.f3 ♗h5 14.exf5. It's harder for black to defend in this case.

12...	f7-f5
13.f2-f3	...

The bishop should be deflected from defending e6.

13...	♗g4-h5
14.e2-e4	♗h5-g6
15.f3-f4	f5xe4
16.♘c3xe4	♘e7-f5?

A mistake that forces black to give up a pawn. He should have played 16...♗xe4 17.♗xe4 exf4 18.♘xf4 ♘c5 19.♗g2 ♘g6, and black can hope for a successful defense.

In this line, white gets a big advantage after 19.♘e6! ♘xe6 (or 19...♘xe4 20.♕d4) 20.dxe6. Black indeed needed to trade on e4, but after 16...♗xe4 17.♗xe4, he had to settle for the calm 17...c6 with somewhat worse chances.

17.f4xe5	♘d7xe5
18.♘d3xe5	d6xe5
19.♘e4-c5	♘f5-d4

The pawn could be saved with 19...♕d6, but then, after 20.♘e6 ♖f7 21.c5 ♕e7 22.♖ae1, white has a significant advantage. Black is counting on his strong d4 knight to provide some compensation.

20.♘c5xb7	♕d8-e7
21.c4-c5	...

21.♖ae1 was weaker because of 21...♖xf1+ 22.♖xf1 ♖b8 23.♘a5 ♕c5, and black's position is quite active.

21...	♖a8-b8
22.d5-d6	c7xd6
23.♘b7xd6	♕e7-c7
24.b2-b4	...

It turns out that black has nothing for the pawn.

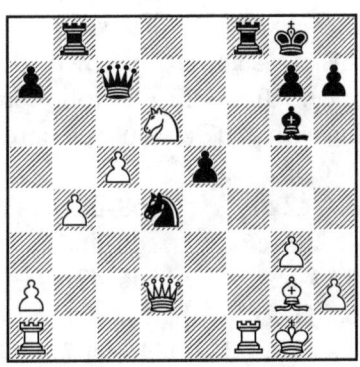

24...	♖f8-d8

After 24...♘c2, there's 25.♖xf8+.

25.a2-a3	♔g8-h8

Not 25...♘b3 due to 26.♕d5+.

26.♖a1-e1 ...

A sloppy move that allows black to trade the d6 knight. The correct move was 26.♕g5, and black would have likely lost quickly.

26... ♘d4-f5
27.♖e1xe5 ...

White misses a decisive blow, as 27.♖xf5! ♗xf5 28.♖xe5 ♗g6 29.h4 h6 30.♕d4 would clearly win.

27... ♘f5xd6
28.c5xd6 ...

The fantastic 28.♕f4!! would win more effectively.

28... ♖d8xd6
29.♕d2-e3 h7-h6
30.♕e3-c5 ♕c7-d7
31.♖e5-d5?! ...

Exchanging a pair of rooks helps black. 31.♖e1 ♖d1! would also give him chances to hold. On the other hand, after 31.♗h3! ♕d8 32.♕xa7 ♖a8 33.♕e3 white would win convincingly.

31... ♖d6xd5
32.♕c5xd5 ♕d7xd5?

This is signing his own death sentence. After 32...♕e8 followed by waiting with ♔h7 it would be hard for white to progress.

33.♗g2xd5 ♖b8-d8
34.♗d5-c6 ♖d8-d6
35.b4-b5 ♖d6-d3
36.♖f1-a1 ...

36.a4 ♖a3 37.♖f8+ ♔h7 38.♖a8 was simpler.

36... ♖d3-b3
37.a3-a4 ♗g6-d3
38.♖a1-e1 ♖b3-a3
39.♖e1-e3 ♖a3-a1+

40.♔g1-f2 ...

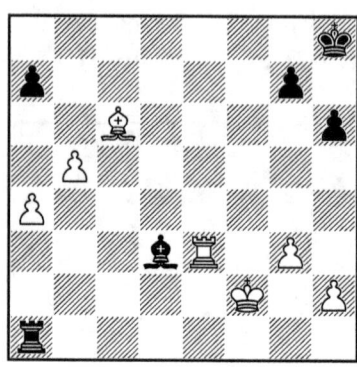

40... ♗d3-c2

After 40...♖a2+ 41.♔f3 ♗c2, white wins with 42.♖e8+ ♔h7 43.♖a8 ♗xa4 44.♗e4+ etc.

41.♖e3-e7 ...

41.♖e8+ ♔h7 42.♖a8 was even more precise, and black can't play 42...♗xa4 due to 43.♗e4+.

Black resigned, but prematurely, because after 41...♖xa4 42.b6 axb6 43.♗xa4 ♗xa4 black had chances to hold.

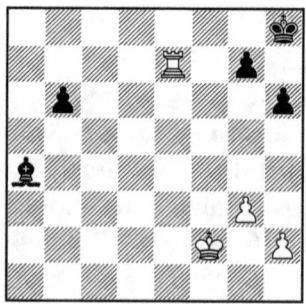

White probably still wins, but black had chances as the next position is a draw:

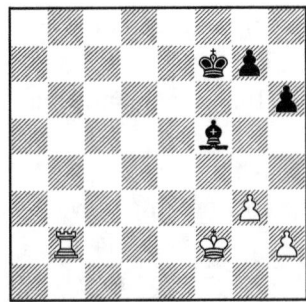

Black to play (Tibor Karolyi)

1...g5! 2.♔e3 ♗h7!!

a) 3.♖b7+ ♔g6! 4.♔d4 ♗g8 5.♔e5 ♗c4! 6.♖b6+ ♔g7 7.♔f5 ♗d3+

b) 3.♔d4 ♗g8! 4.♔e5 ♔g7 5.♖b6 (5.♔f5 ♗h7+=; 5.♖b7+ ♔g6=; 5.h4 gxh4 6.gxh4 ♔g6=)

5...♗c4! 6.♖d6 ♗a2 7.♖a6 ♗c4 8.♖c6 and 8...♗a2 or 8...♗g8 draws.

No. 23. Sergei Belavenets – Vasily Panov
Moscow Championship, 1938
Queen's Gambit D31

1.d2-d4	d7-d5
2.c2-c4	c7-c6
3.♘g1-f3	e7-e6
4.♘b1-c3	♘b8-d7

Black obviously intends to play the Stonewall system and preemptively protects the e5 square. However, the immediate f7-f5 was more logical, because white's next move radically prevents this.

| 5.e2-e4 | d5xe4 |
| 6.♘c3xe4 | ♘g8-f6 |

After 6...♗b4+ 7.♗d2 ♗xd2+ 8.♕xd2, the threat ♘d6+ is rather unpleasant.

| 7.♗f1-d3 | ♗f8-b4+ |
| 8.♔e1-f1 | ... |

Without a doubt, the best move. White avoids simplifications and gets a very open position. After 8.♗d2 ♗xd2+ 9.♕xd2 ♘xe4 10.♗xe4 ♘f6 11.♗c2 0-0, it's much easier for black to equalize.

The engine recommends 8.♘c3 or 8.♗d2, but it doesn't like the king move too much.

| 8... | ♘f6xe4 |

The e4 knight is positioned just too well. It's necessary to eliminate it.

9.♗d3xe4	♘d7-f6
10.♗e4-c2	b7-b6
11.♗c1-f4	...

11.h4 ♗b7 12.♖h3 ♗d6 13.♕e2 ♕c7 14.b3 0-0-0 15.♗b2 h6 16.♘e5 *was worth considering, with somewhat better chances for white, Alekhine – Kunerth, Lublin/Warsaw/Krakow 1942*

11...	♗b4-d6
12.♘f3-e5	♗c8-b7
13.♕d1-e2	...

Overprotecting the e5 knight, which could be useful in case of, say, ♕c7 (this can be countered with c4-c5), and preventing ♘h5 at the same time.

| 13... | ♕d8-e7 |

After 13...♕c7, as already stated, white had 14.c5, and if 14...bxc5 15.dxc5 ♗xc5, then 16.♘g6, winning an exchange.

Alas, this doesn't work because of 16...♕b6! 17.♘xh8 ♗a6 18.♗d3 ♗xd3 19.♕xd3 ♕xb2. Therefore, white would have to settle for 14.h4 with slightly better chances.

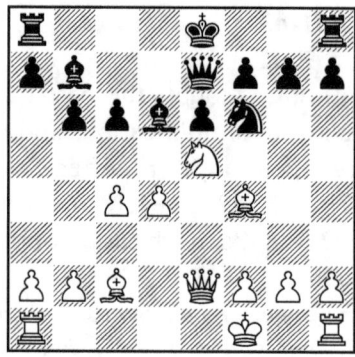

14.♗c2-a4 ...

White is trying to prevent his opponent from castling long – kingside castling would be too dangerous. However, the game move is still dubious, because the bishop takes up a passive position. The same idea could be executed with 14.a3, because if 14...0-0-0, then 15.b4, with an attack unfolding easily. Short castling with the bishop remaining on c2 was obviously bad.

14... ♖a8-c8

After 14...♕c7, 15.c5 doesn't work due to 15...bxc5 16.dxc5 ♗xc5 17.♘g6 ♕b6, threatening ♗a6. However, 15.b4 is possible: 15...♗xb4 16.♘g6.

15.h2-h4 ...

A typical way to develop the h1 rook in this opening.

15... h7-h6?

Black had a playable position, but this mistake makes it very difficult. If 15...♘d7, then 16.♕g4 0-0 and black would be doing OK, but not 16...g6? 17.♖d1, and then 17...♘xe5 is bad for black, because after 18.dxe5 ♗c5 19.♗g5, the white bishop invades f6.

Probably the best continuation was 15...0-0, and white has no forced continuation for his attack. For instance, 16.♗c2 c5, and black can still fight.

16.♖h1-h3! ...

A superb attacking move.

16... ♘f6-d7

Short castling would have allowed white to attack with g2-g4-g5.

17.♕e2-g4 ...

17.♖d1! is clearly stronger.

17... g7-g6

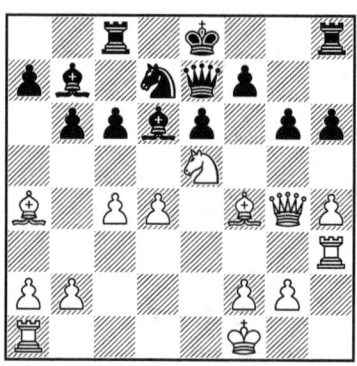

18.♖h3-e3? ...

This gives black an opportunity to defend seriously. White should have played the quiet 18.♖d1. After 18...♘xe5 19.dxe5 ♗c7, there's 20.h5 g5 21.♗h2, and black's position is difficult because of the threat f4.

18.h5 was bad because of 18...g5 (18...♘f6?! 19.♕f3 ♘xh5 20.♘xc6 is better for white).

18... ♘d7xe5

19.♗f4xe5 ...

After 19.dxe5, the rook's move to e3 would have been rendered unnecessary, so white goes for a more open position. Interestingly, the pawn capture is still the stronger recapture as it gives the black pieces less room.

19...	♗d6xe5
20.♖e3xe5	h6-h5
21.♕g4-f4	♔e8-f8
22.♖a1-e1?!	...

22.♗c2! is more precise.

| 22... | ♔f8-g7? |

22...♗a6! would avoid a clear loss.

| 23.♗a4-c2 | ... |

The break 23.d5 cxd5 24.cxd5 doesn't work because of 24...♕c7! 25.dxe6 f6 26.♖d1 ♗a6+ 27.♔g1 ♕xe5. Now white threatens ♗xg6.

| 23... | ♕e7-f6 |
| 24.♕f4-g3 | ... |

Again threatening ♗xg6.

| 24... | ♖h8-h6 |

The more committal move 24...♔h6 is met with 25.♖1e4, threatening 26.♖f4 ♕e7 27.♖xh5+ ♔xh5 (or gxh5) 28.♖xf7! So, black has to put his rook on an awkward square.

There's an even stronger move: 25.♗xg6! ♕xg6 26.♖g5 ♕f6 27.♖ee5 *or* 25...fxg6 26.♖xe6 ♕f5 27.♕e3+ ♔g7 28.♖e7+, *winning.*

| 25.♔f1-g1 | ♖c8-d8 |

25...c5 only creates new weaknesses after 26.dxc5. Thus, black goes for a waiting strategy, especially considering that it's rather hard for white to open any lines.

| 26.♖e1-e4 | ♕f6-e7 |
| 27.♕g3-c3 | ♔g7-h7 |

The immediate 27...♔g8 would lose as well.

| 28.♖e4-f4 | ♔h7-g8 |
| 29.b2-b4 | ... |

White's plan is to push the queenside pawns. Black, in return, prepares counterplay on the kingside.

| 29... | ♖h6-h7 |
| 30.a2-a4 | ♖h7-g7 |

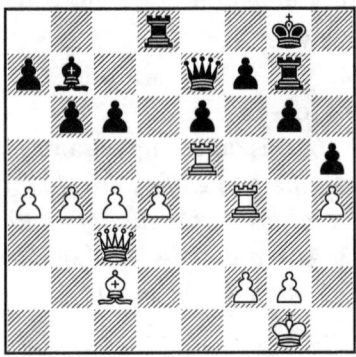

Natural, but not good. Black had to play 30...a6. In this case, he could meet 31.c5 with 31...b5, and white wouldn't have achieved much.

| 31.c4-c5 | ♗b7-c8 |

Now 31...b5 would have been met with 32.axb5 cxb5 33.c6, and white is better. Black defends the e6 pawn in advance, intending to open up play on the kingside.

| 32.c5xb6 | ... |

Preparing the action would be stronger, for example 32.♗b3 would be decisive.

32...	a7xb6
33.a4-a5	f7-f6
34.♖e5-e1	b6xa5
35.b4xa5	g6-g5?

This loses, whereas black could resist with 35...f5 or 35...♔h7.

| 36.h4xg5 | ♖g7xg5 |
| 37.♗c2-b3 | ... |

Creating pressure on the e6 pawn.

| 37... | ♔g8-g7 |
| 38.♖f4-e4 | ♕e7-a3 |

39.♖e1-a1 ...

Less clear was 39.♕xc6 ♕xa5 (39...♕xb3 40.♕c7+) 40.♗xe6 ♗xe6 followed by 41...♕d5, and white wouldn't be certain of converting his extra pawn.

39... ♕a3-d6
40.♕c3-e3 ...

40.a6 c5 is quite unpleasant.

Still, the straightforward 40.a6 led to the goal faster, because after 40...c5 there's 41.♖a5! cxd4 42.♖xg5+ fxg5 43.♕a5 with decisive threats.

40... c6-c5
41.d4xc5 ...

41.♖d1 would end the game quickly.

41... ♕d6-c6!

The only chance. After 41...♕xc5 42.♕xc5 ♖xc5 43.a6, the a-pawn decides matters.

42.♖a1-c1 ...

The only move that keeps the advantage. The more natural 42.f3 leads to unpleasant complications after 42...♕b5!

42... e6-e5
43.♗b3-a4 ♕c6-a8

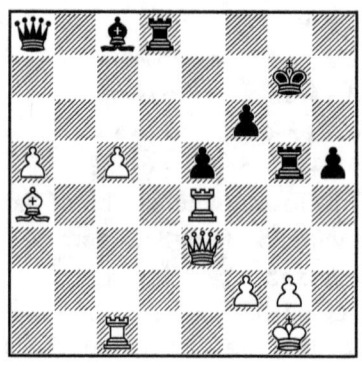

44.c5-c6 ...

By giving away the a-pawn, white eliminates all of black's attacking resources. The strong c6 pawn gives him an advantage.

44... ♕a8xa5
45.♕e3-a3? ...

45.c7 was worse because of 45...♖d6, and it's unclear how white can improve his position.

The improvement plan is to put the bishop on f3, then play ♖h4 and organize an attack on the king. There would be no defence for black.

45... ♕a5-c7

White was threatening ♕e7+, but black could have allowed it with 45...♕d5! and suddenly he would have realistic chances to hold.

46.♗a4-d1 ...

Both preventing ♖g4 and preparing ♗f3 and ♖a4.

46... ♖d8xd1+!!

Black finds a great saving resource in a difficult position.

He could have played 46...♗f5 as well, and if 47.♖a4 then 47...♖xd1+ and equal chances. Had white met 46...♗f5 with 47.♖ec4 then black could stay alive with 47...♗e6. It seems that white's best option is 47.♖h4 e4 48.♗e2 ♗g6 and black would struggle, but is not necessarily lost.

47.♖c1xd1 ♕c7xc6
48.♕a3-e7+ ♔g7-g6?

The losing move. Instead, the brilliant 48...♔h6!! would keep black in the game. Now on 49.♖d6 black could rescue himself with 49...♖xg2+!. White could also have played 49.f3, and if 49...♖xg2+, then 50.♔xg2

♕c2+ 51.♔g3 ♕xd1 52.♕xf6+ ♔h7 53.♔h4!, winning. However, after *49... ♗h3! black draws, for instance: 50.♔h2 ♖g7! 51.♖d6 (51.♕f8 ♕c2!) 51...♖xe7 52.♖xc6 ♗f5 53.♖b4 ♔g5 and black holds.*

49.♖d1-d6	♖g5xg2+
50.♔g1-h1!	♕c6xe4
51.♕e7xf6+	♔g6-h7
52.♕f6-h6+	♔h7-g8
53.♖d6-d8+	♔g8-f7
54.♖d8-f8+	♔f7-e7
55.♕h6-f6+	♔e7-d7
56.♖f8-f7+.	

Black resigned.

No. 24. Sergei Belavenets – Ilya Rabinovich
11ᵗʰ Soviet Championship
Leningrad 1939
Ruy Lopez C76

1.e2-e4	e7-e5
2.♘g1-f3	♘b8-c6
3.♗f1-b5	a7-a6
4.♗b5-a4	d7-d6
5.c2-c3	♗c8-d7
6.0-0	g7-g6
7.d2-d4	♗f8-g7
8.♖f1-e1	...

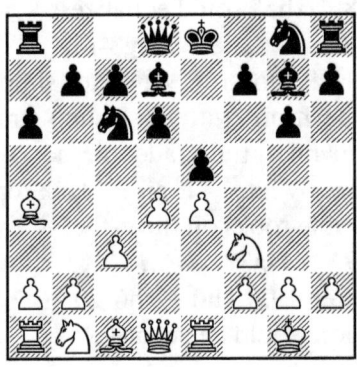

8... ♕d8-e7

In the 1930s, it was thought that 8...♘f6 didn't work because of 9.♗xc6 ♗xc6 10.dxe5 ♘xe4 *(10... dxe5 11.♕xd8+ ♖xd8 12.♘xe5 ♗xe4 13.f3 ♗xb1 14.♘xg6+)* 11.exd6 ♕xd6 12.♕xd6 cxd6 13.♘g5 0-0 14.♖xe4 ♗xe4 15.♘xe4 ♖fe8 16.♘bd2 d5 17.♘g3 ♖e1+ 18.♘gf1! with the subsequent ♘b3 and ♗d2, which is why Rabinovich played 8...♕e7 – to prevent this combination. However, subsequent analyses added a number of improvements to the line above: for instance, even in the final position, black still has a good game after 18...d4!, but there are some improvements "along the way" as well. All in all, 8...♘f6 proved its right to exist – together with 8...♕e7, 8...b5 and 8...♘ge7 (currently the most popular move).

In addition, deferring the development of the g8 knight, black doesn't let up the pressure on the d4 pawn, interfering with white's development as well.

9.h2-h3 ...
Preventing a possible ♗g4.
9... h7-h6
Continuing with the same waiting strategy.
10.♗a4-c2 ...
White didn't want to play 10.d5 because it would have made black's counter-strike f7-f5 stronger. He also didn't like 10.♗e3 because he intended to keep this square for his knight. However, he should have played 10.♗e3 after all, because the

quiet 10.♗c2 allows black to launch a kingside attack.

10...   g6-g5

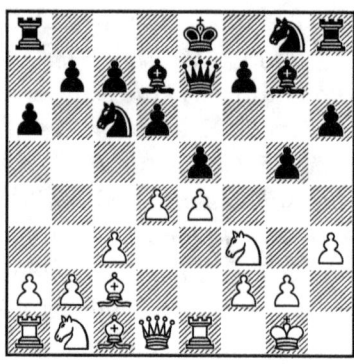

11.d4xe5   ...

The beginning of an erroneous plan. Even now, white should have played 11.♗e3, preventing h6-h5 and avoiding opening the d-file, which will be seized by black.

11...   d6xe5
12.♘b1-d2?   ...

A careless move. 12.b4 would be stronger.

12...   h6-h5!

This pawn move exploits white's mistake.

13.♘d2-f1   g5-g4
14.♘f3-h2   0-0-0!
15.♕d1-e2   ...

15.♘e3 gave white nothing: 15... gxh3 16.g3 ♗g4 17.♘d5 ♕d7 18.f3 (18.♘xg4 hxg4 19.♘e3 is better, but black still has the advantage) 18... ♗e6, and white has to retreat with his d5 knight, because 19.c4 cedes the d4 square to black. Or if 19.♗b3, then 19...f5.

15...   g4xh3

16.g2-g3   ...

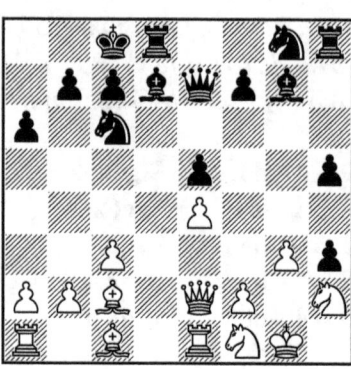

White had this position in mind when he made his 10th move. He thought that the f1 and h2 knights defended the kingside very well, and a pawn storm of the black king's position could be successful. This evaluation, however, turned out to be not entirely correct.

16...   ♗g7-h6
17.b2-b4   ...

17.♘e3 would be preferable.

17...   ♘c6-b8?

To avoid b5, opening the b-file. Black would be clearly better after 17...♗xc1! 18.♖axc1 h4 19.g4 ♕g5.

18.a2-a4?   ...

18.♕xh5! would equalize.

18...   ♘g8-f6

Black doesn't want to simplify the position with a bishop trade. Meanwhile, the trade on h6 is no good for white – it gives black tempi to double rooks on the g-file.

19.♗c1-a3?   ...

After 19.♗xh6 ♖xh6 20.♘e3 the position would be equal.

19... ♕e7-e6

19...♕e8 was stronger, and if 20.♗b2, then 20...♕e6, or since the bishop is positioned worse on b2 than on a3, then if 20.♘f3 black replies 20...♗g4.

20.b4-b5   a6-a5
21.♖a1-b1   ♖d8-g8

The immediate 21...h4 would be just about winning for black, for example after 22.♗b3 ♕b6! 23.g4 ♖hg8.

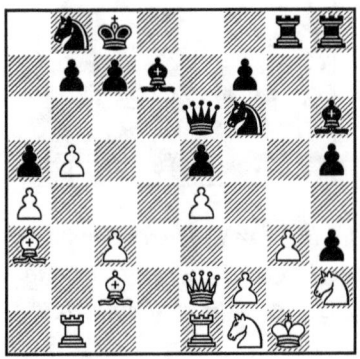

22.c3-c4?   ...

The preliminary 22.♗b3! was stronger, forcing the queen to take up a passive position on e8.

22...   h5-h4
23.♔g1-h1   ...

Black threatened 23...hxg3 24.fxg3 ♘h5, and white can't play 25.♕xh5 because of 25...♗e3+.

23...   h4xg3
24.f2xg3?! ...

24.♘xg3 would be less bad.

24...   ♘f6-g4

24...♗f4!! 25.gxf4 exf4! intending ♖g2 would win.

25.c4-c5   c7-c6

Or else c5-c6 destroys the black king's position.

This cautious move loses a large part of the advantage. 25...♘xh2 26.♔xh2 ♕f6! was much stronger, for example: 27.♗b3 (27.c6? ♗g4) 27...♗f4 28.c6 ♗xg3+ 29.♘xg3 ♖xg3 30.cxd7+ ♘xd7, and black is winning.

26.♗c2-b3   ♕e6-g6
27.♘h2-f3   ...

A mistake that allows black to increase the pressure. White should have played 27.bxc6 ♘xc6 (27...♗xc6?! 28.♘xg4 ♕xg4 29.♗xf7) 28.♗d5 with double-edged play.

27...   h3-h2!

Now white constantly has to reckon with the threat ♘f2+. His only chance is to complicate matters on the queenside. It's too dangerous to open up the h-file with 28.♘xh2.

28.b5xc6   ♗d7xc6
29.♗b3-d5   ...

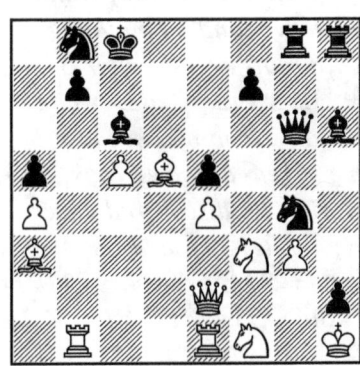

29...   ♗h6-f4

A flashy, but incorrect move. The right continuation was 29...f5!. White can't capture the g8 rook because of the weakness of the h1-a8 diagonal.

A white queenside counter-attack wouldn't have worked either, because black could easily defend the b7 square by placing the rooks on the seventh rank.

After 29...f5 white can more or less hold after 30.♘h4 ♕f6 31.♗xc6 ♘xc6 32.♘xf5. However, black had a stunning combination 29...♗xd5 30.exd5 ♕d3!! at his disposal, after which white's chances of drawing are remote.

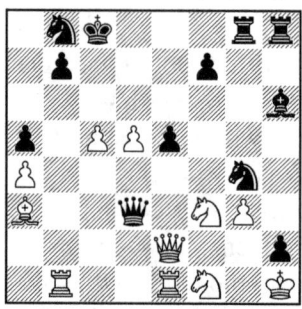

Now, if the a3 bishop moves, black simply plays 31...♕xd5, winning a second pawn and eliminating all of white's threats. While after 31.♕xd3 ♘f2+ 32.♔xh2 ♘xd3, white loses at least an exchange, because he has no time to retreat the e1 rook: 33.♖e2 is met with the discovered check 33...♗c1+, while 33.♖ed1 is met with 33...♗e3+ 34.♘h4 (34.♔g2 ♘f4#!) 34...♖xh4+ 35.gxh4 ♗g1+ 36. ♔h1 ♘f2#!

Well, in 2024 we can say that black has another incredible way to attack: 29...♗e3!! 30.♘xe5 ♕ex4! would win. Or 30.♘xe3 ♘xe3 31.♕xe3 ♕xg3 32. ♖b2 ♕g1+ and black checkmates on the next move.

30.♗d5xc6 ...
30.gxf4 loses: 30...♘f2+ 31.♕xf2 ♕g1+ 32.♕xg1 hxg1=♕#.
30... ♘b8xc6

After this mistake, white gets good counterplay on the queenside. Both players thought that 30...♕xc6!! was impossible because of 31.gxf4, but then black had a beautiful tactical blow.

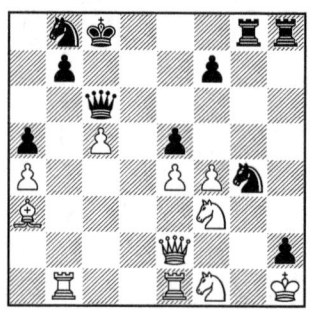

a) 31...♕xe4! The queen cannot be captured because of mate in one, and 32.c6 is met with a simple, but pretty combination, 32...♘f2+ 33.♕xf2 ♕xf3+! 34.♕xf3 ♖g1#. Thus, white should protect the g1 square with 32.♘1d2, but after 32...♕xf4, black already has three pawns for the piece, and the king on h1 is still in grave danger. White's only chance is to try and create mutual threats with 33.c6! ♘xc6 34.♖ec1.

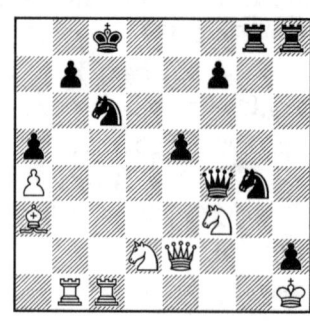

If now black blunders 34...♕g3??, he gets checkmated after 35.♖xc6+! bxc6 36.♕a6+. 34...♕g6 is met with 35.♖c4, after which both 35...♕h6 36.♘e4 and 35...♕g3 36.♖xc6+! ♖xc6 37.♘e4 ♕f4 38.♘d6+ lead to an unclear position. Nevertheless, black retains the advantage with 35...♕e3. However, in the last diagram position, the most precise move is 34...♖h6!, because now 35.♖c4 ♕g3 36.♖xc6+ ♖xc6 37.♘e4 is met with 37...♘f2+! (in 2024 we can say that 37...♕f4 wins) 38.♕xf2 ♕xf2 39.♘xf2 ♖f6, and white has to give up one of his knights (40.♖b3 ♖g3).

b) Well, in 2024 we can say that black has another, better tactical blow as well: 31...exf4!! 32.♖b2 ♘d7 and black then wins with ♘de5.

31.♕e2-b2   ♘c6-b4

If 31...♘d8?, then 32.c6, and black can't play 32...♕xc6 due to 33.♖ec1. If 31...♔d8 then 32.♖e2 ♗xg3 33.♘xg3 f2 34.♖xf2 ♕xg3 with a balanced position.

32.♗a3xb4   a5xb4
33.♖e1-e2   f7-f5
34.♕b2xb4   ♖h8-h7

34...♕c6! was stronger, both protecting b7 and blocking the c5 pawn.

35.♕b4-a5   ...

Mind-boggling complications occur after 35.c6!? ♕xc6 36.♕b3 ♖gg7! 37.♖c2 ♔b8!, for instance: 38.♖xc6 ♘f2+ 39.♔g2 h1=♕+ 40.♔xf2 fxe4 with mutual chances. The game move is enough to maintain the balance.

35...   ♔c8-b8
36.♖b1-b6   ♕g6-h5

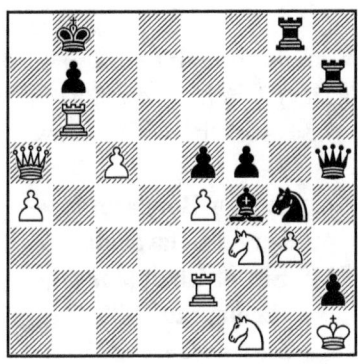

37.♖b6-a6!   ...

Black has created a number of serious threats (♘e3 and ♕h3), so white has no time to waste.

37...   b7xa6
38.♖e2-b2+   ♖h7-b7

Forced: after 38...♔c8 39.♕xa6+ black will be mated.

39.♖b2xb7+   ♔b8xb7
40.♕a5-b6+   ♔b7-c8
41.♕b6-e6+   ...

And a draw was agreed because of the following:

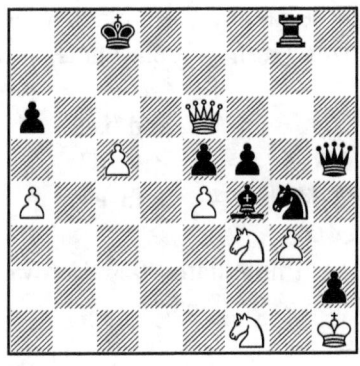

41...♔d8 (otherwise, there's perpetual check) 42.♕xg8+ ♔c7 43.♘3xh2! (43.♘1xh2 ♗xg3 44.♔g2 with equality) 43...♗xg3 44.♕e6!

♘f2+ (44...♘xh2 45.♘xg3 loses, but 44...♗xh2 is enough to draw) 45.♔g1 (not 45.♔g2 ♕h3+ 46.♔g1 ♘xe4) 45...♘h3+ 46.♔h1 with a draw.

No. 25. Igor Bondarevsky – Sergei Belavenets
11th Soviet Championship
Leningrad 1939
Slav Defense D45

1. d2-d4   ♘g8-f6
2. c2-c4   e7-e6
3. ♘g1-f3   d7-d5
4. ♘b1-c3   c7-c6
5. e2-e3   ♘b8-d7
6. ♘f3-e5   ...

Rubinstein's move. It doesn't promise white much of an advantage, but it allows him to avoid the double-edged Meran Variation.

Sometimes white plays 6.b3 with the same intention, but after 6...♗b4 7.♗d2 0-0 8.♗d3 dxc4 9.♗xc4 (9.bxc4 e5!) 9...♕e7 with the subsequent e6-e5 black quickly equalizes (Kan – Belavenets, round 7).

6...   ♘d7xe5
7. d4xe5   ♘f6-d7
8. f2-f4   ♗f8-e7
9. c4xd5   ...

The immediate 9.♗d3 wasn't good due to 9...♘c5.

9...   e6xd5

After 9...cxd5, the pawn structure in the center became immobile, and white could transfer his knight to the excellent d4 square.

10. ♗f1-d3 ♘d7-c5
11. ♗d3-c2 f7-f5

It's necessary to prevent the unpleasant threat f4-f5. White's protected passer on e5 does not pose a serious danger, because white can't move it forward. Chances are roughly equal. The move 6.♘e5 was not dangerous for black.

12. 0-0   0-0
13. b2-b3   g7-g6
14. ♗c1-b2 ...

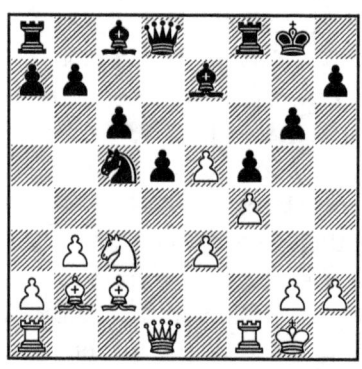

14...   ♘c5-e4

The most solid continuation. White's kingside initiative after the knight trade is not dangerous for black. Instead of 14...♘e4, black could choose a more difficult plan with 14...♘e6, intending b7-b6, ♗b7 and c6-c5. This would lead to unclear play, because white could launch a kingside attack with g2-g4.

14...b6 is bad due to 15.b4 ♘e4 (if 15...♘e6, then 16.b5) 16.♗xe4 dxe4 17.♕b3+ with a clear advantage for white (Makogonov – Yudovich, round 7), although 16...fxe4! leads to a somewhat smaller disadvantage for black.

15.♘c3xe4   d5xe4

After 15...fxe4, the position would be balanced as well.

16.♕d1-e2   ...

The queen trade 16.♕xd8 ♖xd8 17.♖ad1 ♗e6 doesn't give white any advantage. Black's extra queenside pawn provides enough compensation for the white e5 passed pawn.

16...   ♗c8-e6
17.g2-g4   ♕d8-e8
18.g4xf5   g6xf5
19.♔g1-h1   h7-h6
20.♕e2-g2+   ♔g8-h7
21.♕g2-h3   ♗e7-c5

Black has found the weakness in white's position – the e3 pawn. Now the sacrifice 22.♗xe4 fxe4 23.f5 gives white nothing, so he tries to use his last chance and transfer his bishop to h5.

22.♖f1-g1   ♕e8-f7

22...♕e7 was less precise, as it allowed 23.b4! and 23...♗xb4? runs into 24.♖g5! as 24...♖g8 loses to 25.♖xf5, whereas the queen on f7 stops this threat.

23.♗c2-d1   ...

If 23.b4?, black can just take the pawn.

23...   ♖f8-g8
24.♗d1-h5   ♕f7-e7
25.♖a1-d1   ...

Black's position is completely defended, and white can't improve his position. Trying to transfer his second bishop to h4 gives him nothing. After 25.♗c3 ♖ad8 26.♖xg8 ♖xg8 27.♗e1 ♕g7, he can't play 28.♗h4 because of 28...♗xe3!.

25...   ♖g8xg1+
26.♖d1xg1   ♖a8-g8
27.♖g1xg8   ♔h7xg8
28.♕h3-g3+   ♕e7-g7
29.♗b2-d4   ...

Without the dark-squared bishop trade, the weak e3 pawn would have been a liability for white. But now black also gets a protected passed pawn.

29...   ♗c5xd4
30.e3xd4   ♔g8-f8

It's not beneficial for black to trade queens, because after 30...♕xg3 31.hxg3, white can play g3-g4 and create two connected passed pawns.

31.♔h1-g2   ♕g7-e7

Threatening to invade on a3 or b4 with the queen, which is unacceptable for white. With this move, black forces a queen trade on g7.

32.♕g3-g6   ♕e7-g7
33.♕g6-g3   ♕g7-e7
34.♕g3-g6   ♕e7-g7
35.♕g6xg7+   ♔f8xg7
36.♗h5-d1   b7-b5

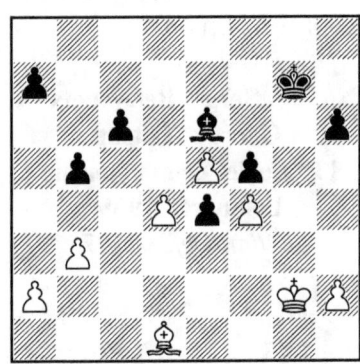

The simplest way to draw. Black prevents the white king from getting to the queenside. White can't break through on the kingside either, because the h5 square can always be defended with the bishop.

37.a2-a3　a7-a5
38.b3-b4　a5xb4

Even though almost all black pawns are on light squares, the endgame is still drawn. The e4 passed pawn greatly limits the mobility of white's pieces.

39.a3xb4　♔g7-f7
40.♗d1-h5+　♔f7-e7
41.♗h5-g6　♔e7-d7
42.♔g2-f2　♔d7-e7
43.♔f2-e3　♔e7-d7
44.d4-d5　c6xd5
45.♔e3-d4　♔d7-e7
46.♗g6-h5　♗e6-d7
47.♔d4xd5　♗d7-e6+
48.♔d5-d4　♗e6-d7

A draw was agreed after a few more moves. Black just holds passively, protecting the b5 and f5 pawns with his bishop. White will never win the b5 pawn, because the white king won't be able to catch the e4 pawn after capturing on b5.

No. 26. Sergei Belavenets – Georgy Lisitsin
11th Soviet Championship
Leningrad 1939

Sicilian Defense B75

1.e2-e4　c7-c5
2.♘g1-f3　d7-d6
3.d2-d4　c5xd4
4.♘f3xd4　♘g8-f6
5.♘b1-c3　g7-g6
6.f2-f3　♗f8-g7
7.♗c1-e3　♘b8-c6
8.♗f1-e2　...

Even though black doesn't threaten 8...d5 yet due to 9.♗b5, the most precise move here was still 8.♘b3, preventing the trade that happened in the game.

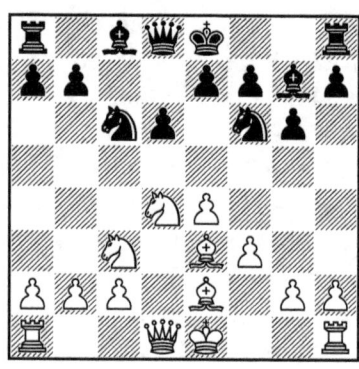

8...　♘c6xd4

This development system in the Sicilian Dragon was developed by Master Lisitsin himself. It's no worse than the usual 8...0-0 with the subsequent 9.♘b3 d5! 10.exd5 ♘b4 11.d6 ♕xd6 12.♗c5 ♕xd1+ 13.♖xd1 ♘c6 and a roughly equal game. However, in the game Yudovich – Chekhover, after 9.♘b3, instead of 9...d5, black played 9...♗e6 10.♘d5 ♘d7 and managed to prove that his position was no worse. I still think that the last line is somewhat better for white.

9.♗e3xd4　0-0
10.0-0　e7-e5

After 10...♗e6 with the subsequent ♕a5, ♖c8 etc., white doesn't have any advantage. This was the simplest way to equality. With the pawn structure in the game, white's chances are more tangible.

11.♗d4-e3	♗c8-e6
12.♘c3-d5	♘f6xd5
13.e4xd5	♗e6-d7
14.c2-c4	...

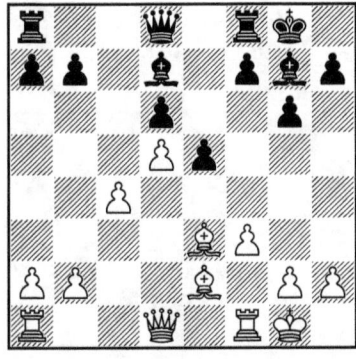

The plans of both players are clear. White should attack on the queenside, and black on the kingside. White's initiative is more effective, and he gains an advantage.

14...	b7-b6
15.♕d1-d2	...

White finishes development before pushing his pawns.

15...	f7-f5
16.♖a1-c1	f5-f4
17.♗e3-f2	g6-g5?!

The position would be balanced after 17...♗f5 18.b4 e4.

18.b2-b4   ♖f8-f6?

This move is aimed at enabling black both to attack on the kingside and block or attack white's coming passed d-pawn. However, black should play 18...♕f6 with a smaller disadvantage than in the game.

19.c4-c5!   b6xc5

It's unlikely anyone would have been satisfied with the position after 19...♖h6 20.c6 ♗c8 21.b5 ♕e8 22.♔h1 ♕h5 23.♗g1, and white is protected against direct threats, while the c6 pawn is very strong.

20.b4xc5	d6xc5
21.♗f2xc5	♕d8-e8
22.d5-d6	...

A correct move. The d6 pawn, despite running ahead of the pack, is not weak because it can always be defended adequately. On the other hand, black continuously has to watch out for its possible movements.

22...   ♔g8-h8

Avoiding checks on c4 and d5 that can potentially play an important tactical role.

23.♖f1-d1   ♖a8-d8

After 23...♗a4, white immediately wins with 24.d7!. Now, however, black threatens ♗a4 and then ♗f8.

24.♕d2-a5	♗g7-f8
25.♖d1-d5	...

The most active defense against ♗a4. White threatens to win a pawn with 26.♖xe5.

25...   ♖f6-e6

25...♗e6 was bad because of 26.♖xe5 ♗xd6 27.♗d4! After 25...♗c6, white would have still played 26.♖xe5 ♕xe5 27.♕xd8.

26.♗c5-a3   ...

Preventing 26...♗c6, which is now met with 27.♖xc6.

26...	♖d8-b8
27.♗e2-d3	...

27...♗c6 is still impossible due to 28.d7! ♗xd7 29.♗xf8, and wins. All white pieces are very well-placed, so black's planned sacrifice is his best practical chance. If black plays passively, white wins easily by piling on the pressure with ♗f5 or ♖c7, etc.

27... ♗f8-g7
28.♗d3-f5 e5-e4

28...♖h6 29.♗xd7 ♕xd7 30.♕c7 is obviously hopeless, with an easy win for white.

29.f3xe4 ♖e6xe4

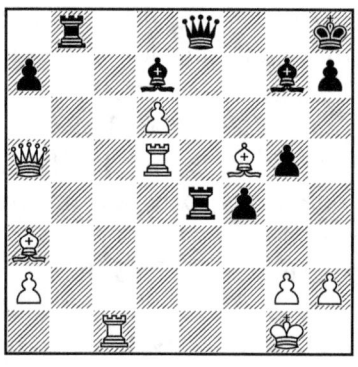

30.♗f5xe4 ...

White would win with 30.♗xd7 as well. 30...♕xd7 31.♕c7 ♕e8 (both 31...♖d8 32.♕xd7 and 31...♕xc7 32.dxc7 ♖c8 33.♖d8+ ♖e8 34.♖xe8+ lose quickly) 32.♕xb8! (32.♖dd1 ♖d8 is unclear, and white can't play 33.d7 due to 33...♗d4+!) 32...♕xb8 33.d7 ♕b6+ (the best. If 33...♕d8, then 34.♖c8 ♗f6 35.♗b2! wins) 34.♗c5 (34.♔h1? ♗f6!, and now it's black who wins) 34...♕d8 (or 34...♗d4+ 35.♖xd4!) 35.♗e7! ♖xe7 36.♖c8 ♖e1+ 37.♔f2, and black loses his queen and e1 rook.

30... ♕e8xe4
31.♖c1-e1 ...

White could also play 31.♕d2, gradually converting his material advantage. For example: 31...f3 32.♕d3!, and now black either has to trade queens or lose the f3 pawn.

The cleanest way to win was probably 31.♕xa7 ♖b1 32.♖dd1 ♗c6 33.♕f2 ♖xc1 34.♗xc1.

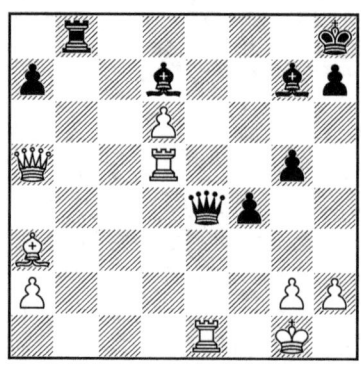

31... ♗g7-d4+?

Perhaps 31...♖b1! gave black better practical chances. Now white can't reply 32.♗c1 because of 32...♖xc1 33.♖xc1 ♕e3+. While after 32.♖dd1 ♗d4+ 33.♔h1 ♖xd1 34.♖xd1 f3, black checkmates by force.

After 31...♖b1, white's only move is 32.♕d8+ ♗e8 33.♕xe8+! ♕xe8 34.♖xb1 with good winning chances. For instance: after 34...♕e3+ 35.♔f1 ♕xa3? (if 35...f3, then 36.♖b8+ followed by ♖xf8+ and ♖xf3; *the most resilient is 35...♗f6, and after 36.♗c5 ♕e4 37.♖bd1, white has no big advantage because of 37...f3!)* 36.♖b8+ ♗f8 37.♖xf8+ *(after 37.d7 ♕c1+ 38.♔e2 ♕e3+ 39.♔d1 ♕g1+ 40.♔c2*

♕xg2+ 41.♖d2 ♕c6+ 42.♔b2 ♕f6+, white can't escape perpetual check) 37...♔g7 38.♖e8! ♕c1+ 39.♔f2 black soon runs out of checks, and the d6 passed pawn decides matters.

32.♔g1-h1   ♖b8-b1
33.♗a3-c1!   ...

Chasing beauty with 33.♕d8+ ♗e8 (33...♔g7!? is also fine) 34.♕xe8+ would lead to the opposite result after 34...♕xe8 35.♖xb1 ♕e4!.

33...   ♖b1xc1

There are no other ways to continue the attack.

34.♕a5-d8+   ♗d7-e8
35.♖e1xc1   f4-f3
36.♕d8xg5   ...

White also won after 36.♖xg5 f2 37.♕e7! (but not 37.♖f1? ♕e2).

36...   ♗e8-c6

An inventive resource, but even this is not enough.

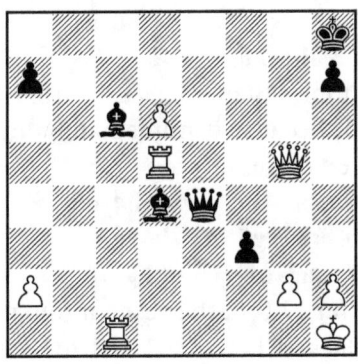

37.d6-d7!   ...

The simplest way to eliminate all of black's threats.

37...   f3xg2+
38.♕g5xg2   ♕e4xg2+
39.♔h1xg2   ♗c6xd5+

40.♔g2-f1   ♗d4-f6

The complications have ended, and white is an exchange up.

41.♖c1-c8+   ♔h8-g7
42.a2-a3   ...

The a-pawn has to be saved.

42...   a7-a5
43.d7-d8=♕   ♗f6xd8
44.♖c8xd8   ♗d5-b3
45.♖d8-d6   h7-h5
46.♔f1-f2   a5-a4
47.♔f2-g3   ♔g7-h7
48.♔g3-h4   ♔h7-g7

Or 48...♗f7 49.♖d7 ♔g7 50.♖a7.

49.♔h4xh5   ♔g7-h7
50.♖d6-d7+.

Black resigned.

**No. 27. Sergei Belavenets –
Vyacheslav Ragozin
11th Soviet Championship
Leningrad 1939**
Queen's Gambit D44

1.d2-d4   d7-d5
2.c2-c4   e7-e6
3.♘b1-c3   c7-c6
4.♘g1-f3   ♘g8-f6
5.♗c1-g5   d5xc4
6.e2-e4   b7-b5
7.e4-e5   h7-h6
8.♗g5-h4   g7-g5
9.♘f3xg5   ♘f6-d5

A double-edged line. Here, neither 10.♕h5 hxg5 11.♕xh8 gxh4 nor 10.♘f3 ♕a5 11.♕d2 ♗b4 12.♖c1 ♘d7 with the threat ♘d7-b6-a4 are good for white. The game move is the only way for white to still play for advantage.

10.♘g5xf7   ♛d8xh4
11.♘f7xh8   ♝f8-b4

11...♘xc3? 12.bxc3 ♝g7 loses to 13.♕c2! (but not 13.♘g6 ♕e4+ 14.♝e2 ♚d8!) 13...♝xh8 14.♕h7.

12.♕d1-d2   ...

If 12.♕c2, then 12...♕xd4.

Another promising theoretical line was 12.♖c1 ♕e4+ 13.♝e2 ♘f4 followed by 14.♕d2 or 14.a3.

12...   c6-c5

Necessary. As long as white has pawns on d4 and e5, black can't create an attack.

13.d4xc5   ...

This is probably the strongest move, even though 13.0-0-0 wasn't bad either, for instance:

1) 13...cxd4 14.♕xd4 ♕g5+ (or 14...♕xd4 15.♖xd4 ♘xc3 16.bxc3 ♝xc3 17.♖g4 ♝xe5 18.♖g8+) 15.f4 ♘xf4 16.♕d2;

2) 13...♘xc3 14.bxc3 ♝a3+ 15.♔b1 ♝b7 16.♝e2 (16.dxc5!?) 16...♘d7 17.♔a1 (Lilienthal – Ragozin, Leningrad 1947), with a clear advantage for white in both cases.

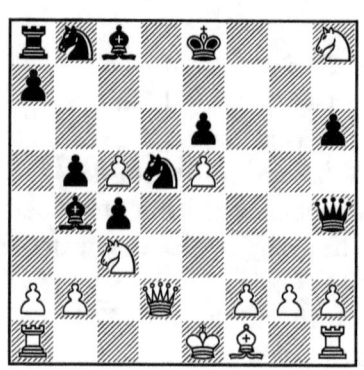

13...   ♝c8-b7

Too sluggish, allowing white to defend with relative ease. The best move was 13...♘d7, threatening both ♘xc5 and ♘xe5. In this case, it's not clear how to prove white's advantage.

The clear way to an advantage was found only almost half a century later: 14.g3! ♕h5 15.♝g2 ♝b7 (15...♕xe5+ 16.♔f1) 16.0-0 0-0-0 17.♕c2 (17.♘f7!? ♕xf7 18.♘xb5 ♝xd2 19.♘d6+ ♔c7 20.♘xf7) 17...♖xh8 (17...♘xe5 18.♕e4!!; 17...♝xc3 18.bxc3 ♖xh8 19.a4 etc.) 18.♘xb5 ♝xc5 19.♕xc4 Finegold – Waddingham, Oakham 1986.

14.♝f1-e2?!   ...

White has better moves here: 14.0-0-0! or 14.g3 ♕h5 15.♝e2 ♕xe5 16.♘g6, and black can't exploit the weakness of the a8-h1 diagonal. There's a beautiful possible line here: 16...♕f6 17.♝h5 ♘xc3 18.♘e7+! ♔xe7 19.♕d6#.

14...   ♘b8-d7
15.♘h8-g6   ...

Simpler than 15.g3 ♕h3 16.0-0-0 ♘xc5, because it immediately forces a queen trade.

15...   ♕h4-g5
16.♕d2xg5   h6xg5
17.♖a1-c1   ...

After 17.0-0, the best continuation for black is 17...♘xc3 18.bxc3 ♝xc3 19.♖ad1. Black equalizes after 19...♝e4! 20.c6 ♘c5 21.♝h5 ♔f7.

17...   ♔e8-f7
18.♝e2-h5   ♔f7-g7
19.0-0   ♝b4xc3

19...♔h6 20.g4 ♝xc5, with unclear play, was quite interesting.

If, for instance, 21.♘xb5, then 21...♘7b6 22.b3 ♖g8 23.bxc4 ♘b4, or 21.♘e4 ♖g8 22.♘xc5 ♘xc5 23.f4 ♖xg6 24.♗xg6 ♔xg6 25.fxg5 ♘d3, and the endgame is much more pleasant for black than the one he got in the actual game.

From the computer's point of view, if we continue the first line with 24.♘d6, then black's position is just bad. The most resilient reply was 19...♘xc3 20.bxc3 ♗xc5.

20.b2xc3   ♔g7-h6?!

The position would be equal after 20...♘c5 21.f4 ♘d3 22.fxg5 ♘xc1.

21.g2-g4   ♖a8-g8

There's nothing else. White threatens to free his stuck g6 knight with 22.f4 or 22.h4.

22.f2-f4   ♖g8xg6

After 22...gxf4 23.♘xf4 ♘e3, white simply plays 24.♘xe6.

23.♗h5xg6   ♔h6xg6

24.f4xg5   ...

24.f5+ is obviously bad due to 24...♔f7, when the black knight gets the strong f4 square.

24...   ♘d7xc5

In case of 24...♔xg5 25.♖f7 ♘xc5 26.♖cf1, white creates dangerous mating threats. For instance: 26...♘xc3 27.♖1f6!, 26...♔g6 27.h4, or 26...♗c6 27.♖g7+ ♔h6 28.♖ff7 with the subsequent h4. 24...♘xe5 is also bad because of 25.♖ce1 and then ♖xe6+, with an unstoppable double-rook attack. Thus, out of three pawns – g5, e5 and c5 – black can only capture one.

25.h2-h4   ♘c5-d3

26.♖c1-c2   ...

26.♖cd1 was also possible, intending to meet 26...♘5f4 with 27.♖xd3 ♘xd3 28.♖f6+ ♔g7 29.♖xe6 with a won position. However, instead of 26...♘5f4, black could play 26...♘xc3 or 26...♘e3 with great complications. Still, white is better in these cases, for instance:

1) 26...♘xc3 27.♖f6+ ♔g7 28.♖cf1 ♘xe5 29.♖xe6 ♘e2+ 30.♔h2 ♘f3+ (30...♘xg4+ 31.♔h3) 31.♖xf3 ♗xf3 32.h5, and white should win.

2) 26...♘e3 27.♖f6+ ♔g7 28.h5 ♘xd1 29.h6+ ♔g8 30.g6 ♘xe5 31.h7+ ♔g7 32.♖f7+ ♔xg6 33.h8=♕ ♘xf7 34.♕g8+ ♔f6 35.g5+, and black loses a piece after 35...♘xg5 36.♕d8+.

3) 26...a5!? was interesting, retaining control over the f6 square. But here, white has a strong exchange sacrifice, 27.♖f6+! ♘xf6 28.exf6 ♔f7 29.h5, and it's unlikely that black can save the game.

26...   ♘d5-f4

27.♔g1-h2   ...

It's necessary to kick the f4 knight away to invade the opponent's camp with the rook.

27...   ♗b7-e4

28.♔h2-g3   ♘f4-d5

Forced – white threatened to play 29.♖h2 ♘d5 30.h5+ ♔xg5 31.h6. Now 29.♖h2 doesn't work because of 29...♘xe5 30.♖e1 ♘xc3 31.♖xe4 ♘xe4+ 32.♔f4 ♘xg5!, and only black has practical chances of winning (despite what the computer may say).

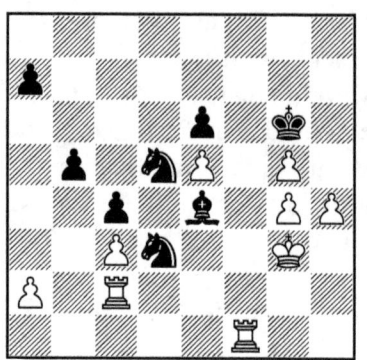

29.♖f1-f6+! ...

The correct way to win. After 29...♘xf6 30.exf6, black won't be able to stop the passed pawns.

29... ♔g6-g7
30.h4-h5 ...

30.♖xe6 would be a mistake because of 30...♘3f4!

30... ♘d3xe5
31.♖c2-e2 ♘d5xc3
32.♖e2-e3 b5-b4

32...♘d3 was hopeless too: 33.♖xe6 ♗d5 (33...♘c5 34.♖e5) 34.h6+ ♔h7 35.♖e7+ etc.

33.♖f6xe6 ♘e5-d3
34.♖e3xe4 ♘c3xe4+
35.♖e6xe4 ...

It's not hard for white to win with an extra exchange. There followed:

35... c4-c3
36.♖e4-e7+ ♔g7-g8
37.♖e7-c7 a7-a5
38.g5-g6 ♘d3-e5
39.♔g3-f4 ♘e5-d3+
40.♔f4-f5 c3-c2
41.♖c7xc2. Black resigned.

For the sake of completeness, we should point out that instead of simply capturing the pawn, white could have given a fun mate in three: 41.♖c8+ ♔g7 42.g5! c1=♕ 43.h6#.

**No. 28. Sergei Belavenets –
Alexander Tolush
Masters Training Tournament
Leningrad 1939**
Sicilian Defense B72

1.e2-e4 c7-c5
2.♘g1-f3 d7-d6
3.d2-d4 c5xd4
4.♘f3xd4 ♘g8-f6
5.♘b1-c3 g7-g6
6.♗f1-e2 ♗f8-g7
7.♗c1-e3 ♘b8-c6
8.f2-f3 ...

The idea of white's opening structure is to seize the d5 square, and to do that, he needs to strengthen the e4 pawn. Now black can't play 8...d5 due to 9.♗b5, and white gains a material advantage.

8... 0-0

Now black threatens d6-d5 with full equality.

9.♘d4-b3 ...

Trying to stop the d-pawn from moving.

9... ♗c8-e6?

After this natural move, white implements his ideas and gains a positional advantage. Despite the fact that white has mechanically stopped the d-pawn, the move d5 is still possible. In the game Belavenets – Levenfish, played several rounds later, black played 9...d5! 10.exd5 ♘b4, and white could find nothing better than 11.d6 (if 11.♗c4, then 11...♕c7 12.♕e2 ♘xc2+) 11...♕xd6 12.♗c5 (12.♕xd6 exd6 13.0-0-0 ♖e8 14.♗f4 is bad due to 14...♘xa2+) 12...♕xd1+ 13.♖xd1 ♘c6 with a roughly equal game.

10.♘c3-d5! ...

Now black doesn't have the counterplay shown above. It's also hard for him to create threats along the c-file, because the white c-pawn can always move to c3 or c4.

10... ♗e6xd5?!

After this slight mistake white stands somewhat better.

Nowadays, another plan is more popular for black – 10...♘d7 with the subsequent f7-f5. Black could also consider 10...a5.

11.e4xd5   ♘c6-b4
12.c2-c4   ♕d8-c8?!

A waste of time, as it turned out later. *After 12...b5! 13.a3 bxc4 14.♗xc4 ♖c8 15.♖c1 ♖xc4 16.♖xc4 ♘bxd5 17.♗xa7 ♗h6 black got some counterplay for the exchange. Now, however, his position is very passive.*

13.♕d1-d2   ♘b4-a6
14.♘b3-d4 ...

Now and in the next few moves white could consider placing the f1-rook on d1 to have an effect if black decides on playing e6.

14...   ♘a6-c7
15.0-0   ♕c8-d7
16.a2-a4   a7-a6

16...e6! would be stronger.

17.a4-a5 ...

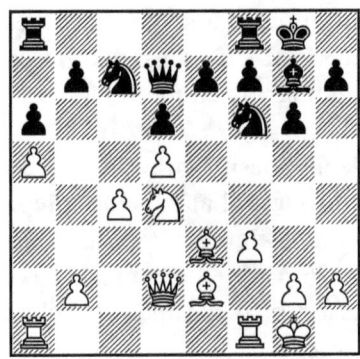

White has an advantage on the queenside. His plan is to push the b- and c-pawns, which should greatly limit black's mobility.

17...   ♖a8-e8?

This mistake makes a somewhat worse position lost. Black had only one attempt to create counterplay, by playing 17...e6 18.dxe6 ♘xe6. He probably missed his opponent's reply. By avoiding e6, black cedes the game without much resistance. He loses two tempi.

18.♗e2-d1!   ♖e8-c8
19.♗d1-a4   ♕d7-d8
20.♖a1-d1 ...

To push the queenside pawns, it made more sense to play 20.♖fd1, but white expected black to reply 20...e6. In this case, after 21.dxe6 fxe6, it would be best to place the white rooks on d1 and e1. However, it turned out that black wasn't even thinking about e6.

20...   ♘f6-d7
21.b2-b4   ♘d7-e5
22.♕d2-e2   ♘c7-e8
23.♖d1-c1   ♘e8-f6
24.♖f1-d1?! ...

This move was somewhat careless, 24.♗b3 or 24.♔h1 would win easily by stopping any counterplay.

24...   ♖c8-c7?

Black doesn't prevent the c4-c5 breakthrough that's being prepared by white. After 24...♘xc4! 25.♖xc4 ♘xd5 26.♕d2 ♘xe3 black has two pawns for the piece and some chances to draw.

25.♘d4-b3   ♕d8-c8
26.c4-c5   ...

Now white has a winning advantage. 26.♗b6 ♖xc4 27.f4 ♖xc1 28.♖xc1 ♕g4 led to unnecessary complications that allowed black to avoid material losses.

26...   ♕c8-f5

26...dxc5 27.♗f4 ♘fd7 28.♗xd7 lost immediately – black gives up either an exchange or a full piece.

27.c5-c6   b7xc6
28.d5xc6   ♖f8-a8
29.b4-b5   a6xb5
30.♗a4xb5   ...

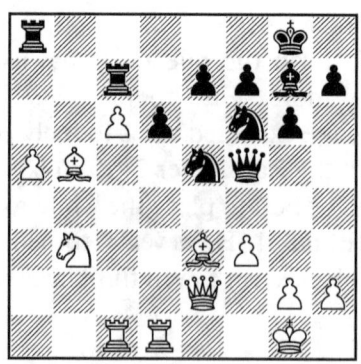

White's passed pawn should win the game for him. Knowing that, black launches a desperate kingside attack, but all his threats are easily repelled.

30...   ♘f6-h5
31.♗e3-b6   ♘h5-f4
32.♕e2-f1   ♖c7-c8
33.c6-c7   ♕f5-g5

Threatening ♘xf3+.

34.♔g1-h1   ♕g5-h5
35.♘b3-d4   g6-g5
36.♘d4-c6   ♘f4-g6
37.♘c6-a7   ...

Black's attack is not serious enough. White can just go and grab some material.

37...   g5-g4
38.♘a7xc8   g4xf3
39.♘c8-a7   ♘e5-g4
40.c7-c8=♕+   ♖a8xc8
41.♖c1xc8+   ♗g7-f8
42.h2-h3   ♕h5-e5
43. h3xg4.

Here, black noticed that he was two rooks and a bishop down and resigned.

**No. 29. Paul Keres –
Sergei Belavenets
Masters Training Tournament
Leningrad 1939**

Nimzo-Indian Defense E43

1.d2-d4   ♘g8-f6
2.c2-c4   e7-e6
3.♘b1-c3   ♗f8-b4
4.e2-e3   b7-b6

The current main line is 4...0-0 5.♘f3 d5 6.♗d3 c5, which eventually leads to one of the "tabiyas of the 20th century".

5.♗f1-d3   ♗c8-b7

6.♘g1-f3   0-0

Immediate attempts to play in the center, 6...c5, 6...d5 or 6...♘e4, are interesting as well. Black chooses the most solid reply.

7.0-0   ♗b4xc3
8.b2xc3   d7-d6

It's now considered that the more energetic 8...♗e4 gives equality to black (used by Alekhine against Reshevsky in the well-known Amsterdam AVRO tournament, 1938).

9.♕d1-c2   ♘b8-d7
10.e3-e4   e6-e5
11.♘f3-d2   ...

White is planning his queenside play, while black is trying to create some counterchances.

11...   ♘f6-h5
12.g2-g3   ♕d8-f6
13.♘d2-b3   ♖a8-e8
14.f2-f3   ...

Since black is putting indirect pressure on the e4 pawn, this move is necessary.

14...   ♕f6-e6
15.a2-a4   a7-a5

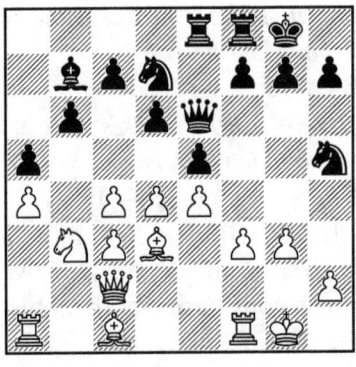

16.c4-c5   ...

Probably too premature. This break would have been much stronger after some preparation, including ♖b1, ♗e3 and ♕e2. After 16.♖b1, for instance, it was too reckless to play 16...♗a6 17.c5! ♗xd3 18.♕xd3 dxc5 19.dxc5 ♘xc5 *(19...bxc5!? is better, even though white still has better chances after 20.c4)* 20.♘xc5 bxc5 21.♗a3 with a big advantage for white.

16...   d6xc5
17.d4xc5   ♘d7xc5

Black needs to trade his bad knight.

18.♘b3xc5   b6xc5
19.♗c1-a3   ♖e8-b8
20.♗a3xc5   ♖f8-d8
21.♗d3-b5   ♗b7-a6

21...♗c6 with the subsequent ♘h5-f6-e8-d6 was more precise.

The computer, however, fully approves of the game move.

22.♕c2-e2   ...

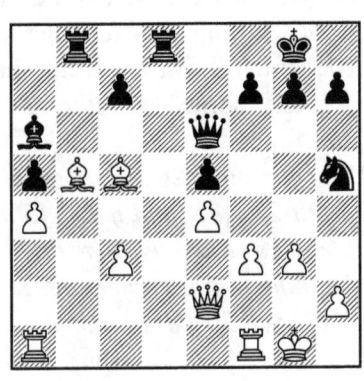

22...   ♕e6-c6

An ingenious reply to a cunning trap: 22...♗xb5 23.axb5 ♕b3 24.c4 ♖d3!? 25.♖a3 ♕xc4 26.♖xd3 ♕xc5+ 27.♔g2 with an extra exchange and a better position.

23.♗b5xc6	♗a6xe2
24.♖f1-b1	...

This energetic pawn sacrifice allows white to retain the initiative.

24.♖f2 ♗c4 is worse, leaving the white c6 bishop trapped.

24...	♗e2xf3?

After this hasty capture, black gets into a difficult situation. 24...♖xb1+ 25.♖xb1 h6! was much stronger – after ensuring his king's safety, black can now meet 26.♗e7 or 26.♔f2 with 26...♖d2!, getting great counterplay.

25.♗c5-e7	♖d8-c8

After 25...♖xb1+ 26.♖xb1 ♖d1+ 27.♖xd1 ♗xd1 28.♗d8, the black pawns fall. Black has a slight chance to survive by sacrificing an exchange with 25...g5 or 25...♘f6.

26.♖b1-b5	...

White wants to win the game "comfortably", but this is a rare privilege in practice. He should have settled for winning the exchange with 26.♗d7, which, however, would have given black some counterchances after 26...♗xe4.

White can meet 26...♗xe4 with the unpleasant 27.♖e1, and if 27...f5 then 28.♗e6+ (it's always useful to drive the opposing king into a corner) 28...♔h8 29.♗xc8 ♖xc8 30.g4!, winning.

26...	♖b8-b6
27.♗c6-d5	♘h5-f6
28.♗e7xf6	g7xf6
29.c3-c4	♖b6xb5
30.a4xb5	f6-f5!

Breaking up white's pawn chain just in time. Black uses all his available chances for his defense.

31.♖a1xa5	♗f3xe4
32.♗d5xe4	f5xe4
33.♖a5-a6	...

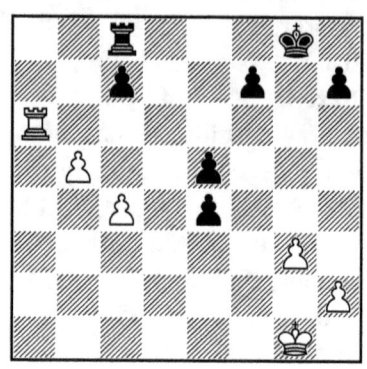

33...	♔g8-f8

White threatened 34.♖c6. 33...♖d8 34.♖c6 ♖d7 35.g4 was rather passive, but black could still hold. Black's position is still worse, so he needs to be precise in defense.

34.♔g1-f2	♔f8-e7
35.♔f2-e3	f7-f5
36.g3-g4	f5xg4
37.♔e3xe4	♖c8-g8

37...c6! would reach the draw more quickly. The pawn endgame after the trade on c6 is drawn, and white can't achieve anything if he keeps the rooks on the board, either.

38.c4-c5	...

After 38.♖h6!, black's task would have been much harder.

38...	g4-g3

Activating the rook just in time. White already threatened ♔d5, which was worth considering both on his 38th and 40th moves.

39.h2xg3	♖g8xg3

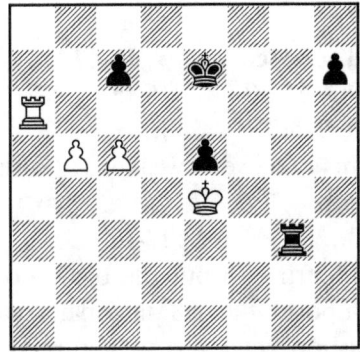

40.♖a6-a7 ...

Losing the last chance to put the king on d5, which would have made black's task harder. Now black has time to put his king on c8, and the draw becomes obvious.

40...	♚e7-d8
41.♔e4-d5	♚d8-c8
42.♔d5xe5	♖g3-g5+
43.♔e5-d4	♖g5-g4+
44.♔d4-c3	♖g4-g3+
45.♔c3-b4	♖g3-g4+
46.♔b4-a5	♖g4-g1
47.♖a7-a8+	♚c8-b7
48.♖a8-h8	♖g1-a1+
49.♔a5-b4	♖a1-b1+

Draw.

"In this game, Belavenets showed great tenacity and perseverance in defense." (Iglitsky)

No. 30. Sergei Belavenets – Salomon Flohr
Masters Training Tournament
Leningrad 1939
Caro-Kann Defense B15

1.e2-e4	c7-c6
2.d2-d4	d7-d5

If Spielmann is called "the knight of the King's Gambit", then we can deservedly crown Flohr with the high title of "King of the Caro-Kann".

3.♘b1-c3	d5xe4
4.♘c3xe4	♘g8-f6

Lately, black almost always plays 4...♗f5 or 4...♘d7, avoiding doubled pawns.

5.♘e4xf6+	e7xf6

Moreover, Flohr believes in his technique and opening knowledge when he chooses this quiet move with a great positional disadvantage: white gets a queenside pawn majority, which makes almost any endgame better for him.

6.♗f1-c4	♗f8-d6
7.♕d1-e2+	♗f8-e7

Black, of course, politely declines the endgame "invitation".

8.♘g1-f3	0-0
9.0-0	♗c8-g4
10.♖f1-e1	♗e7-d6
11.♕e2-d3	♘b8-d7
12.h2-h3	...

Even though it certainly won't hurt to have a luft, this move wasn't really necessary, because the black bishop is even better-positioned on h5. White should have played 12.♗b3 immediately.

12...	♗g4-h5
13.♗c4-b3	...

13.♘h4 was probably stronger.

13...	a7-a5
14.c2-c3?!	...

White's best move is 14.a4 with a slight edge. Another good option was 14.a3, even though after 14... a4 15.♗a2 ♗g6 (the consequence of 12.h3), the white queen would have been forced onto the awkward c3 square. Now black uses a tactical blow to achieve the bishop pair advantage and seizes the initiative.

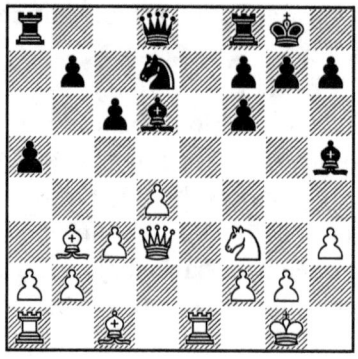

14...	♘d7-c5!
15.♕d3-d1	...

Of course not 15.dxc5? ♗h2+, winning the queen.

15...	♘c5xb3
16.♕d1xb3	...

16.axb3 created a weak pawn on b3, which could have become a liability down the road. On the other hand, the potential kingside weakness after 16.♕xb3 ♗xf3 17.gxf3 can be easily defended.

16...	♕d8-d7
17.♘f3-h2	...

17...♗xf3 was a threat, and white probably didn't like another defense, 17.c4, because of the b7-b5 break that dramatically weakens the light squares in the center, which is rather unpleasant in the absence of the light-squared bishop.

17...	a5-a4
18.♕b3-c2	♗d6-c7
19.♗c1-e3	f6-f5
20.f2-f4?!	...

This move weakens white's position.

20...	f7-f6

Preparing to put the bishop onto the important a2-g8 diagonal. Again, the bishop's position on h5 turned out to be very fortunate!

21.♘h2-f1	♗h5-f7
22.c3-c4	♖f8-e8

22...b5! would be even stronger.

23.♕c2-d3	g7-g6
24.b2-b3	b7-b5

Increasing the pressure. Black has the initiative, but white tenaciously defends his difficult position.

25.g2-g3	♗c7-a5
26.♖e1-d1	♖a8-d8
27.♖a1-c1	♗a5-b6
28.♔g1-f2	...

Coolly involving the last piece, the king, in his defense. However, 28.♗f2 would lead to a smaller disadvantage for white.

28...	♕d7-a7

Threatening a tactical blow, 29...♖xe3. However, as it turns out several moves later, black's decision to force matters was too premature. White has no counterplay, so black could, for instance, just play 28...h6, preparing the unpleasant pawn break g6-g5.

29.♔f2-g2	♕a7-a8
30.♔g2-f2	♕a8-a7
31.♔f2-g2	♕a7-b7
32.♔g2-f2	...

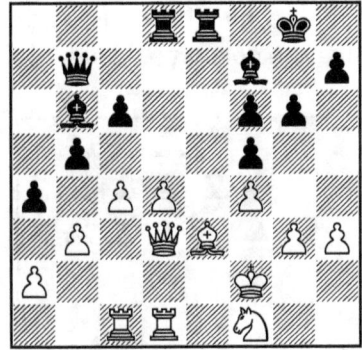

**32...   b5xc4
33.b3xc4   ♗b6xd4**

Black's combination doesn't bear any fruit. White's calculation was correct, and he repels the attack.

The simple 33...♖e4 wins.

**34.♗e3xd4   c6-c5
35.♕d3-c3   c5xd4
36.♖d1xd4   ♕b7-a7**

Perhaps black overlooked that 36...♖e2+!? doesn't work because of 37.♔xe2 ♕g2+ 38.♔d1! (but not 38.♔d3? ♕e4+ or 38.♔e3? ♖e8+) 38...♕xf1+ 39.♔c2 ♕e2+ (39...♕f2+ 40.♖d2 also wins for white) 40.♔b1! (40.♕d2! is also winning) 40...♖b8+ 41.♔a1, and the white king safely escapes in the corner.

37.c4-c5?   ...

White blunders.

37...   ♗f7xa2

37...♖xd4! 38.♕xd4 ♗xa2 39.♕xf6 a3 and black wins.

**38.♖d4xd8   ♖e8xd8
39.♕c3xf6   ♖d8-c8**

Another mistake that seemingly leads to overwhelming difficulties. Black should have played 39...♖f8.

Indeed, 39...♖f8 is better than the game move, but 39...♖b8 was probably even stronger.

**40.♘f1-e3   a4-a3
41.c5-c6   ...**

Now the white c-pawn is much stronger than its black counterpart on the a-file.

This move could have led to dire consequences for white. He should have played 41.♕d6 with the idea of ♘d5, and the position is close to equality.

41...   ♗a2-d5??

A severe mistake that dramatically changes the situation on the board. After 41...♖e8 42.♕c3 ♗e6, white has to find 43.c7 a2 44.g4! to keep the position balanced.

42.c6-c7   ...

It's hard to say what exactly Flohr missed (maybe he didn't see that 42...♖e8 here is met with 43.♕e5!), but now his rook is tied to c8, and white threatens the deadly check 43.♕d8+.

**42...   ♕a7-a5
43.♖c1-d1   ♕a5xc7
44.♖d1xd5   ♖c8-e8
45.♕f6-d4   a3-a2
46.♖d5-d7**

"Black resigned, because after 46...a1=♕, white simply plays 47.♕d5+ and 48.♖xc7. The whole game is an example of tenacity and inventiveness in difficult defense." (Iglitsky)

No. 31. Sergei Belavenets – Vasily Panov
Moscow Championship, 1939
Old Indian Defense A54

1.d2-d4   ♘g8-f6

2.c2-c4   d7-d6
3.♘b1-c3   e7-e5
4.♘g1-f3   ...

4.dxe5 dxe5 5.♕xd8+ ♔xd8 leads to full equality.

4...   ♘b8-d7
5.g2-g3   ♗f8-e7
6.♗f1-g2   0-0
7.0-0   ♖f8-e8
8.♕d1-c2   c7-c6
9.♖a1-b1   ...

Preparing to move the b-pawn to make the g2 bishop stronger.

9...   ♕d8-c7
10.b2-b4   ♘d7-f8
11.♖f1-d1   ♘f8-g6

Panov often uses this development system. The black knight is well-positioned on g6, defending the e5 pawn.

12.b4-b5   ♗c8-d7
13.b5xc6   b7xc6

Black could also play 13...♗xc6 14.♘b5 ♗xb5 (14...♕c8!?) 15.♖xb5; white has the bishop pair and a good position, but black has some counterchances because of the weak c4 pawn.

14.♗c1-a3   h7-h6

Black waits for events to unfold. In the meantime, he prevents the potential maneuver ♘f3-g5-e4.

15.d4xe5   ...

Trying to exploit the somewhat weak d6 square.

15...   d6xe5
16.c4-c5   ...

16.♗xe7 ♘xe7 didn't give white much, since the e7 knight would be well-positioned, defending the c6

pawn. Now white threatens to transfer his knight to d6 after ♘f3-d2-c4.

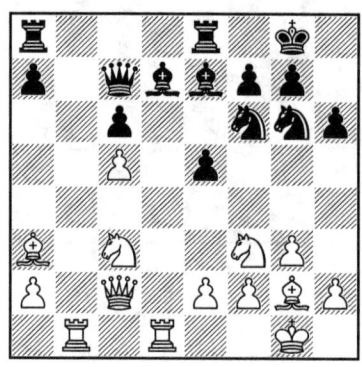

16...   ♖e8-b8

Black opts for quiet defense and ultimately gets a somewhat worse position. Maybe 16...♕c8 17.♘d2 ♗h3 18.♗h1 ♕a6 was better, with unclear chances. 16...♕a5 gave black nothing because of the simple 17.♗b4.

17.♘f3-d2   ♗d7-e6

17...♕a5 is still bad because of 18.♘c4 ♕a6 19.♕a4 with an advantage for white.

18.♕c2-a4   ...

But now, 18...♕a5 was a threat.

18...   ♘f6-d5
19.♘d2-e4   ♖b8xb1

If 19...f5, then 20.♘xd5 cxd5 21.♖xb8+ ♗xb8 22.♘c3, and black's position is difficult, because after 22...♗xc5, there's 23.♘xd5 ♕c8 24.♖c1.

White also has an advantage after 19...♘xc3 20.♘xc3, because it's hard for black to defend the c6 pawn.

20.♖d1xb1   ♖a8-d8

After 20...♗f5, white can play 21.♖b2 or 21.♖d1. For instance:

21.♖d1 ♗xe4?! 22.♘xe4 f5 23.♘d6 with an overwhelming position.

21.♘c3xd5   ♗e6xd5?

A serious mistake that gives white an overwhelming advantage in the endgame. Black had to play 21...cxd5, and if 22.♘c3, then 22...♗xc5. While after 22.♘d6 ♖b8 23.♖xb8+ ♕xb8, the white passed c-pawn is not nearly as dangerous as in the game. For instance, after 24.♕e8+ ♕xe8 25.♘xe8 d4 26.♘c7 ♗xa2 27.♘d5, black has an extra pawn as compensation for the worse position.

In this line, it is better to play 24.♕b3 with an advantage.

22.♘e4-d6   ♖d8-b8

23.♖b7 was a threat.

23.♖b1xb8+   ♕c7xb8
24.♗g2xd5   c6xd5
25.♔g1-g2   ...

Preventing any first-rank checks, which could have played an important tactical role. The endgame after 25.♕e8+ ♕xe8 26.♘xe8 ♔f8 27.♘c7 d4 is better for white, but this advantage is most likely not enough for a win.

25...   ♘g6-f8

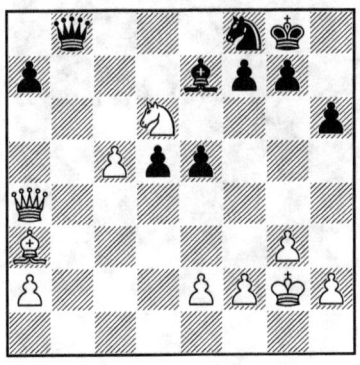

26.♘d6-f5   ...

With this move, white begins a combination. However, it was totally unnecessary. The simple 26.♕c6 d4 27.♕d5 ♗xd6 28.cxd6 ♘d7 29.♕c6 should win.

26...   ♗e7-f6

26...♗d8 is very bad because of 27.♕e8.

27.♕a4-b3   ♕b8-c8

The queen trade loses quickly: 27...♕xb3 28.axb3 ♘e6 29.c6 ♘c7 30.♗d6 ♗d8 31.♘e7+ ♗xe7 32.♗xc7 etc.

28.c5-c6?   ...

28.♘d6! was more forceful, but to play that, after 28...♕a6, you need to find the resource 29.e4!, and black's counterplay dries up quickly, for instance: 29...♘e6 30.exd5 ♘d4 31.♕b8+ ♔h7 32.♕b1+ ♔g8 33.♗b2 etc.

28...   ♘f8-g6

Now the pawn is promoted. 28...♕xf5 didn't help either because of 29.c7, then ♕b8 and c8=♕.

The only decent chance to save the game was 28...♕xc6 29.♕b8 d4+ 30.♔g1! *(after 30.♔h3, there's 30...♕h1!, and the king cannot escape perpetual check)* 30...♔h7 31.♕xf8 ♕c2, and it's hard for white to convert his extra piece, because the black king's position is super solid.

29.♕b2-b7!   ♕c8xf5
30.c6-c7   ♕f5-e4+

30...♘f4+ 31.gxf4 ♕g4+ 32.♔h1 doesn't help either.

31.♔g2-g1   ♕e4xe2

32.c7-c8=♕+, and black resigned after a few moves.

Selected Games of Ludmila Belavenets

Ludmila Belavenets

Vera Nikolaevna Tikhomirova:
"What can I say about Belavenets? A most sweet woman. Interesting. Unique. Has a way with words. I remember her and Kushnir as two tomboy teens. Very talented girls. Back then, I thought they were very cheeky, but now, I'd rather say "energetic". Time changes your thinking... In 1975, I was the arbiter of the Soviet championship won by Belavenets. The youngsters sat in a small group and analyzed each other's games. And then someone said, very surprised, 'Wow, Ufimtsev is still alive!' I sat beside them, and I answered, even more surprised, 'Of course he's still alive, I played against him.' And then Lyusia said, 'But you're also from the Hereafter...' And back then, I was younger than she is now. So, now we're both from the 'Hereafter'... But never mind, I just decided to moan a bit. Seriously though, she was a fine chess player. Right now, she's doing great work with children. A very good journalist. I always read her articles with pleasure." (2005)

***

I mainly show my correspondence games here, because they're my most memorable ones, I experienced them the most. I lived with them for several years, had to think constantly about these games, and they became my best because of that.

I got interested in correspondence chess back in the 1960s. In 1965, I played in the first ladies individual world correspondence chess championship. As a member of the USSR team, I won three team world championships. I liked correspondence chess very much, it was more exciting for me than over-the-board chess. A tournament game lasts for a few hours, and then you just forget about it. But correspondence games last for months, you play several of them at once, and you constantly "spin" the positions inside your head. I often caught myself analyzing games at a party, at the cinema or the theater. I even found some interesting moves in my dreams. This happened to other correspondence players as well.

Correspondence chess allows you to be constantly involved with your favorite game and take part in competitions without traveling or taking leave from your main job.

When there were no computers and modern communications technologies (did we really live in such a time?!), the games were played by mail. You would send a postcard with your move and then wait patiently. The post from abroad wasn't delivered particularly quickly, so even the most energetic and quick attack on the king could take a year and a half. And the world championship that I won ran for almost six years! That's how slow our time was.

You spend all your free time with a pocket chess set. At home, you have a demonstration board with some problematic position that prevents you from sleeping peacefully and should always be before your eyes. Even in your dreams, you can't escape calculating lines, because all the games are played simultaneously, and you have just three days to think on your next move. You're very lucky if your opponent makes some mistake, and the game ends quickly.

No. 32. Mieke Van Elst – Ludmila Belavenets
2nd Ladies Correspondence Chess Olympiad
1975 – 1980
Sicilian Defense B80

1.e2-e4	c7-c5
2.♘g1-f3	e7-e6
3.d2-d4	c5xd4
4.♘f3xd4	♘g8-f6
5.♘b1-c3	d7-d6
6.♗c1-g5	...

A relatively rare move that's not considered particularly dangerous for black.

6...	♗f8-e7
7.♕d1-d2	a7-a6
8.0-0-0	♘b8-d7

Black implements a standard plan – preparing for a queenside attack. The knight will be better placed on d7 than on c6: it doesn't shut off the c-file and is ready to move to c5 at any time, increasing pressure on the e4 pawn.

9.f2-f4	♕d8-c7
10.♗f1-d3	b7-b5
11.f4-f5	...

This is a poor move. 11.a3 or 11.♔b1 should be played.

11...	e6-e5
12.♘d4-f3	♗c8-b7

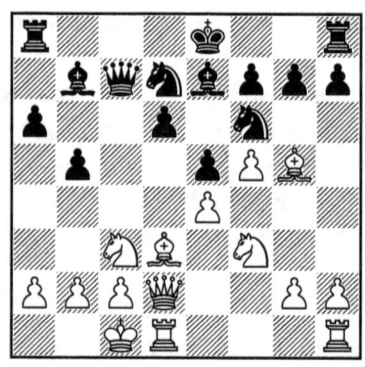

13.a2-a3? ...

During my lessons with children, I usually explain how pernicious such moves really are. The a3 pawn becomes a "hook" that allows black to eventually open another file on the queenside.

On 13.♖he1 black would take control with 13...b4! 14.♘d5 ♘xd5 15.exd5 f6! 16.♗e3 ♗xd5 and a clear advantage.

13... ♗b7-c6

A typical Scheveningen restructuring: the queen heads to b7 to increase the pressure on the e4 pawn and prepare to open the file with b5-b4.

14.h2-h4 ♕c7-b7
15.b2-b4? ...

Suicidal. White had a good continuation, 15.g4! ♘xg4 16.♗xe7 ♔xe7 17.h5 with compensation.

15... a6-a5!

Now black's attack basically plays itself.

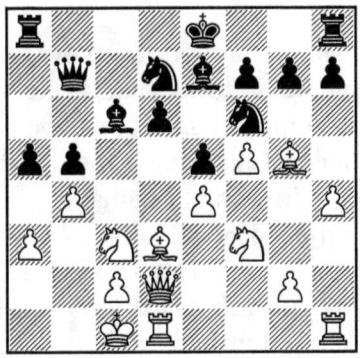

16.♕d2-e2 0-0
17.♗d3xb5 a5xb4
18.a3xb4 ♖f8-b8
19.♗b5xc6 ♕b7xc6
20.♘c3-d5 ♘f6xd5
21.e4xd5 ♕c6-c3!

Mate is inevitable, and black resigned.

No. 33. Ludmila Belavenets – Ildiko Szalai-Horvath
3rd Ladies Correspondence Chess Olympiad
1986 – 1991
Scandinavian Defense B01

1.e2-e4 d7-d5
2.e4xd5 ♕d8xd5
3.♘b1-c3 ♕d5-a5
4.d2-d4 c7-c6
5.♘g1-f3 ♗c8-g4
6.h2-h3 ♗g4xf3
7.♕d1xf3 e7-e6

7...e6 and 7...♘f6 are equally good here. Both moves are planned by black anyway.

8.♗c1-d2 ♕a5-c7

This move somewhat worsens the position. 8...♘d7 is reasonable.

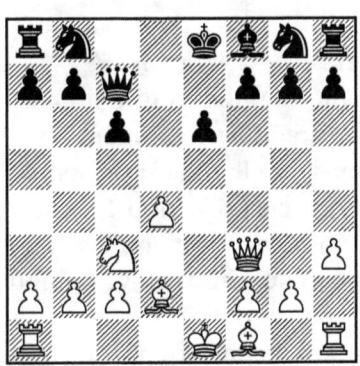

9.♘c3-e4! ...

The centralized knight is very strong, preventing black from fully developing her pieces. However, the immediate 9.♗f4, continuing to harass the black queen, was also possible. After 9...♗d6?, there's an unexpected double attack 10.♕g3! ♗xf4 11.♕xg7. Now, to save the exchange, black has to return the bishop: 11...♗d2+ 12.♔xd2 ♕f4+ 13.♔d3 ♕f6 14.♕xf6 ♘xf6 15.♗e2. As a result, white gets a healthy extra pawn in the endgame.

9... ♘b8-d7
10.♗d2-f4 ♕c7-a5+
11.c2-c3 ...

11.♗d2 was better.

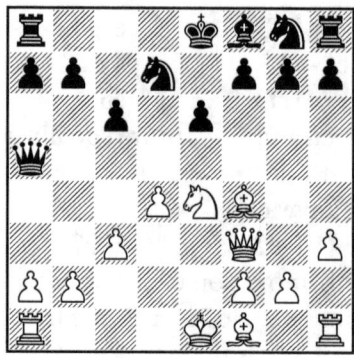

11... e6-e5?

White wanted to give a check on d6 and trade her opponent's second bishop as well. Black prevents this, but at the cost of seriously worsening her position (she opens up the position despite being behind in development).

It was better to play 11...♘gf6, even though white still has a pleasant position after the simple 12.♗d3 ♘xe4 13.♗xe4 – the bishop pair and space advantage will allow white to prepare an attack on any area of the board.

12.d4xe5 ♘d7xe5
13.♗f4xe5 ♕a5xe5
14.0-0-0 ...

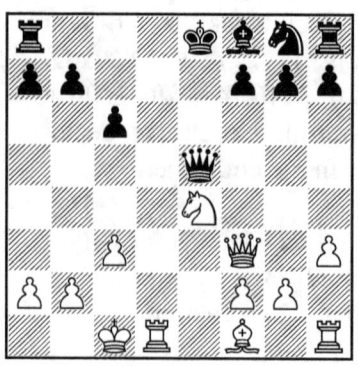

14... ♗f8-e7

Black is catastrophically behind in development, while white is increasing the pressure with simple developing moves. For instance, after 14...♖d8 15.♗c4 ♖xd1+ 16.♖xd1 ♘f6, an invasion along the d-file decides matters: 17.♕d3 ♗e7 18.♘xf6+ gxf6 19.♕d7+ ♔f8 20.♖d4.

15.♗f1-c4 ...

A simple and strong move, even though, as it turns out, white also had a computer-like blow available 15.♗a6!. Capturing the bishop leads to irreparable damage – 15...bxa6 16.♘d6+ ♗xd6 17.♕xc6+ ♔e7 18.♖he1 ♖d8 19.♖xe5+ ♗xe5 20.♕b7+ ♔e8 21.♖xd8+ ♔xd8 22.♕d5+. Further, after 15...♕c7, white creates decisive threats with the simple 16.♖he1 ♔f8 17.♗c4.

15... ♘g8-f6

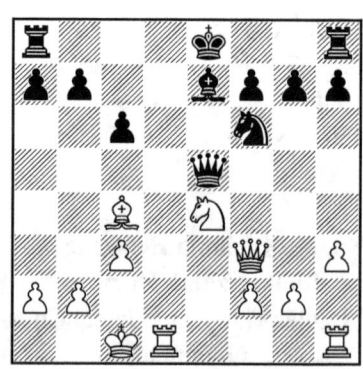

16.♘e4-d6+! ...

White wins the queen for a rook and knight and still has good attacking prospects on the kingside.

16... ♗e7xd6
17.♖h1-e1 0-0

18.♖e1xe5   ♗d6xe5
19.g2-g4   ...

I managed to calculate the consequences of this move accurately and precisely.

19...   ♖a8-d8
20.♖d1xd8   ♖f8xd8
21.g4-g5   ♘f6-d5
22.♗c4xd5   c6xd5

Black has to break up her pawn chain, because after 22...♖xd5 white wins a pawn with 23.♕f5 (the computer recommendation 23.♕e3!? may be even stronger).

23.♕f3-e3   ♗e5-b8
24.♕e3-e7   ♗b8-f4+
25.♔c1-c2   ♖d8-b8
26.h3-h4   ...

The black pieces are very passive and material losses are inevitable, so she resigned.

No. 34. Ludmila Belavenets – J. M. Cunningham
4th Ladies World Correspondence Chess Championship
1984 – 1990
Alekhine Defense B04

1.e2-e4   ♘g8-f6
2.e4-e5   ♘f6-d5
3.d2-d4   d7-d6
4.♘g1-f3   g7-g6
5.♗f1-c4   ♘d5-b6
6.♗c4-b3   ♗f8-g7
7.♘f3-g5   d6-d5
8.f2-f4   ♘b8-c6
9.c2-c3   ...

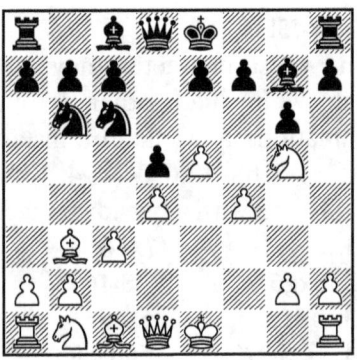

9...   h7-h5

Black wants to put her bishop on f5 and prevent g2-g4. However, this significantly weakens her g6 pawn. Instead of that, she had to play 9...f6, driving the active g5 knight away. After 10.♘f3, white's position is of course more pleasant (she has a space advantage), but the main struggle is still ahead.

10.e5-e6!   ...

I think that it won't be an exaggeration to say that black's position is already lost after this move.

10...   0-0?

This is a bad mistake. 10...♗xe6 is black's only chance to resist. 11.♘xe6 fxe6 12.♘d2! would be white's best response, and if 12...g5 then 13.♕c2 could be played.

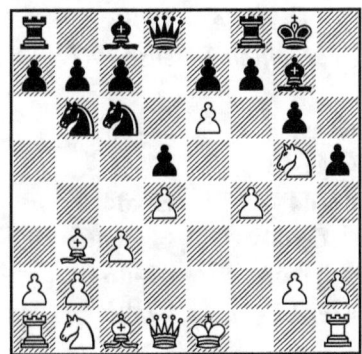

11.f4-f5! ...

The most energetic move, even though white had other tempting continuations as well. For instance, 11.exf7+ ♔h8 12.0-0 ♗g4 13.♕e1 ♕d6 14.♗c2 with a big advantage.

11...	f7xe6
12.f5xg6	♖f8-f6
13.♕d1xh5	e6-e5
14.♘g5-f7!	♕d8-e8
15.♕h5-h7+	♔g8-f8
16.♗c1-h6.	

Black resigned.

In correspondence chess, you usually play many games at once, so it's important to reach the culmination at different times. Many experienced correspondence players even deliberately choose their openings in such a way that some games go slowly (those games usually don't require much exertion), while in other games, the crisis comes quickly.

So it was a true joy when several games ended "lightning-fast", just 12 to 18 months after they started!

No. 35. Ludmila Belavenets – Traute Manthey
4th Ladies World Correspondence Chess Championship
1984 – 1990
Sicilian Defense B81

1.e2-e4	c7-c5
2.♘g1-f3	e7-e6
3.d2-d4	c5xd4
4.♘f3xd4	♘g8-f6
5.♘b1-c3	d7-d6
6.g2-g4	h7-h6
7.h2-h4	♘b8-c6
8.♖h1-g1	h6-h5
9.g4xh5	♘f6xh5
10.♗c1-g5	♕d8-b6

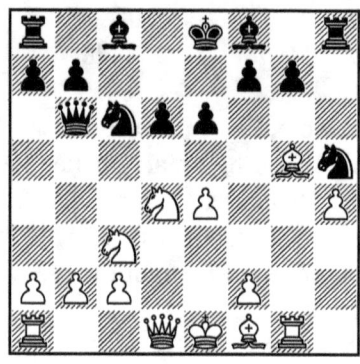

We have played the double-edged Keres Attack. The main line here is 10...♘f6. By leaving the knight on h5, black makes it harder for white to play f2-f4, because this is met with f7-f6, winning the bishop. However, the knight is usually ill-positioned on the edge of the board, and black will eventually have to spend some time evacuating it.

11.♘d4-b3	a7-a6

Black needs to cover the b5 square, or else the threat ♘b5 (immediately or after ♕d2 and ♗e3) might become quite unpleasant.

12.♕d1-d2	♗c8-d7
13.0-0-0	♕b6-c7
14.♕d2-e2!?	...

Back then, we didn't have computer databases, and free creativity began around these moves. The idea of this move is to maintain constantly the threat of ♘d5.

14...	b7-b5

A more restrained plan was worth considering — 14...♘f6 with subsequent queenside castling.

15.a2-a3   ♘c6-e5?

I expected this move and prepared to push the f-pawn in reply. The knight move is a mistake, though, and black should play 15...♖b8.

16.f2-f4   ♘e5-c4
17.f4-f5   ♖a8-c8

An important subtlety: 17...♘xa3? doesn't work because of 18.♘d5!, and black loses at least a piece (and not 18...♕xc2+? 19.♕xc2 ♘xc2 20.♘c7#).

18.f5xe6   ...

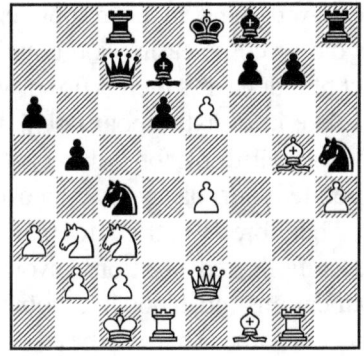

18...   ♗d7xe6

I think that this is a mistake that immediately makes black's position very difficult. For better or for worse, she had to take on e6 with the pawn, preventing the white knight from invading on the dangerous d5 square.

After 18...fxe6, I planned to play 19.e5 d5 (after 19...♘xe5? white plays 20.♘d4 with the subsequent ♗h3, targeting the e6 pawn) 20.♖e1! (white prepares the blow on d5, which doesn't work immediately: 20.♘xd5?! exd5 21.e6 ♗c6 22.e7 ♗xe7 23.♖e1 ♘f6, and black can still hold, even though it's clear that white has great compensation for the piece) 20...♘xb2 (if 20...♘xa3, then white just ignores the knight and piles on the pressure on the kingside: 21.♕f3 ♗c6 22.♗d3 ♕f7 23.♖ef1!, and black is in trouble).

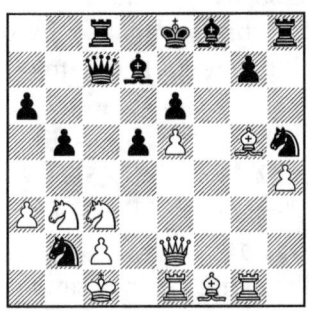

21.♘xd5! ♕a7 (capturing the knight, 21...exd5, is just bad because the e-pawn crushes black's position like a battering ram: 22.e6 ♗c6 23.e7 and wins) 22.♔xb2 ♕xg1 23.♕d2 — white has sacrificed an exchange but has created too many threats for black to deal with. The latter's position is now hopeless.

In addition to 19.e5, there's a strong computer move 19.♕f3! ♘e5 (after 19...♘xa3, white has a quiet reply 20.♗e2! with the deadly threat ♕xh5+; after the forced 20...♗e7 21.♗xe7 ♔xe7 22.♕e3, black's position falls apart) 20.♕f2 (white just creates more threats; she wants to play ♗e2 and ♖df1 or ♘d4 and ♗h3; the black king is stuck in the center, and she has no counterplay) 20...♘f6 21.♗xf6 gxf6 22.♕xf6 — white has an extra pawn and a strong position.

All in all, when I got the move 18...♗xe6 in the mail, I sighed in relief, because now I didn't have to check and double-check all those sharp lines.

19.♘c3-d5   ♕c7-a7

After 19...♗xd5 20.exd5+ ♘e5, there's 21.♗h3 ♖a8 22.♘d4, and white pieces dominate the board.

20.♘b3-d4   ...

The white knights have got everything they could dream of!

20...	♗e6-d7
21.♗f1-g2	♘c4-e5
22.♗g2-f3	♘e5xf3
23.♕e2xf3	♖c8-c4
24.♖g1-f1	...

At this point, as they say, all roads lead to Rome. White could also play 24.♗e3 ♕b7 (24...♕b8 25.♖g5) 25.e5! ♗c6 26.♘xc6 ♕xc6 27.♖gf1, winning.

24...	♗d7-c8
25.e4-e5!	...

On the postcard I sent to my opponent, I included the following beautiful mating line:

25...	d6xe5

If 25...♖xd4, then 26.♖xd4 ♕xd4 27.♕xf7#.

26.♘d4xb5!	a6xb5
27.♘d5-c7+	♕a7xc7

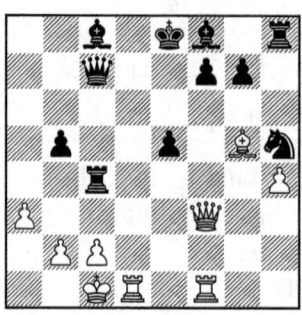

28.♕f3xf7+!   ♕c7xf7
29.♖d1-d8#.

After checking that there was no salvation, black admitted her defeat.

However, much more often the games would drag on for long. Sometimes you find a solution in a complicated middlegame, other times you have to outplay the opponent in an endgame.

You had to play for a win in every game. I took part in three Olympiads, and for the Soviet team, any place other than first wasn't considered merely a setback – it was an abject failure. And wins in correspondence chess didn't come easily: you couldn't expect blunders, and there's no surprise effect, like in over-the-board play. The opponent will think for a day, analyze and refute your flashy but incorrect idea. Therefore, we tried to play for more complicated positions, avoiding simplifications and, if possible, going for a better endgame. That was the advice of Alexander Konstantinopolsky, a great chess player and outstanding coach who worked with the correspondence chess team for a long time.

No. 36. Ludmila Belavenets – Zvonka Praznik-Pezdirc
4th Ladies World Correspondence Chess Championship
1984 – 1990
Pirc Defense B07

In that tournament, I had one bad position, and that essentially meant that I had to win all the other games to compete for first place. It's hard to win right out of the opening, so I had to devise a way to get some long game without forcing matters too much.

1.e2-e4	d7-d6
2.d2-d4	♘g8-f6
3.♘b1-c3	g7-g6
4.g2-g3	...

An unassuming move. It doesn't exactly give white a big advantage, but you have to let your opponent play and show what she is capable of.

As a result, I managed to obtain a small advantage, but I feared dropping it. Sometimes such things happen: you're too anxious to chase the two birds in the bush because you might catch neither, but then you pluck and pluck the bird in your hand until you see that nothing is left of it...

4...	♗f8-g7
5.♗f1-g2	0-0
6.♘g1-e2	e7-e5
7.0-0	♘b8-d7
8.h2-h3	e5xd4
9.♘e2xd4	♖f8-e8
10.♖f1-e1	♘d7-c5
11.♘d4-b3	...

This move was recommended to me by Rudolf Kimelfeld. After the knight trade, white is better.

11...	♘c5xb3
12.a2xb3	♗c8-d7
13.♗c1-e3	♕d8-c8
14.♔g1-h2	♗d7-c6
15.♗e3-d4	a7-a6
16.♕d1-d2	...

White has more freedom in her position, even though the advantage is certainly not great. But still, black has to play too, make some moves.

16...	♖e8-e6
17.♖e1-e2	♕c8-f8
18.♖a1-e1	♖a8-e8
19.f2-f3	...

I wanted to play f4, but I feared that black might attack the e4 pawn. So I decided to overprotect it.

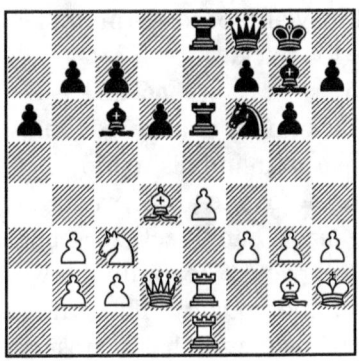

19...	♘f6-d7

She wants to trade another pair of pieces. But the game doesn't end after that!

20.♗d4xg7	♕f8xg7
21.♖e2-e3	h7-h5
22.h3-h4	♘d7-f6
23.♘c3-e2	...

I wanted to put my knight on d4 or f4. I was quite good at creating small threats.

23...	♖e6-e5
24.♘e2-f4	♕g7-h6

I'm not sure about this move. The computer proposes the sharper 24... g5!?, but I would have been quite happy with the resulting endgame after 25.♘d3 ♖5e7 26.hxg5 ♕xg5 27.♖3e2 ♕xd2 28.♖xd2: the black h5 pawn is now isolated, and maybe I'd be able to exploit that somehow. Playing for a small advantage – just a year and a half more!

25.♘f4-d3   ♖e5-e7
26.♕d2-a5!   ...

White starts creating small threats. In some lines, the c7 pawn is hanging; white also underscores the black queen's miserable position on h6. ♘b4 may also become an unpleasant move for black.

26...   d6-d5?!

Black finally cracks under pressure and makes an impulsive move.

26...♗b5 27.c4 ♗c6 was stronger; now, black can meet 28.♘b4 with an unexpected beautiful blow 28...♖xe4!! and equality. That said, after 28.♗h3, white still has a considerable advantage.

27.e4-e5   ♗c6-b5
28.♕a5-c3   ♗b5xd3
29.♕c3xd3   c7-c6
30.♗g2-h3   ♘f6-d7

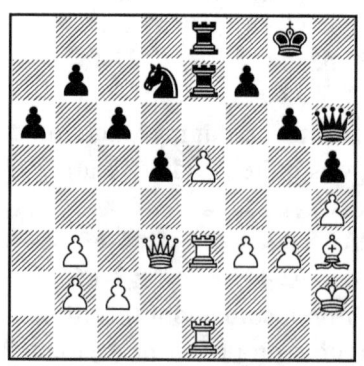

31.e5-e6?!   ...

During the game, I thought that this move was winning, but later, the computer found an unexpected defense. So, the objectively best move was 31.♕d4, for instance: 31...♘f8 and white can choose between 32.c4 or 32.f4, or 31...♕g7 32.f4 with a small advantage for white.

31...   ♘d7-c5?

Black had to boldly capture the pawn – 31...fxe6, and after 32.♖xe6 (32.♗xe6+ ♔h8 is unlikely to trouble black, besides, the bishop is now pinned), black has a move that would have made Steinitz happy – 32...♔f7! As the first world champion taught, the king is a strong piece that can protect itself. After 33.♖xe7+ ♖xe7 34.♖xe7+ ♔xe7, chances were roughly equal.

However, black's game move loses.

32.e6xf7+   ♔g8xf7
33.♖e3xe7+   ♖e8xe7
34.♖e1xe7+   ♔f7xe7
35.♕d3-c3   ♔e7-d6

After 35...♘d7, white could consolidate her advantage with 36.f4. The line 36.♕b4+ c5 37.♕xb7 ♕d2+ 38.♗g2 a5 etc is less convincing, where black has more chances to draw.

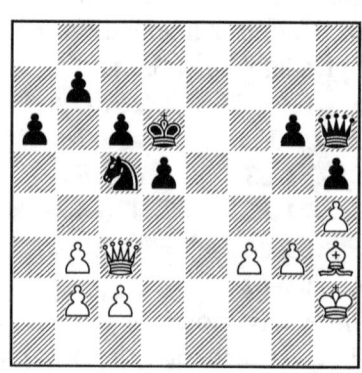

36.f3-f4 ...

White had a quicker win: 36.♕f6+! ♔c7 37.♕e5+ ♔b6 38.♕d4, and black loses a piece. But I thought that 36.f4 was a solid enough way to win.

36...	♘c5-d7
37.♕c3-b4+	♘d7-c5
38.♕b4-d4	♘c5-d7
39.♕d4-a7	...

White achieves her aim — capturing one of her opponent's pawns.

39...	♕h6-h8
40.♕a7xb7	♘d7-c5
41.♕b7-f7	♕h8-d4
42.♕f7xg6+	♔d6-c7
43.♕g6xh5	♕d4-f2+
44.♗h3-g2	♕f2xc2
45.♕h5-e5+	♔c7-b7
46.h4-h5	♘c5-d3
47.♕e5-e7+	♔b7-b6
48.h5-h6	♘d3-f2
49.h6-h7	♘f2-g4+
50.♔h2-h3.	Black resigned.

Some people assume that you have all the time in the world to think on your moves in correspondence chess. But, and it's a big "but", you also have a life, and this life includes things such as your main job, over-the-board tournaments, and so on. Therefore, you actually don't have *that* much time to analyze the position. I, for instance, analyzed a lot of positions while traveling in the subway on my pocket chess set; this makes travel much more fun.

**No. 37. Nina Orlova —
Ludmila Belavenets
4th Ladies World Correspondence
Chess Championship
1984 – 1990**
Sicilian Defense B85

The decisive game for the women's world champion title. This game was incredibly important, because it's so hard to get a second shot at the correspondence world championship. Who knows how many years you will need to wait...

My opponent's husband was Sergei Mironovich Sokolov, a strong master from Moscow. It's quite a dangerous union! I realized clearly that my results in over-the-board tournaments were much better than hers, I'm a stronger player than she is (for illustration, her level was Moscow championship semi-final, while I played in ten Soviet championship finals). But correspondence chess is a very different beast; if you have somebody at home who can help you, this plays a huge role.

1.e2-e4	c7-c5
2.♘g1-f3	e7-e6
3.d2-d4	c5xd4
4.♘f3xd4	♘b8-c6
5.♘b1-c3	a7-a6

With this move order, black avoids the Keres Attack.

6.♗f1-e2	♕d8-c7
7.0-0	d7-d6
8.f2-f4	♘g8-f6
9.♗c1-e3	♗f8-e7
10.♕d1-e1	0-0
11.♕e1-g3	♘c6xd4

12.♗e3xd4	b7-b5
13.a2-a3	♗c8-b7
14.♔g1-h1	♗b7-c6
15.♖a1-d1	...

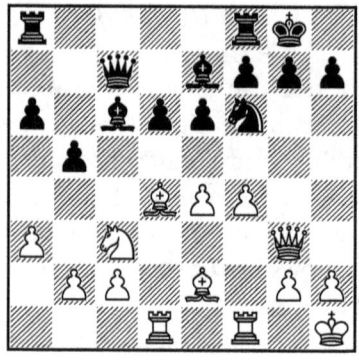

15...	♖a8-c8

The Sicilian Defense again, a classical Scheveningen. I think that if you need to play for a win with black, this is the only opening you can choose. Today, of course, life is very different, there's a lot more information available, and white can now draw even in the Sicilian if she wants. But back then, you had to piece the information together bit by bit — from magazines, from *Chess Informant* and so on.

I don't think that black's last move was very good — the rook has nothing to do on the c-file. It's no accident that other moves are more popular: 15...♕b7, 15...♖ad8 or 15...♖ae8.

16.♖f1-e1	g7-g6
17.♗e2-f3	♕c7-b7
18.♖d1-d3	a6-a5

I saw no other plan: black launches a queenside attack, kicks the knight away from c3 and puts pressure on the e4 pawn. Meanwhile, white continues to create threats on the kingside.

19.♕g3-h3	...

White indirectly protects the e4 pawn by laying a trap.

19...	b5-b4
20.a3xb4	a5xb4
21.♘c3-d1?!	...

A poor retreat that allows black to seize the initiative. White had a more principled (and simply stronger) move available: 21.e5 dxe5 22.fxe5. Now 22...♘d7 is bad due to 23.♗xc6 ♕xc6 24.♘e4 with dangerous threats for white. However, she did have 22...♘h5! 23.♘e4 (23.♗xh5? bxc3 24.♗e2 cxb2 25.♖b3 ♕d7 is better for black) 23...♖fd8 (black has an amusing queen sacrifice here: 23...♘f4?! 24.♕h6 ♗xe4 25.♗xe4 ♘xd3 26.♗xb7 ♘xe1, but the final position of this line — 27.♗xc8 ♖xc8 28.♕d2 — is better for white, and she still has some resources to play for a win) 24.c3 (24.♗xh5? ♗xe4 is still bad) 24...bxc3 25.bxc3 with mutual, roughly equal chances.

21...	♘f6-d7

Black wants to play e6-e5 and close off the long dark-squared diagonal.

A question for lessons with children: why can't black capture the e4 pawn? And a pretty line as an answer: 21...♘xe4? 22.♗xe4 ♗xe4 23.♕xh7+! ♔xh7 24.♖h3+ ♔g8 25.♖h8#.

22.f4-f5	e6-e5
23.♗d4-f2	...

White wants to put her bishop on h4, trade bishops and exploit the weakness of the dark squares.

23... ♖c8-d8
24.♗f2-h4 ...

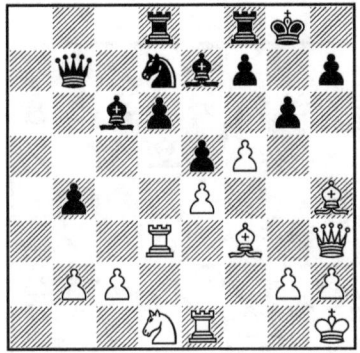

24... g6-g5!

I decided against this move at first, but after a lot of wood-pushing, decided that it wasn't too bad.

25.f5-f6? ...

This pawn sacrifice is poor, because white can't use the freed up f5 square for anything. She should have just retreated with the bishop — 25.♗f2, even though black's position is still more pleasant after 25...♚h8.

25... ♗e7xf6
26.♗h4-f2 ♗f6-g7!

White's plan could work after 26...♗e7? 27.♘e3! ♖fe8 (27...♗xe4? 28.♗xe4 ♕xe4 29.♘d5 loses) 28.♘f5 ♘f8 29.♕h5! with dangerous threats, for instance: 29...♘g6 30.♕h6 ♗f8 31.♕xg5. White regains the pawn while maintaining strong pressure.

With the game move, black immediately returns the pawn but regroups her pieces.

27.♖d3xd6 ♘d7-f6

Black is attacking the e4 pawn, and the white knight will have to change its route and go to f2 instead of e3, so it doesn't reach the coveted f5 square.

28.♗f2-c5? ...

This is a losing move. White should play 28.♖xd8 ♖xd8 29.♘e3 with a small advantage for black.

28... ♖d8xd6
29.♗c5xd6 ♖f8-e8

Now it's not clear what white should do. Her bishop is stuck in the opponent's camp, while the e4 pawn needs protection.

30.♘d1-f2 ♗c6-d7

30...♕b6 was also very strong, for example: 31.♘d3 b3 32.♗xe5 bxc2 33.♕f5 ♗b5 with an advantage for black. But I liked my other idea, with more forced play.

31.♕h3-g3 ♕b7-b6

The bishop is "arrested"!

32.♖e1-d1 ...

White doesn't want to take the pawn because of 32.♗xe5 ♖xe5! 33.♕xe5 ♘g4, and a smothered mate looms over the board; as a result, white will have to give up her queen.

32... ♖e8-e6

Black forces her opponent to take on e5 anyway.

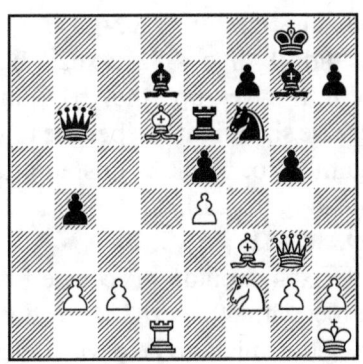

33.♗d6xe5   ♖e6xe5
34.♕g3xe5   ♘f6-g4
35.♘f2xg4   ...

There's nothing better.

35...   ♗g7xe5
36.♘g4xe5   ♗d7-e6
37.h2-h3   ...

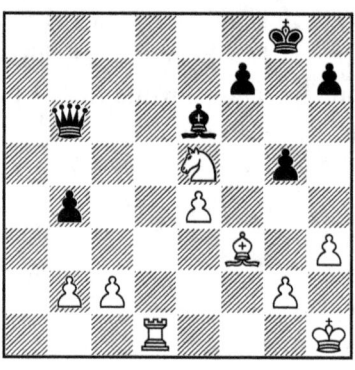

Formally, material is equal: a queen for a rook, knight and pawn. However, white's pieces are poorly coordinated and not too active (her bishop, for instance, is blocked by its own e4 pawn), while a queen is highly dangerous in positions with weaknesses on both flanks. Objectively, black's position is won, it's just a matter of technique.

37...   ♕b6-c7
38.♘e5-d3   ♕c7-g3

I didn't like 38...♕xc2: black shouldn't give up the b4 pawn, otherwise she might not be able to win the game. So, black begins an attack on the king instead.

39.♖d1-f1   ...

39.♘xb4 would, of course, have been met with 39...♗xh3. The attempt to bring the knight to help with defense 39.♘e1!? doesn't work because of 39...h5 40.♗xh5 ♗xh3 41.♗e2 ♕f2 42.♗d3 ♗g4 43.♖b1 ♗e2, and black wins.

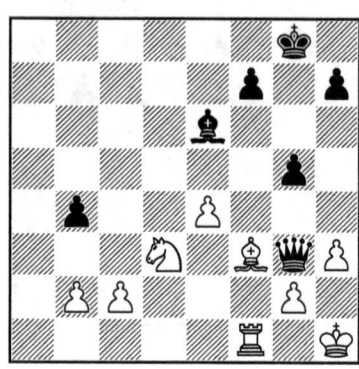

39...   b4-b3!

Depriving the d3 knight of its defense.

40.c2xb3   h7-h5

I didn't like the line 40...♗xh3 41.gxh3 ♕xh3+ 42.♔g1 ♕g3+ 43.♔h1 g4 44.♗xg4 ♕h4+ 45.♔g1 ♕xg4+: even if I manage to scoop up all the white pawns, it's hard to win with the disconnected f- and h-pawns against a rook and knight.

The game move is much better: black just wants to give checkmate. The h5 pawn cannot be captured because of the loose knight.

41.e4-e5   g5-g4
42.♗f3-e4   ...

White can't trade on g4 – she will get crushed after ♕h4+ and hxg4-g3.

42...   ♕g3-e3
43.♖f1-e1   ♕e3-d2
44.♖e1-f1   ♗e6xb3

My bishop destroys white's defensive structure, the d3 knight and e4 bishop, from behind.

45.h3xg4	h5xg4
46.♖f1-f4	♗b3-d1

Of course, black shouldn't part with the g4 pawn.

47.♔h1-h2	♗d1-e2
48.b2-b4	...

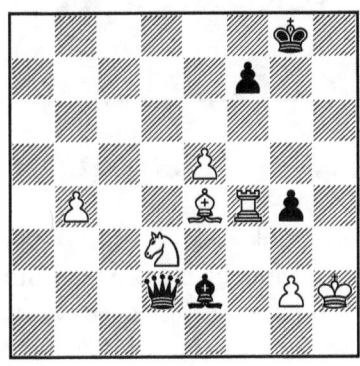

48...	♕d2-e3!

Black will capture the piece in the most beneficial situation and keep the g-pawn. The main aim was to avoid some kind of queen versus rook fortress; I've studied a lot of such positions.

49.♗e4-f5	g4-g3+
50.♔h2-h3	♗e2xd3
51.♖f4-g4+	♔g8-f8
52.♗f5xd3	♕e3xd3
53.♔h3-h4	♕d3-e3

White resigned.

No. 38. Rodica Vizdei – Ludmila Belavenets
3rd Ladies Correspondence Chess Olympiad, 1986–1991

Sicilian Defense B81

1.e2-e4	c7-c5
2.♘g1-f3	e7-e6
3.d2-d4	c5xd4
4.♘f3xd4	♘g8-f6
5.♘b1-c3	d7-d6
6.g2-g4	h7-h6
7.h2-h4	♘b8-c6
8.♖h1-g1	h6-h5
9.g4xh5	♘f6xh5
10.♗c1-g5	♘h5-f6

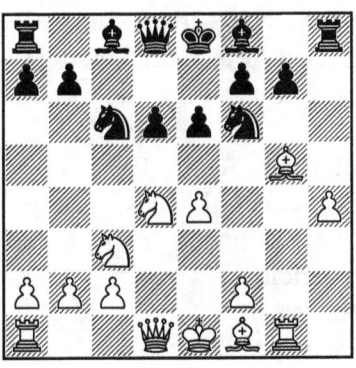

11.♖g1-g3	...

The purpose of this maneuver is to put the rook on d3 in some lines, increasing pressure on the d6 pawn. This move is not without poison, but still, white usually plays more natural moves, such as 11.♕d2 or 11.♗e2.

11...	♗f8-e7
12.♕d1-d2	a7-a6
13.0-0-0	♕d8-c7
14.♗f1-e2	♗c8-d7
15.f2-f4	♘c6xd4
16.♕d2xd4	♖a8-c8?

This move prevents black from having a safe place for his king. 16...0-0-0 was preferable.

17.h4-h5?!	...

This push weakens the h-pawn. After 17.♔b1! black would be in trouble, as on 17...b5 18.e5 dxe5 19.fxe5 ♘d5 20.♕d2 white has a big advantage, while against other moves white could gradually build her position without resistance and, sooner or later, would open up the black king decisively.

17... ♕c7-c5
18.♗g5xf6?! ...

A dubious decision. She could have played 18.♕d2 ♘xh5 19.♗xh5 ♖xh5 20.♗xe7 ♔xe7 21.♖xg7 with some advantage for white.

18... g7xf6?!

After 18...♗xf6! 19.♕xd6 ♕xd6 20.♖xd6 ♗c6 black's bishop pair would allow her to hold despite the pawn deficit.

19.♕d4-d2 ♗e7-f8
20.♖g3-d3?! ...

White is seeking direct pressure, but waiting and building would be much more testing. 20.♔b1! ♗h6 (20...♗c6 21.♗g4!) 20.a3 ♗c6 21.♗f1 and black has no decent plan to follow.

20... ♗d7-c6
21.♗e2-f3 b7-b5
22.♘c3-e2 b5-b4
23.♘e2-d4 ♗c6-a4
24.♘d4-b3?! ...

Controlling the b5 square longer with 24.♔b1 would be preferable, and only on 24...a5 should she play 25.♘b3. White would retain an edge.

24... ♕c5-b6
25.♔c1-b1 ♗a4-b5!
26.♕d2xb4 ...

After 26.♖e3 e5, black is still better. Now, she can deliver a pretty tactical blow.

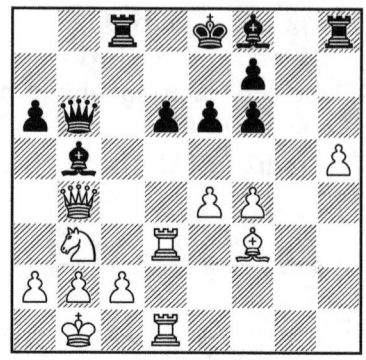

26... ♖c8xc2!
27.♘b3-d4 ...

The rook is obviously taboo. Ludmila thought black was winning after the capture on c2. However, in 2024 we can say that white's move in the game was not losing, and, further, that 27.♖d4 ♖f2 28.♗g4 would keep the position balanced.

27... d6-d5!
28.♕b4-b3 ♗b5xd3!
29.♕b3-a4+?? ...

This is the losing blunder. Black had a small advantage after 29.♕xb6 ♖c6+ 30.♖xd3 ♖xb6 31.exd5 e5 32.fxe5 fxe5 33.♘c6 ♗g7.

29... ♕b6-b5
30.♕a4xb5+ a6xb5
31.♖d1xd3 d5xe4
32.♗f3xe4 ...

32.♔xc2 exd3+ 33.♔xd3 b4 is hopeless.

32... ♖c2-f2
33.♘d4xb5 f6-f5
34.♗e4-c6+ ♔e8-e7
35.a2-a4 ♖h8xh5
36.♘b5-c3 ...

If 36.a5, then 36...♖hh2 37.♖b3 ♗g7, targeting b2.

36...	♖h5-h2
37.♖d3-d7+	♔e7-f6
38.♖d7-b7	...

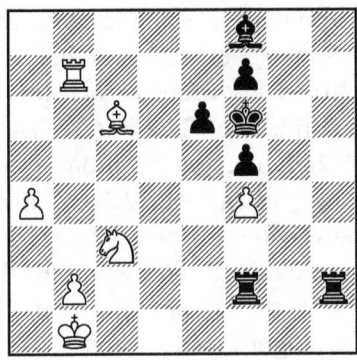

38... ♗f8-a3!?

Who would miss a chance to make such a spectacular move? The computer winning line is much less pretty, in my opinion: 38...♖f1+ 39.♔a2 ♖xf4 40.a5 ♖c4 41.♗e8 ♖xc3 42.♖xf7+ ♔e5 43.♖xf8 ♖c5, winning.

39.a4-a5 ...

39.♔a2 ♗d6 (39...♗xb2 40.♘d1 ♗d4 wins with more effort) 40.a5 ♖c2 doesn't save white either.

39...	♖f2xb2+
40.♖b7xb2	♖h2xb2+
41.♔b1-a1	♖b2-c2
42.a5-a6	♖c2xc3

Another way to win was 42...♗c5 43.♘b5 ♖c4 44.♔b2 ♖a4.

43.a6-a7	♗a3-c5
44.a7-a8=♕	♖c3-a3+
45.♔a1-b1	♖a3xa8
46.♗c6xa8	♗c5-d6

White resigned.

No. 39. Ludmila Belavenets – Rita Heigl
4th Ladies World Correspondence Chess Championship
1984 – 1990
Sicilian Defense B99

1.e2-e4	c7-c5
2.♘g1-f3	d7-d6
3.d2-d4	c5xd4
4.♘f3xd4	♘g8-f6
5.♘b1-c3	a7-a6
6.♗c1-g5	e7-e6
7.f2-f4	♗f8-e7
8.♕d1-f3	h7-h6
9.♗g5-h4	♕d8-c7
10.0-0-0	♘b8-d7
11.♗f1-e2	...

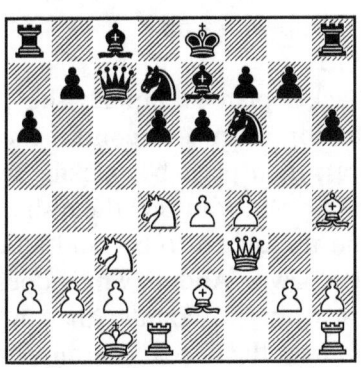

11... g7-g5?!

This move has almost fallen out of use; perhaps it was refuted somewhere along the way. The database shows that the most popular moves now are 11...♖b8, 11...b5, 11...0-0 and even 11...♖g8.

12.f4xg5	♘d7-e5

These moves were made in full accordance with the latest theory of the time – I think they were taken from the

Yugoslavian *Sahovska Enciklopedija*.

13.♕f3-e3   ♘f6-g4
14.♗e2xg4   ♘e5xg4
15.♕e3-d2   ♘g4-e5
16.♘d4-f3   ...

This is still theory. The knight, of course, should be driven off e5.

16...   h6xg5
17.♗h4xg5   f7-f6

Obviously, black can't trade the bishops – her position would have been simply hopeless.

18.♘f3xe5   d6xe5
19.♗g5-e3   ...

The position is not that simple to play as white. Black has the bishop pair and many pawns in the center, and it's not that easy to reach her king. In this game, I had to think a lot to come up with a plan.

19...   b7-b5

Black's plan is simple: she puts her bishop on d7 (to control the a4 square), then plays b4, kicking away the c3 knight, transfers the bishop to c6 and the queen to b7, and attacks the e4 pawn. And if white doesn't find anything to counter that in the meantime, the black central pawns will become very dangerous.

20.♘c3-e2   ...

I wanted to transfer the knight to g3 to create some threats on the kingside. Of course, white has other possibilities too, but I couldn't figure out how to play it. 20.a3! followed by g4 and g5 would be stronger.

20...   ♗c8-b7

Of course, I examined the move 20...♕c4! and intended to reply 21.♔b1 (21.♕d3 ♕xa2 22.♘c3 ♕a5 is better for black) 21...♕xe4 22.♗c5, to trade the dark-squared bishops and weaken the king on e8. However, the computer has since found a most unpleasant resource 22...♕d5!, forcing white to trade queens as well (on the other hand, after 22...♕c6? 23.♗xe7 ♔xe7 24.♖hf1, the position is close to won). Instead of 22.♗c5, it was probably better to play 22.♘g3 with the approximate continuation 22...♕c6 23.♕d3 f5, but this is not, of course, a fight for an advantage.

21.♘e2-g3   ♖a8-d8?!

Advancing the b- or a-pawn would be stronger and keep the position balanced.

22.♕d2-e2   ♖d8xd1+
23.♖h1xd1   ♖h8-h4?

The pawn cannot be taken: 23...♖xh2? 24.♕g4!, and the black king falls under a crushing attack. Black should play 23...b4!.

24.♗e3-f2? ...

White should defend the a-pawn and, after 24.♔b1! ♕c4 25.♕d2, she would stand better.

24...   ♕c7-c4
25.♕e2-d2   ...

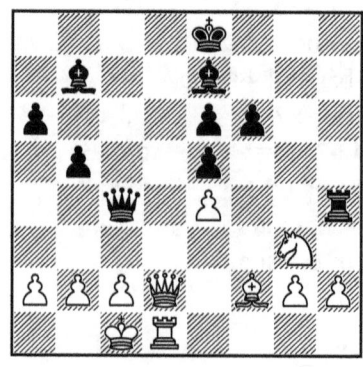

25... ♗b7xe4?

Black has hurried too much with regaining the pawn. Her move is very impractical and she should play 25...♗c6!, then after 26.b3 (26.♔b1 ♖xh2) 26...♕b4 27.c3 ♕a3+ 28.♔b1 ♖xh2 29.♕e2 ♕a5, the position becomes very sharp.

26.♘g3xe4   ♖h4xe4
27.♕d2-h6!   ...

White has finally got what she wanted: an attack on the black king that's stuck in the center. Now black has to find a string of only moves.

27...   ♖e4-g4

27...♖e2? loses by force to 28.♕h5+ ♔f8 29.♕h8+ ♔f7 30.♕h7+ (white has defended from the mate on c2 with checks and now involves her rook in the attack as well) 30...♔f8 31.♖d7! (31.♗c5 ♕xc5 32.♕h8+ ♔f7 33.♕h5+ ♔f8 34.♕xe2 was enough to win, too).

28.♕h6-h5+   ♔e8-f8
29.♗f2-e3   ...

29.♗c5? doesn't work due to 29...♖h4! 30.♗xe7+ (30.♖d8+? ♔g7 even loses) 30...♔xe7 31.♕g6 ♕f4+ 32.♔b1 ♕g4 – black repels the attack and equalizes.

29...   ♖g4xg2
30.♗e3-h6+   ...

Forced play begins.

30...   ♔f8-g8
31.♕h5-e8+   ♔g8-h7
32.♕e8xe7+   ♔h7xh6
33.♕e7xf6+   ♔h6-h5

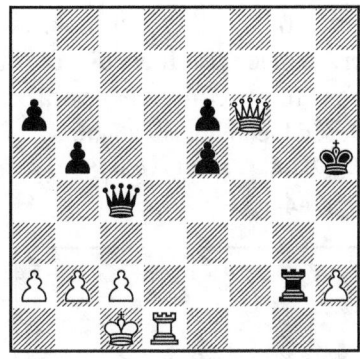

34.♕f6xe5+   ...

When I looked at this position from afar, I thought that I would checkmate the black king after 34.♕h8+ ♔g4 35.♕g7+ ♔f3 36.♖d3+? Thankfully, I noticed the refutation in time: 36...♕xd3! 37.♕xg2+ ♔xg2 38.cxd3 ♖xh2 39.♔d2 ♔g2 40.♔e3 ♔f1, and it's black who wins. Of course, after 36.♕b7+ white could give perpetual check.

34...   ♔h5-g6
35.c2-c3   ♖g2-g5?

This move loses. It was necessary to trade queens – 35...♕e2 36.♕xe2 ♖xe2 37.♖d6 a5 38.h4. Of course, the rook ending is difficult for black, but she would most likely be able to save a half-point.

36.♕e5-d4?   ...

I only realized that this was an error after sending the move. White had to retreat with the queen to another square, 36.♕e3! If black now takes on a2, then we transpose to the game. Otherwise, white just gets an extra pawn and can slowly build up pressure.

36...   ♕c4xa2?

Black had to trade queens – 36...♕xd4 37.♖xd4 e5, and the e-pawn, supported by the king and rook, would be very dangerous. It would be quite hard for white to convert her extra pawn.

37.♕d4-e4+   ♔g6-h6
38.h2-h4   ♖g5-f5
39.♕e4-e3+   ...

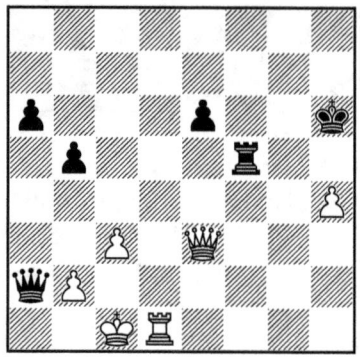

39...   ♔h6-g7

Other king retreats lose as well: 39...♔h5? 40.♖g1 ♕d5 41.♕e2+ ♔h6 42.♕g4, and mate is unavoidable, or 39...♔g6? 40.h5+! (opening the file for the attack) 40...♔xh5 (black can't just leave this pawn be: 40...♔f6 41.♕d4+ e5 42.♕d6+ ♕e6 43.♕f8+ ♔g5 44.♕g7+ ♔f4 45.♖f1+) 41.♕h3+ ♔g6 42.♖g1+ ♖g5 43.♕d3+ ♔h6 44.♖h1+, and I think we can stop the line here and believe the computer: black has no defense from the mating attack.

40.♕e3-d4+   ♔g7-h7

Unfortunately, a beautiful line was not played out: 40...e5 (I couldn't find how to counter this move for a long time) 41.♕g4+ ♔f6

a) 42.h5? (Ludmila thought this move was winning, but she had not found the resource 43...♕a4+! shown below) 42...♕a1+ 43.♔c2

a1) 43...♖f2+ 44.♔d3 ♕xb2.

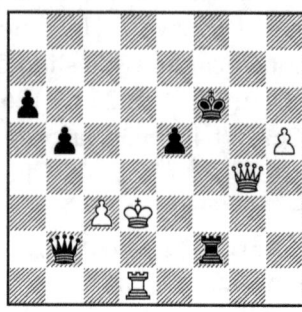

It might seem that black is now on the offensive, and white must give a perpetual check before it's too late. However, white has a fantastic resource: 45.♔e3!. The white king attacks the f2 rook, and now black can't give any checks. Meanwhile, white threatens to give the deadly check 46.♖d6+. White wins! I'm so proud of this line; it's a pity that my opponent didn't go there. The game would have ended a whole year earlier.

a2) 43...♕a4+! 44.♕xa4 bxa4 45.h6 ♖h5 and black holds the rook ending.

b) 42.♖d6+! ♔e7 43.♕xf5 ♔xd6 44.♕f6+ ♔d7 45.h5 ♕a1+ 46.♔c2 ♕a4+ 47.♔d2 ♕e4 48.♕f7+ ♔d8 49.b4 and the queen ending is clearly winning for white.

41.♖d1-g1   ...

41.♕g4 ♕a1+ 42.♔c2 ♕a4+ 43.♕xa4 bxa4 44.♖d6! led to a similar endgame.

41...   e6-e5
42.♕d4-e4   ♕a2-a1+
43.♔c1-c2   ♕a1-a4+

I think that the queen ending after 43...♕xg1 44.♕xf5+ ♔h6 45.♕xe5 is completely hopeless for black; in a rook ending, there's more hope for some kind of swindle.

44.♕e4xa4   b5xa4
45.c3-c4!   ...

The passed pawn goes forward, and His Majesty the king walks after it.

45...   ♖f5-f4

After 45...♖f2+ 46.♔c3 ♖f3+ 47.♔b4 ♖b3+ 48.♔xa4 ♖xb2 49.♖c1, black has to give up her rook for the c4 passer, and white has just enough time to stop the e5 pawn. The lines are quite long, but straightforward, and they aren't that difficult to calculate: 49...♖h2 50.c5 ♖xh4+ 51.♔a5 ♔g6 52.c6 ♖h8 53.c7 ♖c8 54.♔xa6 ♔f5 55.♔b7 ♖h8 56.c8=♕+ ♖xc8 57.♖xc8! ♔e4 (or 57...e4 58.♖e8 ♔f4 59.♔c6 ♔f3 60.♔d5 e3 61.♔d4 e2 62.♔d3 and the pawn is stopped just in time) 58.♔b6 ♔d3 59.♖d8+ ♔c3 60.♖e8 ♔d4 61.♔b5 e4 62.♔b4 ♔d3 63.♔b3 e3 64.♖d8+! — an important technique that allows the white king to get to the passed pawn and stop it.

46.♔c2-c3   a6-a5
47.c4-c5   ♖f4xh4

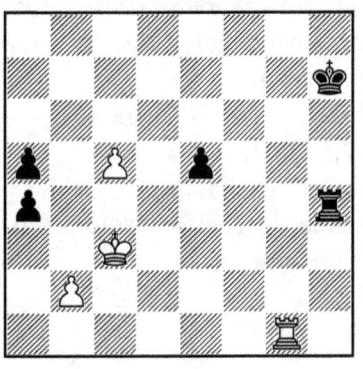

48.♖g1-e1   ...

48.♖g2 e4 49.♔c4 e3+ is just as straightforward for white, as she wins after 50.♔d5! or 50.♔b5! However, if 50.♔d3 ♖h5 she can still spoil the win with 51.♖c2? as 51...♔g7 would hold, which is also the case if white chooses 51.♔c4? ♖e5!, but 51.♔d4! ♖h5+ 52.♔d5 would still be winning.

48...   ♔h7-g6

After 48...e4, I planned 49.♖c1!

49.♖e1xe5   ♔g6-f6
50.♖e5-e2   ♖h4-b4
51.♔c3-d3   ...

Now white is threatening to push the c5 pawn and support it with her rook from behind. Black's desperate attempt to create her own passed pawn and get some counterplay is too late.

51...   a4-a3
52.b2xa3   ♖b4-a4
53.c5-c6   ♖a4xa3+
54.♔d3-c4   ♖a3-a1
55.♔c4-b5   ♖a1-c1
56.♖e2-e4!   ...

The last subtlety: white threatens to erect a bridge on c4.

56...   a5-a4

56...♔f5 would have been met with 57.♖c4!, and the pawn endgame is lost for black: 57...♖xc4 58.♔xc4 ♔e6 59.♔c5 a4 60.♔b6 a3 61.c7, and the pawn queens with a check.

57.♖e4xa4   ♔f6-e6
58.♖a4-d4.

Her king is cut off from the passed pawn, so black resigned.

No. 40. Zsuzsa Makai – Ludmila Belavenets
2nd Ladies Correspondence Chess Olympiad
1975 – 1980
Sicilian Defense B25

1. e2-e4　c7-c5
2. ♘b1-c3　♘b8-c6
3. g2-g3　g7-g6
4. ♗f1-g2　♗f8-g7
5. d2-d3　d7-d6
6. f2-f4　e7-e6
7. ♘g1-f3　♘g8-e7
8. ♗c1-e3　♘c6-d4
9. 0-0　0-0
10. ♖a1-b1　...

The most popular tabiya of the Closed Sicilian occurs after 10.e5 ♘ef5 11.♗f2 etc. But the game move is well-known, too.

10...　♘e7-c6
11. ♘c3-e2　...

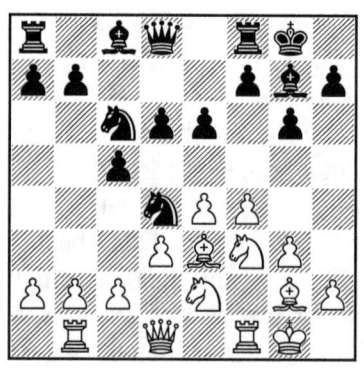

11...　e6-e5!?

A relatively rare move (black much more often trades on f3 or e2 to free the square for the second knight), but Rybka rather liked it in 2012 and Stockfish doesn't have a problem with it in 2024 either. My opponent has weakened her control over the d5 square, and black immediately launches an operation in the center.

12. c2-c3　♘d4xf3+

12...♘xe2+!? 13.♕xe2 exf4 14.♗xf4 ♗g4 15.h3 ♗e6 led to a position with mutual chances.

13. ♖f1xf3?!　...

The natural capture 13.♗xf3 was probably stronger.

13...　f7-f5!?

Black is trying to sharpen the position as much as possible. 13...♗g4 14.♖f2 exf4 15.♗xf4 ♗e6 16.a3 ♖c8 also looked promising.

14. ♖f3-f2　♗c8-e6
15. f4xe5　...

15.exf5!? was more cautious, at the very least.

15...　♘c6xe5

Black probably shouldn't be tempted by the a2 pawn: after 15...fxe4 16.♖xf8+ ♗xf8 17.♗xe4 ♗xa2 18.♖a1 ♗f7 19.exd6 ♕xd6 20.♘f4, white is no worse.

16. e4xf5　...

It seems that 16.♘f4! ♗xa2 17.♖a1 ♗f7 18.exf5 gxf5 19.♘d5 was better – white gets a decent initiative for the pawn.

16...　♗e6xf5
17. ♖f2xf5　...

This exchange sacrifice is unjustified. 17.♘f4 would keep the position balanced.

17...　♖f8xf5
18. ♗g2xb7　...

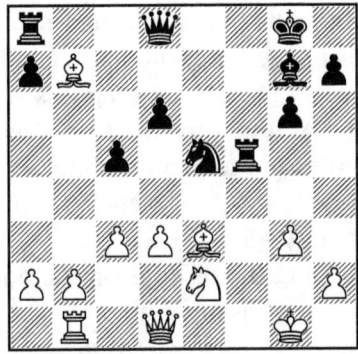

18... d6-d5?!

Black is ready to give the exchange back (and lose a pawn) to gain control over the kingside light squares. However, after 18...♖b8! 19.♗e4 ♖f8 20.♘f4 ♕d7 white had virtually nothing for the exchange.

19.♗b7xa8 ...

This continuation was fine, but there were also good alternatives: 19.♘f4! d4 20.♗f2 ♖b8 21.♗e4 ♖f6 22.cxd4 cxd4 with a double-edged position, or 20.♘e6 ♕b8 21.♗xa8 ♕xa8 22.♗f4 ♘xf3 23.♔f2 with equality.

19... ♕d8xa8
20.d3-d4? ...

Now white faces serious difficulties. 20.♗f4 was stronger, with the following approximate lines:

20...♘f3+ 21.♔g2 d4 22.♕b3+ c4! 23.♕b8+ (23.♕xc4+ ♔h8 24.♔f2 ♘e5 loses) 23...♕xb8 24.♗xb8 cxd3 25.♘xd4 ♘xd4 26.cxd4 ♗xd4 27.♖d1 ♗b5 (or 27...♖f2+ 28.♔h3 ♖xb2 29.♖xd3 ♗g1 30.♖d8+ ♔f7 31.♗xa7! and white equalizes) 28.♖xd3 ♖b8 29.♖xd4 ♖xb2+ 30.♔f3 ♖xa2 31.♖d8+ ♔g7

32.♖d7+ ♔h6 33.h4 ♖a3+ and black cannot claim to be better.

20... ♘e5-f3+
21.♔g1-g2 ...

21.♔f2 was met with 21...♘d2+ 22.♘f4 ♘xb1 and Black wins.

21... ♕a8-e8!
22.♘e2-f4 ♘f3-h4+

A cleaner way was 22...♕e4 23.♕xf3 ♕xb1 with an overwhelming position.

23.♔g2-f2 ...

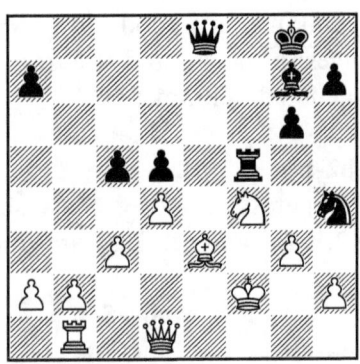

23... g6-g5?!

And here, the queen invasion on e4 would have decided matters. However, black had to find the following pretty line: 23...♕e4 24.gxh4 cxd4 25.cxd4 ♗h6 26.♕h1 ♕c2+ 27.♔g3 ♗xf4+ 28.♗xf4 ♕d3+ 29.♕f3 ♕xb1, winning.

24.g3xh4 g5xf4
25.♗e3-d2 ♕e8-e4
26.d4xc5 ...

26.♕g1 ♕d3 27.♖d1 cxd4 28.♕g4 would have prolonged the struggle.

26... f4-f3!
27.♗d2-g5 h7-h6

White resigned.

No. 41. Ludmila Belavenets – Milena Skacelikova
2nd Ladies Correspondence Chess Olympiad
1975–1980
Alekhine Defense B04

1.e2-e4	♘b8-c6
2.♘g1-f3	♘g8-f6
3.e4-e5	♘f6-d5
4.c2-c4	♘d5-b6
5.d2-d4	d7-d6
6.e5-e6!	...

I think this is a good move: white sacrifices a pawn and freezes her opponent's development.

6...	f7xe6
7.h2-h4	...

An aggressive move. Stats show that 7.♘g5 and 7.♘c3 are more popular.

7...	e6-e5
8.d4-d5	♘c6-d4
9.♘f3xd4	e5xd4
10.♕d1xd4	e7-e5
11.♕d4-d1	♕d8-f6
12.♘b1-c3	♗f8-e7

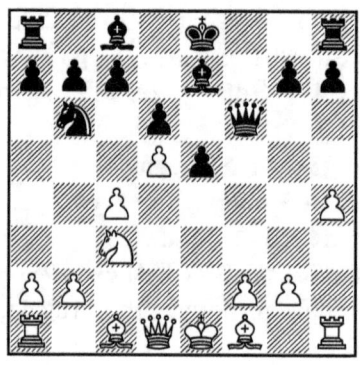

13.♗f1-d3	...

I thought that white had to have an advantage here: she has a good e4 square, and the black knight is stuck on b6. At the very least, it's much more pleasant to play as white.

13...	♗c8-f5
14.♗c1-g5	...

Keeping the bishops on the board with 14.♗e3! is preferable.

14...	♕f6-g6
15.♗d3xf5	♕g6xf5
16.♗g5xe7	♔e8xe7

I wasn't averse to trading pieces, thinking that if the black king is stuck in the center, it ought to be in trouble. However, white's advantage is small.

17.♕d1-e2	♖a8-f8
18.♘c3-e4	♕f5-f4?

After 18...♘d7! the position would be virtually equal.

19.♘e4-g5?!	...

When I made this move, I was totally sure that the c4 pawn couldn't be captured. However, white's best move is 19.c5 dxc5 20.0-0 with reasonable compensation.

19...	♖f8-c8?

My opponent came to the same conclusion and didn't capture the pawn. Nevertheless, computer analysis shows that this capture was possible: 19...♕xc4 20.♕xc4 ♘xc4 21.♖c1 ♖f4 22.b3 (22.g3 ♖d4 23.b3 h6 transposes to the same line) 22...h6 23.g3 (black has good counterplay in the line 23.♘f3 ♖e4+ 24.♔d1 ♘b6 25.♖xc7+ ♔f6 26.♖xb7 ♘xd5) 23...♖d4 24.♘f3 ♖e4+ 25.♔f1 ♖f8! (an important Zwischenzug that allows black to get the second rook into play) 26.♔g2 ♘b6 27.♖xc7+ ♔f6 28.♖xb7 ♖f7. Black has very good compensation for the pawn: all her pieces are active, and the d5 pawn is weak and requires defending.

20.b2-b3　　　c7-c6

Black has no good moves here.

21.d5xc6　　　b7xc6
22.g2-g3　　　♕f4-f5

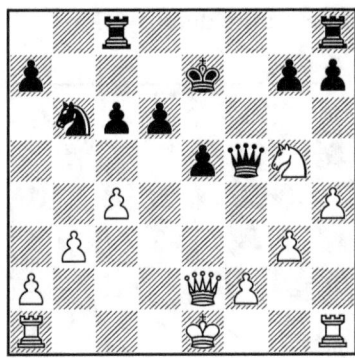

23.c4-c5!　　　...

My opponent probably missed this move that allows white to destroy her pawn structure in the center.

23...　　　h7-h6?

After 23...dxc5 24.0-0 h6 white's advantage is obvious, but black still had hopes to survive.

24.♘g5-e4　　　d6xc5
25.0-0　　　♖h8-d8
26.f2-f4　　　...

If the enemy king is stuck in the center, you have to open lines. However, 26.♖ac1 was a bit stronger.

26...　　　♖d8-d5

Black has nothing else.

27.♖a1-e1　　　♕f5-h3?

This move is losing. Instead, white's advantage would be small after 27...♘d7 28.♕a6 and then either 28...♖b8 or 28...♖f8.

28.f4xe5　　　♖c8-e8

After 28...♖xe5 29.♕f2 white seizes the f-file and quickly invades black's position.

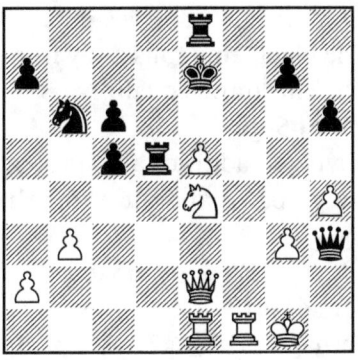

29.♕e2-h5?　　　...

I thought it was important to capture the g7 pawn. I honestly admit that I didn't give much consideration to the move 29.e6!, pointed out by the computer. The following lines are beautiful: 29...♔d8 (after 29...♕xe6, there's 30.♘f6!) 30.♖f8! (an unexpected and powerful blow) 30...♕xe6 (30...♖xf8 loses to 31.e7+ ♔e8 32.♘d6+ ♖xd6 33.exf8=♕+ ♔xf8 34.♕e8#)

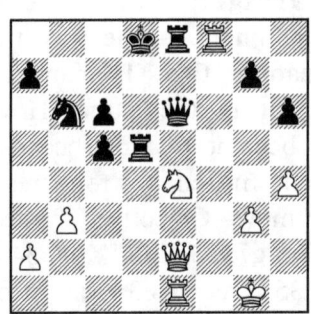

31.♘f6!! The final chord of the combination: white transposes into an endgame with an extra exchange. 31...♕xe2 32.♖xe8+ ♕xe8 33.♖xe8+ ♔c7 34.♖e7+ (the concluding little subtlety) 34...♔d8 35.♘xd5, and black's position is hopeless.

29... ♔e7-d8!

The black king runs away from the center. This move equalizes.

30.♕h5-g6 ...

Giving additional protection to the g3 pawn and attacking the g7 pawn.

30... ♖d5xe5

31.♖e1-d1+ ...

Perhaps 31.♕xg7 was stronger, since black cannot capture the knight: 31...♖xe4? 32.♖xe4 ♖xe4 33.♖f8+ ♖e8 34.♕f6+ ♔d7 35.♖f7+ ♔c8 36.♕xc6+, with mate next move. Therefore, black would have most probably replied 31...♘d7, and after 32.♘f2 ♕e6 33.♖xe5 ♕xe5 34.♕xe5 ♘xe5 35.♖c1, white kept some advantage in the endgame. However, I wanted to continue the attack, so I unpinned the knight.

31... ♘b6-d7

32.♘e4-f2 ♕h3-e6

33.♕g6xg7?! ...

Launching the trading combination that I managed to implement in the game. However, it only became possible because my opponent missed a strong resource on her move. Objectively, instead of taking on g7, 33.♖d6 ♕xg6 34.♖xg6 ♖8e7 35.♖xc6 ♖e3 was stronger. The chances are mutual, but it's more pleasant to play as white, in my opinion.

33... ♔d8-c8?!

Black's desire to get her king to safety is understandable, but she could actually launch an immediate counter-attack – 33...♖e3! After 34.♔h2 (34.♘h1?! looks very sad) 34...♔c7 (34...♖e2!? is also good) 35.♕g4 ♘e5 36.♕xe6 ♖xe6, white has to go on the defensive.

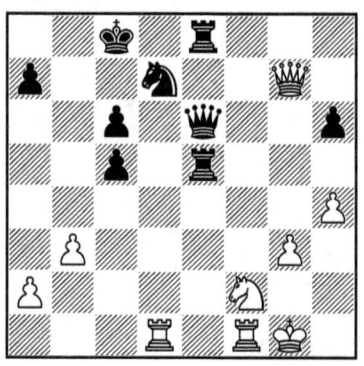

34.♕g7xd7+! ♕e6xd7
35.♖d1xd7 ♔c8xd7
36.♘f2-g4 ...

White regains the exchange and obtains a substantial advantage because of her better pawn structure. I finally breathed a sign of relief.

36... c5-c4?

Black gets rid of her doubled pawns and launches queenside counterplay. However, the sacrifice is somewhat premature. After 36...a5! 37.♘xe5 ♖xe5 38.♖f7+ ♔e6 39.♖a7 (39.♖h7 h5) 39...c4 40.bxc4 ♔f6 black would draw.

37.b3xc4 ♖e5-c5
38.♘g4-f6+ ♔d7-e7

39.♘f6xe8   ♚e7xe8
40.♖f1-f6   h6-h5
41.♔g1-f2   ♚e8-e7

41...♖xc4 42.♖f5 ♖c2+ 43.♔f3 ♖xa2 44.♖xh5 led to similar consequences, with good winning chances for white.

41...♚d7 42.♖h7 a5 43.♔e3 would also win for white.

42.♖f6-h6   ♖c5xc4
43.♖h6xh5   ♖c4-c2+
44.♔f2-f3   ♖c2xa2
45.♖h5-h7+ ♚e7-e6
46.g3-g4   ...

The white pawns are further advanced; in addition, white's passers are connected, while the black ones are disjointed. I tried to play this endgame very accurately, fearing to spill the advantage. It was most pleasant to learn many years later that Rybka approved almost all of my moves at the conversion stage. I also hope that nobody would accuse me of cheating!

Shortly before this game was played, Dr. Max Euwe, ex-world champion and mathematics professor, said, "Of course we can suppose that a computer will defeat a human, but I think that it will happen 100 or so years later." Just a couple of decades later, the computer destroyed the best human chess players. Euwe couldn't anticipate that technology would evolve so fast.

Back then, Botvinnik was working on the problem of the artificial chess player. He asked to be allowed to travel to America, he was even ready to pay for the travel of his whole group out of his own pocket. Mikhail Moiseevich wanted to read lectures there and spend the earnings to pay for lodging. But his higher-ups disagreed: how can that be, how can we let our group go to the U.S. to work on their computers?!.. We would show everyone that American technology is far more advanced than Soviet technology! Such trips had to be signed off by many authority figures, and I don't know a single one who would have agreed to that.

And later, CPU performance became the main factor — simple brute force. The machine shouldn't think like a human — it has its own advantages, and the humans their own. Comparing old computers with modern ones is like comparing a turtle with a jet plane. When I began my job at the institute, we had a Ural-4 vacuum-tube machine. We programmed it with a command system — we wrote, "Take the number from A cell, add it to the number from B cell and store the result in C cell", and so on, describing every action. A 120 square-meter room was needed to host this huge machine. It stood there in the great hall, shining with all its lamps. We fed it tasks through punch cards, then checked them with a special grid. It was most amusing to see the machine swallow these punch cards. Then, the ANPU (alphanumerical printing unit) would spit out a special tape with the printout. Whereas now, an ordinary laptop is already considered unwieldy!

Technology has made such huge leaps in such a short time. I was already an adult when I worked in the research institute, and I'm still alive now! My aunt worked as an accountant, and she maintained the accounts with an abacus. I remember playing in Lithuania, I was around 30 at the time. A German guy pointed at the abacus in some store and asked, "What is this?" Someone answered, "Russian calculator!"

We would ride the huge abacus in our home like a sleigh. The beads were sturdy, and the wires were made of steel. My aunt got angry, but for me and my sister, it was just harmless fun. I remember all that well. Then arithmometers appeared, then the first calculating machines, such as Vega. It was such a miracle at the time. I remember how someone brought my husband a programmable calculator as a birthday gift. This is progress, you can't hide from it. That's why computers can now easily find moves such as 29.e6!. With mild annoyance, I have to admit that I couldn't find it, even though I moved the pieces a lot in that position.

46...	a7-a5
47.g4-g5	a5-a4
48.g5-g6	♖a2-d2
49.♔f3-g4	...

The piece roles are reassigned: the king runs to help its pawns, while the rook will hold the opponent's passer.

49...	a4-a3
50.♔g4-g5	a3-a2
51.♖h7-a7	♖d2-g2+
52.♔g5-h6	c6-c5

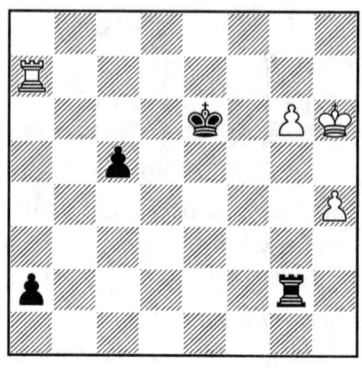

53.h4-h5	c5-c4
54.g6-g7	♔e6-e5
55.♖a7xa2	♖g2xa2
56.g7-g8=♕	♔e5-d4
57.♔h6-h7	♖a2-d2
58.♕g8-d8+	♔d4-c3
59.♕d8-c7	♔c3-b3
60.h5-h6	c4-c3
61.♔h7-g6	♖d2-g2+
62.♔g6-f5.	Black resigned.

The Czechoslovakian women's team was always a difficult opponent at all the Olympiads, and they made it that much harder for the USSR to take 1st place. Back then, any place but first was considered an abject failure. Winning the next game greatly improved our team's chances to take gold.

No. 42. Krystyna Hołuj-Radzikowska – Ludmila Belavenets
3rd Ladies Correspondence Chess Olympiad
1986 –1991
King's Indian Defense E99

1.d2-d4	♘g8-f6
2.c2-c4	g7-g6
3.♘b1-c3	♗f8-g7

4.e2-e4	d7-d6
5.♘g1-f3	0-0
6.♗f1-e2	e7-e5
7.0-0	♘b8-c6
8.d4-d5	♘c6-e7
9.♘f3-e1	♘f6-d7
10.♘e1-d3	f7-f5

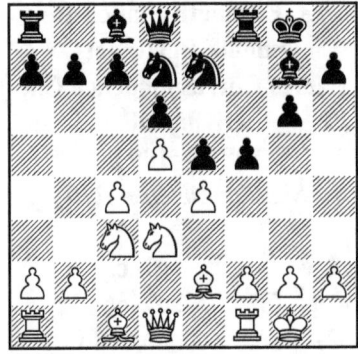

This classical line of the King's Indian was deeply studied even back then. White has a space advantage, and she systematically prepares for a queenside attack. Black, on the other hand, looks for her chances in the attack on the king, usually not fearing to sacrifice material.

11.♗c1-d2	♘d7-f6
12.f2-f3	f5-f4
13.c4-c5	g6-g5
14.♖a1-c1	♘e7-g6
15.c5xd6	c7xd6
16.♘c3-b5	♖f8-f7
17.♕d1-c2	♘f6-e8
18.a2-a4	h7-h5
19.♘d3-f2	♗g7-f8
20.h2-h3	♖f7-g7
21.♕c2-b3	♘g6-h4
22.♖c1-c2	a7-a6
23.♘b5-a3	♘e8-f6

24.♖f1-c1?! ...

It's hard to recall now where exactly we left the theory of the day, but, at any rate, both sides were playing logically enough up to that point. As far as I know, 24.♗e1 is now recommended instead of the game move, but in such sharp positions it's better to double-check recommendations.

24...	g5-g4
25.f3xg4	h5xg4
26.h3xg4	♗c8xg4

There was another tempting move – 26...♘h5!? with the subsequent ♘g3.

27.♗e2xg4	♘f6xg4
28.♘f2xg4	♖g7xg4
29.♗d2-e1	...

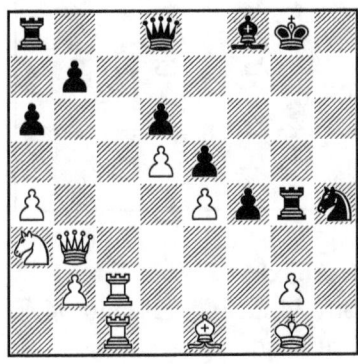

29...	♕d8-g5

Later, 29...f3 was tried in this position, but I think that the game move is stronger. Black has the initiative, she's obviously ahead of her opponent.

30.♗e1xh4	♕g5xh4
31.♖c2-f2?	...

This move loses. After 31.♕xb7!,

there's a tactic – 31...f3 with the idea 32.♕xa8 fxg2 33.♖xg2 ♖xg2+ 34.♔xg2 ♕xe4+ 35.♔f2 ♕f4+ 36.♔e2 ♕xc1, and the endgame is unpleasant for white. However, it seems that 31...♖e8 was even stronger, involving the second rook in the attack as well. Black would be better, but not winning.

31...   ♕h4-h7!

Black defends the b7 pawn and threatens to play ♖h4, reaching the white king.

32.♖c1-c4   b7-b5!
33.a4xb5   a6xb5

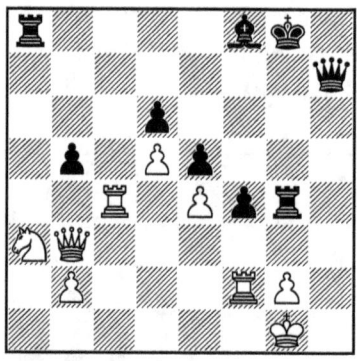

34.♕b3xb5   ...

Both 34.♖c3 ♕xe4 and 34.♘xb5 ♖a1+ are bad.

34...   ♖g4-h4
35.♔g1-f1   ♕h7-h5!
36.♔f1-e1   ♖h4-h1+
37.♔e1-d2   ...

After 37.♖f1, black wins with 37...♕h4+ 38.♔e2 ♕g4+ 39.♔e1 ♕g3+.

37...   ♕h5-d1+
38.♔d2-c3   ♕d1-e1+
39.♖f2-d2   f4-f3!
40.♕b5-d7   f3xg2

41.♕d7-g4+   ♔g8-h8
42.♕g4xg2   ♗f8-h6
43.♘a3-c2   ♗h6xd2+
44.♔c3-d3   ♕e1-c1
45.♘c2-e3   ♕c1-b1+
46.♔d3xd2   ♕b1xb2+

White resigned.

No. 43. Elizabeth Staller-Reis – Ludmila Belavenets
3rd Ladies Correspondence Chess Olympiad
1986 – 1991
Sicilian Defense B40

1.e2-e4   c7-c5
2.♘g1-f3   e7-e6
3.c2-c3   ♘g8-f6
4.♗f1-d3   d7-d5
5.e4-e5   ♘f6-d7
6.♗d3-c2   ...

White wants to play d2-d4 and get a French-type position, but with her bishop on the b1-h7 diagonal. Black prevents that with her next move.

6...   d5-d4
7.0-0   ♘b8-c6
8.♕d1-e2   ♗f8-e7
9.d2-d3   0-0

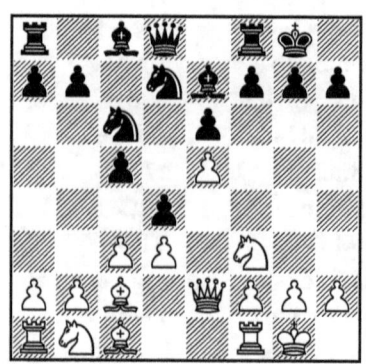

10.♖f1-e1 ...

White has wasted several tempi on moving her light-squared bishop, but it ultimately gets stuck on c2. I think that it made some sense to play ♗a4, either immediately or on the next few moves, and then trade this ill-fated piece to relieve the pressure on the e5 pawn.

10...	b7-b6
11.c3xd4	c5xd4
12.a2-a3	♗c8-b7
13.♘b1-d2	♖a8-c8
14.♘d2-c4	...

The knight goes the wrong way... It was better to transfer it to g3 through f1, with hopes to mount a piece attack on the black king later.

14...	b6-b5
15.♘c4-d6	...

Retreating is unpleasant, but the jump ahead loses a pawn.

15...	♗e7xd6
16.e5xd6	e6-e5
17.♘f3-g5?	...

White had a playable position after 17.♗g5 f6 18.♗d2.

17...	♘d7-f6
18.f2-f4	...

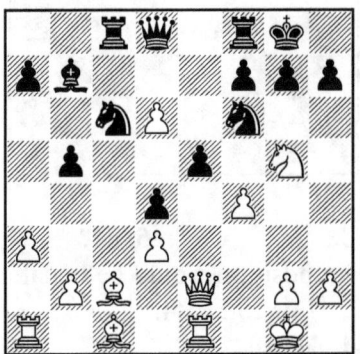

White is trying to muddy the waters, but her initiative quickly hits a brick wall.

18...	♕d8xd6
19.f4xe5	♕d6xe5!
20.♕e2-d1	...

After 20.♕xe5 ♘xe5 21.♖xe5 ♖xc2, the hanging bishop on c2 proves to have been even more of a liability. Frankly, it didn't do much good for white.

20...	♕e5-c7
21.♗c2-b3	♘c6-a5
22.♗b3-a2	h7-h6
23.♘g5-f3	♘f6-g4
24.♖e1-e2	♖f8-e8
25.♗c1-d2	♗b7xf3
26.g2xf3	♘g4-e3
27.♕d1-e1	♘a5-c6
28.♖a1-c1	♕c7-d7
29.♕e1-f2	♘c6-e5

White resigned.

No. 44. Ludmila Belavenets – Hana Modrova
3rd Ladies Correspondence Chess Olympiad
1986 – 1991
Ruy Lopez C78

1.e2-e4	e7-e5
2.♘g1-f3	♘b8-c6
3.♗f1-b5	a7-a6
4.♗b5-a4	♘g8-f6
5.0-0	b7-b5
6.♗a4-b3	♗c8-b7
7.♖f1-e1	♗f8-c5
8.c2-c3	d7-d6
9.d2-d4	♗c5-b6
10.♗c1-g5	h7-h6

11.♗g5-h4   ♕d8-e7

My opponent played the Arkhangelsk Variation, which was popular back then. An important theoretical crossroads is now on the board. Black also plays 11...g5, 11...♕d7 and 11...0-0 here.

**12.a2-a4   g7-g5
13.♗h4-g3   h6-h5**

Black boldly attacks with her kingside pawns, even though she realizes that she will be forced to leave her king in the center.

**14.a4xb5   a6xb5
15.♖a1xa8+   ♗b7xa8
16.h2-h4   g5-g4
17.♘f3-g5   ♘c6-d8
18.f2-f4!?   ...**

This interesting and logical-looking move (white wants to clarify the situation in the center immediately) hadn't been studied much. The common move here is 18.♘a3.

worth considering, as Gennadi Kuzmin and Evgeny Vasiukov used to play.

19.g2xf3   ♘f6-h7

19...c5!? was an interesting alternative, since white can't close the center off with 20.d5 due to 20...c4 with check. This allows black to activate her bishops somewhat.

**20.♘g5xh7   ♖h8xh7
21.♔g1-h2   ♘d8-e6
22.♘b1-a3   ♗a8-b7**

22...exd4 23.♘xb5 dxc3 24.♘xc3 is clearly better for white – her knight finally becomes a strong piece.

23.♘a3-c2   ...

The correct decision: white isn't tempted by the pawn and strengthens her center instead. 23.♘xb5 was simply met with 23...♖g7, developing the kingside. And white would have to leave her knight awkwardly placed on b5 to defend d4.

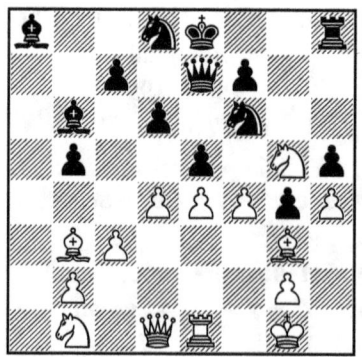

18...   g4xf3

Black opens up the white king's file, but the key e4 pawn is still securely defended. 18...♘d7 was

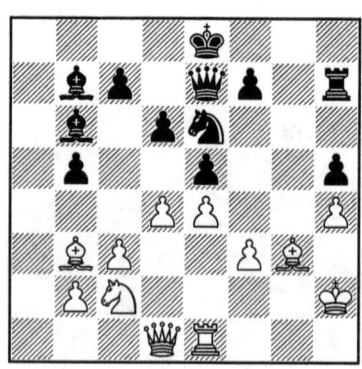

23...   e5xd4?

The position would be equal after 23...♖g7 or 23...♘f4.

24.♘c2xd4?!   ...

White misses a chance. After 24.♘b4! c5 (24...c6 25.♘d5!) 25.♘d5 ♕d8 26.♘xb6 ♕xb6 27.♗d5 white had a clear advantage.

24... ♘e6xd4
25.c3xd4 ♕e7-d7?

A reckless, losing move. It was much better to spirit the king to f8 or play 25...♔g7, and then, in the line 26.e5 d5 27.f4, black needs to find an important resource 27...♖g4, protecting the h5 pawn and preparing a sacrifice on h4 or f4.

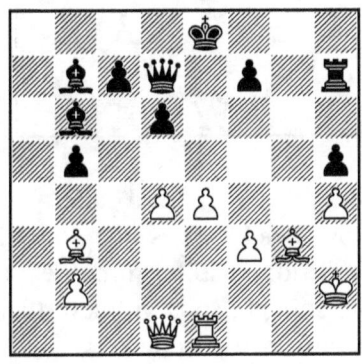

26.e4-e5! d6-d5
27.f3-f4 ♗b7-c8?!

Another inaccuracy, met with another blow by white.

28.e5-e6! f7xe6
29.f4-f5 ♕d7-g7
30.♗g3-e5 ...

30.♗xd5 ♕xd4 31.♕f3 looked very strong as well, but in this case, the position remains sharp enough. Now, though, white is not averse to trading queens.

30... ♕g7-g4
31.♕d1xg4 h5xg4
32.♔h2-g3 ♔e8-f7

33.f5-f6 ...

33.fxe6+ ♗xe6 34.♖f1+ looks tempting too, but this opens up the position, and black's bishops can break free. With the game move, white strengthens her grip.

33... ♖h7-h6
34.♖e1-f1 c7-c6
35.♗b3-c2 ♗b6-d8
36.h4-h5 ...

By sacrificing the rook pawn, white deflects attention from the passed f6 pawn. However, the more straightforward 36.♔xg4 was also possible. Now, 36...♗xf6 37.h5 ♔e7 38.♗g6 ♗xe5 39.dxe5 looks very bleak, as the black pieces are awfully passive. It's better to sacrifice the exchange with 36...♖xf6, but even here, after 37.♗xf6 ♗xf6 38.h5 ♔e7 39.h6, white is close to winning.

36... ♖h6xh5
37.♖f1-a1 ♗d8-b6
38.♖a1-a8 ♖h5-h8
39.b2-b4! ...

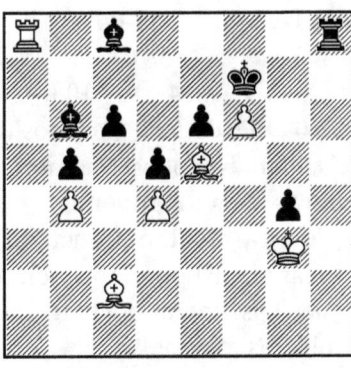

Black is two pawns up, but she has big trouble finding moves.

39... ♖h8-d8
40.♔g3-f4 ...

Accurately bypassing the trap 40.♔xg4 ♗xd4, even though white could even walk straight into it: 41.♗xd4 e5+ 42.♖xc8 ♖xc8 43.♗xe5, and it's hard to imagine that black would be able to save this position.

40... g4-g3
41.♗c2-d1 ♖d8-h8
42.♔f4xg3 ...

Black resigned.

No. 45. Inge Kattinger – Ludmila Belavenets
3rd Ladies Correspondence Chess Olympiad
1980 – 1986

Sicilian Defense B23

1.e2-e4 c7-c5
2.♘b1-c3 e7-e6
3.g2-g3 d7-d5
4.e4xd5 e6xd5
5.♗f1-g2 ♘g8-f6
6.d2-d3 ♗f8-e7
7.♘g1-e2 d5-d4
8.♘c3-e4 0-0

8...♘xe4 9.♗xe4 ♘d7 10.0-0 ♘f6 11.♗g2 0-0 leads to a transposition. White's plan is not very ambitious: she allows her opponent to grab space, counting on the strength of her light-squared bishop. However, one good piece is not enough to create real problems for black.

9.0-0 ♘f6xe4
10.♗g2xe4 ♘b8-d7
11.♗e4-g2 ♘d7-f6
12.♘e2-f4 ...

It seems that white overestimates her chances. A more restrained move, such as 12.♖e1, was preferable.

12... ♗c8-g4
13.♗g2-f3 ♕d8-d7
14.♘f4-d5 ...

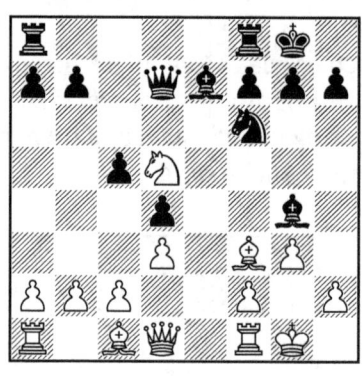

14... ♕d7xd5!

Now black seizes the initiative. The position is still symmetrical and simple enough, so it will nevertheless be hard to achieve anything substantial.

15.♗f3xg4 ♘f6xg4
16.♕d1xg4 f7-f5
17.♕g4-h5 ♗e7-d6
18.♗c1-d2 ♖a8-e8
19.b2-b3 ...

White is improving her pawn positions on the queenside. However, she has kept putting off the useful move a2-a4...

19... g7-g6
20.♕h5-g5 ♗d6-e7
21.♕g5-h6 ♗e7-f6
22.♖f1-e1 ♗f6-e5
23.♕h6-h3 ♕d5-f3
24.♕h3-g2 ♕f3xg2+

25.♔g1xg2   ♚g8-f7

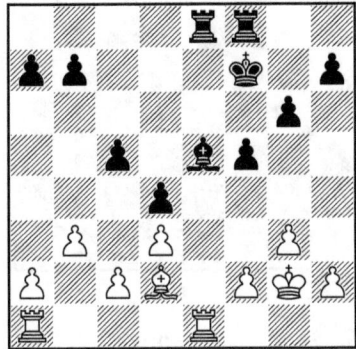

The endgame is unpleasant for white, because she lacks counterplay. However, her position is solid, so patient, accurate defense would probably have saved her half a point.

26.♖e1-e2   ♝e5-d6
27.♖a1-e1   ...

White could consider moving the pawn to a4 — 27.♖xe8 ♖xe8 28.a4, not fearing 28...♖e2, because after 29.♖d1 the black rook can't stay on the second rank for long.

27...   ♖e8xe2
28.♖e1xe2   b7-b5
29.♔g2-f3   ♖f8-c8
30.♝d2-f4   ♝d6-e7

Black doesn't need new trades. Formally, white controls the only open file, but it gives her nothing; black, meanwhile, prepares a queenside attack.

31.h2-h4   ♖c8-c6
32.♝f4-e5?   ...

This move is the losing mistake. White could hold passively with 32.♖e1 and if 32...♖a6 33.♖a1 black cannot crack white's fortress-like position.

32...   b5-b4

Fixing the weak a2 pawn.

33.g3-g4?   ...

A desperate attempt to complicate things. Alas, it's impossible to save the pawn: 33.♖e1? is met with 33...♖e6! 34.♔g2 (34.♖e2 ♖a6) 34...♝f6 35.f4 ♝xe5 36.fxe5 ♖a6 37.♖a1 ♔e6 — black wins the pawn and gets an overwhelming position.

33...   f5xg4+
34.♔f3xg4   h7-h5+
35.♔g4-g3   ♖c6-a6
36.f2-f4   ♖a6xa2
37.f4-f5   g6xf5
38.♔g3-f4   ...

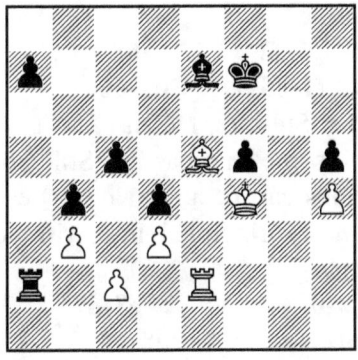

38...   c5-c4!
39.♖e2-g2   ...

White has no defense against the pawn breakthrough. 39.bxc4 loses to 39...b3, while 39.dxc4 loses to 39...d3.

39...   c4xb3
40.♖g2-g7+   ♔f7-e6
41.c2xb3   ♖a2-f2+
42.♔f4-g3   ♝e7xh4+

| 43.♔g3xh4 | ♔e6xe5 |

White resigned. That's how you had to wait for a mistake for a year or two to get some chances. Such hard work!

**No. 46. Doina Berbecaru –
Ludmila Belavenets
3rd Ladies Correspondence Chess Olympiad
1980 – 1986**
Ruy Lopez C62

Having black was especially difficult. Sometimes you get nothing out of the opening, but you still have to come up with something, searching for a chance to outplay your opponent.

1.e2-e4	e7-e5
2.♘g1-f3	♘b8-c6
3.♗f1-b5	d7-d6

The Steinitz Defense is a solid line, if somewhat passive. Still, sharp positions can occur if white goes for the most principled line with long castling.

4.0-0	♗c8-d7
5.d2-d4	e5xd4
6.♘f3xd4	g7-g6
7.♘b1-c3	♗f8-g7
8.♗c1-e3	♘g8-f6
9.f2-f3	0-0
10.♕d1-d2	♖f8-e8
11.♖a1-d1	a7-a6
12.♘d4xc6	♗d7xc6

After 12...bxc3 13.♗c4, white's position is more pleasant.

| 13.♗b5-c4 | b7-b5 |
| 14.♗c4-b3 | a6-a5 |

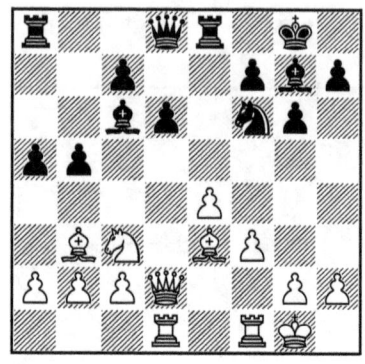

15.a2-a4	b5xa4
16.♗b3xa4	♗c6xa4
17.♘c3xa4	♕d8-b8

Objectively, the stronger move was 17...d5!? 18.exd5 ♕xd5 19.♕f2 (or 19.♕xd5 ♘xd5) 19...♕b5 20.b3 ♘d5 with roughly equal chances, but this simplified the position too much.

| 18.♗e3-d4 | ♕b8-b4 |

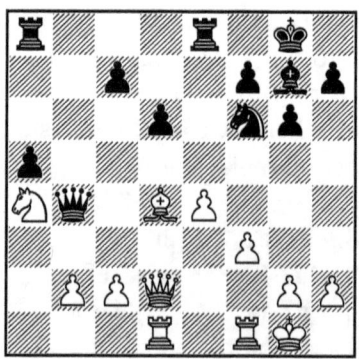

| 19.♕d2xb4? | ... |

White probably thought that this was the simplest way to draw, but she was wrong as it worsens white's position, leaving it equal. The correct move was 19.b3, with black slightly worse.

| 19... | a5xb4 |
| 20.b2-b3 | ♖a8-a5 |

21.♖f1-e1	♘f6-d7
22.♗d4xg7	♔g8xg7
23.♖d1-d4	♖e8-b8
24.♖e1-d1	♘d7-c5
25.♖d4-d5	♖b8-b5
26.♘a4xc5?!	...

26.♘b2 ♖a2 27.♖b1 would be equal.

26...	♖b5xc5
27.♖d5xc5	♖a5xc5
28.♖d1-d2	...

Reducing the number of pawns with 28.♖d4 would be preferable.

| 28... | ♔g7-f6 |

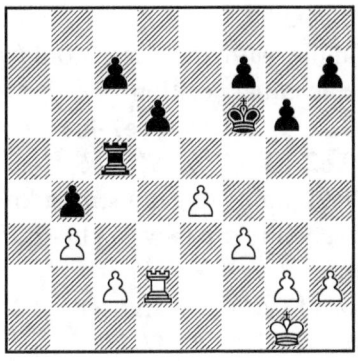

The black pieces are more active, and the white c2 pawn is somewhat weak. It's still not enough to win, but black can continue improving her position.

29.♔g1-f2	♔f6-e5
30.♔f2-e2	g6-g5?!

30...h5! with ♖c3, h4 and ♔f4 would give black excellent winning chances.

31.♔e2-d1	h7-h5
32.♖d2-d3	h5-h4
33.g2-g3?!	...

33.♔d2 ♔f4 34.♖d4 holds.

33...	h4-h3
34.♔d1-d2	f7-f6
35.♖d3-e3	♖c5-a5
36.♔d2-d3	♖a5-a1
37.♖e3-e2?	...

White could grab a practical chance: 37.f4!? ♔e6 38.fxg5 ♖d1+! (38...fxg5 39.g4!) 39.♔c4 and not 39...fxg5? because 40.g4 holds, but 39...♖d2! and black should still win.

| 37... | ♖a1-f1 |

Black has paralyzed white.

38.♔d3-e3	c7-c6
39.♖e2-d2	d6-d5
40.e4xd5	c6xd5
41.f3-f4+	...

White can't withstand the pressure so she decides to eliminate her opponent's active rook and transpose into a pawn ending, but it turns out to be hopeless. However, there was nothing better, for example 41.♔e2 ♖g1 42.♔e3 d4+.

41...	g5xf4+
42.g3xf4+	♖f1xf4
43.♖d2xd5+	♔e5xd5
44.♔e3xf4	♔d5-d4

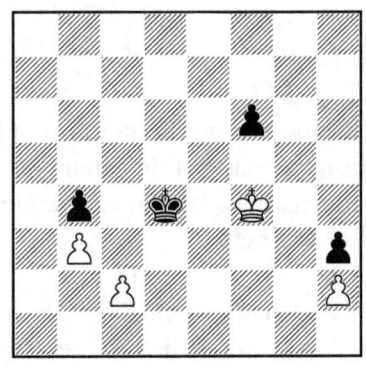

| 45.♔f4-g3 | ♔d4-e3! |

Had the king headed the other way, it would have led to a drawn queen endgame.

46.♔g3xh3   f6-f5
47.♔h3-g2   f5-f4
48.♔g2-f1   ♔e3-f3!

White resigned. She either loses the h-pawn or has to allow the f-pawn to promote.

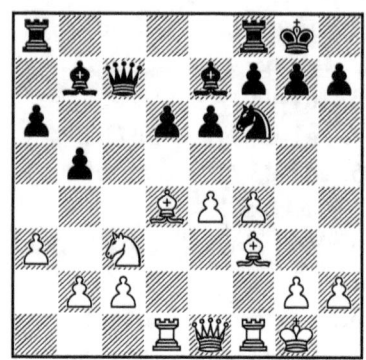

No. 47. Liisa Vayrynen — Ludmila Belavenets
4th Ladies World Correspondence Chess Championship semi-final, 1980 — 1984
Sicilian Defense B85

1.e2-e4   c7-c5
2.♘g1-f3   e7-e6
3.d2-d4   c5xd4
4.♘f3xd4   ♘g8-f6
5.♘b1-c3   d7-d6
6.♗f1-e2   ♘b8-c6
7.0-0   ♗f8-e7
8.♗c1-e3   0-0
9.f2-f4   a7-a6
10.♕d1-e1   ♘c6xd4
11.♗e3xd4   b7-b5
12.a2-a3   ♗c8-b7
13.♗e2-f3   ...

This move is not in the spirit of the position, because white's main idea is to create a kingside attack. Therefore, 13.♕g3 was better.

13...   ♕d8-c7
14.♖a1-d1?!   ...

14.♕g3 was still better. Now black defuses the center, which is beneficial for her.

14...   e6-e5!
15.♗d4-e3   e5xf4
16.♗e3xf4   ♘f6-d7
17.♘c3-d5   ♗b7xd5
18.e4xd5?!   ...

Taking with the rook would give white an equal position.

18...   ♗e7-f6
19.c2-c3   ♗f6-e5

Black wants to get a strong knight against white's passive light-squared bishop.

20.♗f3-e4   ♖a8-e8
21.♕e1-h4   f7-f5!
22.♗e4-b1   ♗e5xf4
23.♖f1xf4   g7-g6
24.c3-c4?!   ...

This inappropriate attempt to create activity only accelerates the loss. However, waiting would be difficult as well.

24...   ♖e8-e2

Black had another tempting continuation: 24...♕b6+ 25.♕f2 ♖e3! 26.cxb5 ♖fe8 27.♖f1 axb5 with an advantage.

25.c4xb5   ♖e2xb2
26.♖f4-b4   ♖b2xb4
27.♕h4xb4   ♕c7-b6+?!

This eases black's grip. 27...axb5! or 27...♖b8 would win.

28.♔g1-h1	a6xb5
29.♗b1-d3	♘d7-e5

After 29...♘c5! 30.♗xb5 ♘e4 white would struggle.

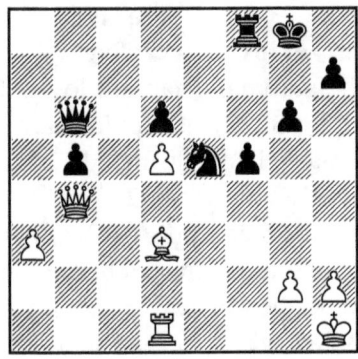

30.♗d3-e2?? ...

30.♕xb5? ♕e3 31.♗e2 ♕xa3 wouldn't make things any easier for white. But after 30.h3! white seems to hold, for example if 30...♖b8 then 31.♗f1 and it is hard for black to progress.

30...	♕b6-e3
31.♖d1-e1	♖f8-c8
32.♕b4xd6?	...

A final mistake. On 32.♗f1 black has many ways to win: 32...♖c1! or 32...♕c3! are the most convincing.

32...	♘e5-d3

White resigned. Black got everything she ever dreamed of in the Scheveningen, even though white didn't exactly resist. I sometimes show this game in my lessons as an example of black's play in this variation.

No. 48. Ludmila Belavenets – Snjezana Bazaj-Bockaj
4th Ladies World Correspondence Chess Championship
1984 – 1990
Sicilian Defense B81

1.e2-e4	c7-c5
2.♘g1-f3	e7-e6
3.d2-d4	c5xd4
4.♘f3xd4	♘g8-f6
5.♘b1-c3	d7-d6
6.g2-g4	a7-a6

A risky reply to the Keres Attack: black fully cedes the initiative on the kingside to create counterplay quickly on the other side of the board.

7.g4-g5	♘f6-d7
8.♗c1-e3	b7-b5
9.a2-a3	♘d7-b6
10.f2-f4	♘b8-d7

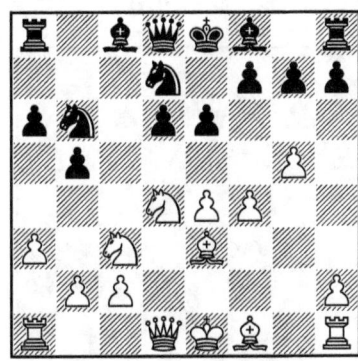

11.f4-f5	e6xf5?

Not a good trade, severely weakening black's position in the center. A stronger move was 11...♘e5 12.fxe6 fxe6 13.♗h3 ♘bc4 with mutual chances, Rutman – Lukin, St. Petersburg 1992.

12.e4xf5	...

This gives white better chances to win than after 12.♘xf5?! ♘e5 13.♗xb6 ♕xb6 14.♘d5 ♕d8 15.h4.

12...	♗c8-b7
13.♖h1-g1	♘d7-e5
14.♕d1-h5!?	...

This is strong, but 14.♕e2! or 14.♖g3! would be even more powerful.

14...	g7-g6
15.♕h5-h3	♘b6-c4
16.♗f1xc4	b5xc4

Black can't get her knight away from the center: 16...♘xc4 17.0-0-0 winning.

17.0-0-0	♕d8-d7
18.♗e3-f4	♗f8-g7
19.♖g1-e1	...

A reasonable move, but not the best. Stepping out of the pin with 19.♕g3! or 19.♕h4! and threatening f6 would win.

19...	0-0

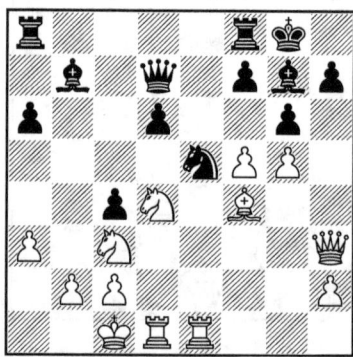

20.♗f4xe5   d6xe5

After 20...♗xe5, white gets an overwhelming position with a small combination: 21.♖xe5 dxe5 22.♘e6 ♕c8 23.♘xf8 ♕xf8 24.f6. Black is trying to get off the hook by sacrificing an exchange.

21.♘d4-e6!	♕d7-e7
22.♘e6xg7?	...

Actually, white could have won by taking the exchange, as after 22.♘xf8 ♕xg5+ 23.♔b1 ♖xf8, black has fewer chances to organize a successful defense.

22...	♕e7xg5+
23.♔c1-b1	♔g8xg7?

The automatic capture loses. The brilliant 23...♗g2!! would narrowly keep black in the game. If 24.♘e4 ♗xh3 25.♘g5 ♗g4! 26.♖d7 ♔xg7 27.♘e6 ♔f6 28.♘xf8 ♔xf8 although white has an extra exchange black would not be worse.

24.♖e1-g1	♕g5-f6
25.♖d1-f1	g6-g5

Black is forced to move the pawn, but it's doomed on the fifth rank.

26.♕h3-h5	♔g7-h8
27.♖g1xg5	♖f8-g8
28.h2-h4	...

28.♖g4! would win.

28...	♗b7-c6?!

28...♗g2! 29.♖e1 ♖xg5 30.hxg5 ♕xf5 and black would be in the game.

29.♕h5-g4	♖g8-c8?

29...h6! still resisted.

30.♖f1-g1	♖a8-b8

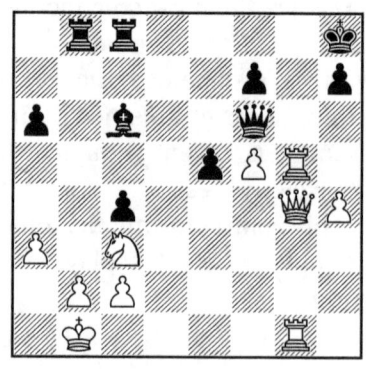

31.♖g5-g7! ...

The decisive invasion – white reaches the h7 square.

31... e5-e4
32.♕g4-h5 ♕f6xg7

Black has to give up the queen, but the black king still can't escape the danger zone.

33.♖g1xg7 ♔h8xg7
34.♕h5-g5+ ♔g7-h8
35.h4-h5 f7-f6

Black can't play 35...♖g8 due to 36.♕f6+ ♖g7 37.h6.

36.♕g5xf6+ ♔h8-g8
37.h5-h6 Black resigned.

No. 49. Peggy Clarke – Ludmila Belavenets
4th Ladies World Correspondence Chess Championship
1984 – 1990
Reti Opening A11

1.♘g1-f3 d7-d5
2.g2-g3 ♘g8-f6
3.♗f1-g2 c7-c6
4.0-0 ♗c8-g4
5.c2-c4 e7-e6
6.c4xd5 ...

After this trade, black doesn't have much trouble. It was better to keep up the tension with 6.♕b3 or 6.b3.

6... e6xd5
7.h2-h3 ♗g4-f5
8.d2-d3 ♗f8-e7
9.♘b1-d2 0-0
10.♘f3-h4 ♗f5-e6

Now white can't even trade her knight for the bishop – the latter has calmly retreated.

11.e2-e4 ♘f6-e8

11...♘fd7 was also possible, for instance: 12.♘f5 ♗xf5 13.exf5 ♗f6 14.♔h1 ♘e5 15.♕c2 ♘a6 16.a3 ♖e8 17.♖b1 ♖c8 with mutual chances, Movsziszian – Campos Moreno, Barbera 1996.

12.f2-f4 ♗e7xh4
13.g3xh4 f7-f5!

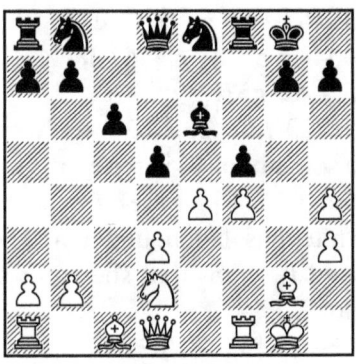

White probably underestimated this move: instead of winning a pawn, black slows down her opponent's kingside attack.

14.♘d2-f3?! ...

14.h5 would lead to an equal position.

14... d5xe4
15.♘f3-g5 ...

Trying to muddy the waters, but this attempt is easily refuted by black.

15... ♗e6-d5
16.d3xe4 f5xe4
17.♗g2xe4 ♘e8-f6
18.♗e4xd5+ ♕d8xd5
19.♕d1xd5+ ♘f6xd5

White's pawn structure is broken, so black has a small but steady advantage in the ending.

20.♖f1-f3?! ...

After 20.♗d2 or 2.f5 white's disadvantage would be smaller than in the game.

20...	♘b8-d7
21.♘g5-e6	♖f8-f7
22.♗c1-d2	♖a8-e8?!

22...♘e5! 23.♖g3 ♘c4 24.♗c3 ♘xc3 25.♖xc3 ♘xb2 with an almost winning position.

23.♖a1-e1	♖f7-e7
24.f4-f5	♘d7-f8
25.♗d2-g5?!	...

25.♖a3 a6 26.♖b3 would give white some hope to survive.

25... ♖e7-f7

White has fallen under a deadly pin, and it seems that she can't save the pawn.

26.♔g1-f2	h7-h6
27.♗g5-d2	♘f8xe6
28.f5xe6	♖f7-e7
29.♖f3-f7	♖e7xf7+
30.e6xf7+	♔g8xf7
31.♖e1xe8	♔f7xe8

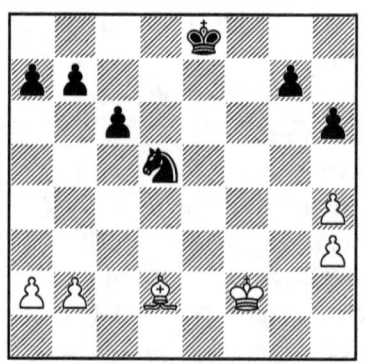

32.♔f2-g3	♔e8-f7
33.♔g3-g4	♔f7-e6
34.♗d2-e1	...

The white king can't go forward, because after 34.♔h5 ♔f5 it gets caught in a mating net (black threatens to give a deadly check from f6 or f4).

34...	♔e6-e5
35.♗e1-g3+	♔e5-e4
36.♗g3-b8	a7-a6
37.a2-a3	♘d5-e3+
38.♔g4-g3	...

White still can't go forward because of 38...♔f5.

38... h6-h5

White loses the h4 pawn as well, so she resigned.

No. 50. Ludmila Belavenets – L. Koroshinadze
Soviet Correspondence Chess Team Championship
1978 – 1980
French Defense C10

I show this miniature, along with those against Voskresenskaya (game 51) and Van Elst (game 32), as examples of unnecessary moves such as a3, h6, etc. that allow the opponent to open the file with the king on it.

1.e2-e4	e7-e6
2.d2-d4	d7-d5
3.♘b1-d2	d5xe4
4.♘d2xe4	♘b8-d7
5.♘g1-f3	♘g8-f6
6.♗f1-d3	♗f8-e7
7.♘e4xf6+	♘d7xf6
8.♕d1-e2	c7-c5
9.d4xc5	♗e7xc5

9...♕a5+ was more solid, taking the pawn with the queen.

10.♗c1-g5   ♗c5-e7?

This move virtually loses. Black should try 10...h6 or 10...♕a5.

11.0-0-0   ♘f6-d7
12.h2-h4!   ...

White has managed to gain a great advantage: she has already finished her development, and it's not easy for black to get all her forces into the game and find a safe haven for her king.

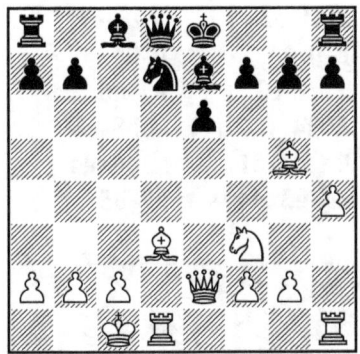

12...   h7-h6

Of course, you don't want to make such a move, creating a "hook" for your opponent to open files, but what else can you do here? After 12...♕a5 13.♗xe7 ♔xe7 14.♔b1, black's position is quite unpleasant, while after 12...0-0 13.♕e4 g6 14.♗b5, she it completely lost.

13.♗g5xe7   ♕d8xe7
14.g2-g4   0-0?!

The king castles right into an unstoppable attack. 14...♘c5 was more resilient, though even here, after 15.♘e5 ♗d7 16.♗e4!?, black's position is still objectively lost.

15.g4-g5   ♘d7-c5

15...h5 didn't save black because of 16.g6 f6 17.♘d4 ♖e8 18.♗b5.

16.g5xh6   g7xh6
17.♖h1-g1+ ♔g8-h8
18.♕e2-e5+ f7-f6
19.♕e5-h5   ...

Black resigned: after 19...♘xd3+ 20.♖xd3 ♕h7 21.♖g6, she loses her queen.

No. 51. Ludmila Belavenets – G. Voskresenskaya
Soviet Correspondence Chess Team Championship
1978–1980
Nimzo-Indian Defense E36

1.d2-d4   ♘g8-f6
2.c2-c4   e7-e6
3.♘b1-c3   ♗f8-b4
4.♕d1-c2   d7-d5
5.a2-a3   ♗b4-e7

Now black gets a Queen's Gambit-like position, but a tempo down. 5...♗xc3+ 6.♕xc3 ♘e4 7.♕c2 c5 etc. was more principled.

6.♘g1-f3   ♘b8-c6?!

The knight's position here is usually bad, as it gets in the way of the c-pawn.

7.♗c1-g5   d5xc4
8.e2-e3   0-0

Black could have tried to justify her opening structure with 8...♘a5.

9.♗f1xc4   h7-h6
10.♗g5xf6   ♗e7xf6
11.0-0-0   a7-a6?

A careless move. Black is clearly behind in development, but she plays like nothing is happening. On 11...

♗d7 12.h4 would give white a winning advantage. Black's best choice is 11...♖b8 and after 12.h4 ♘a5 13.♗a2 b5 black has a very difficult position.

12.♗c4-a2   b7-b5?

12...♗e7 was more tenacious, but even here, after 13.♗b1 f5 14.g4, white's threats are very dangerous.

12...g6 is black's best move, with a tortuous defence.

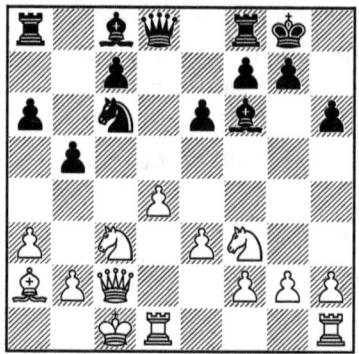

13.d4-d5!   ♘c6-e5

After 13...exd5 14.♗xd5, the pin on the c6 knight decides the outcome: 14...♕e8 (the only move, since white also threatened 15.♗xf7+) 15.♘e4 ♗b7 16.♘xf6+ gxf6 17.♕g6+!, and white wins.

14.d5xe6   ♕d8-e7
15.♘f3xe5   ...

15.exf7+ ♘xf7 16.♘d5 ♕e6 17.♗b1 also won.

15...   ♗f6xe5
16.e6xf7+   ♔g8-h8
17.♗a2-b1   ...

Black resigned.

And, in conclusion, I'll show you some games from over-the-board competitions.

No. 52. Rita Gramignani — Ludmila Belavenets
Roosendaal 1976
Sicilian Defense B85

This game was played at the Interzonal.

1.e2-e4	c7-c5
2.♘g1-f3	e7-e6
3.d2-d4	c5xd4
4.♘f3xd4	♘g8-f6
5.♘b1-c3	d7-d6
6.♗f1-e2	♗f8-e7
7.0-0	0-0
8.♗c1-e3	a7-a6
9.f2-f4	♘b8-c6
10.♕d1-e1	♘c6xd4
11.♗e3xd4	b7-b5

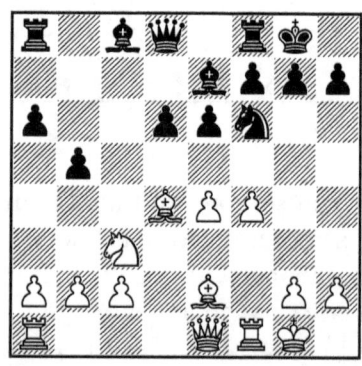

12.♗e2-d3   ...

White chooses a rare continuation in the classical Scheveningen line. 12.a3 or 12.♖d1 are more popular here.

12...   ♗c8-b7
13.a2-a3   ♕d8-c7
14.♕e1-g3   e6-e5
15.♗d4-e3?   ...

A poor decision that forces white to part with her dark-squared bishop.

She should have traded on e5, 15.fxe5, though even here, after 15...♘h5 16.♕f2 (16.♕h3 dxe5 17.♕xh5 exd4 18.♘d5 ♗xd5 19.exd5 g6 is a bit better for black) 16...dxe5 17.♗b6 ♕d6 18.♖ad1 ♘f4, black still has good counterplay and is not worse, Ivkov – Sax, Hilversum 1973.

**15... ♘f6-h5
16.♕g3-h3 ♘h5xf4
17.♗e3xf4 e5xf4
18.♖f1xf4 h7-h6**

18...g6 was more precise, but black is preparing to put her bishop on g5 and wants to protect it beforehand, just in case.

19.♔g1-h1 ...

In the line 19.♘d5 ♗xd5 20.exd5 ♗g5 21.♖ff1 ♖ae8 black has a sustained advantage, and opposite-colored bishops only increase her chances of mounting a successful attack.

**19... ♗e7-g5
20.♖f4-f1 ♖a8-e8
21.♖a1-d1? ...**

After 21.♘d5! white had good chances to hold.

21... ♖e8-e5!

Black prepares to double rooks along the e-file, increasing pressure on the e4 pawn. This move also exploits the fact that the d3 bishop is somewhat useless.

**22.♕h3-g3 ♔g8-h8
23.♖f1-f5? ...**

23.♘d5! ♗xd5 24.exd5 and on 24...♖xd5 25.♖de1 with a reasonable position.

23... ♗g5-f6

It was equally fine to trade rooks first – 23...♖xf5 24.exf5, and only then put the bishop on the long diagonal – 24...♗f6 with an obvious advantage for black.

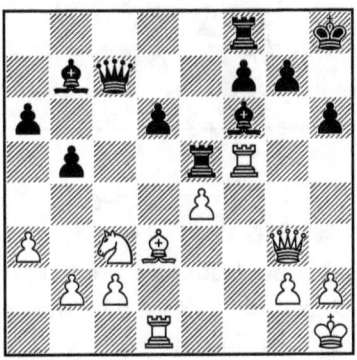

24.♖d1-f1 ...

After 24.♖xf6 gxf6 25.♕f4 ♔g7 26.♘e2 white has insufficient compensation for the sacrificed exchange.

**24... ♖e5xf5
25.e4xf5 ...**

After 25.♖xf5, black has a very unpleasant reply 25...♗e5 and if necessary black will take on c3.

25... ♖f8-e8

I was very satisfied with my position here. Black has two strong bishops on the long diagonals, while the white bishop is "kissing" the f5 pawn.

26.♕g3-f4 ...

If 26.♖e1, then 26...♖e5 and black maintains a clear advantage.

**26... ♕c7-c6
27.♕f4-g3 ...**

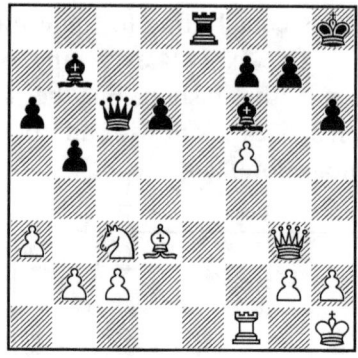

27... ♖e8-e3!
28.♕g3-f2   ♗f6-h4

This move leads to a pretty ending, but objectively, 28...♗d4! was even stronger, for instance: 29.♕d2 ♗e5 30.♕f2 f6, and white's position is hopeless – she'll run out of moves soon.

29.♕f2-d2   ...

For some reason, I was sure that my opponent would make this move. But I still win after the "mundane" 29.♕g1 ♗f6.

29...   ♗h4-e1!

Who misses an opportunity to make such a move?! White resigned.

No. 53. Radmila Popivoda – Ludmila Belavenets
Tbilisi 1979
French Defense C02

This game was played in my last Soviet championship.

1.e2-e4   c7-c5
2.♘g1-f3   e7-e6
3.c2-c3   d7-d5
4.e4-e5   ♘b8-c6

I made this move automatically, without thinking, and got into a French Defense, which I'd never played. Later, I would usually play 4...d4 in this position.

5.d2-d4   ♕d8-b6
6.a2-a3   c5-c4
7.♘b1-d2   ♘c6-a5

I had to wing it in the opening. I only had a general idea of what to do: black should play ♗d7, 0-0-0 and f6 somewhere along the way – as well as showing some semblance of kingside activity...

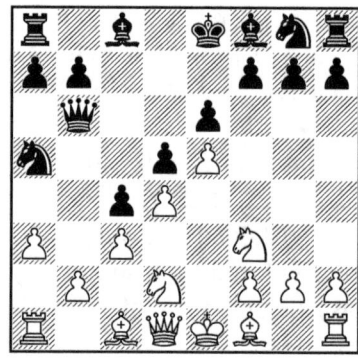

8.b2-b4?!   ...

A sharp move. White's play is usually more restrained here, for example, 8.♗e2, 8.g3 or 8.♖b1. Popivoda probably realized that I didn't know this opening and decided to go for the sharpest continuation.

8...   c4xb3
9.♗c1-b2   ♗c8-d7
10.c3-c4   d5xc4

10...♘e7 looks even better.

11.♘d2xc4   ♘a5xc4
12.♗f1xc4   ♘g8-e7
13.0-0   ♗d7-c6

It looks like I'm doing everything

right: developing my pieces, fighting for the d5 square.

14.♘f3-d2   ♘e7-d5
15.♗c4xb3   ♘d5-f4

To be honest, I didn't know what to do here. Black's position looks fine, but what now? White, on the other hand, wants to play ♕g4 and put pressure on the kingside.

The computer says that black should have continued her development: 15...♗e7 16.♘c4 ♕a6 with better chances.

16.♕d1-g4?!   ...

It made sense for white to insert 16.♘c4! ♕d8 and only then play 17.♕g4, for instance: 17...g5 (not 17...♘xg2? 18.d5) 18.d5! h5 19.♕d1 ♘xd5 20.♖c1 with great compensation for the pawn: black will have to play with the king stuck in the center and constantly have the threat ♘d6+ in mind.

16...   g7-g5
17.d4-d5   ...

The g5 pawn is poisoned: 17.♕xg5 ♘h3+! 18.gxh3 ♗h6! 19.♕g3 ♗xd2 with an extra pawn and an overwhelming position.

17...   h7-h5

Such moves are usually made "by hand", but it was probably better to just capture the pawn: 17...♘xd5 18.♗xd5 ♗xd5 with an extra pawn and a very promising position.

18.♕g4xg5??   ...

This is a losing mistake. After 18.♕d1 ♗xd5 19.♗xd5 ♘xd5 20.♖b1 white has good compensation for the pawn.

18...   ♘f4xd5
19.♕g5-h4   ...

If 19.♗xd5 ♗xd5 20.♗c3 black should win with 20...♖h6!.

19...   ♖h8-g8
20.g2-g3   ♗f8-e7
21.♕h4-c4   ♖g8-g4!
22.♘d2-e4   ...

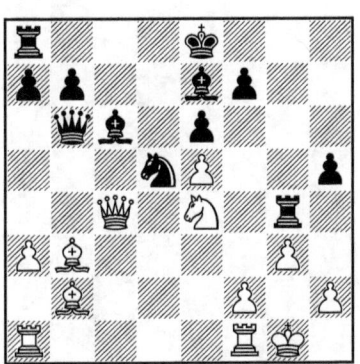

22...   ♘d5-e3!

It's hard not to make such a pretty move, even though I could simply take material and win – 22...♖xe4 23.♕xe4 ♕xb3, retaining all the advantages of my position.

23.f2xe3   ♕b6xe3+
24.♖f1-f2   ♖g4xe4
25.♕c4-c2   ♗e7-c5
26.♖a1-f1   ♗c5-b6

Black had another beautiful way to win: 26...♖h4! Now the rook is untouchable (27.gxh4 ♕f3), but not capturing it is equally hopeless: 27.♖a1 ♕xg3+ 28.♔f1 ♗b5+ 29.♔e1 ♖d8, checkmating.

27.♗b2-c3   ♕e3-f3
28.♗c3-a5   ♖e4-e2

White resigned.

Afterword

At the time the contract to publish this work in English was concluded, in early 2021, Ludmila Sergeevna Belavenets was alive and well. It was agreed that she would write a small update on her professional life to take the reader through to the present day. However, that insidious disease Covid-19 badly hurt the Russian chess community, claiming the lives of Klara Kasparova, Evgeny Sveshnikov, and Yuri Dokhoian among others. Alas, Ludmila Sergeevna, despite being vaccinated, was not spared either and she passed away on 7 November 2021 at the age of 81. She had no children. She was buried at Kalitnikovskoe Cemetery in Moscow.

Still, we have pieced together two major events of the last decade of her life that happened after publication of the Russian version of this book. First, identification of Sergei Belavenets's final resting place and its honoring with a headstone. Secondly, the establishment of the Sergei Belavenets Chess House in Brazil.

Sergei Belavenets's Final Resting Place

Sergei Belavenets was killed in battle on 6 March 1942. Along with fallen comrades, he was buried initially in a war grave in the village of Shishimorovo, near where he died. Later, in 1957, bodies from a number of war graves in villages around Staraya Russa were reburied together in the village of Nagovo. In 2014, Ludmila together with Sergey Yanovsky managed to locate this common war grave at Nagovo and a monument with the names of the buried soldiers engraved on it, including that of Sergei Belavenets. They took the first photo on the next page.

In 2015, the Chess Federation of Russia erected a headstone for Sergei nearby. See the second photo on the next page.

The Sergei Belavenets Chess House in Brazil

In 2018 the Sergei Belavenets Chess House (Casa do Xadrez) was opened in Porto Alegre, Brazil. This was the initiative of a local chess fan, Russian speaker and chess memorabilia collector Fabiano Ferreira, an oncologist by profession. Back in 2014, Dr. Ferreira met Ludmila in Moscow while he was in the process of purchasing an envelope from a seller in Latvia that had been addressed and sent by Sergei to his family on 2 February 1942, just a month before his death. Ludmila wrote an article in *64* (no. 5 / 2014) about their meeting and about the actual letter, which she already had in her possession. Thanks to Dr. Ferreira's interest in the Belavenets family, he

decided to open the Sergei Belavenets Chess House, which is now a thriving chess club and educational center. Ludmila together with Sergey Yanovsky traveled to Brazil to take part in the opening ceremony. Fabiano kindly supplied the following photos from the ceremony, and also from a visit by Alexei Shirov in 2020.

Afterword

www.ingramcontent.com/pod-product-compliance
Lightning Source LLC
LaVergne TN
LVHW021334080526
838202LV00003B/170